W9-CAI-306

ATLAS OF THE

PREHISTORIC WORLD

ATLAS OF THE PREHISTORIC WORLD

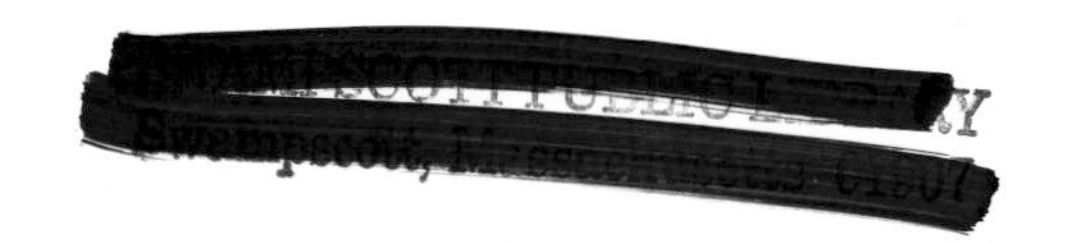

DOUGLAS PALMER

DISCOVERY BOOKS • NEW YORK

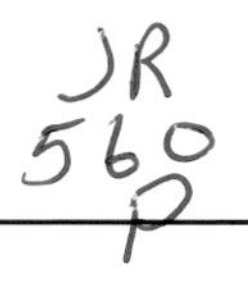

Discovery Communications, Inc.
John S. Hendricks, *Founder, Chairman, and Chief Executive Officer*
Judith A. McHale, *President and Chief Operating Officer*
Michela English, *President, Discovery Enterprises Worldwide*
Raymond Cooper, *Senior Vice President, Discovery Enterprises Worldwide*

Discovery Publishing
Natalie Chapman, *Vice President, Publishing*
Rita Thievon Mullin, *Editorial Director*
Mary Kalamaras, *Senior Editor*
Maria Mihalik Higgins, *Editor*
Heather Quinlan, *Editorial Coordinator*
Christine Alvarez, *Business Development*
Kimberly Small, *Senior Marketing Manager*

Discovery Channel Retail
Tracy Fortini, *Product Development*
Steve Manning, *Naturalist*

Discovery Communications, Inc., produces high-quality television programming, interactive media, books, films, and consumer products. Discovery Networks, a division of Discovery Communications, Inc., operates and manages the Discovery Channel, TLC, Animal Planet, Travel Channel, and the Discovery Health Channel.

Conceived, edited and designed by
Marshall Editions Ltd
The Orangery
161 New Bond Street
London EC1Y 9PA
UK

Marshall Editions Ltd

Project Editor	Tom Ruppel
Editors	Jane Chapman Conor Kilgallon
Consultant Editor	Kevin Padian University of California, Berkeley
Art Editors	Dominic Zwemmer Steve Woosnam-Savage
Design Assistant	Mike Grigoletti
Editorial Advisor	Robert Dinwiddie
Managing Editor	Clare Currie
Managing Art Editor	Patrick Carpenter
Art Director	Dave Goodman
Editorial Director	Ellen Dupont
Editorial Coordinator	Rebecca Clunes
Picture Research	Zilda Tandy
Editorial Assistant	Dan Green
Production	Nikki Ingram

Published in the United States by Discovery Books. Distributed in the United States by Random House, Inc., New York, and in Canada by Random House of Canada Limited, Toronto.

Library of Congress Cataloging-in-Publication Data

Palmer, Douglas
Atlas of the Prehistoric World
Douglas Palmer — 1st American ed.
p. cm.
Includes index
ISBN 1-56331-829-6
1. Paleontology Maps I. Discovery Channel (Firm) II. Title III Title: Discovery Channel Atlas of the Prehistoric World
G1046.C57 P3 1999 <G&M>
912--dc21 99-40212 CIP
MAPS

Discovery Communications, Inc.
Website Address: www.discovery.com

Originated in Singapore
Printed and bound in Germany

10 9 8 7 6 5 4 3 2 1
First Edition

Contents

The Changing Globe

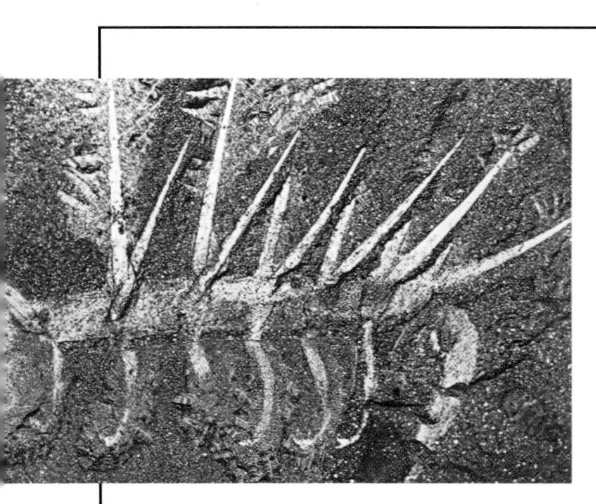

Ancient Worlds

Earth Fact File

Introduction

For four and a half billion years or more, the Earth has been circling the Sun. Our planet hasn't always looked at all as it does now, of course. In fact, almost like a living thing, the Earth's face has changed continually as it has aged. Its oceans and atmospheres have evolved, mountain ranges have risen and crumbled, seas have opened and dried, rivers have run their course and cut great canyons in ancient rocks. And through it all, life on Earth has evolved to keep up with these monumental changes. It seems that whatever changes the Earth goes through, the plants, animals, and microbes manage to change along with it. How do we learn about these changes? History is a story of becoming. But geology and paleontology (the scientific study of fossils) give us the history of how the Earth and its life came to be.

One of the things that draws people to work in the field of paleontology is thinking about the questions of how things came to be. The Earth and all its life bear the marks of its history. Mountain ranges are former seafloors upthrust by tectonic processes, eroded by wind and water, raked by glaciers, shattered by earthquakes. In the same way, humans bear the marks of our evolution. We have elaborate organ systems, notably our kidneys and parts of our hormonal system, that function to simulate our ancestral watery home internally for us. Our forearm and lower leg bones are paired, reflecting their use in rotating the limbs during early land locomotion. Human fetuses even have gills for a while during the early stages of development. These clues to the history of life fascinate paleontologists, and us all.

The Discovery Channel's *Atlas of the Prehistoric World* allows you to follow these changes as they occurred through Earth's long history. First, a series of magnificent maps based on painstaking geological research shows how the continents have moved around the world over the last 620 million years. Next, these maps are related to the fossils that tell you about the plants and animals that lived in the ancient seas and on the unfamiliar lands shown in the maps. Finally, a comprehensive Fact File clearly explains the complex ideas and principles of geology and paleontology.

It is probably fair to say that the Western world really began to study the Earth in the modern sense nearly two centuries ago. At this time there were many "theories" of the Earth that tried to account for the shapes and character of rocks and their contents. It was accepted that fossils were the remains of past organic life, not artifacts or accidents of nature. The presence of fossil seashells on mountainsides, first thought to be remnants of Noah's flood, were revealed to be a succession of strata distributed all over the world, as William Smith and many others in England, then through continental Europe and elsewhere, established the science of stratigraphy.

The next problem was to figure out how old all these rocks were. Clearly the lower ones were deposited before the higher ones, but most places in the world had only a few pieces of the entire succession. It awaited the discovery of radioactivity and the measurement of isotope decay before we could calibrate the age of the rocks in millions of years, though Darwin and many geologists had made reasonable guesses decades earlier. Finally, how did all of these disjunct pieces of real estate reach their far-flung corners? This was the problem of continental drift, first a notion, then a hypothesis, then an established theory that developed into plate tectonics, the unifying concept of geology. As we learned about the movements of continents, the shifting and bucking of plates, and the openings and closings of oceans, we also learned why earthquakes, volcanoes, hot spots, and mountain building were all parts of the same general phenomenon of tectonics. This also helped us to test ideas about the origin and evolution of the atmosphere, the oceans, the Earth itself, and of course its life.

The book you hold is a time traveler's version of a typical atlas. It tells you not so much where things are, but where things were; not so much about the present day inhabitants, but much about those of the past, including their peculiar "habits" and "customs." Above all, it is a book about how these things came to be. How the flowering plants evolved; how a mass extinction wiped out most of the marine life 250 million years ago; how India moved from the southern to the northern hemisphere, throwing up the Himalayas in the process. It is also a book about the amazing creatures that have populated the Earth since the dawn of time, steadily replacing successive fauna and flora and providing today's hunters of the past with a rich tapestry of life.

The Discovery Channel's *Atlas of the Prehistoric World* has been designed to be a compact, informative digest of what we know about the world of the past. It will provide a gateway to further reading and exploration. Its illustrations are meant to inform and delight its readers; its text contains many key words that will open the doors to further knowledge in libraries and on the internet. Whether you are interested in how the continents got to their present positions, who was living in Australia 20 million years ago, or you simply want to brush up your knowledge of the Burgess Shale, this book will get you off to a good start. Happy traveling.

Kevin Padian
Museum of Paleontology
University of California, Berkeley

The Changing Globe

Ours is a world in constant motion, its surface a patchwork of interlocking tectonic plates that carry the continents. The maps in this section trace the movements of the Earth's plates over the last 620 million years, revealing how the continents arrived at their present positions. We see how mountain ranges mark where ancient continents collided and how lands now separated by wide oceans were once clustered together as a giant supercontinent.

The Changing Face of the Earth

VENDIAN TIMES 620 MILLION YEARS AGO (MA)

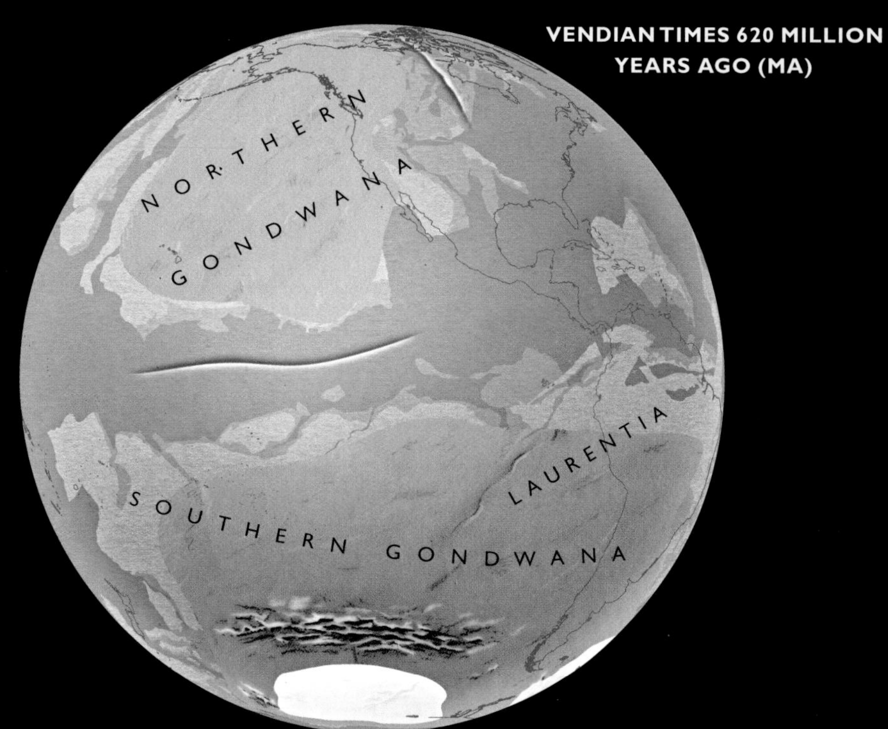

Throughout its long geological history, the Earth has undergone vast changes that have affected the distribution and shapes of its continents, its climate, its lifeforms, and the extent and depths of its oceans. The maps on the following 34 pages illustrate these alterations.

The reason for many of these changes has been movement of tectonic plates—large pieces of the Earth's surface layer. These movements are in turn driven by huge flows of hot semi-molten material within the Earth's interior. Plates consist of continental crust, oceanic crust (seafloor), or both. New oceanic crust is continuously formed at structures called spreading ridges at the bottoms of the oceans. When new oceanic crust is added to a plate that also contains a continent, the continent is pushed away from the formative ridge. Over hundreds of millions of years, sequences of such movements have caused continents to move thousands of miles over the Earth's surface and in some cases to rotate.

Plate movements sometimes cause continents to collide, and the result may be the formation of vast mountain ranges. They also cause oceanic crust to be forced down into the Earth's interior at some plate boundaries, which can cause earthquake and volcanic activity, with widespread effects including climatic change. Climatic fluctuations in turn affect factors such as sea levels and the world distribution of plants and animals.

DEVONIAN TIMES 360 MA

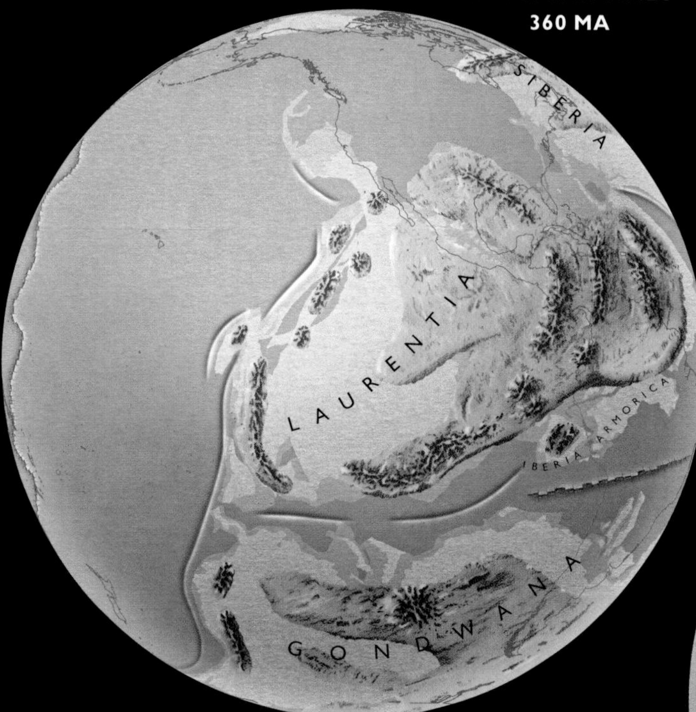

LATE CRETACEOUS TIMES 65 MA

THREE STAGES IN PREHISTORY

The maps on this page show the hemisphere of the Earth now occupied by the Americas at three stages in history. About 620 million years ago or MA (top), two main landmasses existed. By 360 MA (above), these had joined up and rotated to the south, but a separate continent, Laurentia, had broken off to the north. By 65 MA (right), the landmasses were beginning to resemble their present form. Laurentia eventually gave rise to North America and to parts of Europe and Asia, while Gondwana had split up to form most of the other continents.

How to Read the Maps

TIMELINE
At the top of each page is a timeline, divided into periods of 50 MA (millions of years). The small globe marks the point in the Earth's history shown by the maps on that page.

WHOLE WORLD PROJECTION

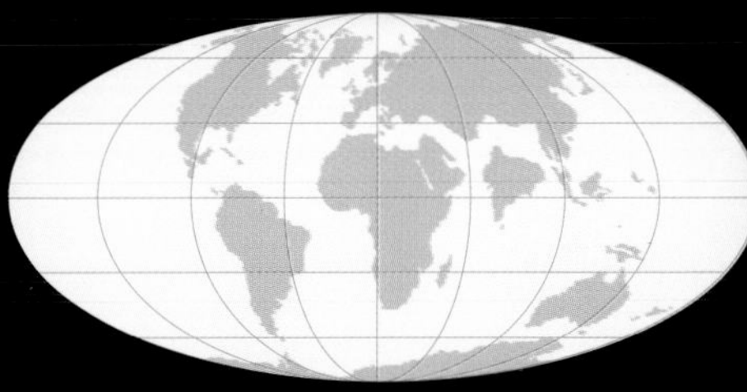

2. ANCIENT CONTINENTAL SEAS
The light blue regions represent areas of the continents covered by shallow seas at the time of the map. Ancient continents were often widely flooded by the sea. The shape of the dry land changed continuously as sea levels rose and fell.

1. MODERN CONTINENTAL OUTLINE
The purple lines represent the modern coasts of continents and islands. They indicate what part of the globe you are looking at, and from what direction (whether looking down on the equator or on one of the poles).

WHOLE WORLD PROJECTION
A small map for each period shows the whole ancient world in one view, making it easy to see how the face of the Earth has changed.

3. ANCIENT MOUNTAIN RANGE
Mountains are shown as they are on physical maps of the modern world—as raised brown areas. Mountains generally form either as a result of volcanic activity or continental collision. Huge mountain ranges of the distant past have since been eroded away to become gentler, more rounded hills.

4. ANCIENT LAND
The green, brown, and yellow regions indicate ancient dry land. The further back into the past, the less these regions resemble the shapes of modern continents.

5. ARID REGIONS
These areas, shown in yellow, contain evaporites (minerals formed by the evaporation of water from salty shallow seas and lakes).

EARLY TERTIARY TIMES 45 MA

6. COAL-FORMING REGIONS
The darker green areas represent lowland forested or swampy regions where peat and coal were deposited.

8. SUBDUCTION ZONE
Solid curved lines in the oceans mark subduction zones, regions where plate movement is causing seafloor to be pushed down beneath a continental crust or (sometimes) other oceanic crust at a plate boundary. Subduction zones are often associated with earthquakes and volcanic activity.

7. SPREADING OCEAN RIDGE
Mid-ocean spreading ridges, marked on the maps as raised, jagged lines, are regions where new oceanic crust (seafloor) is created. The creation of new seafloor, which is pushed slowly away from a mid-ocean ridge as it is formed, is the main driving force for plate movement.

Vendian Times

Maps of the earth some 620 million years ago, at the beginning of Vendian times and at the end of the long Precambrian era, show a planet with an unfamiliar face. Land fills much of the area now covered by the Pacific Ocean, while ancient seas fill the hemisphere where Europe, Asia, and Africa now lie. Two main continents dominate the globe: the northern one (northern Gondwana) is made up of what is now India, Antarctica, and Australia, while the landmass in the south consists of what is now Africa, the Americas, and parts of Asia. Areas that are tropical in modern times, such as West Africa and parts of South America, were clustered then near the South Pole and were heavily glaciated.

1. PASSIVE MARGINS
The coasts of what are now northwestern Australia (in northern Gondwana), northeastern North America (Laurentia), and northeastern Siberia were all "passive margins," zones forming the edges of crustal plates but without the earthquake activity associated with such regions. Extensive sediments built up on the beds of shallow seas in these locations in Vendian times.

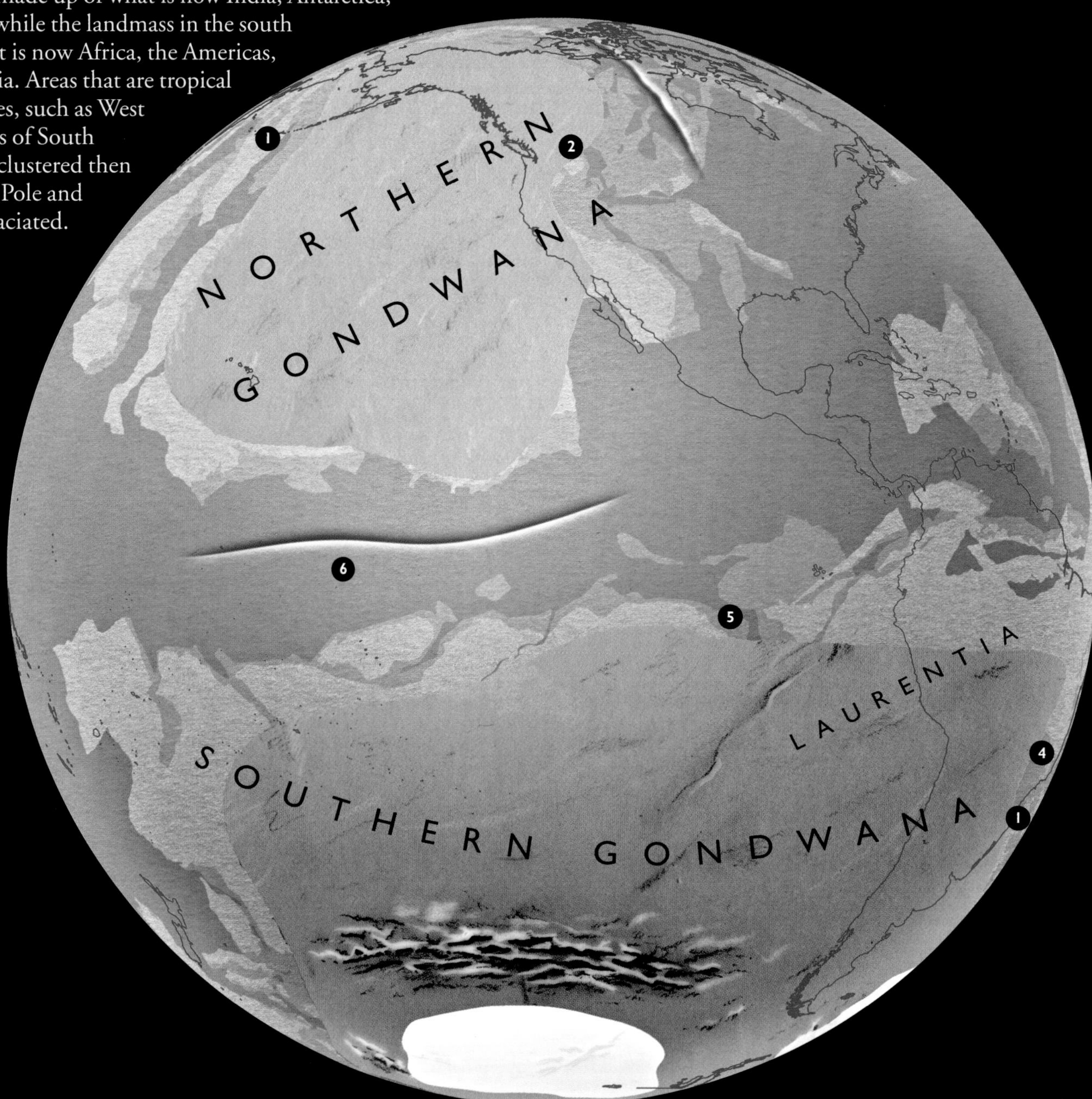

6. DISAPPEARING OCEAN
The ocean between the northern and southern parts of what would one day become the supercontinent of Gondwana was rapidly narrowing. About 580 million years ago, the northern coast of southern Gondwana collided with the southern coast of northern Gondwana to form a landmass called Pannotia, which seems to have lasted for only a few million years.

5. WARM NAMIBIAN WATERS
Namibia, now in southwest Africa, lay in warm shallow equatorial waters for a long period during Vendian times. It is now one of the most famous localities in the world for Ediacaran fossil traces (although they are somewhat younger in age, mostly less than 600 million years old, than the times shown on this map).

2. FLINDERS RANGE, SOUTH AUSTRALIA

Australia lay in the northern hemisphere in Vendian times. It contains excellent examples of the sandstone that is typical of the period, originally laid down on a shallow, sandy seafloor swept by tidal currents. Vendian sandstone preserves the best-known fossils of the period, the Ediacarans. These soft-bodied animals were named for the Ediacara Hills in the Flinders Range of South Australia, where they were first found. They thrived in the shallow seas, anchored to the seabed or burrowed into the sand.

WHOLE WORLD PROJECTION

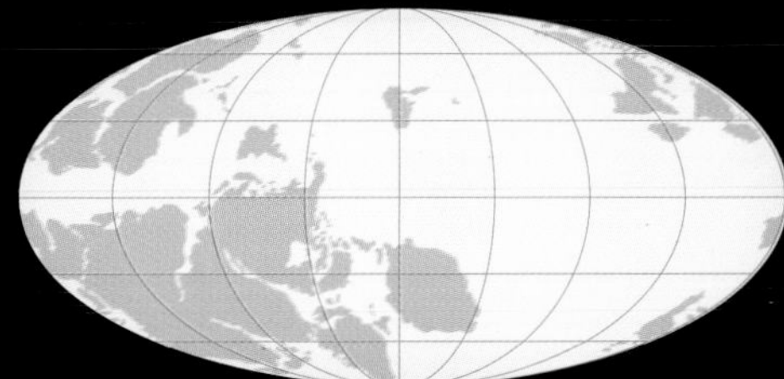

4. NEWFOUNDLAND

The Vendian sandstone rocks of Newfoundland are finer grained than those of Australia. The sediments may have been deposited by successive underwater avalanches called turbidity currents, possibly triggered by submarine earthquakes. Ediacaran fossils are also found here, at locations such as Mistaken Point.

3. CHINESE STRATA

The Nantuo Formation in southern China is made from "tillites," a mixture of mud, sand, large stones, and rock brought together and carried along by ancient glaciers. The presence of tillites in this region shows that it was glaciated in late Vendian times (20 million years after the situation shown in this map, once sea levels had fallen). How much of the world was covered by glaciers is hotly debated. Some specialists theorize that the Earth was almost completely frozen over, while others refute this claim.

Early Cambrian Times

Soon after the start of the Cambrian age, 540 million years ago, the world had already experienced major changes. All the continents of the previous Vendian world had come together briefly to form a supercontinent called Pannotia, which had then broken up. By the early Cambrian times shown in these maps, a remnant of Pannotia, called Gondwana, still stretched almost from pole to pole. It was made up of modern China, India, Australia, Antarctica, Africa, and South America. Two major lands not part of this continent were Laurentia (including most of North America) and Siberia. A growing mid-oceanic ridge between these islands and Gondwana pushed them on a long journey northward.

1. LIMESTONE OF LAURENTIA
Laurentia, including much of North America, part of Newfoundland, Scotland, and Greenland, was surrounded by calm seas, which provided the right environment for limestone to form. This limestone contains fossils of tiny, shelled creatures. Conditions in Siberia also fostered the formation of limestone during this period, but the fossils found there are different from those found in Laurentia, indicating that the two landmasses were widely separated.

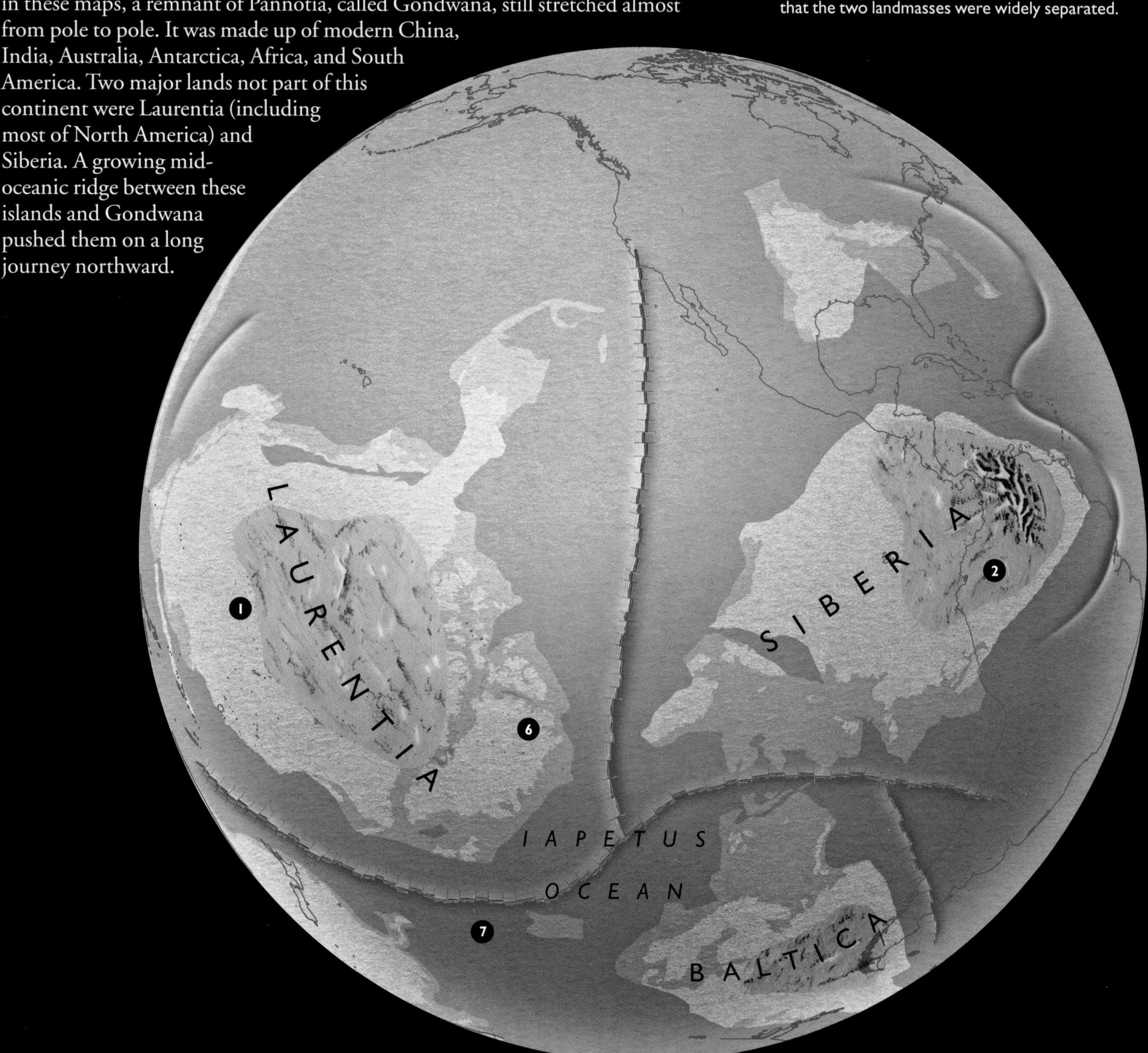

7. IAPETUS OCEAN
In early Cambrian times, a body of water known as the Iapetus Ocean separated Laurentia from Gondwana, Avalonia, and Baltica (which included Scandinavia and eastern Europe). Florida and parts of Central America were on the shores of Gondwana, split off from the rest of North America. East and west Newfoundland also lay on opposite sides of the ocean.

6. TROPICAL GREENLAND
Peary Land, now in the far north of Greenland within the Arctic Circle, lay in much warmer waters during early Cambrian times. Evidence for this comes from limestone and muddy sediments in the region, which contain fossils of arthropods, sponges, brachiopods, and worms, all inhabitants of calm, warm seas.

2. SIBERIAN MOVEMENTS
When rocks form, some of them record the Earth's magnetic field. The record in the rocks of Siberia shows that, during Cambrian times, it moved northward from its previous position near the South Pole. The data also show that the Siberian continental plate was upside-down compared to its present position.

3. NORTH AND SOUTH CHINA
China at this time consisted of two separate and submerged continental masses that lay in warm tropical waters off the coast of the large continent of Gondwana. Both parts of China were slowly moving southward during Cambrian times.

WHOLE WORLD PROJECTION

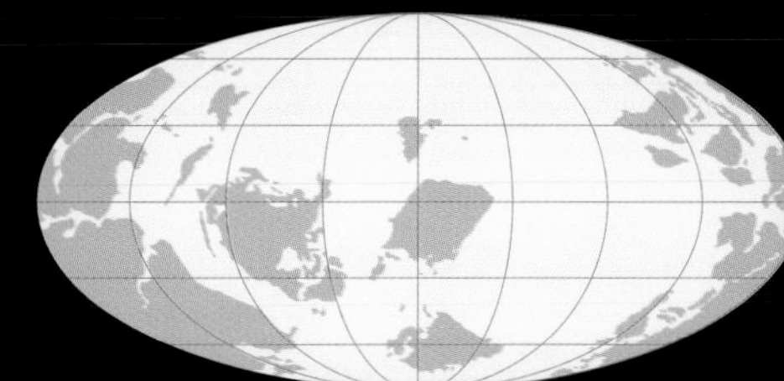

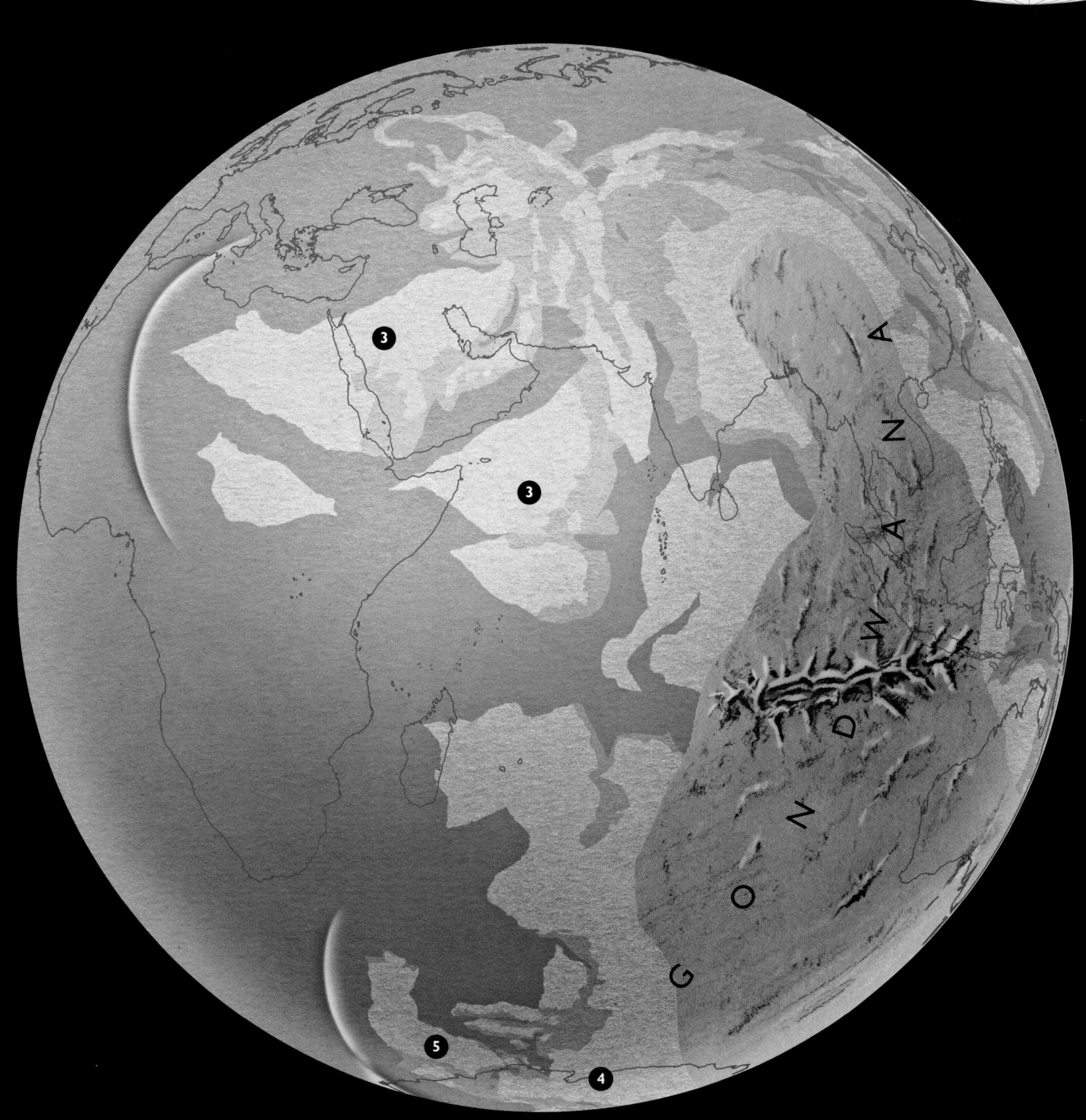

5. CAMBRIAN AVALONIA
Wales was part of Avalonia, a continental fragment off the coast of Gondwana that also carried England, parts of Newfoundland and New England, and Nova Scotia. Cambrian strata were first mapped in Wales, but strata in Newfoundland are now used to define the beginning of the period. The starting point is marked by distinctive trace fossils.

4. NORTH AFRICAN ENIGMA
Analyzing the magnetic field of rocks from Morocco suggests that North Africa lay near the South Pole in early Cambrian times, as shown on this map. Fossil evidence in coral reefs and sandstone, however, suggests that the region was hot during this period and may have lain closer to the equator. This conflict has not been satisfactorily resolved.

Late Cambrian Times

The earth's poles, as seen 500 million years ago, present a surprising view. Today the northern hemisphere (this page, viewed looking down on the pole) is crowded with land, but half a billion years ago it was almost empty, except for a submerged fragment of modern Russia close to the North Pole. The southern hemisphere contained further surprises. Near the South Pole, located underwater off the coast of Gondwana, were Avalonia (parts of Britain, Ireland, and the eastern American seaboard), Iberia (Portugal and Spain), and Armorica (other fragments of western Europe), about 8,000 miles (13,000 kilometers) away from their present positions.

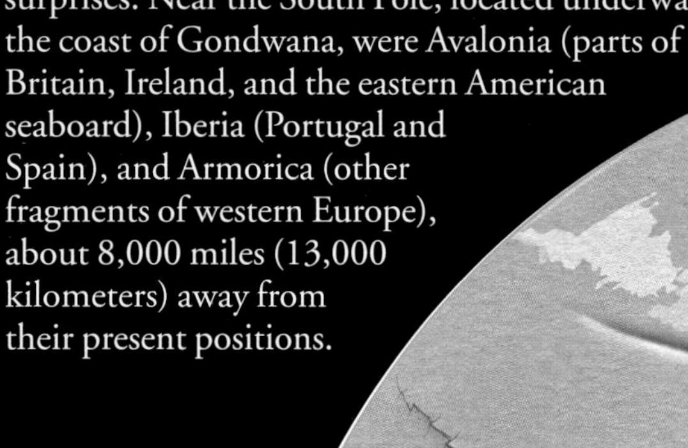

1. AUSTRALIAN BUILDUP
The area that is now eastern Australia was on the northern coast of the great landmass known as Gondwana. It contained a series of mountain belts formed as the ancient core of the continent collided with thin slivers of continental shelf called "microcontinents" beginning about 500 million years ago.

8. BRITISH COLUMBIA
During these times, Laurentia straddled the equator (the perimeter of the globes on these pages). Rising sea levels flooded more and more of the continent during the Cambrian, so that by the end of the period half of the land was under the sea. In the eastern part of modern British Columbia, underwater mudslides trapped the famous fossils of the Burgess Shale.

7. ALASKAN ACCRETION
Laurentia is the ancient continent that now forms the core of North America. In late Cambrian times, what is now the west coast of North America looked different than it does today. Alaska was just a small peninsula. Slivers of land called terranes collided with the coast of Laurentia south of Alaska. Plate movement then pushed these north until they reached Alaska, which gradually increased in size.

2. ROCK OF AGES
Strata from scattered regions of ancient Avalonia and Armorica show how sea levels changed during Cambrian times: the coarser the grains in a sedimentary rock formed underwater, the closer to shore it formed. The earliest Cambrian rock in the region is coarse sandstone. Later rock is mostly mudstone, made of much smaller particles. This shows that sea levels rose during Cambrian times.

3. NAMING TIME
The Cambrian period is named for the Roman word for Wales, "Cambria," because early mapping of rocks from this period took place in north Wales early in the 19th century. These strata consist of slate, sandstone, and some volcanic rocks, and contain fossils of worms and early shellfish.

WHOLE WORLD PROJECTION
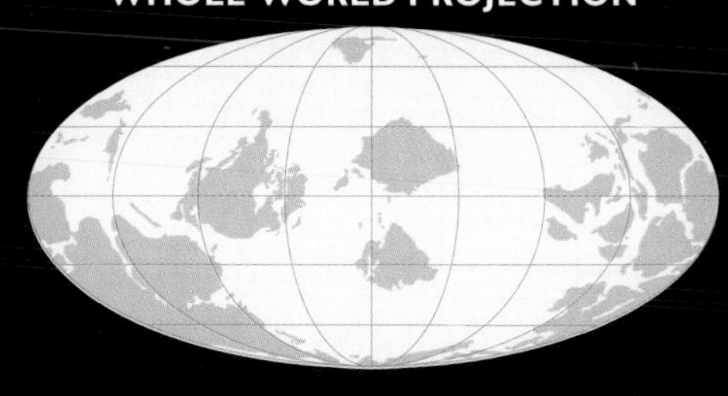

4. MUD DEPOSITS
Piles of sediment, mud, and sand up to 3 miles (5 kilometers) thick were deposited in deep marine basins in north Wales and southeast Ireland. The marine mud of north Wales was later compressed into slate, which is extensively used today as roofing material.

6. BUILDING UP
At the end of the Cambrian period, 495 million years ago, a mountain chain started to appear in Baltica, in the northernmost parts of what is now Scandinavia. The mountains formed as Baltica collided with a series of volcanic islands, the start of a process that later led to the building of the Caledonian Mountains in Scotland and the Appalachian chain in America.

5. OCEAN CROSSING
By late Cambrian times, the Iapetus Ocean was a huge body of water separating Gondwana, Baltica, and Laurentia. Over the next few million years, plate movements detached Avalonia, Armorica, and Iberia from the coast of Gondwana and carried them toward Laurentia, closing Iapetus while at the same time opening up a new sea, the Rheic Ocean.

Ordovician Times

Toward the end of the Ordovician period, 460 million years ago, one ancient sea, the Iapetus Ocean, was beginning to close, while another, the Rheic Ocean, was starting to open. These seas were on either side of thin strips of land close to the South Pole that now form the eastern seaboard of North America. Parts of Gondwana began to break away from the rest of the supercontinent. The remaining parts moved to the south, so that what is now North Africa lay directly over the South Pole. The land areas of many of the continents were growing; episodes of intense volcanic activity added land to the east coast of Australia as well as to parts of Antarctica and South America.

1. NORTHERN ENGLAND
The mountains and hills of the English Lake District are made of rocks that formed about 450 million years ago. They are resistant to erosion and are a mixture of slatelike mudrock, gritty sandstone, and volcanic rocks including lava, ash, and basalt. The ash from erupting volcanoes washed into shallow seas and lakes and settled over time to form rocks. During the last ice age, glaciers carved this bedrock into picturesque hills and wide valleys.

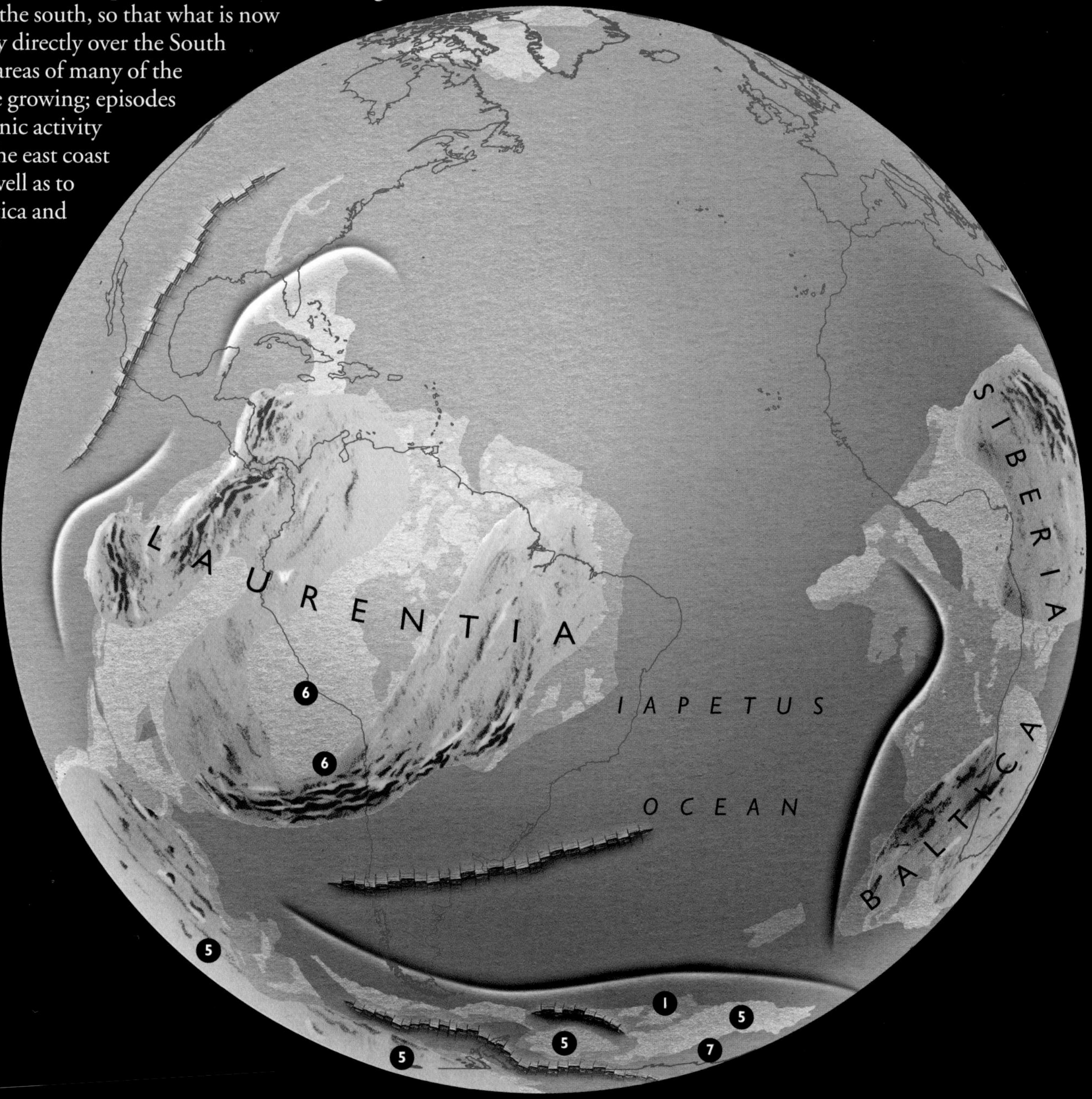

7. AN OCEAN IS BORN
During Ordovician times, Avalonia and Armorica, continental fragments that are now parts of North America and Europe, split away from the ancient supercontinent of Gondwana (which consisted of Africa, South America, Antarctica, Australia, and India). As the fragments moved north, a new ocean appeared behind them, known as the Rheic Ocean.

6. EVIDENCE OF A CATASTROPHE
Near Hagen, Virginia, a layer of volcanic ash dating from the Ordovician period can be seen. The layer stretches all the way from Minnesota and contains 500 times more ash than that created by the eruption of Mount St. Helens in 1980. The huge eruption that produced the ash led to the extinction of many species, with all local echinoderms (ancestors of modern starfish) and cephalopods disappearing.

2. CHINA

At the beginning of the Ordovician period, seas flooded across the several crustal plates that were part of western Gondwana and now make up China. Sediments accumulated to form deposits of limestone, half a mile thick in places. These rocks contain the world's most complete marine fossil record of the period, including corals, trilobites (which resembled king crabs), and nautiloids (relatives of today's squid and octopuses). From time to time, shallow lagoons in the area dried up, leaving behind deposits of minerals such as salt and gypsum.

3. FORGOTTEN SEAS

About 460 million years ago, Australia lay astride the equator. Ordovician sandstone found near Alice Springs in the middle of present-day Australia shows that Australia was partly flooded by shallow seas during Ordovician times. The sediment contains some of the oldest known fish remains.

WHOLE WORLD PROJECTION

4. SOUTH AFRICA

Late Ordovician strata, some 440 million years old, from Clanwilliam in Cape Province, South Africa, are interesting on two counts. They provide evidence for a late Ordovician glaciation and for the body form of the extinct conodonts (eel-like animals with tiny toothlike fossils). The strata contain rocks carrying scratchmarks from glaciers. Above the glacial deposits lies shale that formed in shallow seas. The occasional dropstone (a pebble that has dropped from or through sea-ice) in the shale shows that these waters were sometimes covered by sea-ice or icebergs. The fossil fauna in the shale consists of trilobites and other arthropods, as well as cephalopods (early ancestors of squid), brachiopods (primitive shelled animals), and conodonts. Recent finds show that conodonts had eyes and a notochord (primitive spinal cord).

5. SIGNS OF GLACIATION

Several sites scattered from the Amazon Basin in Brazil, across North Africa and through to Saudi Arabia contain tillites—compacted rock rubble and mud carved out by late Ordovician glaciers. These indicate that part of Gondwana, near the South Pole, was heavily glaciated in Ordovician times. Other signs of glaciation, such as dropstones, are found in many regions, such as France and Spain, which were off the coast of Gondwana at the time.

Silurian Times

Viewing the Earth from an angle almost above the poles (the South Pole on this page, the North Pole opposite), it is clear that 420 million years ago, during the Silurian period, most of the continents lay in the southern hemisphere. The great continent of Gondwana, including modern South America, Africa, Australia, and India, was situated around the South Pole. Avalonia, a continental fragment including much of the eastern seaboard of America, closed up the Iapetus Ocean as it approached Laurentia, which makes up most of modern North America. South of Avalonia, the Rheic Ocean opened up. Greenland and Alaska, lands now near the North Pole, were on the equator during the Silurian period.

1. Defining an Age

The crossover between the Ordovician and Silurian periods of Earth's prehistory is defined in rock strata at Dob's Linn, Scotland. During Silurian times, the area was at the edge of Baltica, a large island that also took in Scandinavia and parts of Northern Europe. Layers of sandstone and shale formed on the seabed, and the boundary between two of these strata marks the changeover point between earlier Ordovician and later Silurian rocks.

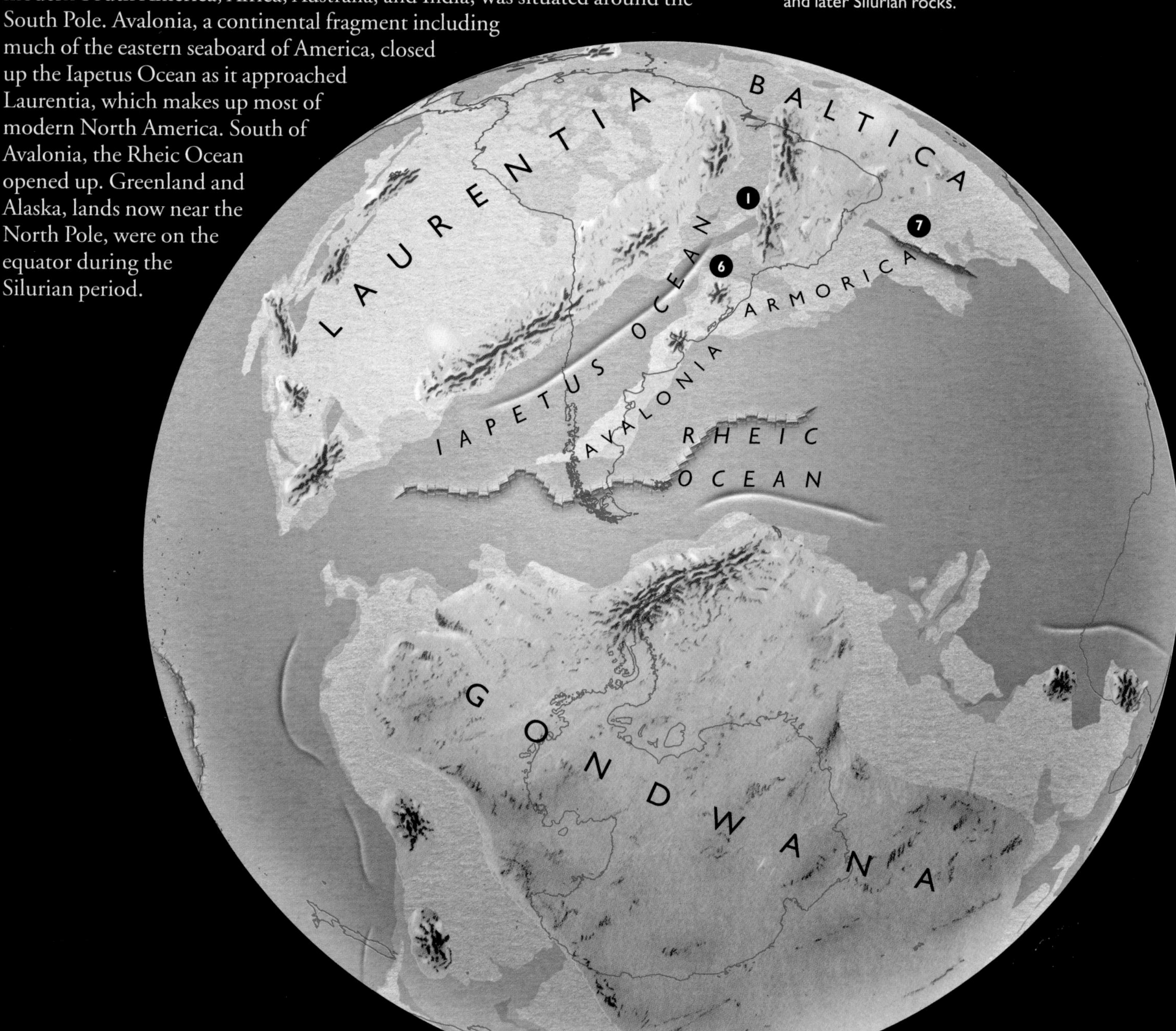

7. Czech Boundary

Shale and limestone strata at Klonk, near Prague in the Czech Republic, are the youngest Silurian rocks, and mark the transition into the next period of geologic time, the Devonian. The rocks in this region contain many fossils, including several thousand species of shellfish, particularly trilobites.

6. Wales and Southern Ireland

In Silurian times, the continental fragment of Avalonia was a series of islands just off the coast of Laurentia. Rocks in Wales and Ireland—then parts of Avalonia—are characterized by fossils of the first plants to colonize the land. These fossils are found in rocks formed on the bed of a shallow sea, not far from the ancient shorelines where the plants once grew.

2. EASTERN AUSTRALIA

Subduction (the movement of one plate under another) on the eastern margins of Gondwana led to the development of active volcanoes as ocean floor rocks were pushed down toward the Earth's mantle and melted. The melted rock forced its way to the surface, erupting to form volcanoes, which spewed out lava and ash. In eastern Australia, extensive volcanic eruptions occurred from mid-Silurian times into the Devonian.

3. THE FOSSIL CLOCKS OF SOUTH CHINA

Silurian strata in southern China contain many different types of fossils called graptolites. Graptolites were tiny creatures that lived in oceans around the world and evolved quickly into different forms. Successive types of graptolites form evolving and well-defined timelines that can be used as yardsticks to match the Silurian strata of China with graptolitic rocks elsewhere in the world.

WHOLE WORLD PROJECTION

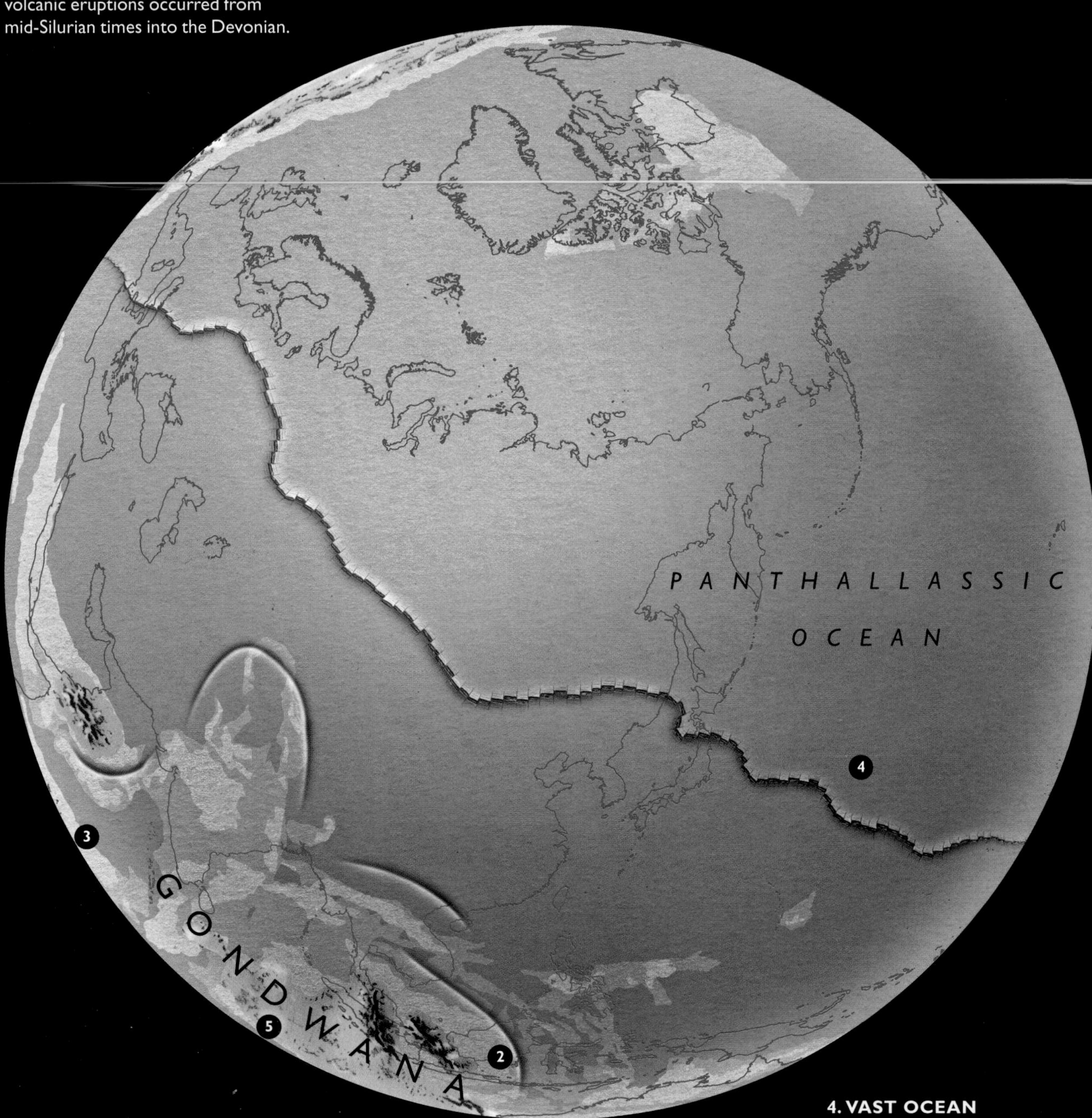

5. TRACKS IN THE DUNES

Trace fossils in the late Silurian sandstones of Kalbarri, Western Australia, tell us much about early land environments there. Trace fossils—the solidified tracks and scratches left by small animals as they moved—were left on the sandy riverbeds and sand dunes. They show that there was no vegetation in the region at the time. The creatures that left the tracks fed instead on a thin film of algae and bacteria.

4. VAST OCEAN

The ocean that covered half the globe from Silurian times through to the Mesozoic era is called the Panthallassic Ocean. It was so vast that from some views in space the Earth would have looked as if it were covered by sea. The growth of the Panthallassic Ocean, and movements of the continental plates on which it lay, must have been controlled by ocean floor spreading from a mid-oceanic ridge; however, the exact location of the ridge shown on this map is not known.

Devonian Times

A look at the earth 360 million years ago shows two massive supercontinents drifting slowly toward each other. In the south is Gondwana, a clustering of the lands that today are called Australia, Antarctica, India, Africa, and South America. The northern supercontinent is Laurentia, which includes the modern lands of North America and northern Europe. The land shape of this continent is not at all familiar, however. Shallow seas flood the area that is the modern American Midwest, while Iberia (modern Spain and Portugal) is an island off Laurentia's south coast.

1. COLLISION ZONE

About 360 million years ago, Baltica (containing modern Scandinavia) collided with Laurentia (modern North America). In the process, great mountain chains were thrown up in Scandinavia. When they first formed, these mountains were many thousands of feet high. The rocks forming the deep roots of the mountains, several miles down, were compressed and heated to form metamorphic rocks such as schists and gneisses. Today, the mountains have been so heavily eroded that these metamorphic rocks are at the surface.

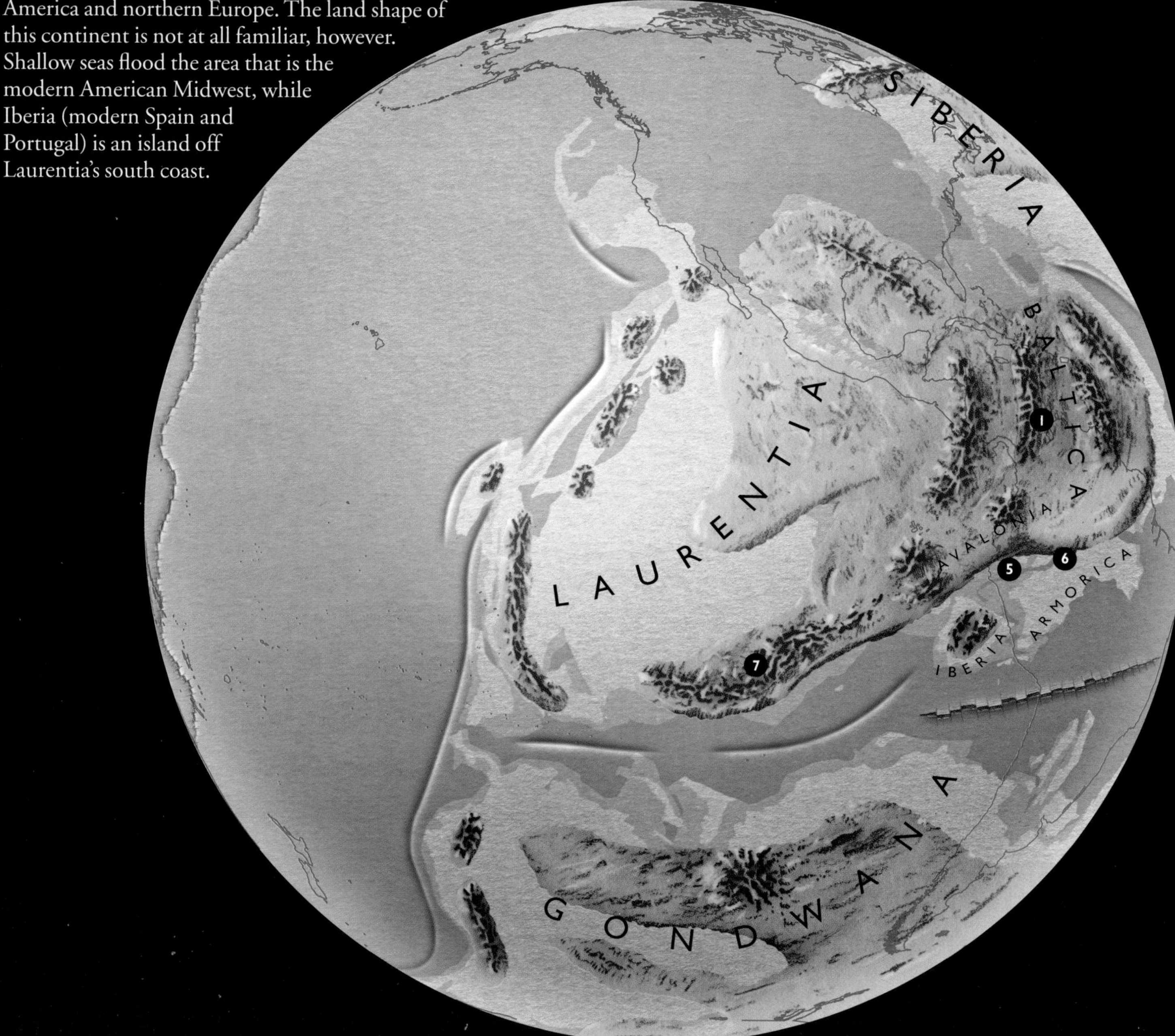

7. AMERICAN MOUNTAINS

About 380 million years ago, an episode of mountain building, or orogeny, took place along the length of the Appalachian mountains in eastern North America. It was called the Acadian orogeny. By late Devonian times, 360 million years ago, rivers had swept eroded rock from these new mountains into deep basins on either side of the range. Over time, these sediments have compacted to form characteristic red rocks.

6. OPENING AND CLOSING SEAS

Armorica (parts of western Europe) collided with Avalonia (England, Wales, and parts of eastern North America) during the Silurian age, but by early Devonian times the lands had again parted. As the gap reopened, a small ocean basin formed. Sediment gradually filled this basin and was compressed to become rock.

2. CHINESE SEAS AND MOUNTAINS

At the beginning of the Devonian period, extensive mountain building took place in China. In most parts of China, which in those times consisted of a series of islands, the process lifted the land above sea level. The northeast and southeast remained covered by shallow seas. They are marked today by Devonian limestone (old, compressed marine sediments), which contain fossils of coral reefs. Elsewhere in China, red sandstones from the Devonian period show that these regions were hot and dry at the time.

3. AUSTRALIA GROWS

During Devonian times, mountain building continued in Australia. The southeast coast of the continent collided with a chain of volcanic islands, forming a chain of mountains. New rivers flowing from these mountains carried sediment to basins in the center of the continent, forming distinctive Devonian rocks.

WHOLE WORLD PROJECTION

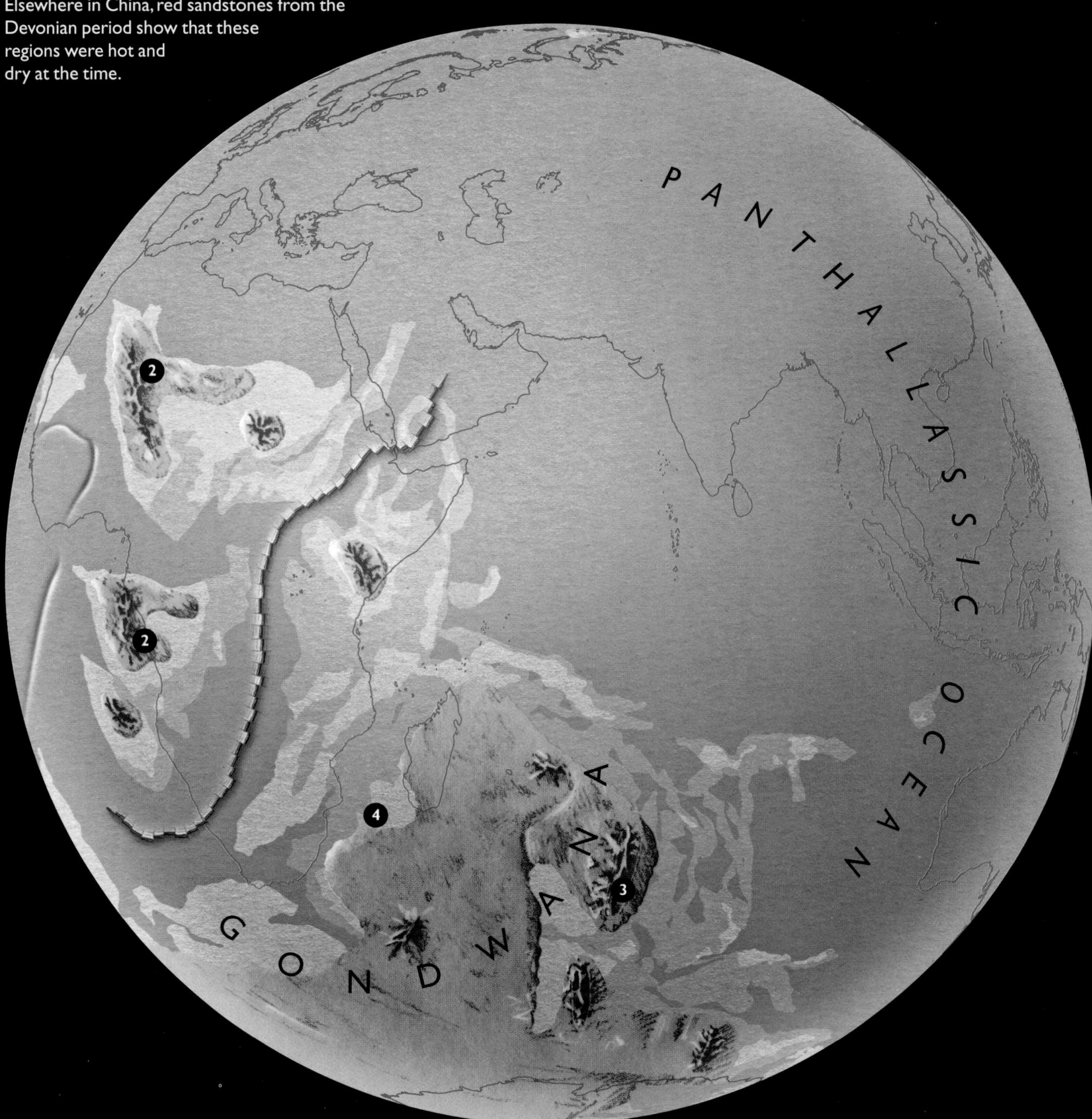

5. NAMING THE DEVONIAN

The Devonian period was named in 1839 for rock strata in the county of Devon in southwest England. The geologists Adam Sedgwick and Roderick Murchison mapped some distinctive layers of rocks found in the county. These rocks, built up from marine sediments, contained fossils different from those found in older Silurian strata and younger Carboniferous strata.

4. WESTERN AUSTRALIAN REEFS

In Devonian times, Australia was part of the southern supercontinent, Gondwana. Parts of Western Australia were covered by shallow seas. Over time, the sea-floor sediments have been compressed to form characteristic reef limestone and mudstone. Fossils of extremely diverse communities of fish and other marine life can be found within these rocks.

Carboniferous Times

The Carboniferous period began 354 million years ago. For the first time the greatest supercontinent of them all, Pangea, can be discerned. Pangea was forming at this time from the collision of Laurentia (North America and Europe) with the old southern supercontinent of Gondwana. Before the collision, Gondwana had rotated clockwise, so that its eastern part (India, Australia, and Antarctica) moved south while its western part (South America and Africa) moved north. This rotation opened a new ocean, the Tethys Ocean, in the east and closed an old one, the Rheic, in the west. At the same time the ocean between Baltica and Siberia was closing, paving the way for another collision of continents.

1. BUILDING CALIFORNIA
Most of North America existed in prehistoric times as the continent of Laurentia. The west coast, however, was not originally part of the continent. It built up by the collision of strings of volcanic islands, formed in the Panthallassic Ocean, with Laurentia's western edge. These islands were drawn toward the coast as seafloor was pushed into the Earth's interior at a subduction zone. During Carboniferous times, the collision of the eastward-moving Antler volcanic island arc with Laurentia prompted a period of rock formation known as the Antler orogeny. The effects of this impact can still be seen in California and Nevada.

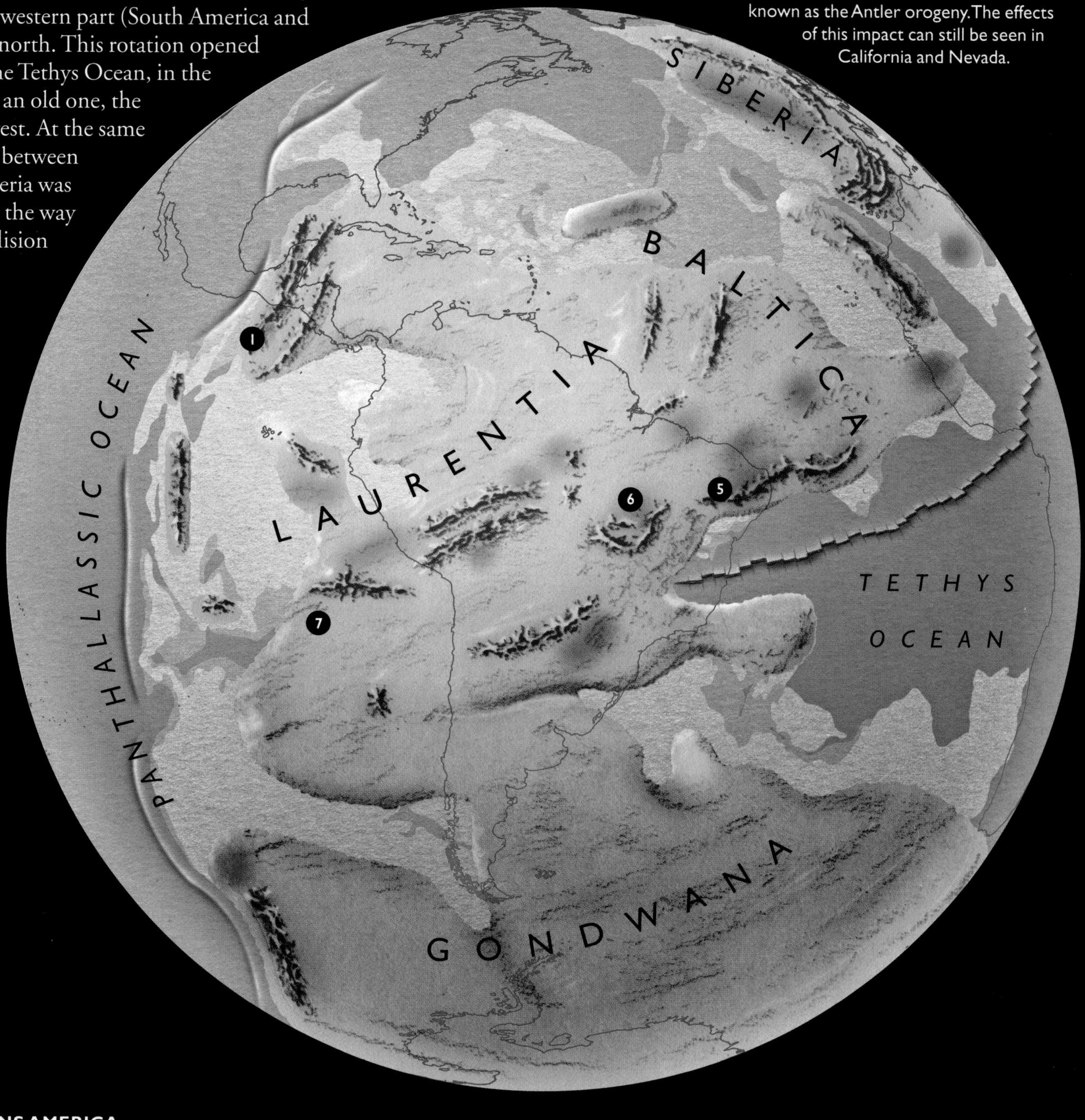

7. FLORIDA JOINS AMERICA
Most of what is now North America was once part of ancient Laurentia. But Florida was originally part of the southern supercontinent, Gondwana. When Gondwana and Laurentia first collided at the end of the Carboniferous period, Florida became joined to the North American continent. It remained there when Gondwana and Laurentia later separated again as the Atlantic Ocean opened.

6. COAL FIELDS
The Joggins coal field in what is now Nova Scotia formed from the remains of a swampy forest that stood in the region during Carboniferous times. Some trunks of giant clubmoss trees from the forest are still preserved in the coal deposits. Similar coal fields lie in what was then a continuous band running from Alabama along the Appalachians and through to Germany.

2. CHINA IN THE CARBONIFEROUS

China in Carboniferous times remained mostly below sea level. Parts of the country were dry land, sometimes inundated by shallow seas. Rocks in the north of the country that date from Carboniferous times are a succession of layers of coal-bearing rocks—formed in swamps on land—and limestone formed from compact sediments that collected on the floor of a shallow sea.

3. AUSTRALIA HEADS SOUTH

In early Carboniferous times, the north of Australia was lapped by seas warm enough for coral reefs to grow. These reefs are visible today as limestone. Dense forests in the eastern part of the continent laid down thin layers of coal. In later Carboniferous times, Gondwana moved south and the climate cooled. Glacial deposits in southeastern Australia are evidence for this movement. In 30 million years Australia moved south by 20 degrees of latitude.

WHOLE WORLD PROJECTION

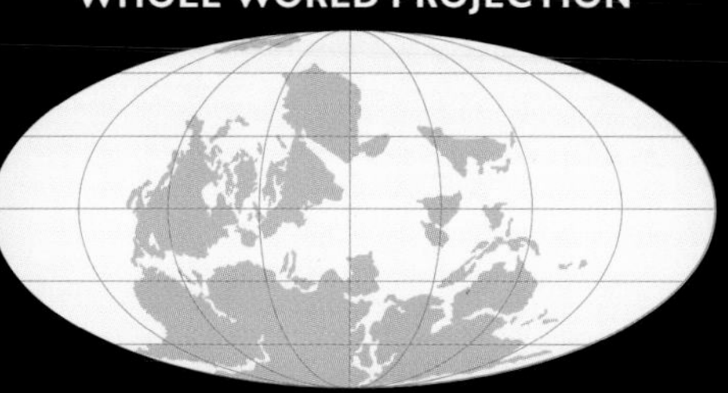

5. EUROPE IN COLLISION

The collision of Armorica (now part of western Europe) and Iberia (Portugal and Spain) with the southern coast of Avalonia (England and Wales) resulted in the Variscan orogeny, the building of a chain of mountains that passed from modern Germany through southern Britain to Ireland. A similar collision between Gondwana and Laurentia in late Carboniferous times produced the Allegheny orogeny, an episode of mountain building that added to the Appalachians.

4. GONDWANA ROTATES

From late Devonian times, Gondwana began to rotate in a clockwise direction. This movement must have been caused by a mid-ocean ridge creating new seafloor to the north and pushing eastern Gondwana south. The location of the ridge shown on this map to the north of Gondwana is not certain.

Permian Times

THE PERMIAN PERIOD LASTED FROM 290 TO 248 MILLION YEARS ago. During this time the great supercontinent of Pangea was finally assembled when the ancient island continent of Siberia joined up with the rest of the world's major landmasses. The enormous jigsaw of crustal plates, which also included Laurentia, Baltica, and Gondwana, thus stretched almost from pole to pole. The end of the Permian was marked by the biggest mass extinction in the history of life. This was probably caused by a sharp fall in sea levels that killed off much of the life in the shallow shelf seas. Huge lava flows in Siberia would also have speeded up climate change.

1. FORMATION OF THE URALS
With the final closure of the ocean separating Siberia and Baltica, the two landmasses collided. The impact compressed the rocks at the edges of the continents, folding and faulting them to form the Ural mountains (the Permian period was named for the city of Perm in the Urals). Rock strata laid down during the building of the Urals are famous for their fossils of ancient relatives of mammals.

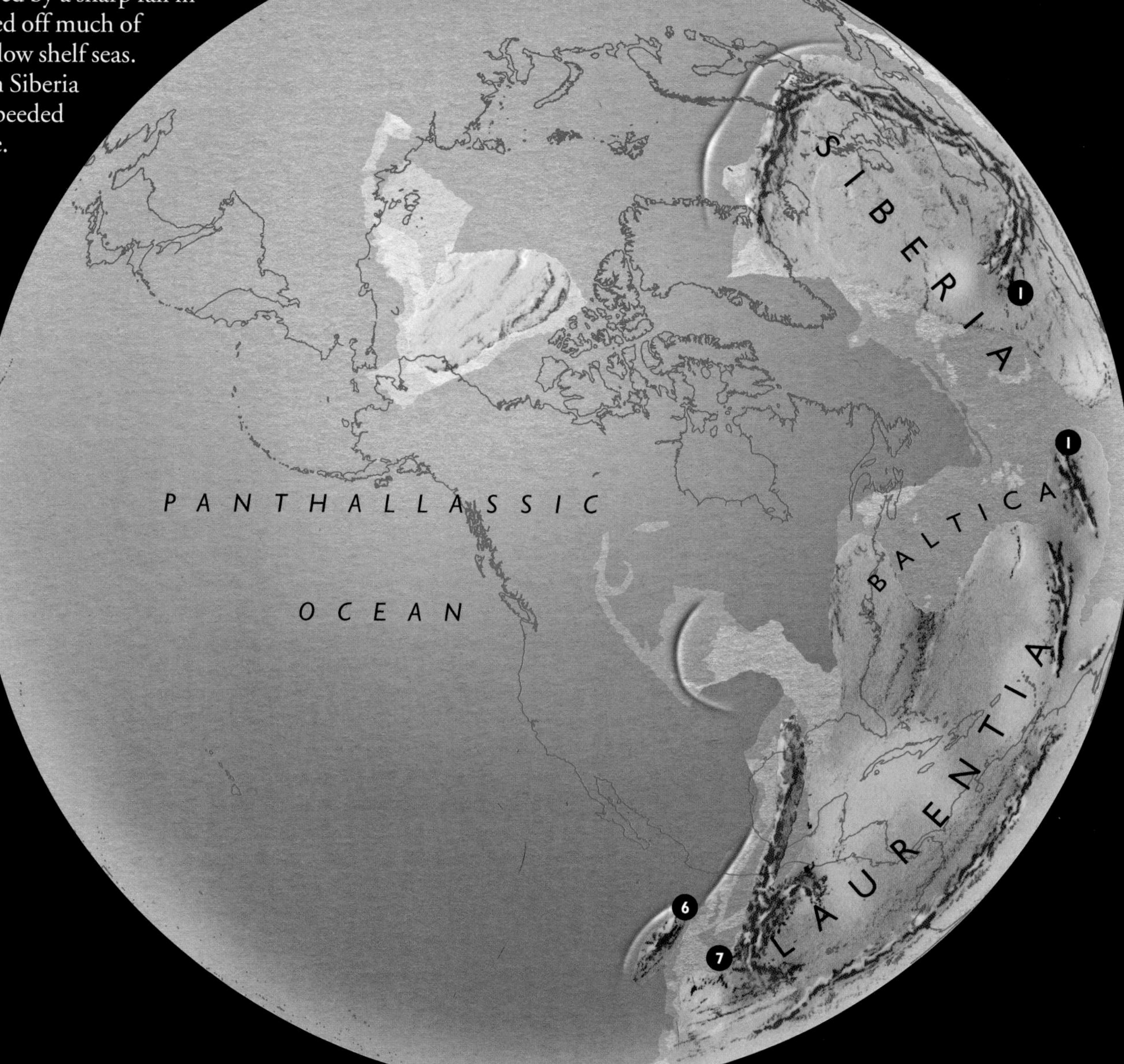

7. SHALLOW SEAS OF AMERICA
At times during the Permian period, shallow seas covered the interior of Laurentia (the core of modern North America). Reefs that built up in these seas from sponges and algae formed the massive Permian limestone of west Texas. At the end of Permian times, temperatures rose, and many of these shallow seas dried out.

6. WEST COAST BUILD-UP
Fragments of continental crust continued to be added on to the west coasts of North and South America, which during Permian times formed the western parts of Laurentia and Gondwana. Ocean floor was subducted (pushed down) below the edges of these continental landmasses to produce a line of volcanoes.

2. GONDWANA BREAKS UP

Just as the supercontinent of Pangea finished forming, fragments began to break off one of its constituent parts, the southern continent of Gondwana. An active ocean ridge opened up, creating new ocean floor. As a newly created sea widened during Permian times, parts of the edges of Gondwana were pushed away from the mainland. The microcontinents that formed and traveled northward in this way included places such as modern-day Tibet and Malaysia.

3. GLACIATION

There is good geological evidence for an extensive southerly icecap during late Carboniferous and early Permian times before the global warming of the mid-Permian. Glacial deposits have been found in South America, southern Africa, Antarctica, and Australia.

WHOLE WORLD PROJECTION

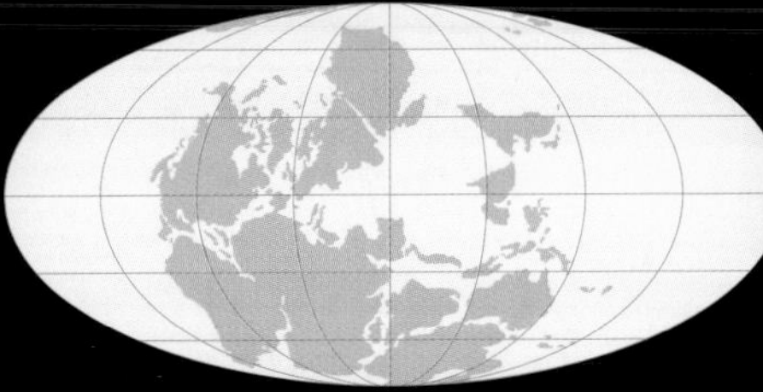

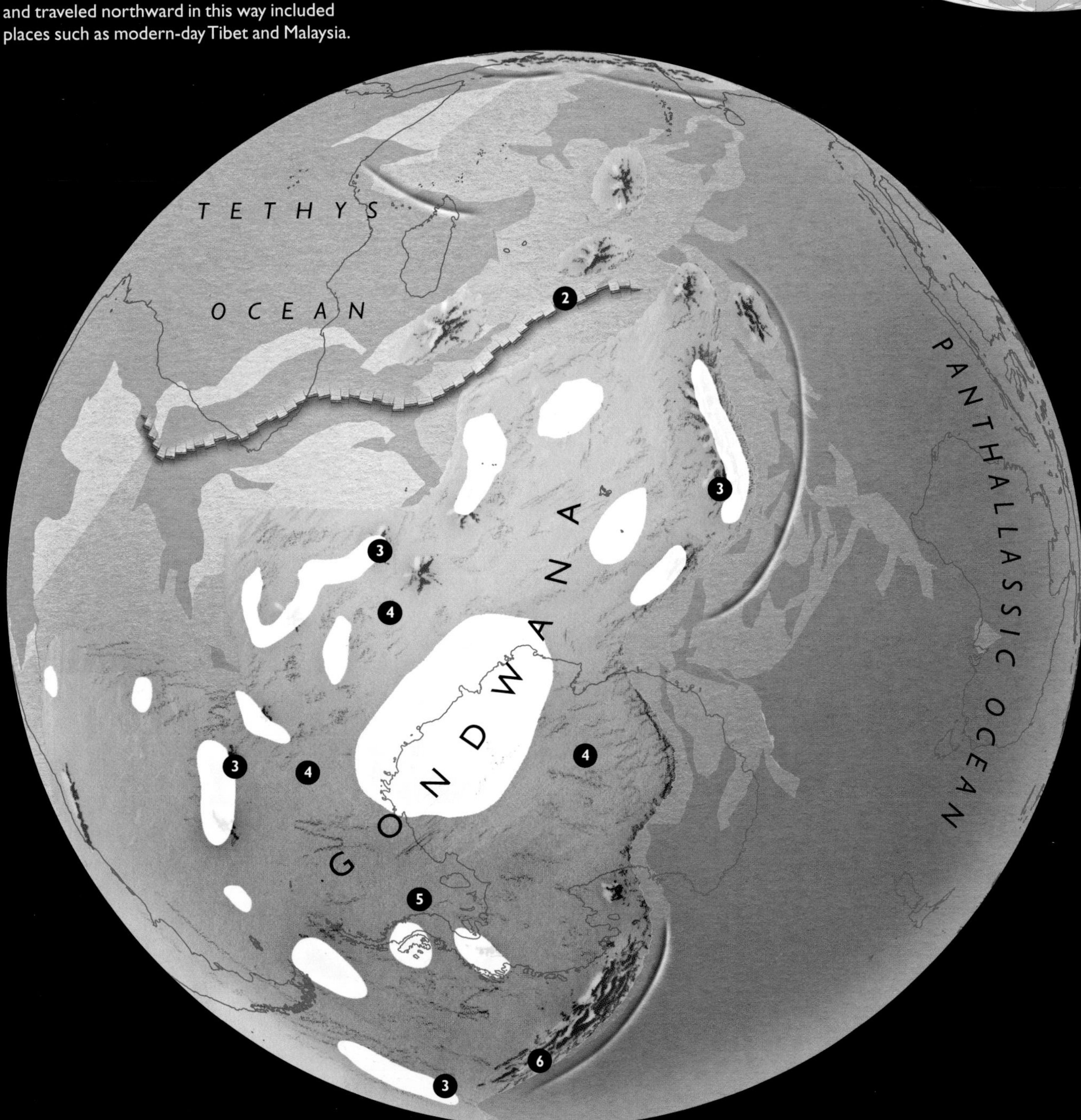

5. SEDIMENTS OF THE KAROO

Huge amounts of sediment built up in the Karoo basin of southern Africa in late Permian times. During this period, the region had a cool climate and was home to a great diversity of animals, including the likely ancestors of mammals. The Karoo basin contained river flood plains crossed by shifting channels that laid down large amounts of sediment. This provided excellent conditions for the preservation of fossils.

4. COOL CLIMATE PLANTS

Permian rock strata in the modern lands that once made up Gondwana contain the remains of plants that are characteristic of cool climates. These prove that the landmasses that are now South America, Africa, India, Antarctica, and Australia were grouped closely together near the South Pole at the time.

Triassic Times

Two views of the Earth 240 million years ago show one hemisphere dominated by a vast ocean and another by a great supercontinent, Pangea. This great landmass included all of what is now North America, Europe, North Asia, Africa, South America, India, Australia, and Antarctica. During Triassic times, Pangea moved gradually northward. At the end of the Permian period, very low sea levels and climate change coincided with a major extinction event. Since then sea levels had risen again allowing a slow recovery of marine life such as corals; on land, tropical coal-forming forests and swamps diminished as climates got warmer and drier.

1. SEAFLOOR CREATION

In Triassic times, a long mid-ocean ridge is thought to have existed in the Panthallassic Ocean. Ridges of this type continuously create new seafloor, which is then pushed sideways from the ridge. At the same time (and approximately the same rate), existing seafloor is forced into the Earth's mantle at subduction zones near the edges of continents. Although seafloor moves away from ridges at a rate of only 0.4 to 4 inches (1 to 10 centimeters) a year, enough time has elapsed since the Triassic for all new seafloor created during the period to have since been destroyed at subduction zones.

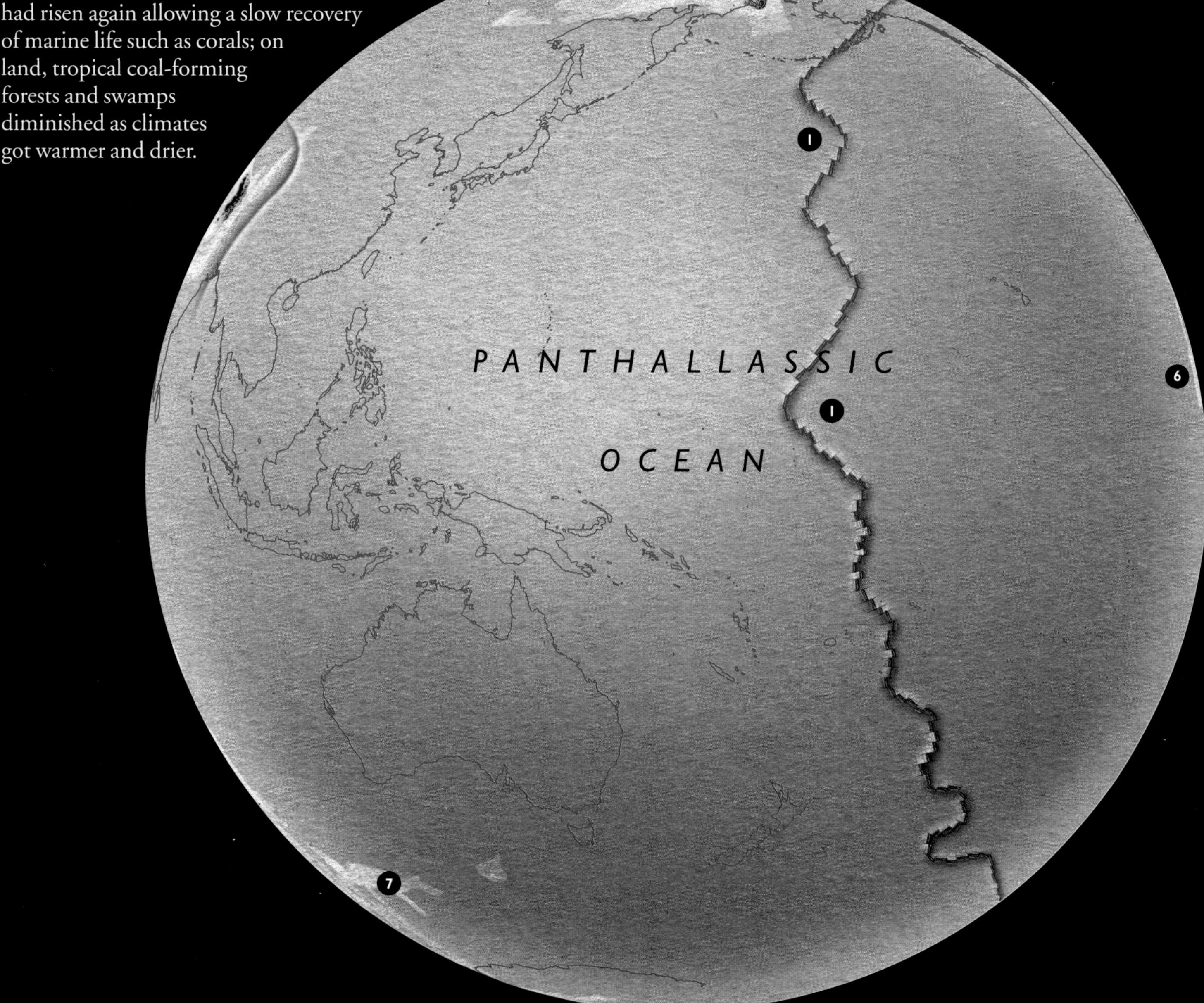

7. SEA LEVELS FALL

At this time, sea levels across the globe were high. However, the end of the Triassic was marked by many extinctions among sea creatures, especially corals. The cause may have been climate change and a marked fall in sea levels. Many of the shallow continental seas in which corals and communities of other creatures thrived became exposed.

6. BUILDING THE WEST COAST

On the eastern edges of the Panthallassic Ocean, a sliver of continental crust consisting of marine sediments and material of volcanic origin impacted with western Laurentia to form today's western Nevada and northern California. Inland, semi-arid climates produced reddened terrestrial sediments such as the Chinle Formation in southern Utah.

2. RISE AND SPREAD OF REPTILES
Triassic times saw an enormous development of reptiles on land and in the air and sea. The first ichthyosaurs (swimming reptiles, similar in shape to modern dolphins) evolved in Triassic times and some grew to 13 feet (4 meters) long in shallow seas off the coasts of Laurentia. Fossil records also exist of early dinosaurs in areas as far apart today as New Mexico (at that time southwestern Laurentia), western Europe (eastern Laurentia), and southern Africa (part of Gondwana).

3. SALT MINES
Warm continental climates dried up the shallow seas of Europe to produce salt lakes and evaporites (minerals deposited from the evaporation of seas and lakes). These are still mined in England, Germany, and Poland. The Triassic is named for strata with salt deposits that have been mined for centuries. These deposits have three distinct divisions, hence the term Triassic, or "three-layered."

WHOLE WORLD PROJECTION

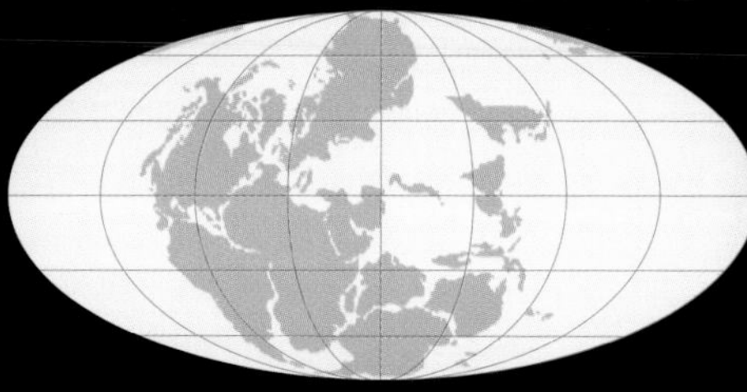

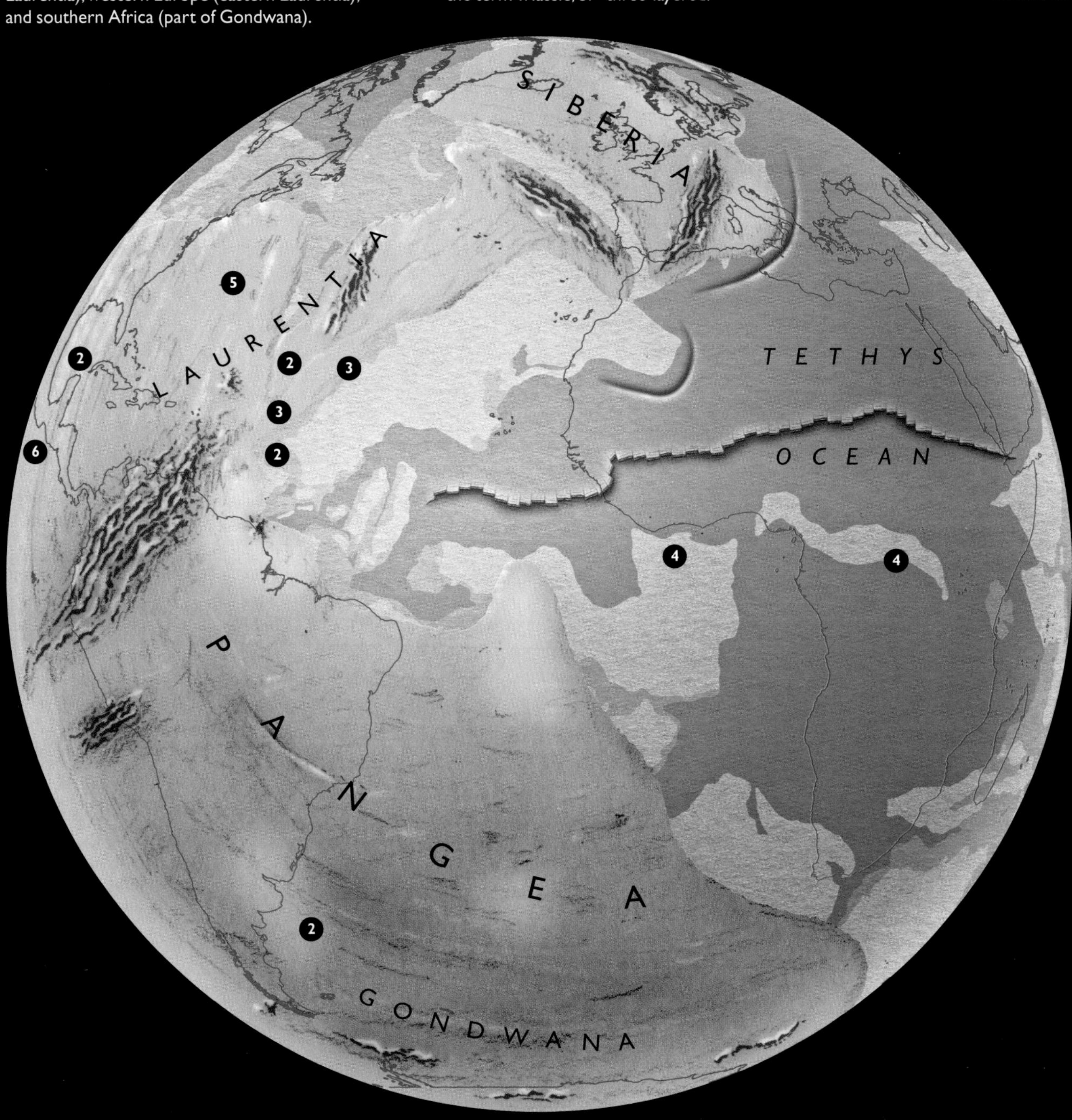

5. IMPACT IN CANADA
A large meteorite smashed into the Earth toward the end of Triassic times, about 209 million years ago, close to the beginning of the Jurassic period. The collision is marked by the Manicougan impact crater in Quebec, Canada. There is no evidence of any disastrous global effects arising from this impact.

4. GONDWANA BREAKS UP
The edges of Gondwana continued to break up, and crustal fragments such as Tibet, Malaya, and southern China moved northward across the Tethys Ocean. Eventually they collided with Siberia and built up to form Asia. In late Triassic times, southern China collided with northern China, forming a range of mountains (the Qin Ling) that is still spectacular today.

Jurassic Times

Seen from above the poles, the Earth 170 million years ago, during the Jurassic period, was a warmer, less varied place than it is today. There were probably no ice caps at the poles for much of the period, and the mild conditions made for much higher sea levels, resulting in a smaller area of dry land but extensive shallow continental seas, which teemed with life. The huge supercontinent of Pangea was splitting up, and familiar modern landmasses such as North America and Eurasia were beginning to appear. Both the South and the North Atlantic Oceans began to open up. At the same time, the ancient Tethys Ocean began to close.

1. WARM POLES

Although no evidence has been found for polar icecaps during the Jurassic period, there was almost certainly winter snow and ice. Dinosaur and plant fossils found in Siberia and Alaska suggest that even lands close to the poles had relatively mild climates. The types of plant fossils, especially, reveal that annual temperatures averaged between 35° and 45°F (2 to 8°C). Even though the world was warm, the short days of the polar winter would still have meant that plant food was scarce for parts of the year.

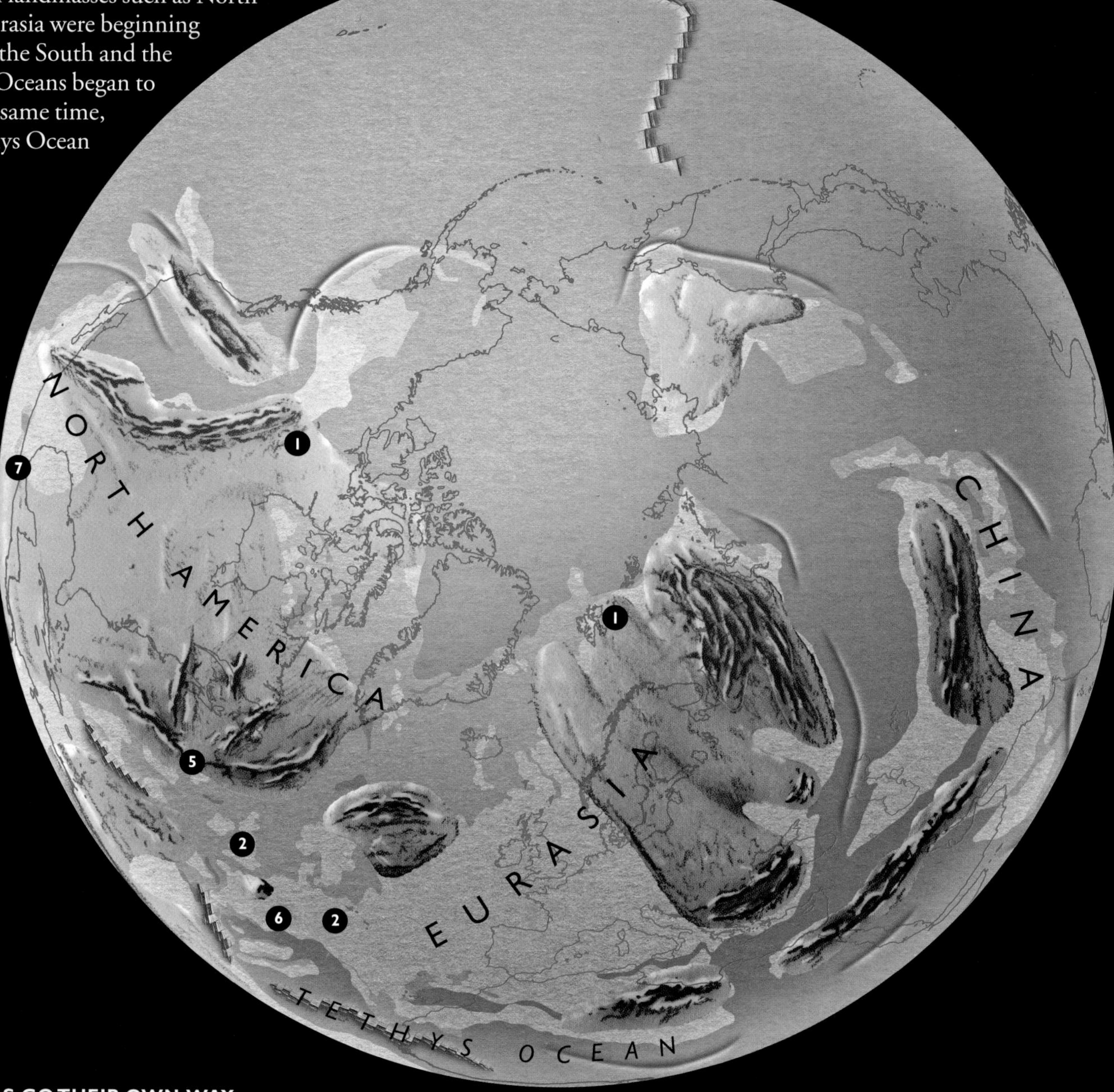

7. THE AMERICAS GO THEIR OWN WAY

During the Jurassic period, the landmasses of North and South America began to split, having previously both been part of Pangea. In the west, rising sea levels resulted in a new sea separating the two continents, while farther east, the Tethys Ocean extended to form the Gulf of Mexico. Marine lifeforms flourished on developing reefs in the shallow seas around the Americas, especially in subtropical regions.

6. NAMING THE JURASSIC

The Jurassic period is named for the limestone hills of the Jura located between France and Switzerland. This limestone formed from the sediment that accumulated in the shallow seas covering the area during that time, and contains an abundance of marine animal fossils, especially ammonites.

2. SHALLOW SEAS OVER EUROPE

Some of the most famous fossils of marine reptiles, such as ichthyosaurs and plesiosaurs, have come from the early Jurassic limestone and shale of England and Germany. The strata were deposited in shallow seas that flooded parts of Europe at this time. The seas formed when a series of rifts in the Earth's crust separated the ancient continent of Laurentia into North America and Eurasia.

3. OPENING THE SOUTH ATLANTIC

During Jurassic times, a plume of hot molten rock rose up from the Earth's mantle. It stretched the crust of the southern supercontinent, Gondwana, in the area of what now comprises southern Africa and eastern South America. This was the prelude to a rift forming and opening up the South Atlantic.

WHOLE WORLD PROJECTION

5. VOLCANIC TURMOIL IN GONDWANA

Massive volcanic eruptions producing huge outpourings of basalt lava occurred in Antarctica, South Africa, and eastern North America at the end of the Jurassic period. The eruptions would have pumped large quantities of smoke and dust into the Earth's atmosphere. The Sun's rays would have been partially blocked, and the global climate would have altered. This could have caused the mass extinction that marked the end of the Jurassic and onset of the Cretaceous periods.

4. PANGEA HEADS NORTH

During Jurassic times, Gondwana moved north. Much of Antarctica, then part of Gondwana, was a considerable distance away from the South Pole. Vegetation flourished on the continent and was sufficiently abundant in places to form thin coal seams. Dinosaur fossils have been discovered in rock layers that are now 2.5 miles (4 kilometers) high in the Antarctic mountains.

Early Cretaceous Times

The Cretaceous period spanned almost 80 million years from 142 to 65 million years ago. During this time the world began to take on a familiar look as lands that had once made up the supercontinent of Pangea pulled apart. The newly formed Atlantic Ocean extended north and southward, separating Africa and Eurasia from the Americas. The continents of Africa, India, Antarctica, and Australia began to move apart about 120 million years ago as new oceans formed between these constituents of ancient Gondwana. Asia still had an unfamiliar form, with lands that are now part of its southern edge, such as Indochina and India, still separate islands.

1. OCEAN CONNECTIONS

The Atlantic Ocean had first begun to open in the Jurassic period. During Cretaceous times, the process continued. The new ocean connected with the western part of the ancient Tethys Ocean (between Eurasia and Gondwana), while at the same time the eastern end of the Tethys Ocean began to close. At the start of the Cretaceous period, land animals could move between the Americas and between Africa and Eurasia. By later Cretaceous times all the connections between these lands had been flooded.

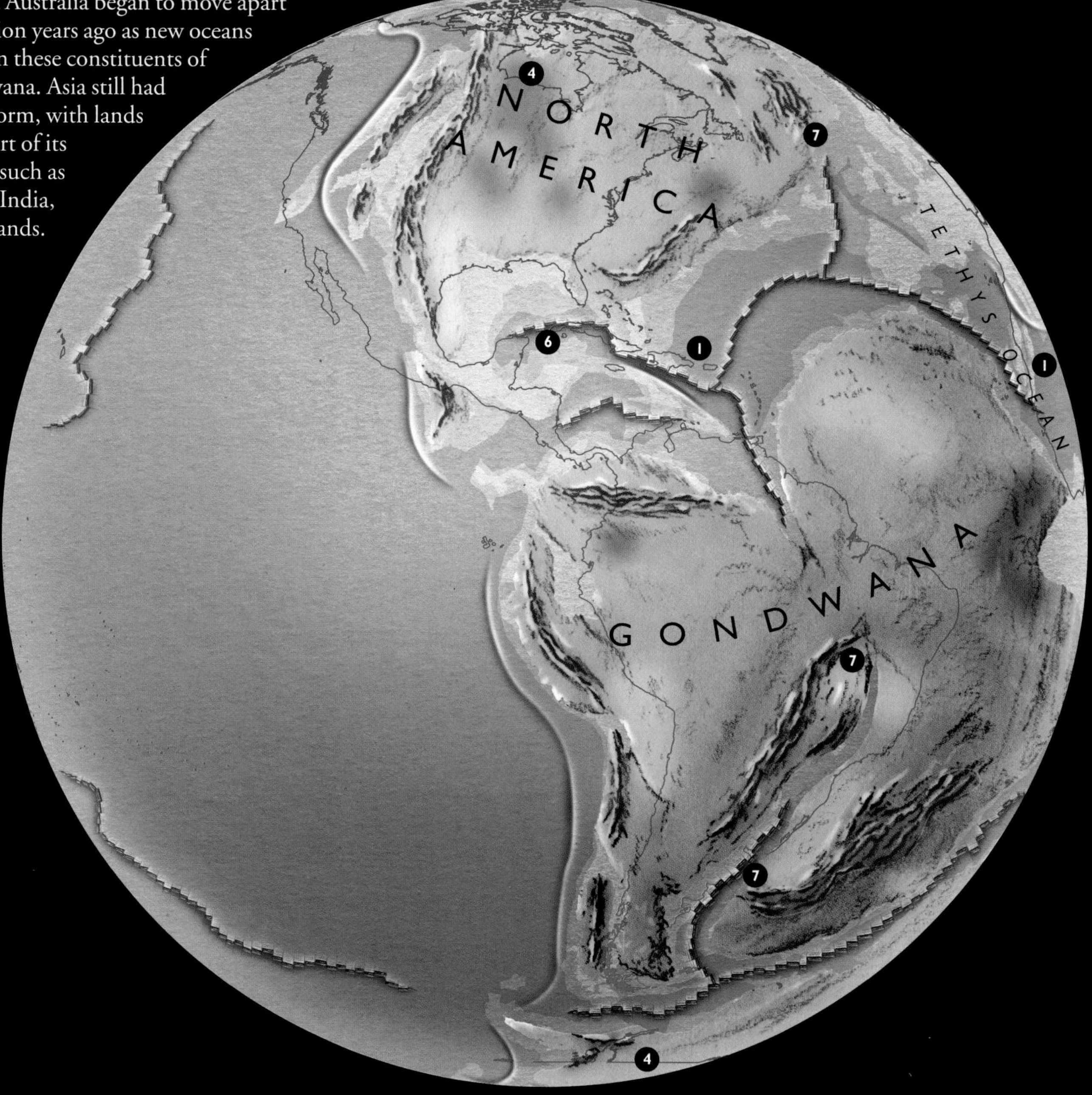

7. THE ATLANTIC CONTINUES TO OPEN

The long process that created the Atlantic Ocean continued through the Cretaceous period. Early Cretaceous flood basalts—rocks created by vast outpourings of lava—are found in rocks in southwest Africa and South America. Similar events occurred at the ocean's northern end, so that by late Cretaceous times 60 million years later, the Atlantic had extended far northward.

6. MAKING OIL IN THE GULF

The shallow shores along the Tethys Ocean supported a flourishing community of sea creatures during the Cretaceous age. In deeper marine basins, vast quantities of decaying planktonic organisms accumulated in muddy sediments. In time these sediments, such as those in the Gulf of Mexico, became black-shale deposits, rich sources of crude oil vital to the modern world.

2. TIBET COLLIDES WITH ASIA

In the early Cretaceous, the land that is now Tibet was made up of separate land fragments, with one of them (at the time shown on this map) still an island. Ocean crust was consumed at a subduction zone to the south of Asia, pulling this island toward an eventual collision with the continent. During the Cretaceous, other fragments of the ancient continent of Gondwana, such as Indochina, also moved northward, continuing the assembly of Asia.

3. CHINA EMERGES FROM THE SEA

During the late Jurassic age and into Cretaceous times, the continental crust of China emerged from the sea. The land that is now the west of modern China became a low-lying region rich in vegetation. It was home to a large variety of dinosaurs, as shown by the many fossils that have been found in the region.

WHOLE WORLD PROJECTION

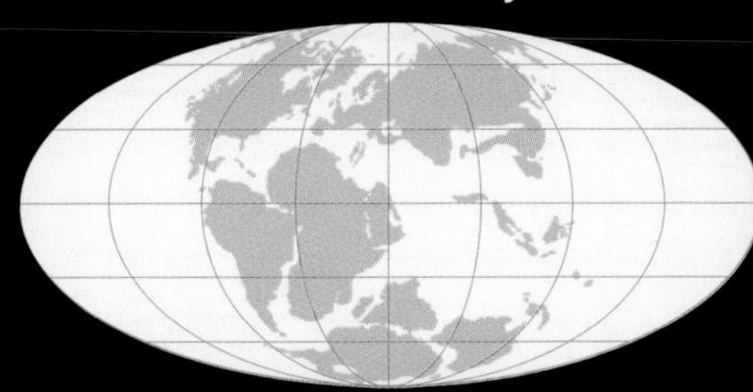

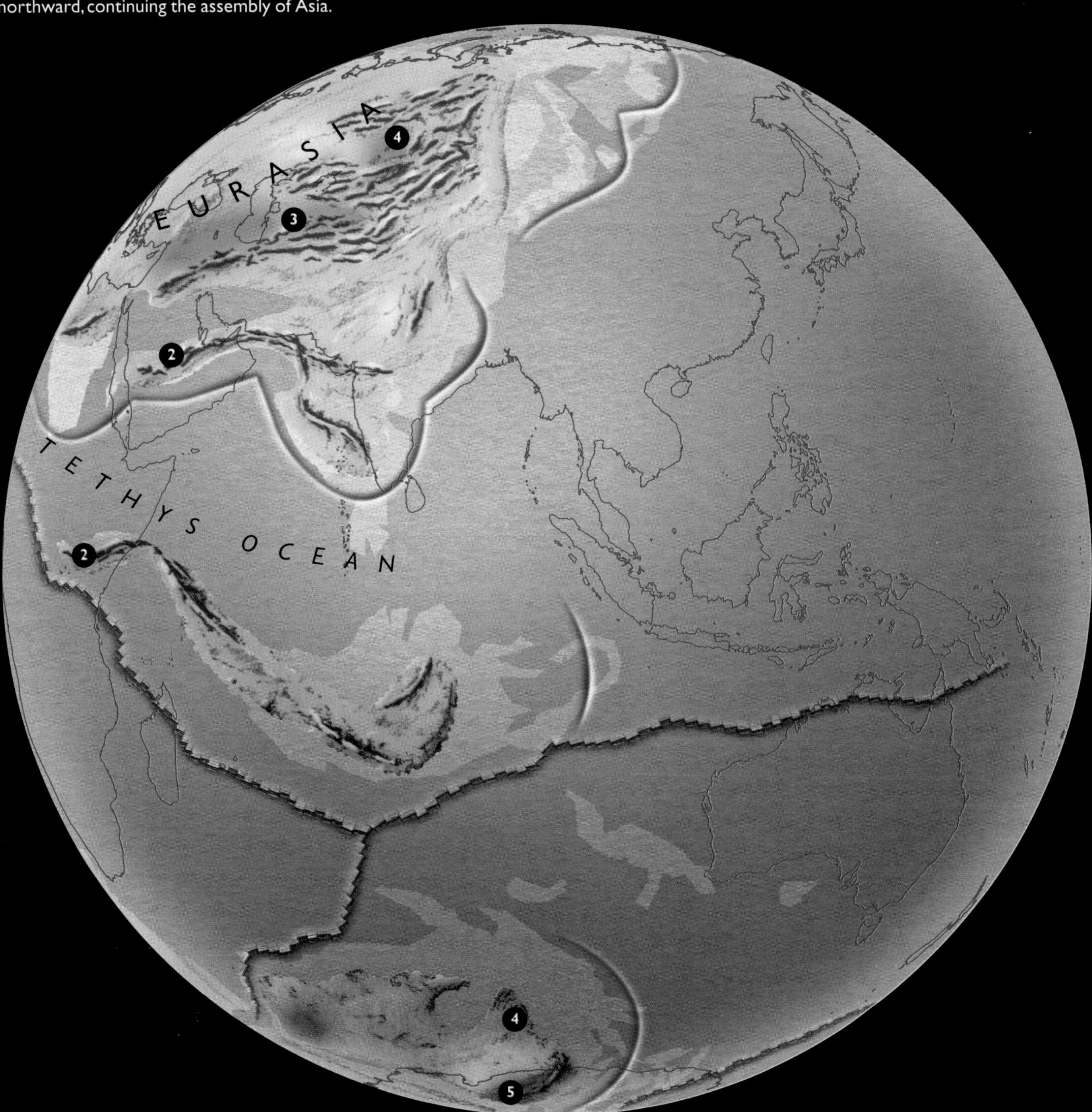

5. COLD EXTREMITIES

Early Cretaceous fossils from Koonwarra, Australia, show signs of fish having died from inadequately oxygenated water. Such conditions occur when a lake is completely covered by a layer of ice. If this was the case, it suggests that despite relatively mild climates farther north, winters in this part of Australia could be extremely cold—a phenomenon that would tally with Australia's position close to the South Pole during the Cretaceous period.

4. WARMER TIMES THAN NOW

Many coal deposits around the world date from the early Cretaceous period. They are found in places that were quite close to the poles at that time, such as Antarctica, New Zealand, northern Australia, Canada, and Siberia. Coal forms from trees and plants that grow in swampy, relatively warm conditions. The coal deposits therefore show that the globe was relatively warm during Cretaceous times.

Later Cretaceous Times

By around 90 million years ago, the distribution of the continents was looking more familiar. The maps shown here depict the Earth as viewed from above the North Pole (this page) and South Pole (opposite). The Atlantic Ocean separated the New World of the Americas from the Old World of Europe, Asia, and Africa. Much of Asia was assembled except for one very important part of the continental "jigsaw" puzzle—India. Australia still languished in the deep south, attached to Antarctica, and India was still attached to Madagascar.

1. FROM CALIFORNIA TO ALASKA
Subduction (movement of ocean crust down into the Earth's mantle at a plate boundary) continued on the west coast of the Americas. A terrane (fragment of continental crust) collided with the west coast of North America in the region of Baja California. It was then forced northward along the western edge of North America. Some terranes have been moved as much as 1,000 miles (3,000 kilometers) by such faults, ending up in Alaska.

7. SEAS ACROSS THE MIDWEST
Sea levels were high during mid-Cretaceous times, and the sea flooded through North America from the Gulf of Mexico to the Arctic Ocean. The formation of the mid-American seaway separated the Rockies in the west from the plains and mountain ranges in the east.

6. OCEAN CONNECTIONS
The Atlantic was connected to the Pacific at its western edge by a tropical seaway between the Americas. At its eastern edge, the Atlantic joined up with the Tethys Ocean. Thus, South America was isolated from North America and Africa was isolated from both Europe and Asia.

2. AUSTRALIA ON ITS OWN

The formation of the Southeast Indian Ridge (a mid-ocean spreading ridge) between Antarctica and Australia began the opening of an ocean between the two continents. Australia was slowly pushed northward as new ocean floor was created and spread on either side of the ridge.

3. MALVINAS MIGRATION

The Falkland Islands are moving between continents. The geology of the islands today clearly shows that they were originally attached to the southwest tip of South Africa but in mid-Cretaceous times were being pulled toward South America. As the South Atlantic and Southern Oceans opened the islands were rotated through 180 degrees.

WHOLE WORLD PROJECTION

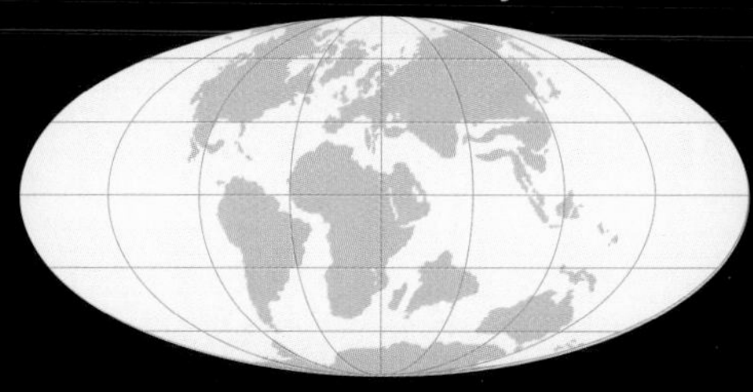

5. ISOLATION OF ANTARCTICA

By the middle of the Cretaceous period, the old southern supercontinent of Gondwana had mostly broken up. Three continents—South America, Africa, and India—that were once joined together were now separate, while Australia and Antarctica remained joined only by tenuous land bridges. The break-up of Gondwana had its origin in a series of spreading ridges that gradually encircled Antarctica, pushing the other continents northward.

4. MADAGASCAR BECOMES AN ISLAND

Madagascar was still joined to India, which had separated from Africa. A rising plume of hot molten material in the Earth's mantle under Madagascar began to stretch the crust. Eventually the crust rifted apart and lava poured onto the surface. This rifting began the separation of India from Madagascar.

K-T Times

THE BOUNDARY BETWEEN THE END OF CRETACEOUS TIMES 65 million years ago and the beginning of the Tertiary period is often referred to as the K-T Boundary. It was marked by a catastrophic meteorite impact at Chicxulub in Mexico that is believed to have contributed to the global extinction of some groups of animals and plants. A coincidental outpouring of lava over the west of India, global cooling, and a significant fall in sea levels, which exposed vast areas of continental shelf, may also have played major parts in the extinction of both marine and land species.

1. RIDGES OPEN THE ATLANTIC
The widening Atlantic Ocean put an ever-greater distance between the New World and Old World. The mid-Atlantic ridge extended into the North Atlantic, the opening of which stretched the western edge of the European crust, causing some areas of continental shelf around the British Isles to sink.

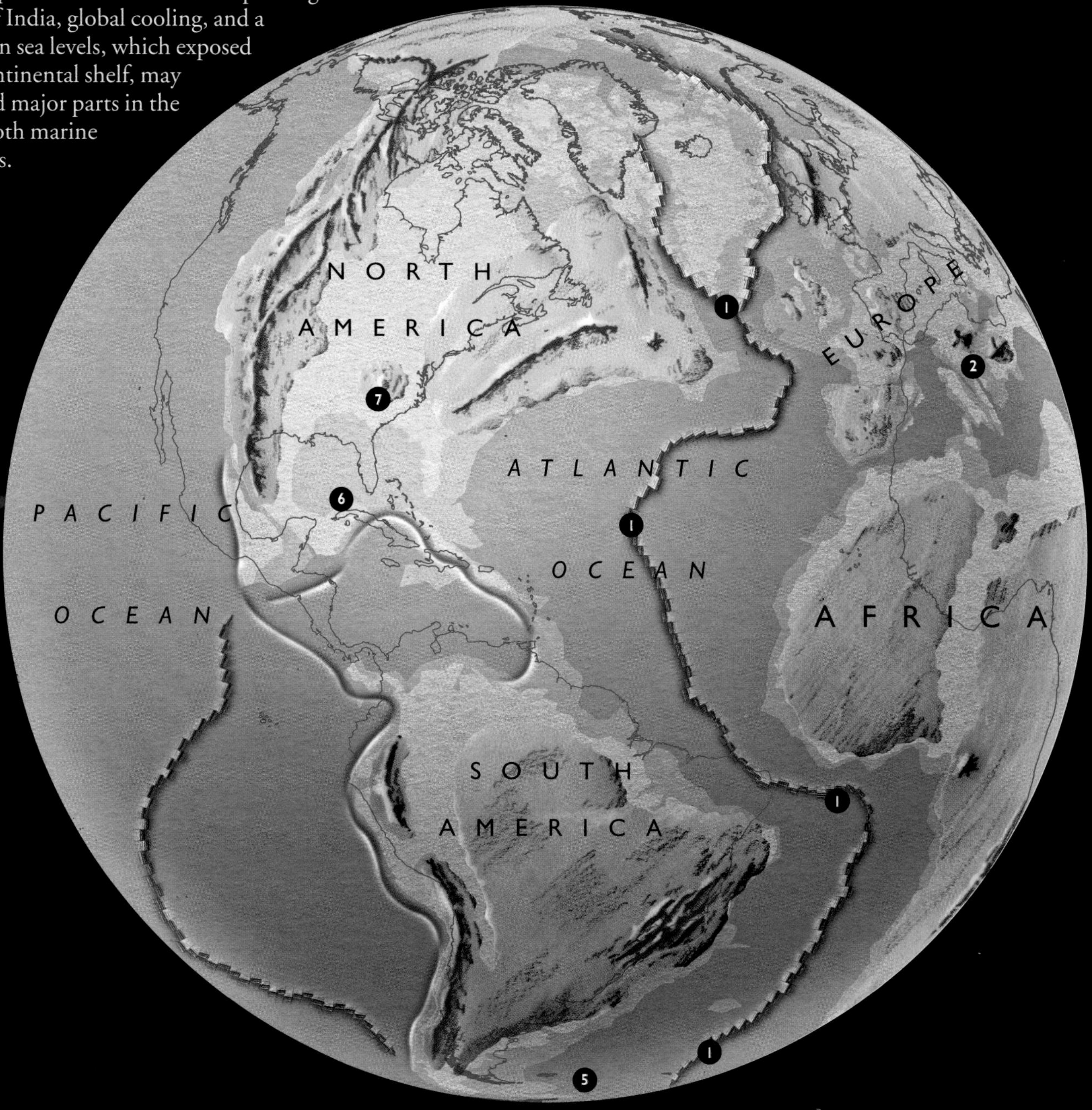

7. EVIDENCE OF A TSUNAMI
A sand layer at the K-T Boundary along the Brazos River, Texas, is thought to have been deposited by a giant tsunami that was generated by the Chicxulub impact. The tsunami wave is estimated to have been over half a mile (1 kilometer) high. It tore up sediment from the floor of the Gulf of Mexico before smashing its way inland all around the Caribbean.

6. CHICXULUB METEORITE
A meteorite about 6 miles (10 kilometers) in diameter slammed into Chicxulub in Mexico. The impact threw up a mountainous rim 5 miles (8 kilometers) high. The rim soon collapsed, creating concentric ridges across the landscape that extended over 90 miles (145 kilometers) from the center of impact. Today, the impact crater is hidden beneath younger sediments that are over half a mile (1 kilometer) thick.

2. SIGNS OF A DISASTER

Marine ocean floor sediments, now preserved at Gubbio in Italy, contain a thin layer of clay at the K-T Boundary. The clay is enriched with the rare metallic element iridium and traces of other metals in a ratio that suggests they came from an asteroid or comet. This iridium-enriched layer, found by Walter Alvarez in the late 1970s, was the first evidence that a large meteorite had hit Earth during K-T times.

3. VOLCANISM IN INDIA

A rising current of hot mantle material under western India produced vast outpourings of lava over the Deccan Plateau in India at the end of the Cretaceous. It is likely that associated global climate changes were partly responsible for the major extinctions that mark the K-T Boundary.

WHOLE WORLD PROJECTION

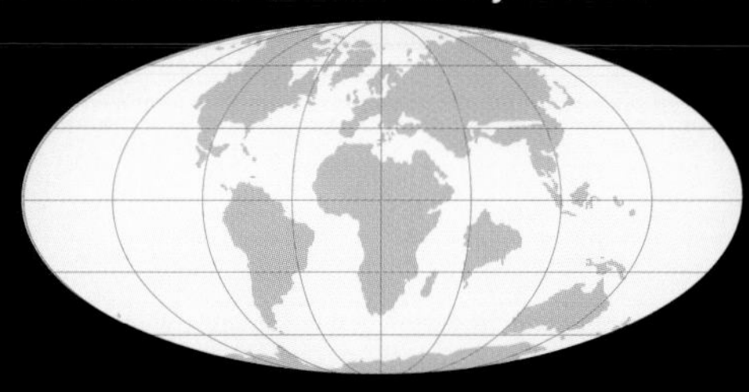

5. EVIDENCE OF GLOBAL COOLING

The rock strata now found on Seymour Island, off the coast of Antarctica, were sediments of a shallow sea in late Cretaceous times. The record of fossils trapped in these rocks shows a gradual reduction in the number of species from a time well before the impact at Chicxulub. Such a steady rate of extinctions over a long period suggests that global cooling was already happening at the end of the Cretaceous, making survival difficult for species that lived in polar regions.

4. NEW ZEALAND ESCAPES

In New Zealand, the record of tiny fossils of marine creatures shows no signs of a mass extinction at the end of the Cretaceous period. In fact, the number of species increased in the region. Possibly, a beneficial change occurred in ocean currents, brought about by the same cooling that doomed animal species in other parts of the globe.

Early Tertiary Times

The end of the Cretaceous period also marks the end of the Mesozoic era of geological time and the beginning of the Tertiary era (from the Latin for third). These maps show the world as it appeared 45 million years ago, with the Atlantic Ocean still widening as the connection between Norway and Greenland severed and the Americas moved westward. Africa slowly pushed in a northeastly direction crumpling southern Europe to form the mountain belts of the Pyrenees and Alps. India continued its progress north, crossing the Equator, while Australia separated completely from Antarctica.

1. SEAS RETREAT IN AMERICA
During the previous Cretaceous period, a shallow sea had filled the midwest of North America. A small remnant, known as the Cannonball Sea, survived into the early Tertiary era. The continuing plate movements that were building up the Rocky Mountains stretched and faulted the land exposed by the retreating seas to form lake basins. One of these, Lake Uinta in Wyoming, accumulated layers of sediment, which now form the rocks of the Green River formation, famous for its exquisite fish fossils.

7. ARABIA PARTS FROM AFRICA
The Red Sea began to rift open as the Earth's crust near northeastern Africa domed and stretched. In the late Eocene age (40 million years ago) lava poured out over a vast area of the Ethiopian plateau and a line of volcanoes appeared along the rift valley.

6. SPAIN AND ITALY JOIN EUROPE
The Bay of Biscay opened as Iberia (Spain and Portugal) rotated counterclockwise. It collided with southern France, crumpling the intervening strata to form the mountains of the Pyrenees. Italy moved north toward southern Europe, pushing the Alps upward in the process.

2. VOLCANISM IN THE ATLANTIC

A "plume" of hot magma from the Earth's interior rose in the North Atlantic between Britain and Greenland. It pushed the crust in the region upward, stretching and rifting it, and in the process huge amounts of lava poured out onto the surface to form new landscapes. Signs of these great eruptions can be seen at the Giant's Causeway in Northern Ireland and Fingal's Cave on the island of Staffa, Scotland.

3. HOT SPOT IN THE PACIFIC

A hot spot in the Pacific produced a chain of volcanic islands, known as the Hawaiian-Emperor seamount chain, as the Pacific plate moved over it. The first volcano erupted from the ocean floor 70 million years ago. Plate movement has now carried the volcano to the northern Pacific. About 43 million years ago, there was a change in the Pacific plate's direction of movement, and this is preserved as a "dog-leg" in the line of volcanoes.

WHOLE WORLD PROJECTION

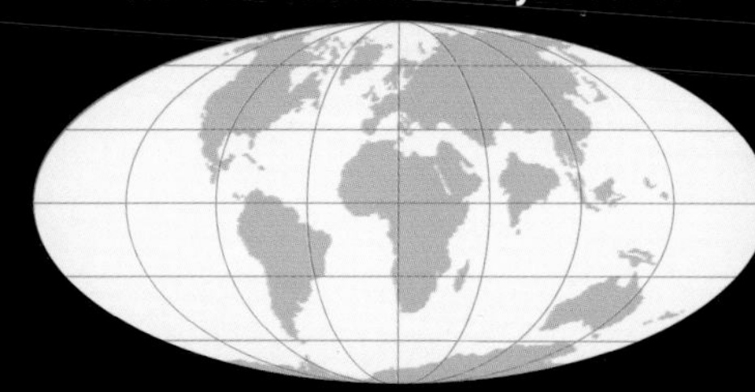

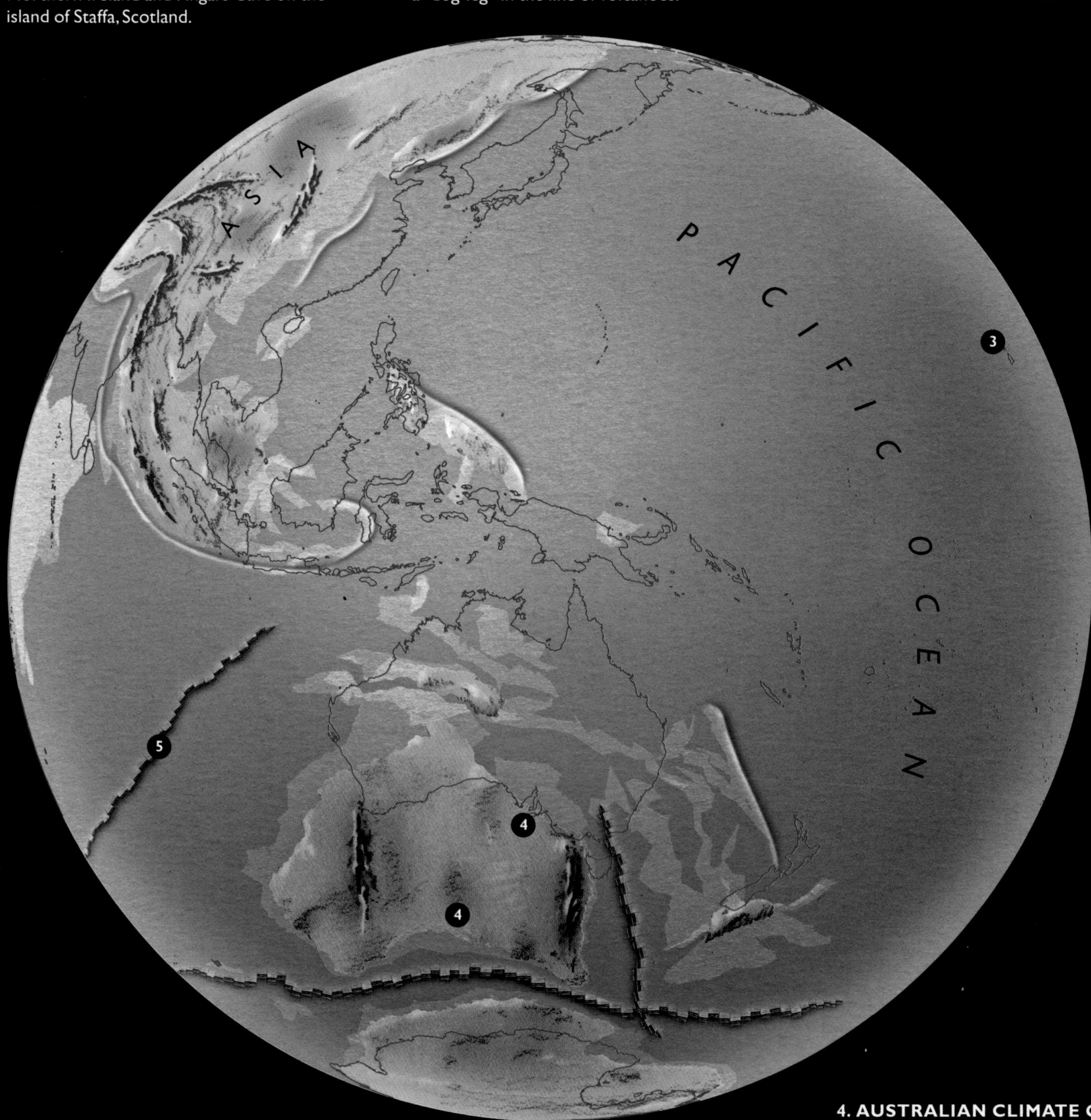

4. AUSTRALIAN CLIMATE CHANGES

Rocks in South Australia and Queensland show that during the early Tertiary era, the climate in Australia changed. Around 55 million years ago it was wet and humid, allowing swampy forests to form that later became reserves of brown coal and oil shale. Layers of sediment from 40 million years ago are thinner, indicating a less rich environment. The rocks that they form are sandstonelike, a sign that the region had become much drier.

5. RIDGE RAISER

In early Tertiary times, the Ninetyeast Ridge was an active transform fault—a region where two tectonic plates slide past each other. The movement between the Indian and Australian Ocean floor plates that produced the ridge stopped when India eventually collided with Tibet. Today, the ridge is inactive but still rises 2 miles (3 kilometers) from the floor of the Indian Ocean.

Mid-Tertiary Times

As Africa approached Europe some 20 million years ago, during Miocene (mid-Tertiary) times, the Tethys Ocean that separated the two continents was squeezed and narrowed. The north-south compression threw up a mountain chain that extended east-west from Turkey through the Balkans. As the ocean floor was pushed down beneath southern Europe, volcanic islands were thrown up as well as mountain belts in the Carpathians and Caucasus (on either side of what is now the Black Sea). Italy, which had been attached to northern Africa as part of Gondwana, was driven into southern Europe, buckling and uplifting the Alps.

1. HAWAII RISES FROM THE WAVES

The volcanic island of Hawaii appeared from the ocean over 5 million years ago. It is the youngest of a chain of volcanic islands that also includes Maui, Oahu, Kauai, and scores of smaller islands that extend for over 3,800 miles (6,100 kilometers) to the northwest. Hawaii rises over 3 miles (5 kilometers) from the ocean floor and a further 13,700 feet (4,170 meters) above sea level, making it the highest mountain on Earth in terms of elevation above base. A new island is currently forming to the southeast of Hawaii, but its summit is still over 3,000 feet (900 meters) below the surface and it is not expected to emerge from the waves for thousands of years.

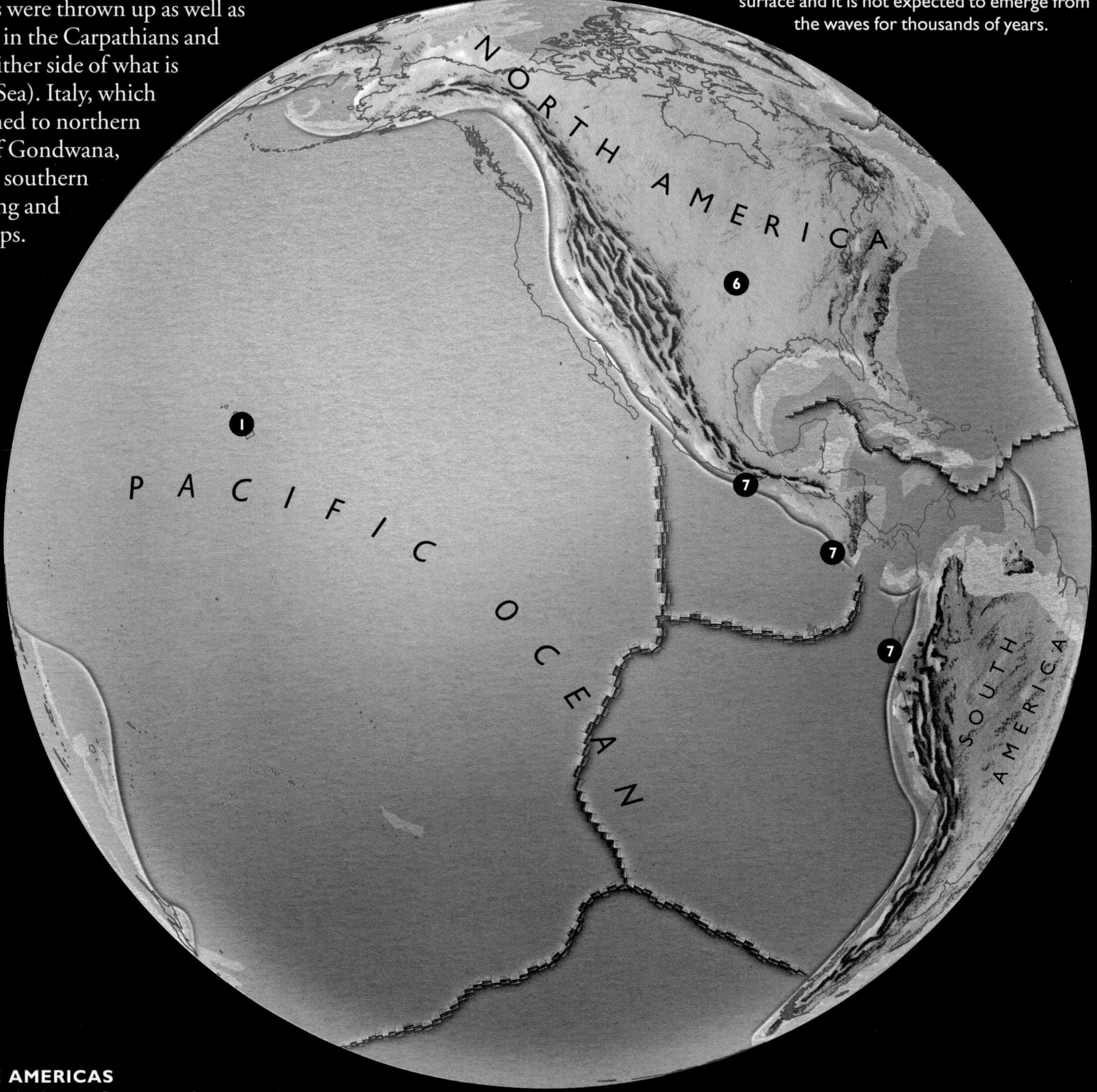

NORTH AMERICA

6

1

PACIFIC OCEAN

7

7

7

SOUTH AMERICA

7. LINKING THE AMERICAS

Plate movements pushed ocean floor crust down into the Earth's mantle in the eastern Pacific, resulting in explosive volcanic eruptions and mountain building along the western edge of Central America and northwestern edge of South America. Some 3 million years ago, sea levels fell and the northern Andes were uplifted, allowing a land corridor between North and South America to form. The two continents are still moving relative to one another and will eventually separate again.

6. CLIMATE CHANGE IN AMERICA

In mid-Tertiary times, the uplift of the Sierra Nevada, Cascade, and Rocky Mountains led to a cooler and drier climate in North America, especially to the east of the mountains. Tropical vegetation was displaced southward, and temperate forests and grasslands replaced them. Increased grass cover led to the evolution of grazing mammals, especially horses, which were very diverse at this time in North America.

2. FORMING THE MEDITERRANEAN
The area between North Africa and southern Europe was pushed down to form a long east-west basin to the south of the newly forming mountain belts of the Alps and Carpathians. The basin filled with seawater to form the Mediterranean. This connected with remnants of the Tethys Ocean that persisted in the Black Sea and Caspian Sea.

3. TAIWANESE ROCK
In Tertiary times, the island of Taiwan alternated between being flooded by the sea and being uplifted to form low-lying swampy land. The rock strata preserve several cycles, alternating between marine and terrestrial deposits with coal seams and layers of volcanic ash and lava.

WHOLE WORLD PROJECTION

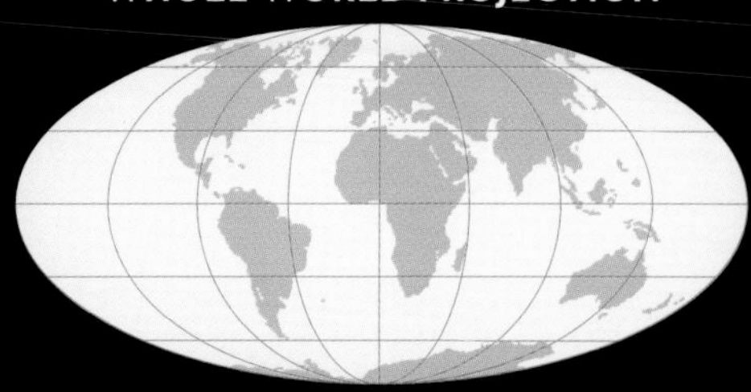

5. JAPAN MOVES EAST
The string of volcanoes forming the Japanese islands was pushed away from the Asian mainland eastward into the Pacific by the opening of the Japan Sea. A deep sea trench off the Pacific coast of the islands marks a subduction zone where ocean floor is being pushed down below the islands. The subduction generates numerous earthquakes in the region. Since their formation, the Japanese islands have moved back and forth from the Asian mainland, pushed and pulled by plate movements.

4. FORMING THE HIMALAYAS
The northward movement of the Indian plate drove India into the southern flank of Asia. The collision crumpled the intervening floor of the Tethys Ocean, pushing it down into the mantle below and up to form the Himalayas. The formation of this great east-west barrier radically changed the regional climate and initiated the seasonal Southeast Asian monsoon.

LATE TERTIARY TIMES

BY THE END OF THE TERTIARY ERA, 5 MILLION YEARS AGO, THE world appeared almost as it does now, with all of the continents more or less in their present positions. A new island, Iceland, had appeared in the middle of the North Atlantic, where the huge ridge at the center of the ocean rose above the surface. The Earth's crust stretched and split in East Africa, where the Great Rift Valley, Red Sea, and the Gulf of Aden were slowly widening. India's northern drive into Asia continued, pushing up the Himalayas and raising the Tibetan plateau. Australia continued its movement northward to reach the tropics.

1. YELLOWSTONE TRAIL

The hot springs and geysers of the Yellowstone National Park in Wyoming are the most recent sign of volcanic activity that has shaped the American northwest for the last 18 million years. At this time, a hot spot—a rising stream of hot magma—forced its way through the North American crust, pouring out lava to form the "layer-cake" landscapes of the Snake River Plateau in Idaho. Due to movements of the North American plate, the hot spot has burned a track some 50 miles (80 kilometers) wide into Wyoming. In 20 million years' time it will cross the Canadian border.

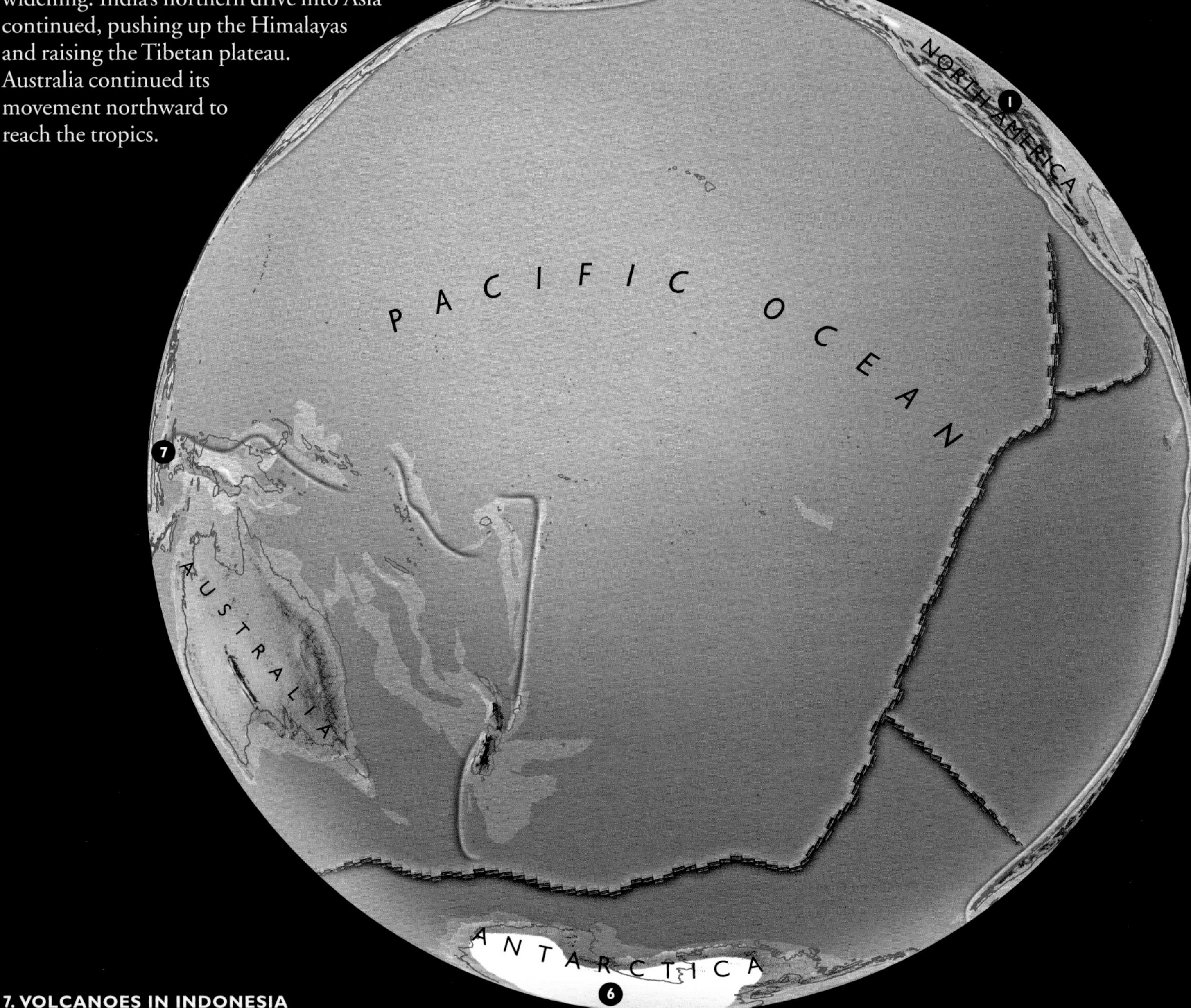

7. VOLCANOES IN INDONESIA

The northward movement of Australia has been a major influence on the development of the Indonesian islands. Over the last 15 million years Australia has moved some 500 miles (800 kilometers) northward. Many volcanic islands have formed near deep ocean trenches to the north, where the oceanic crust is pulled into the Earth's interior. The collision 5 million years ago between the Australian continental plate and Timor resulted in further mountain building.

6. ANTARCTICA FREEZES

By 5 million years ago, Antarctica was completely isolated from the other continents. Plate movement separated South America from Antarctica and allowed the cold circum-Antarctic current to form. The supply of warm water to the region became blocked, so that the land cooled and an icecap formed. The ice caused further cooling because it reflected sunlight so well.

2. THE MEDITERRANEAN DRIES OUT

Less than 7 million years ago, a fall in sea level cut off the Mediterranean Sea from the Atlantic Ocean in the west. During the next 2 million years, the Mediterranean repeatedly reflooded and dried out. Seawater evaporation has left salt deposits over 6,500 feet (2,000 meters) thick in places, while the occasional presence of dry land allowed animals to migrate from Africa into southern Europe. Then, 5 million years ago, a rise in sea level allowed Atlantic waters to flood back into the Mediterranean basin either through the Strait of Gibraltar or across the lowlands of southwest France.

3. ONE STEP UP, ONE STEP DOWN

The Indian plate thrust into the Asian plate at a rate of 2 inches (5 centimeters) a year—nearly 3 miles (5 kilometers) in total after 100,000 years—and pushed up the Himalayas. Although the mountains continued to grow, their total height was kept constant by an increased rate of weathering, which stripped mountain surfaces away.

WHOLE WORLD PROJECTION

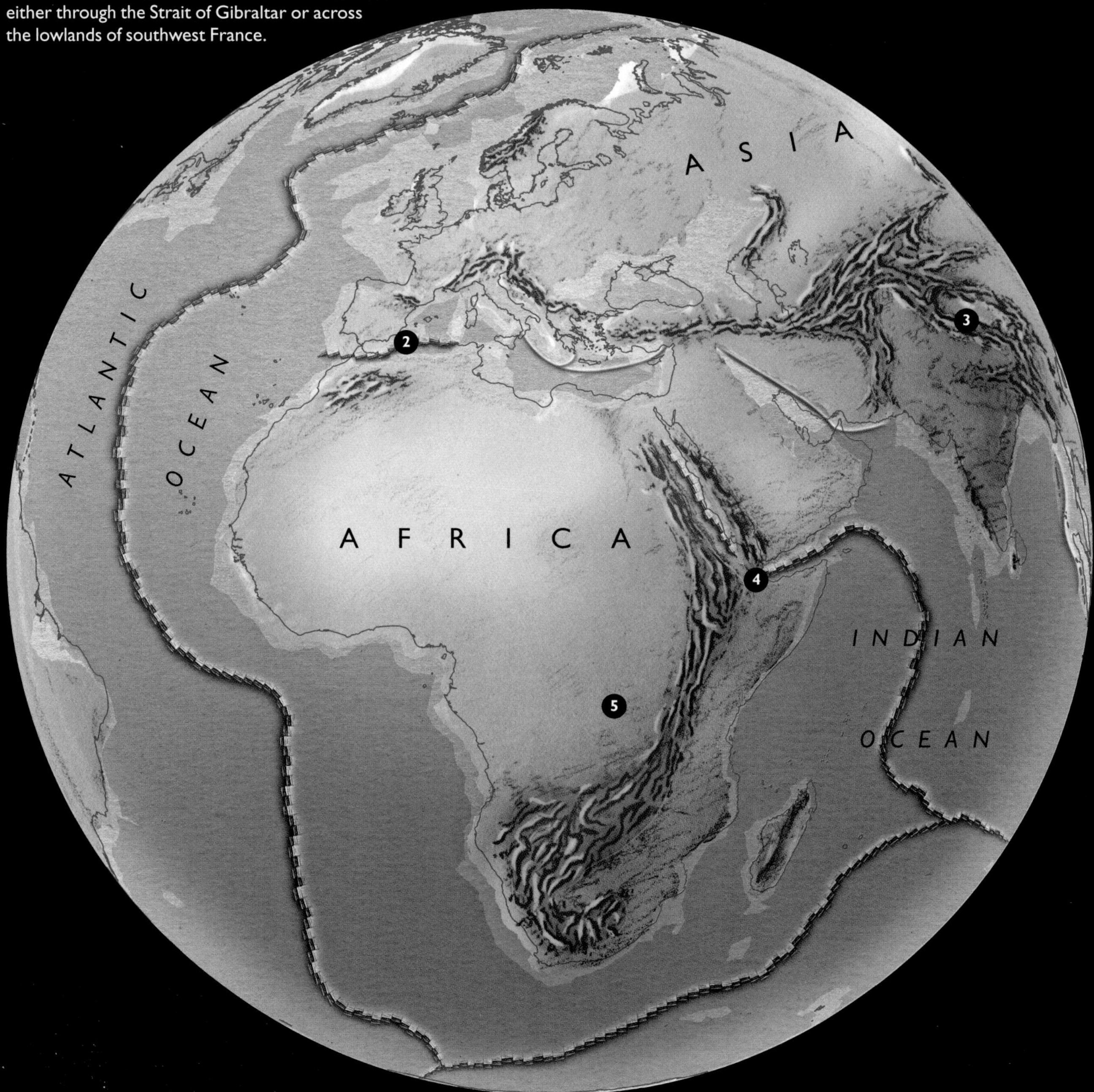

5. AFRICAN CLIMATE CHANGE

The onset of drier and cooler climates 5 million years ago caused important changes in the plant cover of Africa. The woodlands and forests retreated and were broken up into smaller patches with less dense growth. They were replaced by more extensive savanna grasslands. Such changes in vegetation had far-reaching implications for the evolution of African mammals and especially primates. They had to move out of the protection of woodlands into more dangerous open grasslands.

4. RIFTING EAST AFRICA

At the end of the Tertiary era, volcanic rifting was well under way in East Africa. The Red Sea and Great Rift Valley of East Africa are areas of continental crust which then, as now, were breaking apart due to a plume of hot rising magma under Ethiopia that domed and cracked the region. Eventually East Africa will break away from the rest of the continent and move east into the Indian Ocean.

Quaternary Times

The most significant geological force in recent times has been the climate. The Quaternary period, from 1.8 million years ago to the present, has been a long ice age. This does not mean that temperatures have remained constantly colder than average. Instead, fluctuating global temperatures have promoted the growth and retreat of polar icecaps, continental ice sheets, and mountain glaciers, with dramatic effects on the landscape. In the coldest periods, so much water was frozen that sea levels dropped by 330 feet (100 meters), turning shallow seas into extensions of the land.

1. NORTH AMERICAN ICECAP

The North American ice sheet covered 5 million square miles (13 million square kilometers). Its slow, grinding movement scoured the landscapes of northern Canada down to the bedrock created in the Paleozoic and Precambrian eras. The ice and meltwater ploughed the debris southward, dumping it in formations around the Great Lakes.

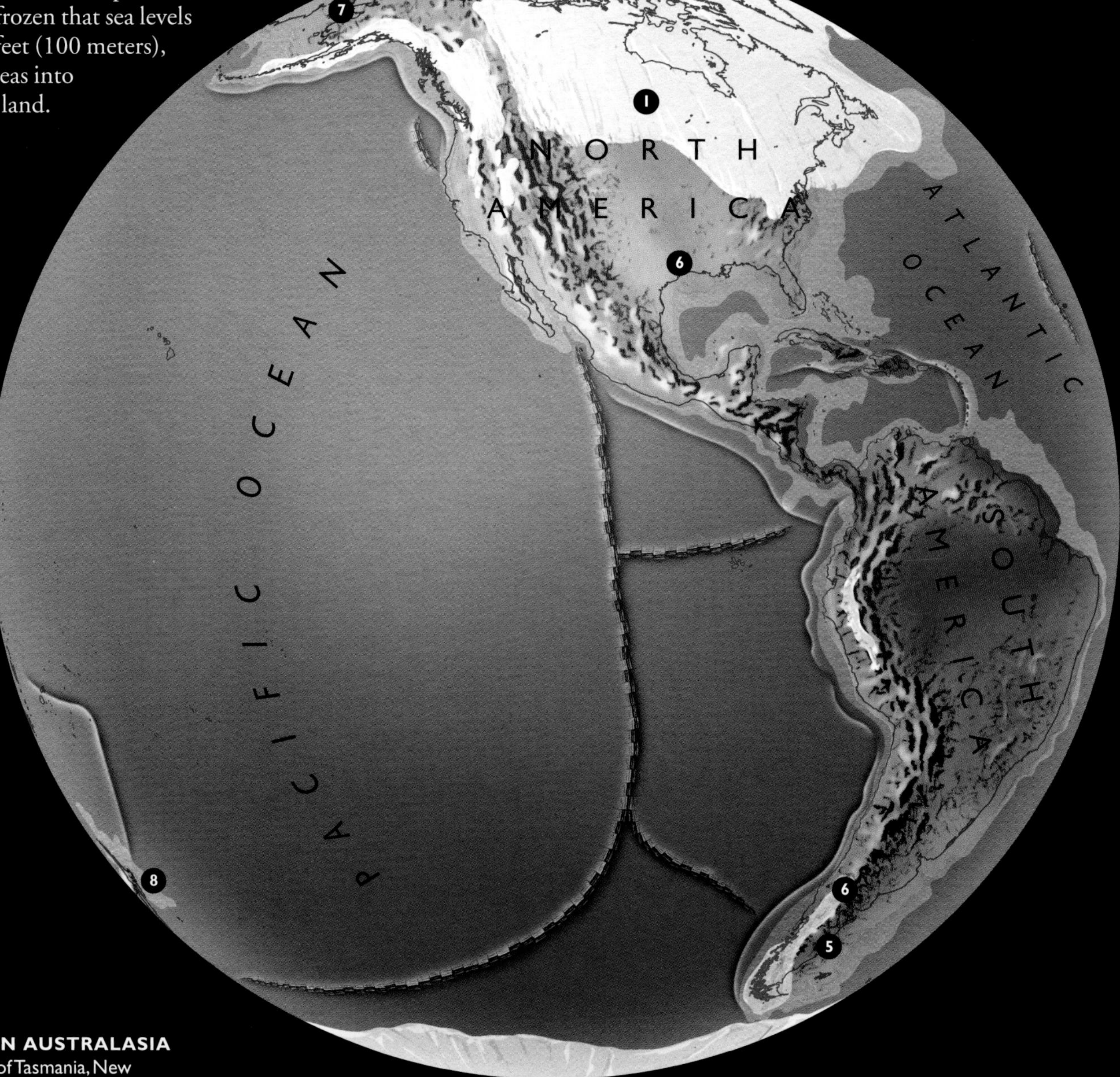

8. GLACIATION IN AUSTRALASIA

The high mountains of Tasmania, New Zealand, and southeast Australia show signs of intense glacial sculpting. Features include U-shaped valleys, cirques (deep semicircular basins), arêtes (sharp ridges of erosion-resistant rock), and horns (peaks formed from the intersection of the walls of three cirques). These provide clear evidence of glaciation during the coldest periods of the last ice age.

7. BERING LAND BRIDGE

With lowered sea levels, Eurasia and America were interconnected by a long, narrow isthmus of land. The opening of this "Beringian freeway" enabled land animals to migrate in both directions. However, the land bridge also prevented the exchange of marine organisms between the Arctic and Pacific Oceans.

2. SCANDINAVIA
The icecap over Scandinavia reached depths of 2.5 miles (4 kilometers), compressing the land beneath. Coasts now lifted clear of the sea show that Scandinavia has "rebounded" upward since the ice melted.

3. EURASIAN ICECAP
The interior of the Eurasian landmass had a climate that was too dry to support a large build-up of ice. Icecaps and sheets were restricted to the coasts and mountains of northwest Europe and a strip along the Arctic coast of Siberia. The total volume of ice and snow is estimated to have been about 4 cubic miles (17 cubic kilometers).

WHOLE WORLD PROJECTION

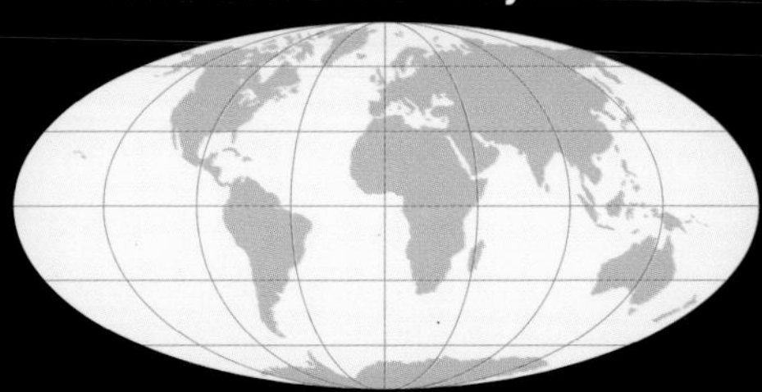

4. MAMMOTH TUNDRA
The vast interior of northern Asia was permanently frozen, but largely free of thick layers of snow and ice. Summer surface melts allowed vegetation to flourish, feeding large migratory herds of mammoth.

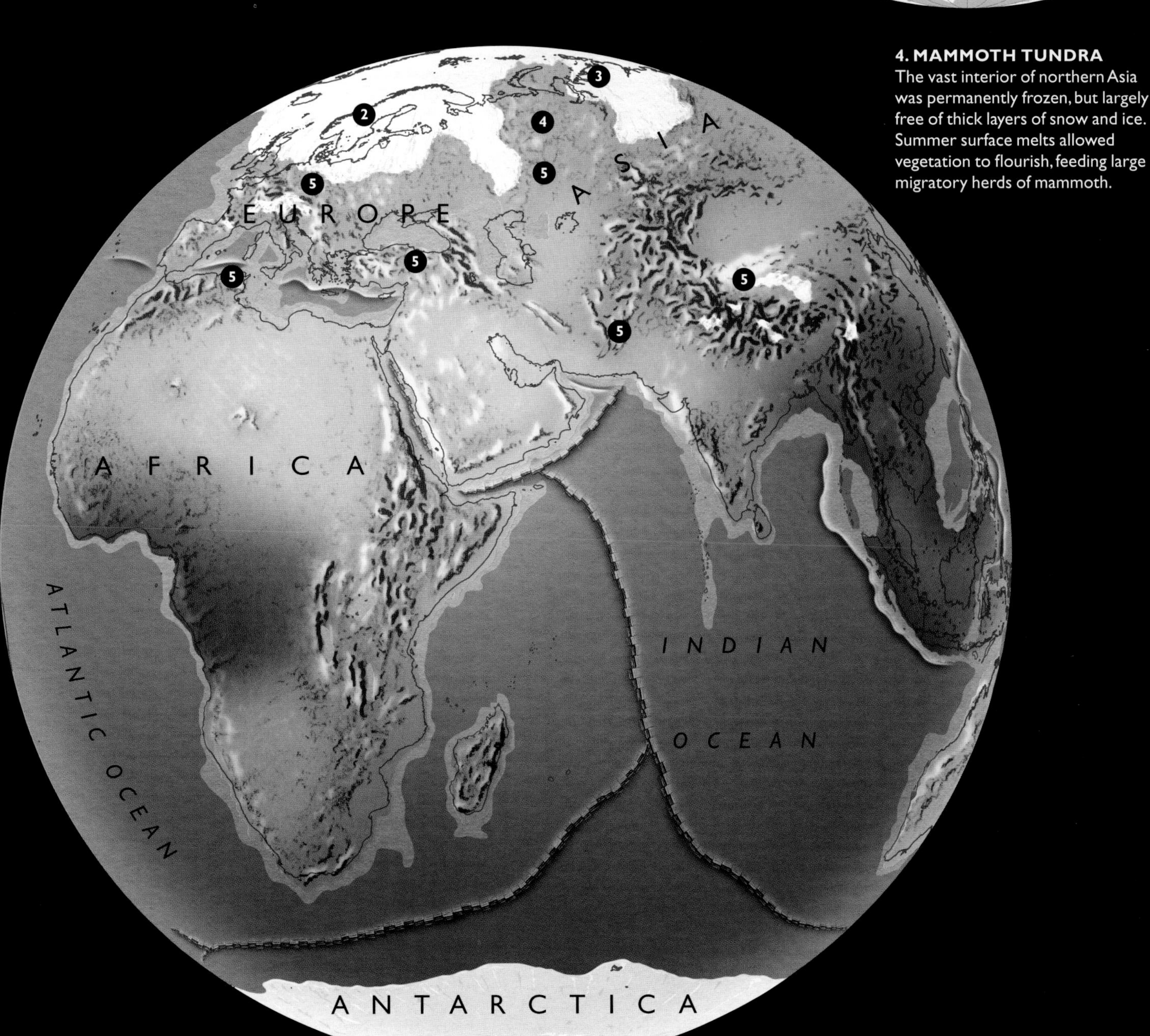

5. LOESS
Fine sand and dust blown from cold, dry plains that fringed areas of permafrost accumulated in parts of Central Europe, Tunisia, Pakistan, Tibet, Central Asia, Patagonia, New Zealand, and the Mississippi valley in America. Called loess, the dust covered the original landscapes and is now shaped into cliffs, which have sometimes been excavated for human dwellings.

6. GLACIATION IN SOUTH AMERICA
Even today, the mountains of the Andes are high enough for glaciers to form on their slopes. At the height of the last ice age, these glaciers carved some of the most spectacular peaks in the world. In southern Chile and Argentina, the glaciers flowed down the mountains to cover much of the southern tip of the continent.

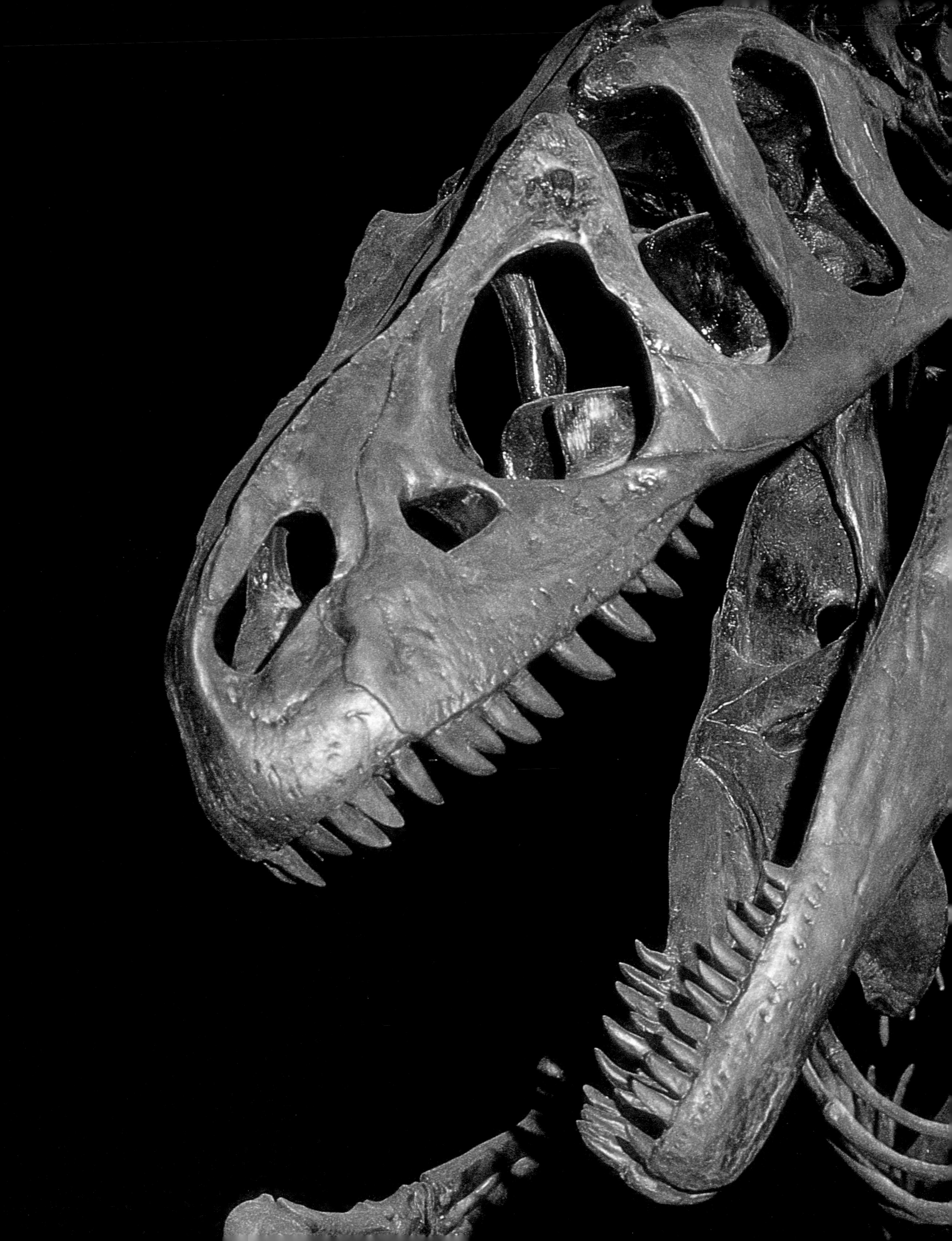

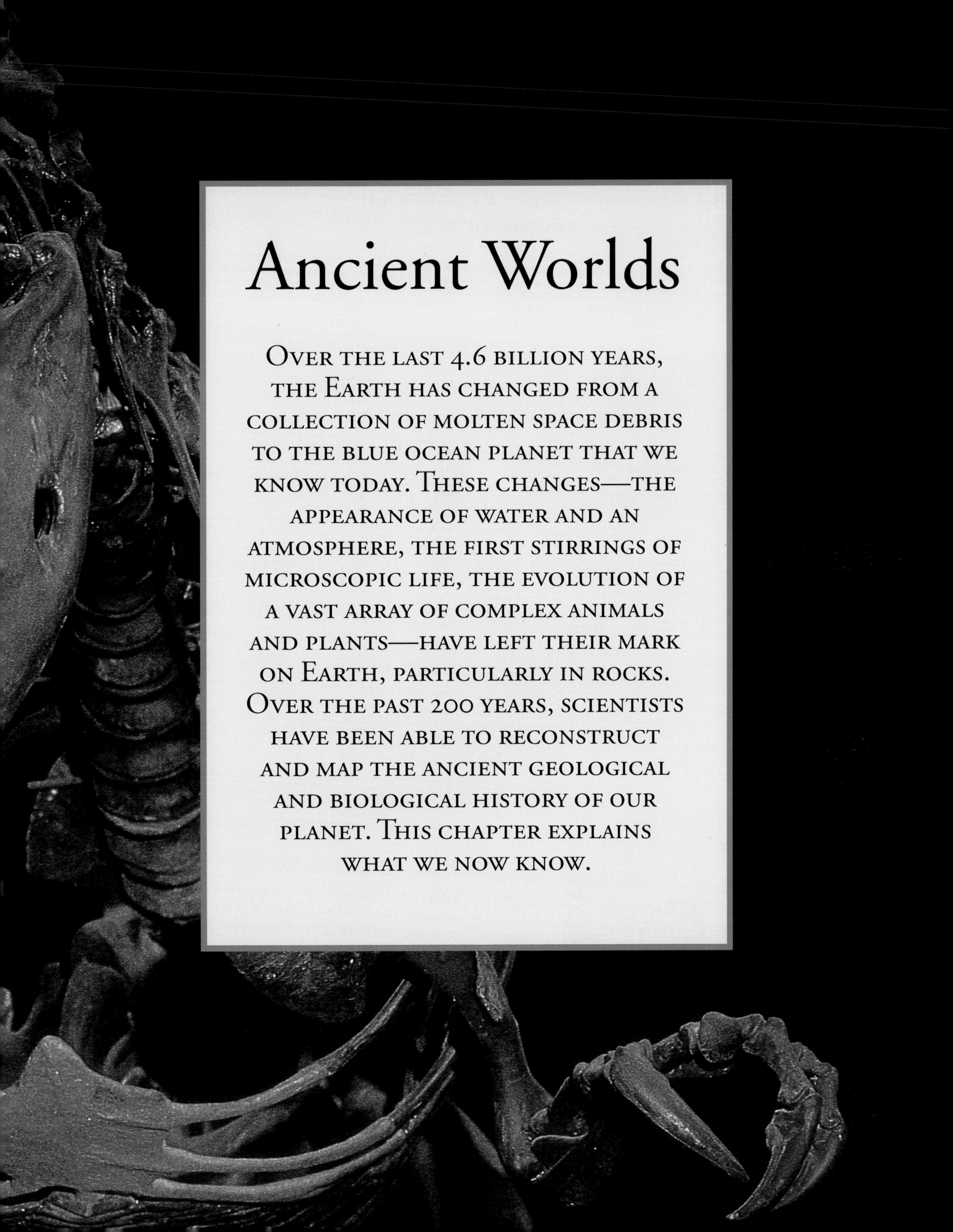

Ancient Worlds

Over the last 4.6 billion years, the Earth has changed from a collection of molten space debris to the blue ocean planet that we know today. These changes—the appearance of water and an atmosphere, the first stirrings of microscopic life, the evolution of a vast array of complex animals and plants—have left their mark on Earth, particularly in rocks. Over the past 200 years, scientists have been able to reconstruct and map the ancient geological and biological history of our planet. This chapter explains what we now know.

The Origin of Life

THE EARLY HISTORY OF THE EARTH IS A STORY OF SLOW BUT DRAMATIC CHANGE, AS ITS FIERY SURFACE COOLED AND PRODUCED THE FIRST SIGNS OF MICROSCOPIC LIFE.

During the formation of our Solar System, the Earth was created by the coalescence of large fragments of rock and ice, along with dust and gas. As these pieces collided 4.6 billion years ago, they released enormous amounts of energy, heating the Earth to 9,000° F (5,000° C).

A "meltdown" followed, lasting 100 million years, during which the Earth's interior assumed its present form. Heavy iron and nickel minerals sank to form a hot, dense core 2,200 miles (3,470 kilometers) in radius. Lighter minerals moved to the surface and formed a rocky outer crust about 4.5 billion years ago. Between the core and the crust, a mass of hot rock, 1,800 miles (2,900 kilometers) thick, called the mantle, formed. Heat convecting upward from this hot interior still shapes the Earth's surface, through, for example, volcanoes and earthquakes.

ATLANTIC SMOKER
Hydrothermal vents have been found on the seabed of the Atlantic Ocean, pumping out mineral-rich water. Early bacteria fed on these minerals.

The planets of the Solar System may have been formed by pieces of orbiting dust and rock colliding and joining together.

The Universe began with the "Big Bang" about 12 billion years ago, when an infinitely small volume of matter with an infinitely large density exploded.

GENESIS OF THE EARTH
About 8 billion years separated the "Big Bang" that created the Universe from the emergence of life on Earth. It would take another 3 billion years for more complex organisms to begin to appear.

About 6 billion years ago, a spinning disc-shaped cloud of gas and dust collapsed inward to create our Solar System.

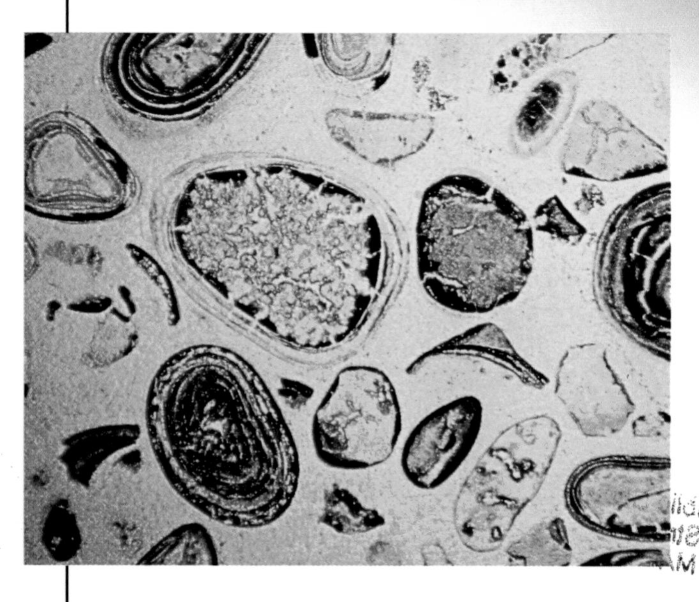

GUNFLINT ROCK
The 1.9 billion-year-old, silica-rich flint sedimentary rocks (flints) of western Ontario contain some of the best-preserved Precambrian microfossils in the world. Detailed cross-sections of the rocks reveal the different structures of the bacteria that lived at the time.

LAND, SEA, AND LIFE

Large-scale volcanic eruptions of gas and steam formed the early atmosphere and the first surface water on the Earth, but geologists are still not sure how the land, or continental crust, grew. The lighter silicate rocks of the crust may have risen high enough to form land "islands" about 4 billion years ago. Collisions between these "islands" are believed to have formed the first large landmasses, about a billion years later.

By 4 billion years ago, the crust had cooled sufficiently for microscopic life to appear. How exactly life originated remains one of the most debated questions in science today. In the early

1950s, Stanley Miller of the University of Chicago showed experimentally that it was possible to create amino acids, one of the basic building blocks of life, given a primitive atmosphere, some water, and a few flashes of lightning. More recently, scientists have speculated that the first organic molecules may have originated elsewhere in the Solar System, and have been brought to the Earth's surface by meteorites that bombarded the Earth about 4 billion years ago. Whatever their origins, the first microbes had to survive extreme conditions, with no oxygen and no protection from the Sun's ultraviolet rays.

THE MOON

Rocks brought back from the Moon by the Apollo missions have been dated as 4.5 billion years old, just younger than the Earth. The Moon is probably a chunk of rock knocked out of the Earth following collision with another planet, but it may be an unrelated body captured by the Earth's gravitational pull.

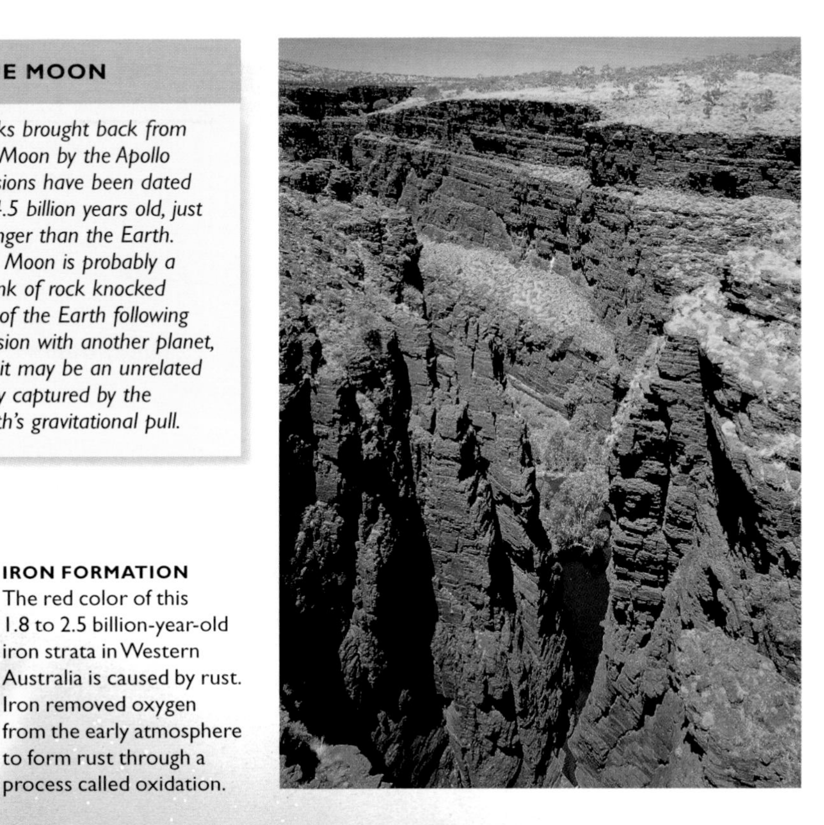

IRON FORMATION
The red color of this 1.8 to 2.5 billion-year-old iron strata in Western Australia is caused by rust. Iron removed oxygen from the early atmosphere to form rust through a process called oxidation.

About 4.5 billion years ago, it is thought that a planet the size of Mars may have crashed into the Earth.

About 3.5 billion years ago, the Earth had cooled sufficiently for oceans and an early oxygenless atmosphere to form.

The Moon may have formed from a ring of material ejected following the Earth's collision with a Mars-sized object.

Aquatic Microbes: Life Begins

The oldest known fossil remains of life on Earth have been found in sedimentary rocks deposited on the seabed about 3.5 billion years ago. These microscopic organisms existed in an environment devoid of oxygen and subject to extremes of temperature and acidity.

LIVING IN EXTREMES

The discovery, since the 1980s, of modern-day primitive organisms living in a variety of extreme conditions has provided valuable insight into how ancient microscopic organisms survived. The springwaters of Yellowstone National Park in Wyoming are home to "thermophilic" bacteria, which thrive in water as hot as 185°F (85°C). At the other extreme, "psychrophile" bacteria prefer Antarctic sea-ice, where the temperature is about 40°F (5°C). "Alkaliphiles" thrive in alkaline lakes and "acidophiles" in acid waters.

The discovery of hot springs at the bottom of the oceans has also revealed the existence of "chemosynthetic" bacteria, which reproduce their cells without the need for sunlight. These bacteria are single-celled and can tolerate temperatures of over 212°F (100°C). They survive on mineral salts dissolved in the boiling water.

All of these "extremophile" bacteria belong to the most primitive group of organisms known, the Archaebacteria. The Archaebacteria and Eubacteria (including the blue-green algae) are both groups of primitive organisms with small cells and no cell nucleus. This differentiates them from more complex lifeforms (such as animals and plants), which have large, nucleated cells. The Archaebacteria are able to survive the extremes of boiling water, ice, acids, alkalines, and darkness. Archaebacteria are also "anaerobes," which means that they can survive without oxygen. In the early

LIVING FOSSILS
In warm shallow seas, such as Mexico's Sea of Cortez, structures called stromatolites are being built today exactly as they were by early lifeforms billions of years ago. Sediments and bacteria bind together to form the curious structures.

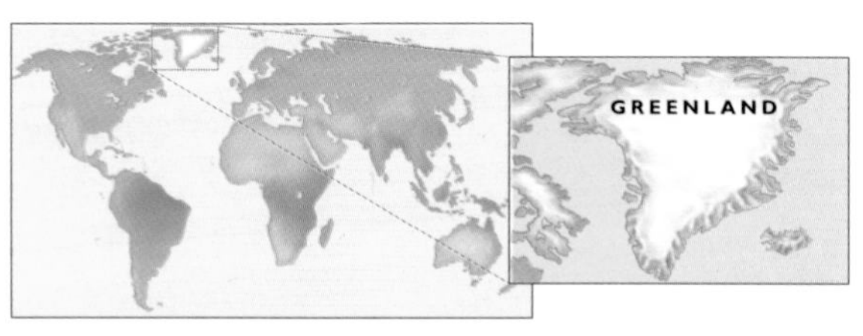

EARLY SIGNS OF LIFE
By 3.5 billion years ago, primitive algae and bacteria had extensively colonized the margins of shallow, warm seas, growing as mats over the surface of the seabed sediment. When these mats were periodically covered by sediment, the primitive organisms migrated upward toward the light, creating a new mat at a higher level. This process eventually formed distinctive "stromatolitic" mounds. These mounds would have been the only visible sign of life in the bare, volcanic early Precambrian scene.

Volcanic hills

Seabed sediment

Precambrian age, the Earth's atmosphere consisted almost entirely of nitrogen and carbon dioxide, so all lifeforms were anaerobic.

STROMATOLITES

The earliest fossil remains visible to the naked eye are stromatolites, curious laminated structures that grew in the shallow, lime-rich, continental shelf seas. The first stromatolites are over 3 billion years old—they are the most common early Precambrian fossils. The stromatolites were built by photosynthesizing blue-green algae, which initially formed mats on the seabed. As the mats were covered in sediment, the organisms would migrate upward, forming a succession of layers that would build into a laminated mound up to 3 feet (1 meter) high and 1 foot (30 centimeters) wide. Similar mounds are still being built today in warm tropical waters. The mounds are very distinctive and easily preserved as fossils.

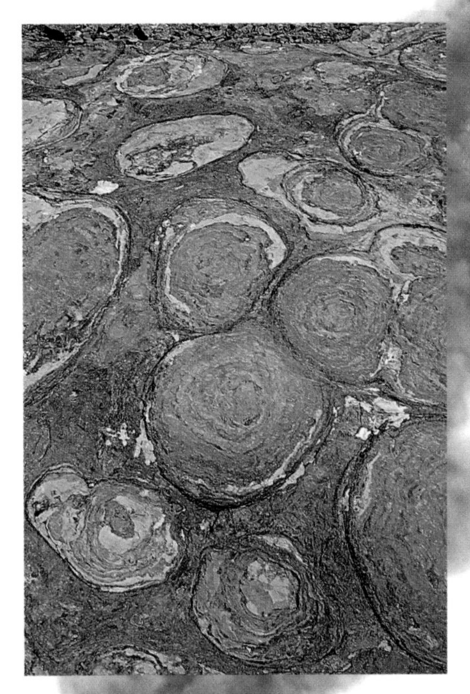

FOSSIL STROMATOLITES These stromatolite specimens come from Precambrian marine strata located in Glacier National Park, Montana.

CARBON TRACES

Although the earliest body fossils are 3.5 billion years old, rocks dating back another 200 million years may reveal traces of even older organisms. These rocks formed when the Earth was still relatively young and so were subjected to the high temperatures and pressures that existed at the time. Fossils could not survive these processes and none exist beyond the 3.5-billion-year limit. However, some of the chemical components of life can survive high temperatures and pressures. So it is possible to find chemical traces of life, even if bodily remains cannot be recovered.

Very few rocks older than 3.5 billion years are visible at the Earth's surface. One of the few places where they are exposed is at Isua, in west Greenland. These 3.7-billion-year-old rocks contain traces of carbon that are believed to be the remains of microscopic photosynthetic bacteria, called photoautotrophs. They lived in the surface waters and their remains dropped down to the seabed, accumulating in the sediments there.

Today, planktonic organisms similar to the ancient photoautotrophs form the basis for most water-based food chains.

OXYGENATING THE ATMOSPHERE

All photosynthesizing bacteria produce oxygen, a by-product of using carbon dioxide, water, and sunlight to replicate their cells. The build-up of atmospheric oxygen did not become significant until about 2.5 billion years ago, when these bacteria became more abundant. Until then, the only significant atmospheric gases were carbon dioxide and nitrogen.

The Vendian Period

FOSSIL EVIDENCE SHOWS THAT MULTICELLED ORGANISMS CAME INTO EXISTENCE IN THE OCEANS OF PRECAMBRIAN TIMES, ONCE REGARDED AS DEVOID OF COMPLEX LIFE.

The Vendian period, which ended 545 million years ago, marked the last section of the Precambrian age. This long period of Earth history was a time of shifting continents and changing atmospheric and ocean chemistry. The continents grew as sedimentary rock accumulated and plates collided and combined. Geologists have good evidence to show that in Vendian times most of the continents were clustered in the southern hemisphere, with northwest Africa situated over the South Pole. Toward the end of the Vendian period the continental plates came together to form a short-lived supercontinent, which has been called Pannotia.

CHANGING CONTINENTS

The Vendian period was once regarded as a geological wasteland of complex and barren rocks, devoid of life. Landscapes did indeed consist of bare rock, rushing rivers, lakes, and vast tracts of sterile rock waste and sediment—an unpromising environment for the development of life. But the oceans were a different matter. Seawater is more protective of life: damaging light rays are filtered out and delicate cell walls are kept moist and supported by the relatively dense water.

That complex life developed and diversified in the Vendian oceans is now clear both from direct fossil evidence and from the diversity of lifeforms found in rocks from the succeeding early Cambrian period, which must have been the result of a long period of evolution in Vendian times.

SOUTH AUSTRALIAN ORGANISM
Spriggina is one of the Ediacaran fossils found in the Flinders Range in South Australia. The Ediacarans were diverse in form and were the first complex organisms to leave a trace in the fossil record, despite having no hard parts. *Spriggina* may have resembled a trilobite.

NAMIBIAN SANDS
The Vendian sandstone of Namibia in southwest Africa contains some of the best-preserved Ediacaran fossils in the world. They were originally deposited in shallow-water seas, and their fossils have not been deformed by later folding or metamorphism of the rocks.

THE FIRST LARGE LIFE

Current research suggests that, in fact, most groups of complex multicelled organisms, apart from the higher plants, must have come into existence in the Vendian oceans. Unfortunately, however, the majority of these animals have left no trace in the fossil record.

The great exception is the Ediacarans, the first larger organisms of which traces have been found, fossilized in seafloor sediments. The Ediacarans had no shells or other hard parts, but they were nonetheless preserved as impressions in the

PRECAMBRIAN OIL

Traces of oil and gas around 2 billion years old have recently been discovered in Australia and South Africa. Since oil and gas are created by the decay of minute marine lifeforms, their presence shows that primitive microorganisms must have been much more abundant in the oceans during Precambrian times than had previously been thought. This microbiota formed a vast potential food resource within the ancient seas and oceans. It is surprising that it took so long for bigger multicellular life, capable of consuming this food, to evolve.

SACLIKE ORGANISM
Among the strangest of the Ediacarans from Namibia, these *Pteridinium* are preserved in a three-dimensional form. They may have lived buried in the seabed, their saclike bodies filled with sand. The small coin provides a sense of scale.

ancient seafloor deposits. They had a wide range of different forms, although many of them looked superficially like jellyfish or worms. The exact place of the Ediacarans in the story of evolution remains a matter of dispute.

LACK OF OXYGEN

The oxygen levels that existed in the Vendian period, 620 million years ago, were still far too low to support life outside water. Primitive forms of bacteria had lived in the oceans from at least 3.8 billion years ago, securing light energy from the Sun and producing oxygen from photosynthesis. But this oxygen was taken up by dissolved iron and deposited as insoluble iron minerals, forming layers of iron-rich sediments, known as "banded iron formations." This oceanic process persisted for nearly a billion years before oxygen levels in the Earth's atmosphere were able to build up to any great extent. By Vendian times, oxygen had risen from 0.2 percent to 17 percent of the atmosphere, close to today's 21 percent level.

EDIACARAN ORGANISM
The flat discs of *Dickinsonia* grew to a length of 2 feet (60 centimeters), making it one of the first "large" creatures. The body is segmented and has a midline symmetry that divides it in two. Its body tissue may have been denser than that of jellyfish or worms.

Complex Organisms Emerge

The first convincing fossil evidence for the existence of complex organisms in late Precambrian times was discovered in the 1940s in South Australia. These "Ediacaran" fossils—named for the Ediacaran Hills in the Flinders Range in Australia where they were first found—are small impressions found in sandy sediments. Hundreds of Ediacarans have now been found all over the world, from Siberia to Namibia, in rocks of Vendian age within the late Precambrian era. They appear as variously shaped blobs, ribbed fronds, and ribbons, ranging in length from about 0.4 inches (1 centimeter) to 3.3 feet (1 meter). Entirely soft-bodied, they apparently had no preservable hard parts, such as shells.

FLINDERS RANGE
The Ediacaran Hills in the Flinders Range in South Australia were made famous in the 1940s by the geologist R. C. Sprigg, who discovered a variety of Precambrian fossils, ranging from 0.4 inches (1 centimeter) to 3.3 feet (1 meter) long.

PRECAMBRIAN "JELLIES"

Originally, the Ediacarans were identified as the ancestors of the main groups of invertebrates (animals without backbones). They were shoe-horned into more or less familiar groups of many-celled invertebrates, such as jellyfish, worms, and seapens. Now this view of their role in evolution has been questioned. Some experts conclude that the Ediacarans as a whole are an extinct group, a failed evolutionary experiment that was neither plant nor animal. Other paleontologists disagree. They claim that some Ediacarans at least may have genuinely belonged to various groups of invertebrates that still exist today. The Ediacarans *Charnia* and *Pteridinium* could be ancestors of the living seapen, while others may be ancestors of the arthropods and annelid worms.

EVOLUTIONARY MYSTERY

The mystery of the true nature of the Ediacarans is part of the wider mystery surrounding the timing of the evolution of the first multicelled

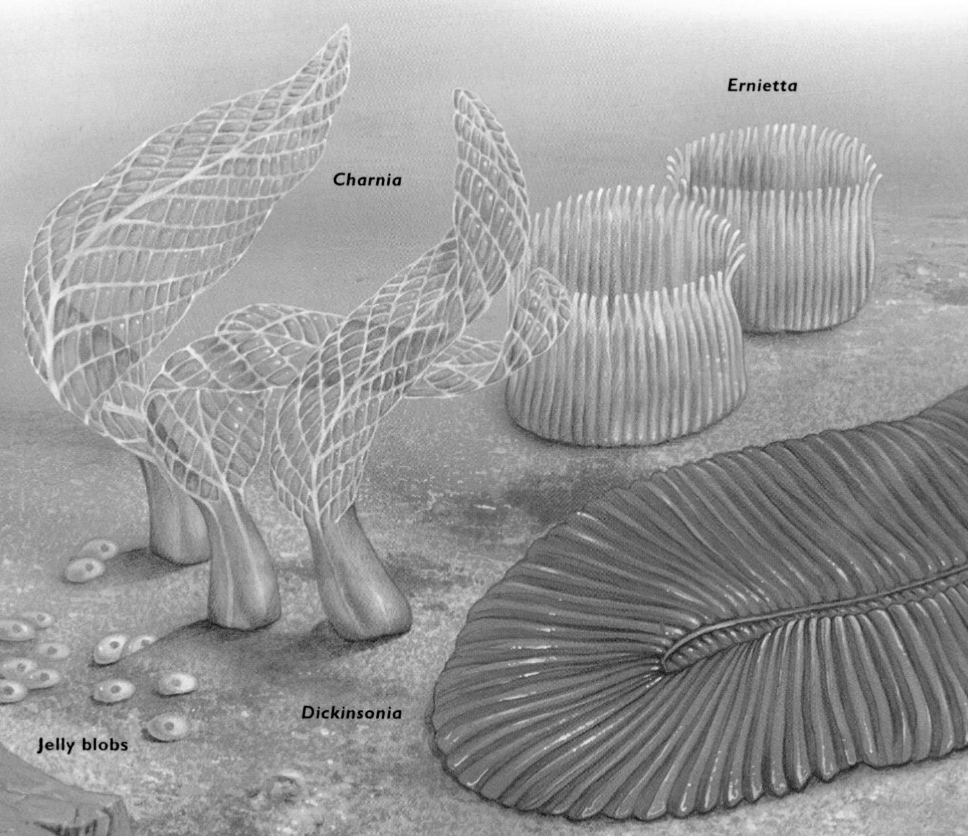

THE VENDIAN SEAWORLD
The organisms that lived in the shallow-water seas of Vendian times have puzzled paleontologists for many years. They were all completely soft-bodied—no trace of any hard parts have been found. At first they were thought to be jellyfish and wormlike creatures. But the way their bodies are preserved suggests they were made of tougher material. Some of them seem to have lived within the seabed and had saclike bodies filled with sand. However, some of the plume-shaped forms, such as *Charnia*, are similar to living seapens and sea-anemones.

creatures, or metazoans. There is good fossil evidence to suggest that single-celled organisms capable of sexual reproduction have been around for a billion years or more. It is argued that Cambrian fossils, from the period after 545 million years ago, are so diverse that they must have begun evolving back in Precambrian times.

Another recent approach to the mystery employs the so-called "molecular clock." Based on known rates of genetic change and the genetic "distance" between major animal groups still in existence today, this theory estimates the origin of the metazoans and the beginning of the divergence of major groups at between 600 million and a billion years ago.

In 1997, fossil evidence to support this idea was uncovered in southern China. Clusters of tiny balls, less than a twentieth of an inch (a tenth of a millimeter) in diameter, were discovered within Precambrian rocks 570 million years old. The balls had a delicate cellular structure that had never before been seen in fossils of such a great age.

The fossils astonishingly turned out to be exquisitely preserved fossil embryos, caught by the processes of fossilization only hours, or even minutes, after fertilization. Just how they were turned to stone remains a mystery. The cellular form of the embryos closely resembles that of early invertebrates, such as metazoan flatworms and arthropods. Their presence in 570-million-year-old strata proves that complex animals must already have been in existence at that time. The fossil remains of adults from similar species have been found only in strata from considerably later geological times.

FOSSIL EMBRYO
Less than one twentieth of an inch (0.1 millimeters) across, this is the embryo of an unknown early organism. Fossilized about 570 million years ago, it was discovered in Vendian strata in China.

MAKING EDIACARAN FOSSILS

Generally, soft-bodied creatures tend to be missing from the fossil record because they do not fossilize in sediment. The Ediacaran fossils are especially puzzling because the creatures' body forms are molded and preserved as squashed but essentially three-dimensional impressions in sandstone. Researchers have carried out experiments in which they buried jellyfish in an effort to replicate the process by which Ediacarans were preserved. These experiments have, however, failed to produce similar traces. This has led many experts to suppose that the bodies of the Ediacarans must have been made of a much tougher material than the bodies of modern jellyfish. Some even suggest that the only organism living today that could be preserved in this way would be a lichen.

Cambrian Explosion

EARLY CAMBRIAN TIMES BROUGHT A DEFINING MOMENT IN THE HISTORY OF LIFE ON EARTH—A BURST IN THE EVOLUTION OF MARINE LIFE, WHICH WE KNOW FROM A WEALTH OF FOSSIL SHELLS.

The Cambrian period, beginning 545 million years ago and lasting for around 50 million years, marks the beginning of a major division of geological time, known as the Paleozoic (meaning "ancient life"). The start of the Cambrian age witnessed the rapid growth of an amazing diversity of lifeforms.

After an incredibly long Precambrian phase of early development—lasting over 3 billion years—a range of fossil forms, unknown in earlier rocks, suddenly appeared in sedimentary rocks in the sea. This important evolutionary event coincided with major environmental changes. There was global warming and sea levels steadily rose following the end of the Vendian glaciation. Seas began to flood the old continents, and in shallow equatorial waters, such as those covering much of the Siberian plate, small fossils composed of calcium carbonate were deposited as limestone. The Sauk Transgression, in the late Cambrian period, was such a time when seas flooded large areas of the continents.

NAMING TIME

The Cambrian period was first defined in 1835 by an English professor of geology, Adam Sedgwick. He mapped a series of marine strata in North Wales and showed that they lay above older rocks (called Precambrian) and below younger Silurian strata. He named them after the Latin for Wales—Cambria.

LAURENTIA
SIBERIA
IAPETUS OCEAN
BALTICA

HOLLOW SHELL
The tiny, hollow cap-shaped shells of the lapworthellids have been extracted from early Cambrian strata in Canada. Lapworthellids may have been a kind of snail-like mollusk.

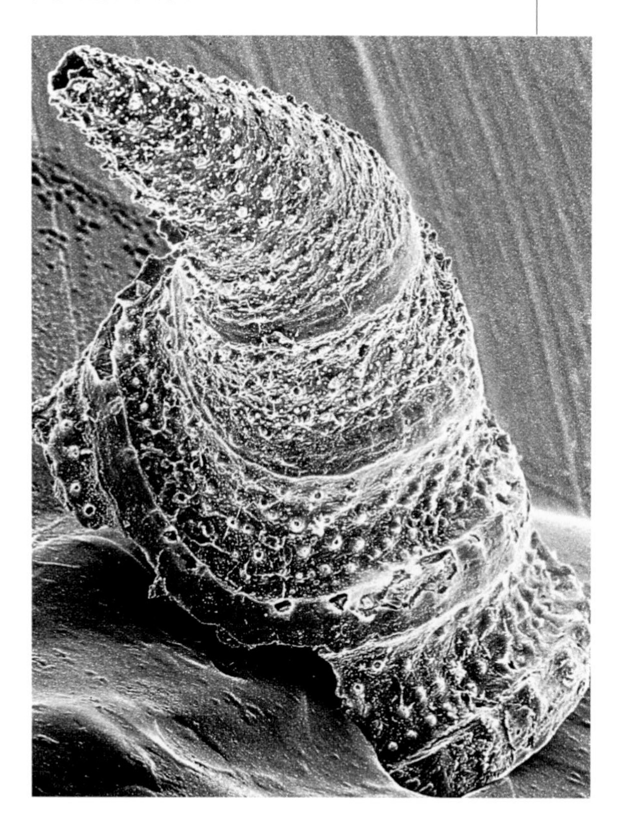

ODD BODY
Halkiera (right), a fossil from early Cambrian strata in Greenland, has a very strange anatomy. The flat, wormlike segmented body, with a brachiopod-like shell at either end, is covered in scales. The mixture of body structures may indicate ancestry to a number of different animal groups.

EVIDENCE OF LIFE

The fossil record shows that, time and again, groups of organisms have evolved and diversified only to become extinct and be replaced by other organisms. The start of the Cambrian period witnessed such a phase of origination and diversification. Evidence of animal activity found in seabed sediment (called trace fossils) show that increasingly complex animals were evolving. Traces include scratch marks of animals with hardened skins (exoskeletons), which were probably the first arthropods—invertebrates with jointed limbs and segmented bodies. Further evidence comes from the 40 different kinds of shelled creatures, no bigger than a millimeter, which have been discovered in marine limestone deposited on top of Precambrian rocks.

Many of these fossils—usually known simply as small shelly fossils—are thought to represent primitive mollusks at an early evolutionary stage. These fossils are mostly simple cones, similar in appearance to today's limpet shells, except that some of them have a curious snorkel-like tube protruding from the side of the cone. It is thought that this tube might represent an early attempt to separate inhalant currents, which bring in water needed for respiration and sometimes filter feeding, from exhalant currents, which are used for passing waste products and reproductive cells out into the sea. Along with these small shelly fossils are slightly bigger conical fossils with porous walls, known as archaeocyathans, which are probably related to the sponges.

These fossils represent the first wave of the Cambrian explosion. Although they eventually declined, to be replaced by other animals, they were widely distributed, with sequences of marine strata around the world revealing comparable remains of these early sea-dwelling creatures.

LIMPET OR BURROWER
Mobergella, a tiny cap-shaped shell from Sweden, is one of the puzzling small shelly fossils found in earliest Cambrian strata worldwide. The paired indentations are thought to be the sites of muscle attachment for a limpetlike animal.

TINY FOSSIL SPINE
This millimeter-sized fossil, *Zhijinites*, was removed chemically from the earliest Cambrian strata found in Sichuan province, China. It was probably one of a number of protective spines embedded in the skin of a larger, and as yet unknown, marine animal.

Early Cambrian Marine Life

The fossils of early Cambrian strata record a curious submarine world, inhabited by minuscule creatures. Organisms had become significantly smaller compared to the earlier Vendian fauna, which had grown up to 3 feet (1 meter) in length. By comparison, the largest organisms of early Cambrian times were small cone-shaped creatures called archaeocyathans, only a few inches high. These animals formed widespread reeflike structures in the shallow tropical waters where they lived. The surrounding seafloor sediment was ploughed by smaller snail-like animals, covered by tiny conical shells. Small worms also lived in the sediment in burrows a few inches deep. Visible life did not exist more than 3 inches (7.5 centimeters) above the seabed.

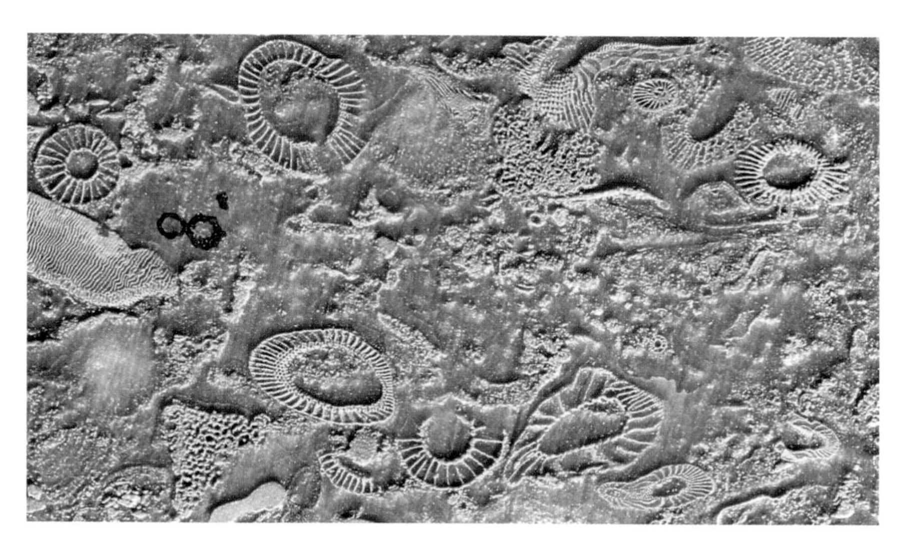

FIRST SHELLS

Shells were an innovation of early Cambrian times. The fossils that mark the boundary between Precambrian and Cambrian strata are trace fossils—the preserved forms of tracks, worm casts, and burrows. However, in strata not far above this boundary, the first fossil shells appear. They fall into two clearly distinct groups: the shells of the archaeocyathans, which were porous cones, and the shells of the so-called "small shelly fossils," a variety of solid-walled cone shapes only 0.2 inches (5 millimeters) in size. In addition, a variety of fossilized spines, studs, and scalelike plates appear, which must originally have been embedded in the skins of different small creatures.

Hard spines, scales, and shells are all familiar defensive devices, suggesting a need for protection. Their appearance in the strata implies that life at this time had suddenly become much more dangerous than in previous ages. If this is true, then a revolution had taken place in the relationships between the organisms of the time. On a miniature scale, a global arms race had begun.

EARLY SHELLED CREATURES

Archaeocyathans were among the earliest fauna with hard parts, producing inner and outer calcareous walls, perforated and porous like a sponge. This double-walled structure can be clearly seen in a cross-section of the fossilized remains of a group of archaeocyathans (above).

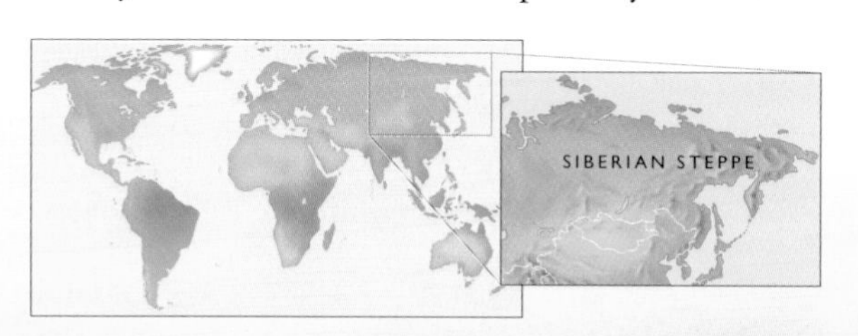

A SMALL WORLD UNDER THE SEA

Tiny mineralized fossil shells and plates from earliest Cambrian sediments show that seabed micro-communities thrived. They included many different kinds of animals that lived on, and perhaps in, the top layer of sediment. Some of these animals belonged to known groups such as the mollusks (*Yochelcionella, Latouchella, Hyolithellus*), brachiopods with bivalved shells, and spongelike archaeocyathans. But others are hard to categorize, such as *Microdictyon*, a soft-bodied arthropod with curious plates embedded in its skin, and *Tommotia*, a strange-shaped mollusk.

Hyolithellus

Yochelcionella

Latouchella

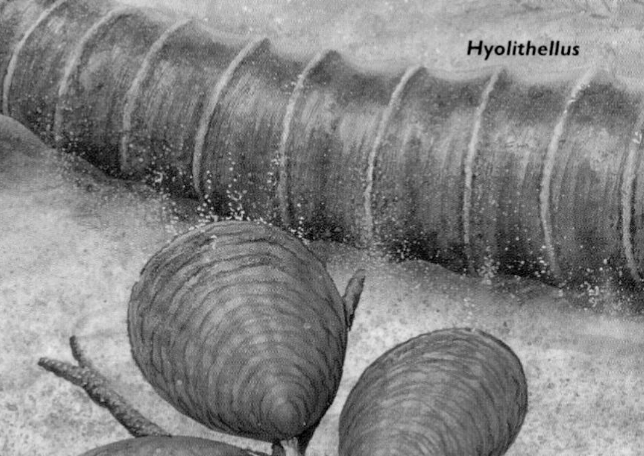

CONTRASTING FUNCTIONS

The shells of the archaeocyathans and the shells of those animals represented by the small shelly fossils had quite different functions. Archaeocyathans primarily used theirs to anchor themselves to the seabed. From here they would grow upward, as sponges and corals do today. They almost certainly also used their shells as feeding devices. The porous walls of the shell would have filtered out microscopic food from the surrounding seawater. Providing protection against predators was probably a less important function.

By contrast, the tiny shells of the small shelly fossils were probably primarily a protective device. The inhabitants of these small shells lived on the seabed and fed by grazing on organic material from the surface of the sediment. There may have been some risk associated with feeding, however. Their exposed fleshy bodies may have made them easy targets for predators swimming in the water above.

Although the archaeocyathans quickly spread worldwide, they did not last for long by geological standards—only some 35 million years—and by late Cambrian times, they were extinct. The animals that lived in the small shells, however, are thought to be related to today's mollusks.

ARTHROPOD ARMOR
Named for their three-lobed shell, trilobites first appeared around 545 million years ago. Trilobites are among the earliest known arthropods, and account for a third of all fossils found in Cambrian rocks. They were some of the first animals to develop an external skeleton.

The "Lilliputian" early-Cambrian seaworld was short-lived. With the rapid formation of shells and other external hard structures, the organisms of that period evolved a great deal in a relatively short time. It was not, however, enough to guarantee their survival. By the end of the early Cambrian period (520 million years ago) an extinction event had wiped many of them out and another wave of diversification was underway.

SHELL THEORIES

Why did early Cambrian organisms evolve shells? The obvious answer is that they needed protection. But it has been pointed out that there were no known predators armed with teeth at this time—so what exactly were these tiny organisms protecting themselves against? One possibility is that predators used other means of attack, such as stinging cells, which left no trace in the fossil record. But it is possible that the shells were not for protection at all. They may have been energy stores, a response to chemical changes in seawater or an anchor for soft body parts.

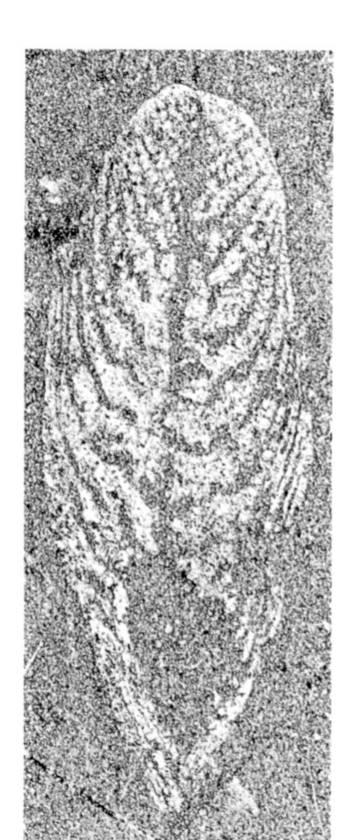

LEAF-SHAPED ANIMALS
This 8-inch (20-centimeter) *Thaumaptilon* fossil, from the Burgess Shale, is very similar to some Vendian leaf-shaped Ediacarans, such as *Charnia*. Some scientists argue that the two are related. It may also be a 560-million-year-old ancestor of the living seapens, which are colonial animals related to the corals.

Late Cambrian Period

THIS PERIOD WAS MARKED BY THE CONTINUING SUCCESS OF ARTHROPODS, SUCH AS THE TRILOBITES, AND THE EMERGENCE OF A POSSIBLE ANCESTOR OF THE VERTEBRATES.

As the world emerged from the "icehouse" state of the glaciated late Precambrian era, the supercontinent of Pannotia, made up of the southern continent of Gondwana, Laurentia (North America), Baltica (Eurasia), Siberia (Asia), and Avalonia (western Europe), continued to break up, creating the Iapetus Ocean, the forerunner of today's Atlantic. Climates warmed to well above today's average temperatures and became humid. The general rise in sea level, which had started at the beginning of the Cambrian age, continued, and lasted into late Cambrian times. By then over half of the North American continent was flooded by shallow seas.

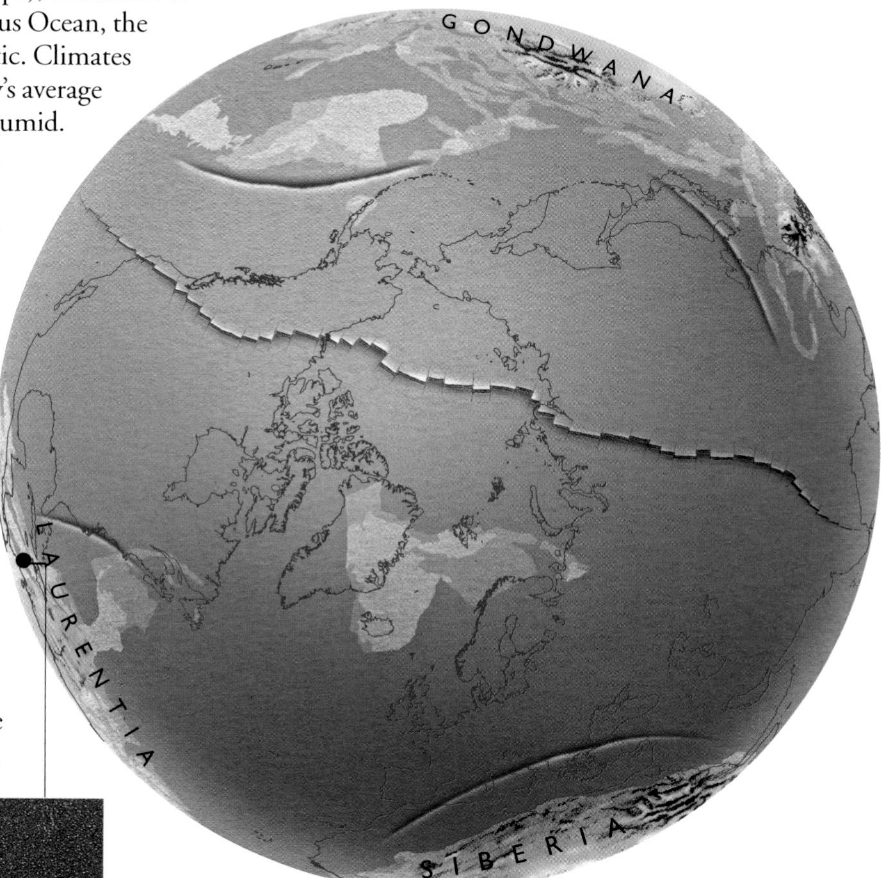

EXTINCTION EVENTS

These warm, light-filled waters were an ideal environment for life to expand and diversify, but progress was not smooth. There were two large-scale extinction events, one at the end of the Precambrian age, and a more drastic one at the beginning of mid-Cambrian times, some 530 million years ago, when up to 70 percent of species disappeared.

Although creatures such as the numerous cone-shaped archeocyathans became extinct, other more

ARMORED SLUG
Scaly armor-plating covers this sluglike creature, *Wiwaxia*, 1.5 inches (4 centimeters) long, from the Burgess Shale, Canada. The scales are hollow and covered with a lattice of intersecting ribs. They may have been iridescent, flashing color signals to attract mates.

MASS EXTINCTION

The mass extinction event that occurred halfway through the Cambrian period seems to have been caused by fluctuating sea levels. As sea levels rose from the low levels of the late Precambrian age, marine animals colonized the expanding shelf seas. Mid-Cambrian sea levels fell again, destroying the shallow-water environments and wiping out large numbers of marine species.

successful and aggressive predatory creatures had evolved by mid-Cambrian times, such as *Anomalocaris* and *Laggania*, which had actively biting mouths. Other carnivorous predators were mostly worms, which swallowed their prey whole.

Arthropods, including the trilobites, were the most common marine organisms of the period, and continued to develop and thrive. Many had increasingly armored bodies, often covered in spines and chainmail-like "sclerites," for defending themselves against predators. Eventually the arthropods covered themselves in hard shells, constructed from the carbonates and phosphates present in the seawater.

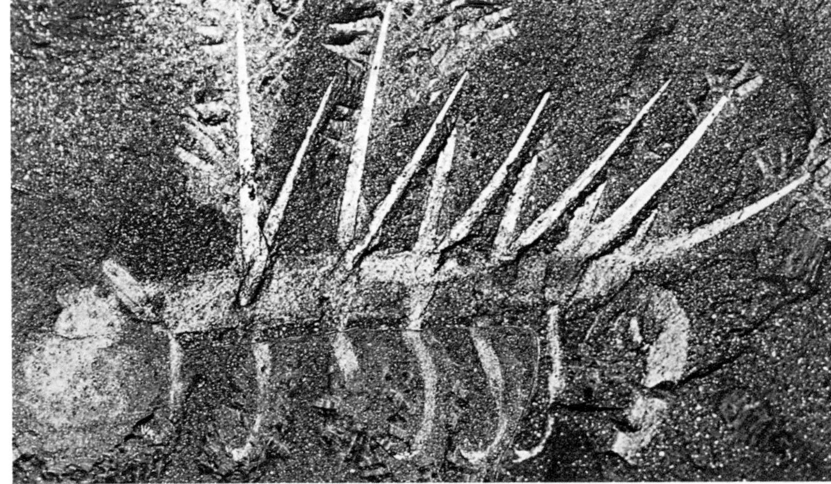

STRANGE, SPIKED CREATURE
This Burgess Shale animal is very strange, as its name, *Hallucigenia*, suggests. The stiff spikes on top were initially thought to be its legs and the flexible appendages underneath its feeding apparatus, but scientists have since turned the creature the other way up. However, it is still not clear which end is the head and which end is the tail.

DETAILED LEG FOSSILS
Trilobites like *Olenoides* were among the most successful arthropods of the time. This Burgess Shale fossil shows *Olenoides*' legs in fine detail, projecting from underneath its hard, crablike covering.

PIKAIA AND THE BURGESS SHALE

The mollusks and brachiopods (two-shelled invertebrates), which had appeared during the early Cambrian period, continued to diversify. But perhaps the most important development of this time, at least in retrospect, was the appearance of a small swimming animal called *Pikaia* (see page 66). This was the first animal to possess the early characteristics of a backbone, in the form of a long, stiffening rod and spinal nerve cord. It is thought that *Pikaia* was the ancestor of all vertebrate animals, including ourselves.

Like animal life, other forms of life were still restricted to the seas. These lifeforms included blue-green algae (single-celled organisms) as well as early multicellular algal seaweeds (green, red, and brown algae).

Information on the creatures of this period has grown enormously since the 1980s. The detailed information from the famous Burgess Shale of Canada has now been added to by information from localities such as Chengjiang in Yunnan Province, China and Sirius Passet, Greenland.

The Burgess Seaworld

THE BEST PICTURE OF THE CAMBRIAN SEAWORLD is provided by the 530-million-year-old mudstone of the Burgess Shale in British Columbia, Canada. This site has now yielded thousands of exceptionally well-preserved fossils, many of them completely intact. Taken together, they provide a vivid insight into life in the Cambrian seas at the time when the arthropods were the dominant lifeform.

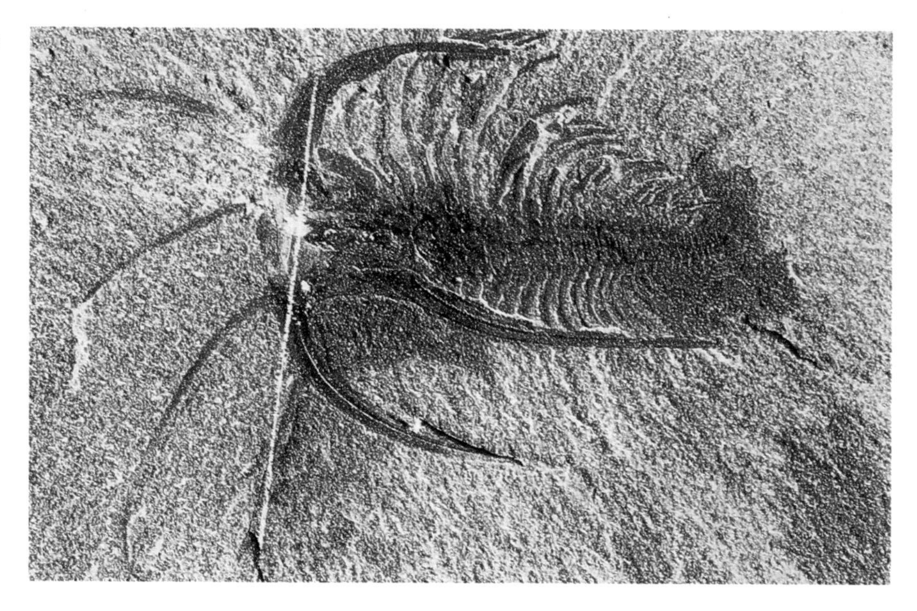

PERFECTLY PRESERVED
This *Marrella* fossil is one of many finely preserved specimens found in the Burgess Shale. Antennae, legs, and delicate gills are clearly visible. Walcott named this creature the "Lace Crab," but it was in fact a primitive shrimplike arthropod.

DISCOVERING THE BURGESS SHALE

The American paleontologist Charles Doolittle Walcott discovered the Burgess Shale by chance on August 31, 1909, as he was making his way across a high ridge in the Rockies that connected Mount Field and Mount Wapta. Walcott spotted a profusion of fossils in a block of hard shale and immediately recognized its importance. Not only were the usual hard parts of the animals preserved, but the soft tissue was also present. Walcott had stumbled upon the largest find of perfectly preserved fossils from any era.

It is generally thought that the creatures in the Burgess Shale were buried by a mudslide from a submarine cliff. The extraordinary anatomical detail present in the fossils, including delicate appendages, indicates that they were buried rapidly, possibly in mud that was low in oxygen. In the absence of oxygen, tissues decompose more slowly and are consequently better preserved.

For eight years after his lucky find, Walcott systematically quarried into the mountainside, excavating thousands of specimens, which he then shipped to the Smithsonian Institute in Washington, DC. Work by paleontologists at the University of Cambridge, England, and the Royal Ontario Museum, Canada, has subsequently revealed the full significance of the find.

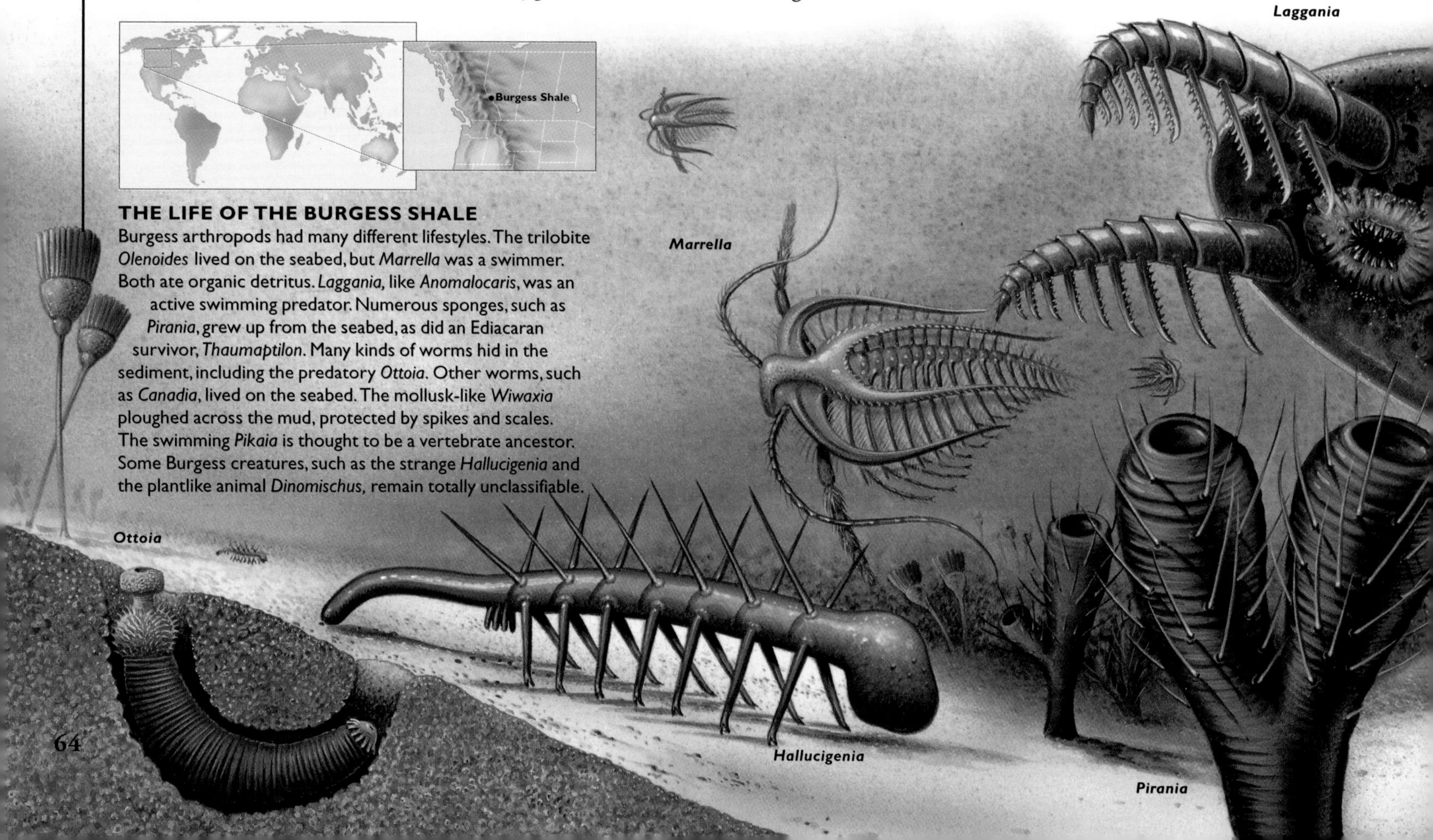

THE LIFE OF THE BURGESS SHALE
Burgess arthropods had many different lifestyles. The trilobite *Olenoides* lived on the seabed, but *Marrella* was a swimmer. Both ate organic detritus. *Laggania*, like *Anomalocaris*, was an active swimming predator. Numerous sponges, such as *Pirania*, grew up from the seabed, as did an Ediacaran survivor, *Thaumaptilon*. Many kinds of worms hid in the sediment, including the predatory *Ottoia*. Other worms, such as *Canadia*, lived on the seabed. The mollusk-like *Wiwaxia* ploughed across the mud, protected by spikes and scales. The swimming *Pikaia* is thought to be a vertebrate ancestor. Some Burgess creatures, such as the strange *Hallucigenia* and the plantlike animal *Dinomischus*, remain totally unclassifiable.

CAMBRIAN SEAWORLD

Study of the fossils found in the Burgess Shale has revealed that approximately 40 different kinds of arthropods accounted for about half of all the preserved animals. A further 30 percent were echinoderms (the family of which the starfish are members), sponges, and priapulid worms. The remainder included brachiopods, mollusks, and a curious swimming creature called *Pikaia*, which may be related to living vertebrates.

There were also "hairy" worms living on the surface of the seabed, such as *Canadia* and *Burgessochaeta*. They literally bristled with thousands of tiny hairlike fibers. These bristles, and many of the finely ridged scales and plates of the Burgess animals, are thought to have acted as reflectors to create display lighting. In the dim light that filtered down from the surface of the water, the reflectors and hairs would have flashed silver as the animals moved about, enabling them to recognize each other. These appendages would also have made them visible to predators, but their spines and scales would have defended them.

The wide variety of creatures in the sea at this time suggests that a structured food web, similar to that found in modern marine ecosystems, had already evolved. Discovering this remarkable diversity and high level of ecological sophistication so early in animal evolution has led scientists to conclude that there must have been a lengthy earlier development of multicelled animals, stretching back to Precambrian times.

THREE-IN-ONE ANOMALOCARIS

The most awesome of the Burgess creatures was the free-swimming predator Anomalocaris, *which grew to around 24 inches (60 centimeters) in length. For over 100 years it was known only from fragmentary remains, and these were thought to belong to three quite different animals, a jellyfish, a shrimp, and a sponge. Finally, in 1985, British paleontologists reassembled the pieces as one animal, and named it* Anomalocaris, *meaning "unusual shrimp."*

IDENTIFICATION
The mouth (left) of *Anomalocaris* was thought to be a jellyfish, the limb (below), a shrimp.

FIERCE WORM
The carnivorous *Ottoia* is one of many priapulid worms found in the shale. They lived in burrows on the seabed and had retractable proboscises with hooks and teeth for grasping their unsuspecting prey.

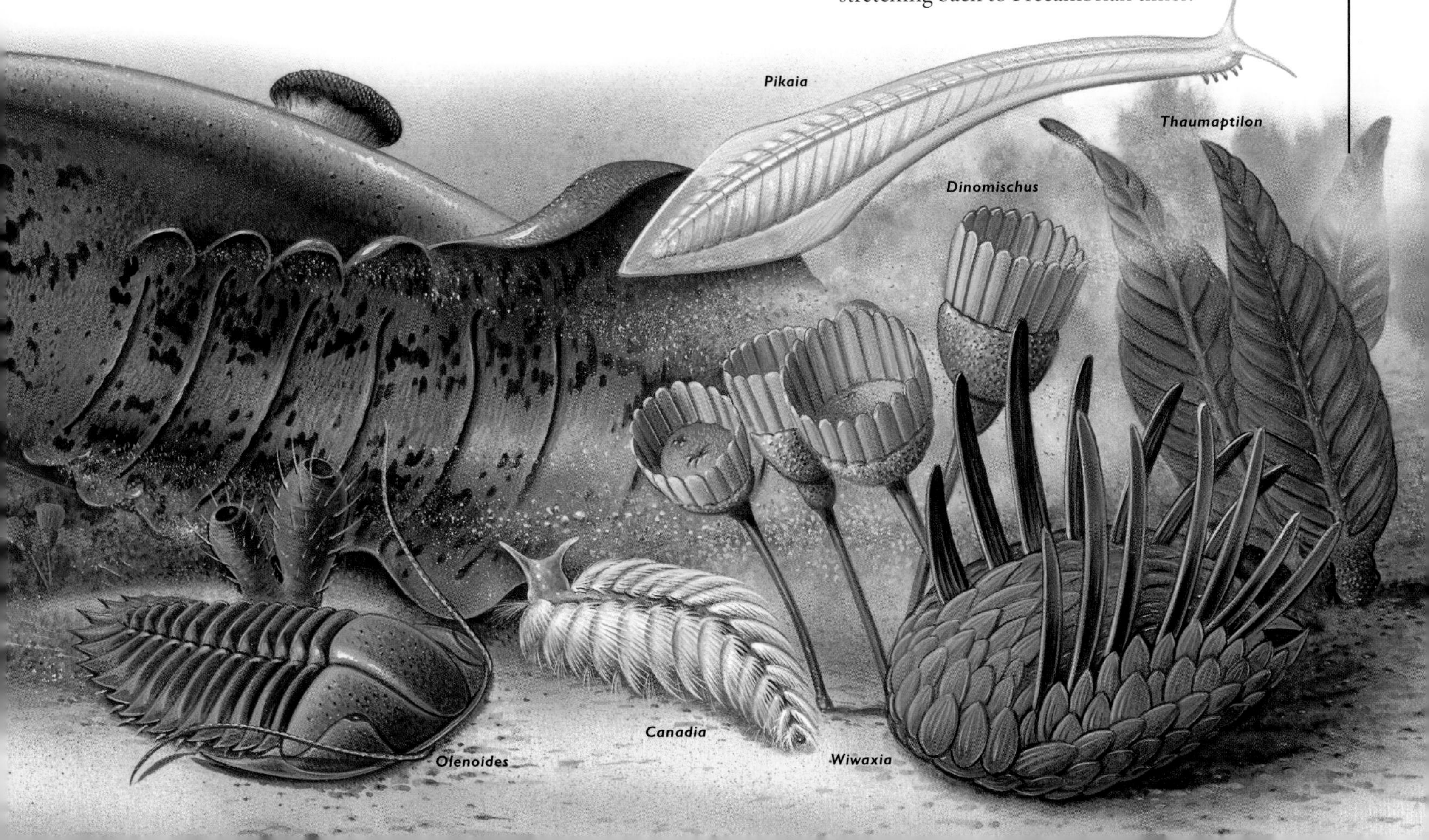

Pikaia—Our Ancestor?

A primitive creature without a well-defined head and less than 2 inches (5 centimeters) long, which swam in the seas during mid-Cambrian times, is close to the ancestor of all backboned animals (vertebrates), from fish to birds to mammals. Called *Pikaia*, it is one of the most interesting of the myriad animal fossils found in the famous Burgess Shale in the mountains of British Columbia.

SEA SQUIRT
The sea squirt, like the *Branchiostoma*, is a most unlikely looking close relation to the vertebrates. Adult sea squirts live permanently attached to the seabed and superficially look like sponges. Their free-swimming larvae, which look like tadpoles, have a body structure that relates them to vertebrates. A long stiffening rod allows the tail to flex for swimming. The larvae attach themselves head first to the seabed and transform into adults.

UNLIKELY ANCESTOR

At first glance, *Pikaia* does not seem like a human ancestor. It looks like a worm that has been flattened sideways. But in detail, these fossils compressed within the Burgess Shale clearly show chordate features such as traces of an elongate notochord, dorsal nerve cord, and blocks of muscles down either side of the body—all critical features for the evolution of the vertebrates.

The notochord is a flexible rod that runs along the back of the animal, lengthening and stiffening the body so that it can be flexed from side to side by the muscle blocks for swimming. In the fish and all subsequent vertebrates, the notochord forms the backbone (or vertebral column). The backbone strengthens the body, supports strut-like limbs, and protects the vital dorsal nerve cord, while at the same time allowing the body to bend.

Surprisingly, a *Pikaia* lookalike still exists today, the lancelet *Branchiostoma*. This curious little animal was familiar to biologists long before the *Pikaia* fossil was discovered. With notochord and paired muscle blocks, the lancelet and *Pikaia* belong to the chordate group of animals from which the vertebrates have descended. Molecular studies have confirmed the lancelet's status as the closest living relative of the vertebrates.

While the lancelet is an advanced chordate, other living and fossil groups, such as sea squirts and graptolites, are more primitive. Called the hemichordates, they have only a notochord at an early stage of their lives.

The presence of a creature as complex as *Pikaia* some 520 million years ago reinforces the controversial view that the diversification of life must have extended back well beyond Cambrian times, deep into the Precambrian era.

Tentacle

PIKAIA ALIVE
Alive, *Pikaia* was a sideways-flattened, leaf-shaped animal. It swam by throwing its body into a series of S-shaped, zig-zag bends, much as snakes do. Fish inherited the same swimming movement, but they generally have stiffer backbones. *Pikaia* has a pair of large head tentacles and a series of short appendages, which may be linked to gill slits, on either side of its head. In these ways, it differs from the living lancelet. Paleontologists are still researching details of *Pikaia*'s anatomy.

PIKAIA FOSSIL
This primitive marine creature shows the essential prerequisites for making backboned animals. The flattened body is divided into pairs of segmented muscle blocks, seen as faint vertical lines. The muscles lie either side of a flexible rod which runs from the tip of the head (bent round at the left) to the tip of the tail (the larger tapering structure to the right.)

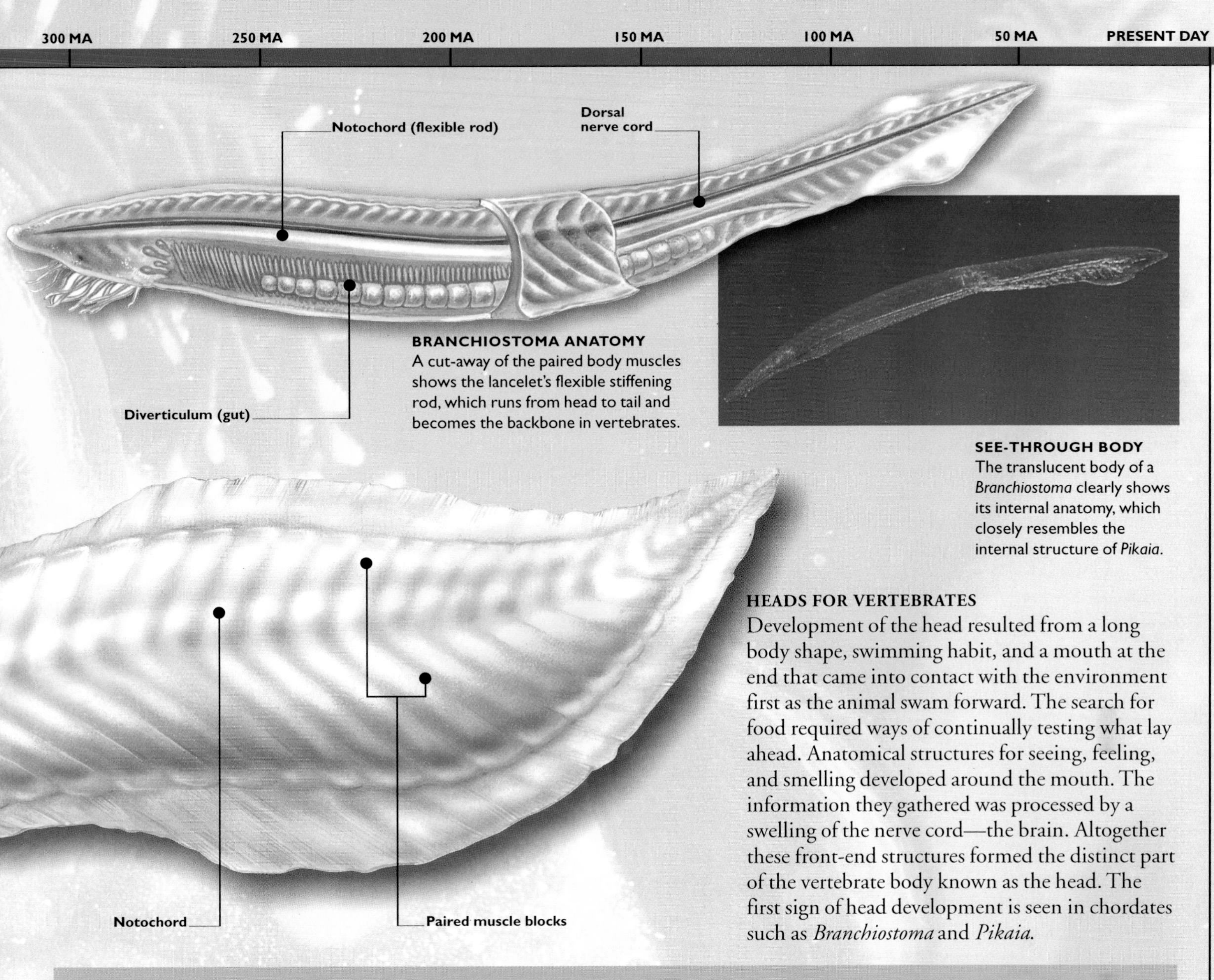

BRANCHIOSTOMA ANATOMY
A cut-away of the paired body muscles shows the lancelet's flexible stiffening rod, which runs from head to tail and becomes the backbone in vertebrates.

SEE-THROUGH BODY
The translucent body of a *Branchiostoma* clearly shows its internal anatomy, which closely resembles the internal structure of *Pikaia*.

HEADS FOR VERTEBRATES
Development of the head resulted from a long body shape, swimming habit, and a mouth at the end that came into contact with the environment first as the animal swam forward. The search for food required ways of continually testing what lay ahead. Anatomical structures for seeing, feeling, and smelling developed around the mouth. The information they gathered was processed by a swelling of the nerve cord—the brain. Altogether these front-end structures formed the distinct part of the vertebrate body known as the head. The first sign of head development is seen in chordates such as *Branchiostoma* and *Pikaia*.

VERTEBRATE RELATIONSHIPS

Understanding the details of animal biology allows scientists to determine how different creatures are related. There are some surprises. For although the connection seems unlikely, starfish (echinoderms) and sea squirts (tunicates) turn out to be closely related to all backboned animals (vertebrates), ranging from fish to humans. The embryos and larvae of sea squirts and echinoderms, before they change to their adult forms, have close similarities to those of the vertebrates. On this biological "family tree" of relatedness, those closest to the vertebrates are chordates with a body stiffening rod (notochord) throughout their lives, as represented by the living lancelet. The 520-million-year-old fossil Pikaia *is sufficiently similar to the lancelets to suggest that it, too, is a chordate, and thus our most distant known ancestor.*

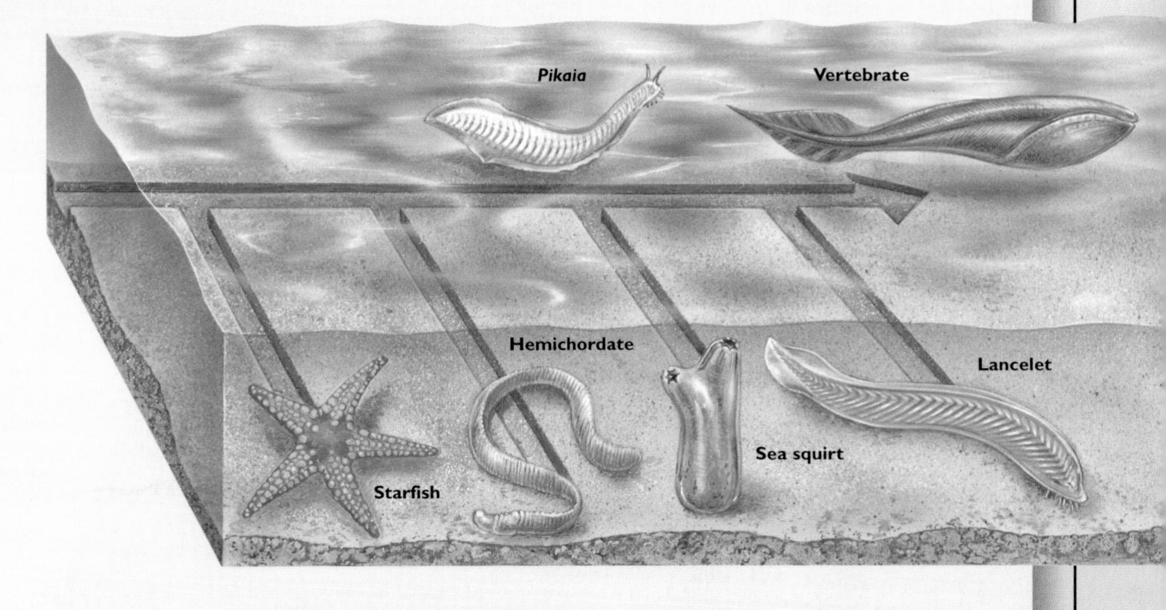

The Ordovician Period

ORDOVICIAN TIMES SAW THE EXPANSION OF MARINE LIFE, UNTIL CLIMATIC CHANGES DESTROYED THE ENVIRONMENT ON WHICH SO MANY SPECIES DEPENDED.

Throughout Ordovician times, the pace of global change quickened. During the period of just over 50 million years that the Ordovician lasted, from 495 to 443 million years ago, Siberia and Baltica moved north, the Iapetus Ocean began to close, and the Rheic Ocean gradually opened to the south. The supercontinent of Gondwana continued to dominate the southern hemisphere, with North Africa at the South Pole.

Much of our knowledge of changes in the Ordovician climate and the position of continents is derived from fossils of small creatures that lived in the seas and oceans. Although primitive plants, along with a few small arthropods, began to invade the land in Ordovician times, life was still concentrated in the sea.

MINIATURE LIFE

Fish had begun to evolve, but most marine life was still remarkably small, with few organisms growing larger than an inch or two. The most common shellfish were the clamlike brachiopods, mostly about 1 inch (2 to 3 centimeters) in size. Altogether, over 12,000 fossil species of brachiopods have been recorded. They lived on the seabed or attached to other creatures, such as sea lilies. Because their shell form varied depending on local conditions, their fossils help reconstruct past environments.

CREATING THE BLUE RIDGE
A collision between the landmasses of Avalonia and Laurentia triggered the formation of what are now the Blue Ridge Mountains of Virginia, deforming earlier sedimentary rocks.

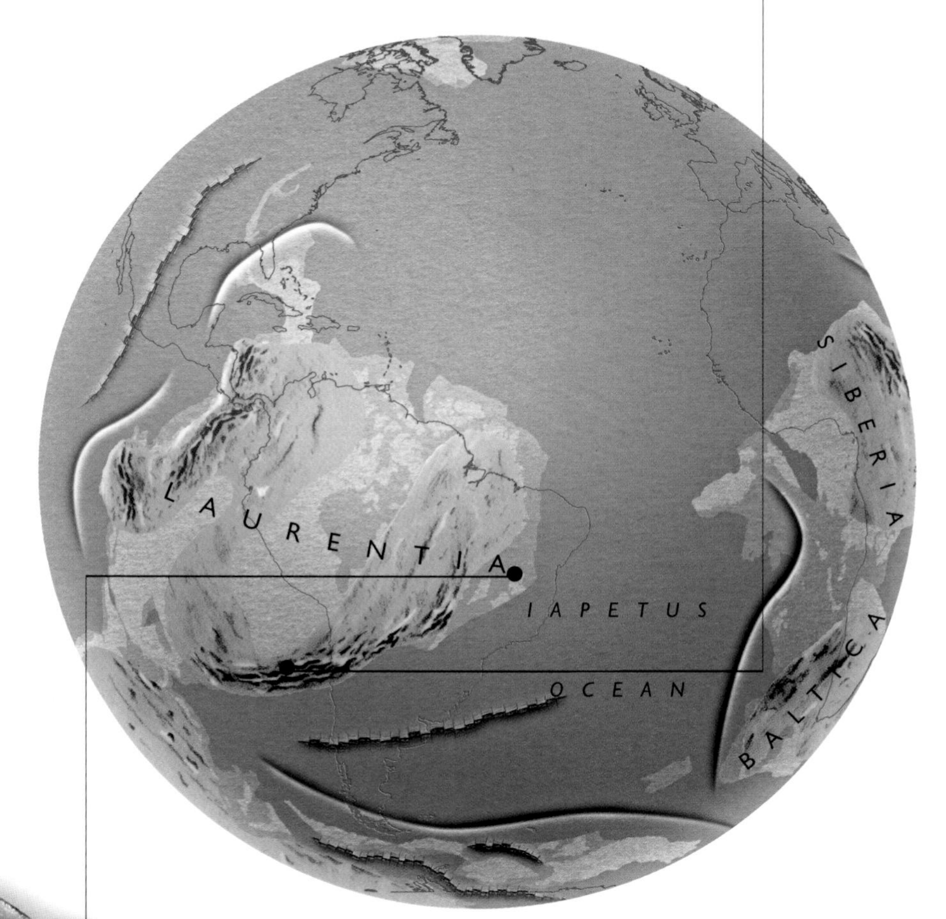

DOB'S LINN ROCK
A shale rock at Dob's Linn marks the boundary between the end of Ordovician time and the start of the Silurian period. This rock, containing well-defined graptolite fossils, was discovered by schoolmaster Charles Lapworth in 1879 in the Southern Uplands of Scotland. Lapworth mapped the complicated succession of ancient marine strata and suggested the identification of a new period between the Cambrian and the Silurian. He named this new period "Ordovician" after a Romano-British hilltribe, the Ordovices.

TRILOBITES AND GRAPTOLITES

Other fossils that help us to understand the Ordovician world include trilobites and graptolites. There were over 4,000 trilobite species, most of them less than 4 inches (10 centimeters) in length. Although trilobites spread through the seas of the world, some regions featured their own particular kinds. The global distribution of trilobite fossils has helped scientists reconstruct the positions of the Earth's crustal plates at the time.

Graptolites were strange creatures that were once even thought to be plants. These once common organisms floated in the seas and consisted of numerous tiny individual, yet interconnected, creatures living in a hollow tubular skeleton and filter-feeding from the plankton.

TUNING FORKS
So-called "tuning-fork" graptolites were small creatures that lived in organized colonies. Each individual animal lived in one of the "cups" formed by the serrated edge of the skeleton. Small tentacles used for filtering food would have projected from the skeleton. This fossil was found in Wales.

GONDWANA

MASS EXTINCTION

The wonderfully diverse marine life of Ordovician times—with over 600 different families of marine organisms—was not destined to last. The global climate became progressively wetter and cooler, descending into an ice age at the end of the period that drove many organisms to extinction. As ocean water was locked up in the polar icecaps, sea levels fell by as much as 1,000 feet (330 meters). The shallow seas of the continental shelves turned into dry plains, killing off many of the creatures that lived there, especially those that could not migrate from the seabed.

GRAPTOLITE BIOZONES

The shape of graptolite skeletons changed as they rapidly evolved. These changes can be used to achieve a precise dating of Ordovician, Silurian, and early Devonian marine strata. In 1879, a Scottish schoolmaster, Charles Lapworth, worked out the correct chronological sequence of graptolites in southern Scotland and used it to establish the correct sequence of strata. Lapworth's graptolite "biozonation" has since been used all over the world.

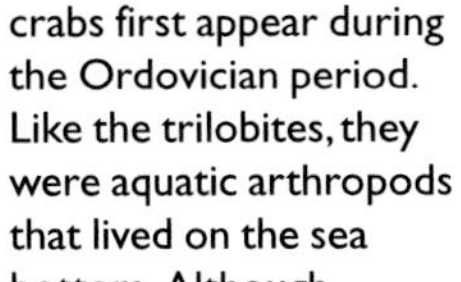

HORSESHOE FOSSIL
Fossils of horseshoe crabs first appear during the Ordovician period. Like the trilobites, they were aquatic arthropods that lived on the sea bottom. Although modern-day horseshoe crabs are sometimes referred to as "living fossils" because they so closely resemble their prehistoric ancestors, none of the species living today date back to Ordovician times.

Life in the Ordovician Seas

The Ordovician period marked a turning point in the evolution of marine life. Many organisms were increasing in size, strength, and speed of movement. Jawless organisms called conodonts, which are extinct today but were common in the Ordovician seas, were particularly significant as they were closely related to the first vertebrates. The appearance of the first fishlike jawless vertebrates was followed by the evolution of the first sharklike vertebrates, which had jaws and teeth, more than 450 million years ago. During this period, there is also evidence that animals began to move onto land.

TINY TEETH
These comblike strands are the tiny fossilized feeding apparatus from the mouth of a conodont (*Promissum*), one of the larger creatures from Ordovician seas. Conodonts are thought to be related to the chordates, including the true backboned creatures, the vertebrates.

CONODONT MYSTERY

Two questions puzzled paleontologists for a long time—what were the conodonts and who were their closest relatives? Until the 1990s, these were difficult questions to answer, since the only fossil remains of the animals were tiny toothlike structures found in rocks from late Cambrian to late Triassic times (520–210 million years ago). No one knew what kind of creature these teeth belonged to until the first conodont with preserved soft tissue was found in Carboniferous rocks in Scotland, and then later in South Africa. These finds have shown that the teeth were indeed a feeding apparatus, positioned below a pair of well-developed eyes. The presence of a nerve cord, a notochord (a flexible rod), and muscle blocks, all located in its back, shows that these animals were actively swimming chordates, closely related to the backboned vertebrates. They also have vertebrate features such as a head and paired eyes moved by muscles. Consequently, some experts argue that conodonts are more advanced chordates than the Cambrian vertebrate ancestor *Pikaia,* and may be closely related to the fishlike jawless vertebrates.

ORDOVICIAN SEAWORLD
The upper waters of the oceans teemed with planktonic life, including the extinct graptolites (*Orthograptus*). On the seabed, there were abundant shellfish such as brachiopods (*Strophomena*), rugose corals, and moss animals (*Strictoporella*). Trilobites (*Triarthrus*) and snails (*Cyclonema*) searched around the seabed for food. More mobile swimming filter-feeders were the first jawless and toothless fishlike vertebrates (*Sacabambaspis*), while the toothed but jawless conodonts (*Promissum*) were active predators, along with the tentacled cephalopods (*Endoceras*) and nautiloids.

SETTING FOOT ON LAND

Animals gained a foothold on land at this time, not directly from the sea, but through the "backdoor" medium of freshwater. Sets of parallel trackways, a centimeter wide, have been found in 450 million-year-old late Ordovician freshwater deposits in northern England. They were probably made by a millipede-like arthropod, an animal with a segmented body, numerous jointed legs, and an exoskeleton. No body fossils have yet been found for this creature. Arthropods were ideally suited to make the transition from the supportive environment of water to dry land, with its desiccating air and primitive vegetation.

ORDOVICIAN JAWLESS VERTEBRATES

Fossils of the very early fishlike jawless vertebrates (agnathans) are rare at first in Ordovician strata but become more common in rocks from the succeeding Silurian and Devonian periods. There is no question, however, that agnathans did exist in Ordovician times.

In 1892, American paleontologist Charles Walcott, famous as the discoverer of the Burgess Shale (see page 64), found a fragmentary agnathan in the Harding Sandstone, Colorado. These strata are over 450 million years old. The same rocks have produced other remarkable vertebrate remains, including the scales of jawed sharklike gnathostomes. The oldest complete agnathan fossils are *Sacabambaspis*, from Bolivia, and *Arandaspis*, from Australia. They are younger, but still Ordovician in age. Their wide geographical separation reinforces the view that their ancestry lies much further back than previously thought, possibly in Cambrian times.

The fossil remains indicate that Ordovician agnathans were very different to the few jawless vertebrates that survive today—the lampreys and hagfish. Typically, they had heads and bodies that were covered with tough leathery plates made of bonelike material. Only the scaly tail had flexibility for swimming. Without jaws and teeth, they must have fed on food that was small and numerous, such as planktonic microorganisms.

CLAM-SHAPED BRACHIOPODS
The most common and successful Ordovician shellfish were the brachiopods. Most brachiopods, like these orthids, were permanently anchored to the seabed or to other shells by a short fleshy stalk called a pedicle, though some lay freely on the seafloor sediment. They lived by drawing seawater through their open shells and filtering out microscopic particles of food. Although they resemble clams, they are not related to them.

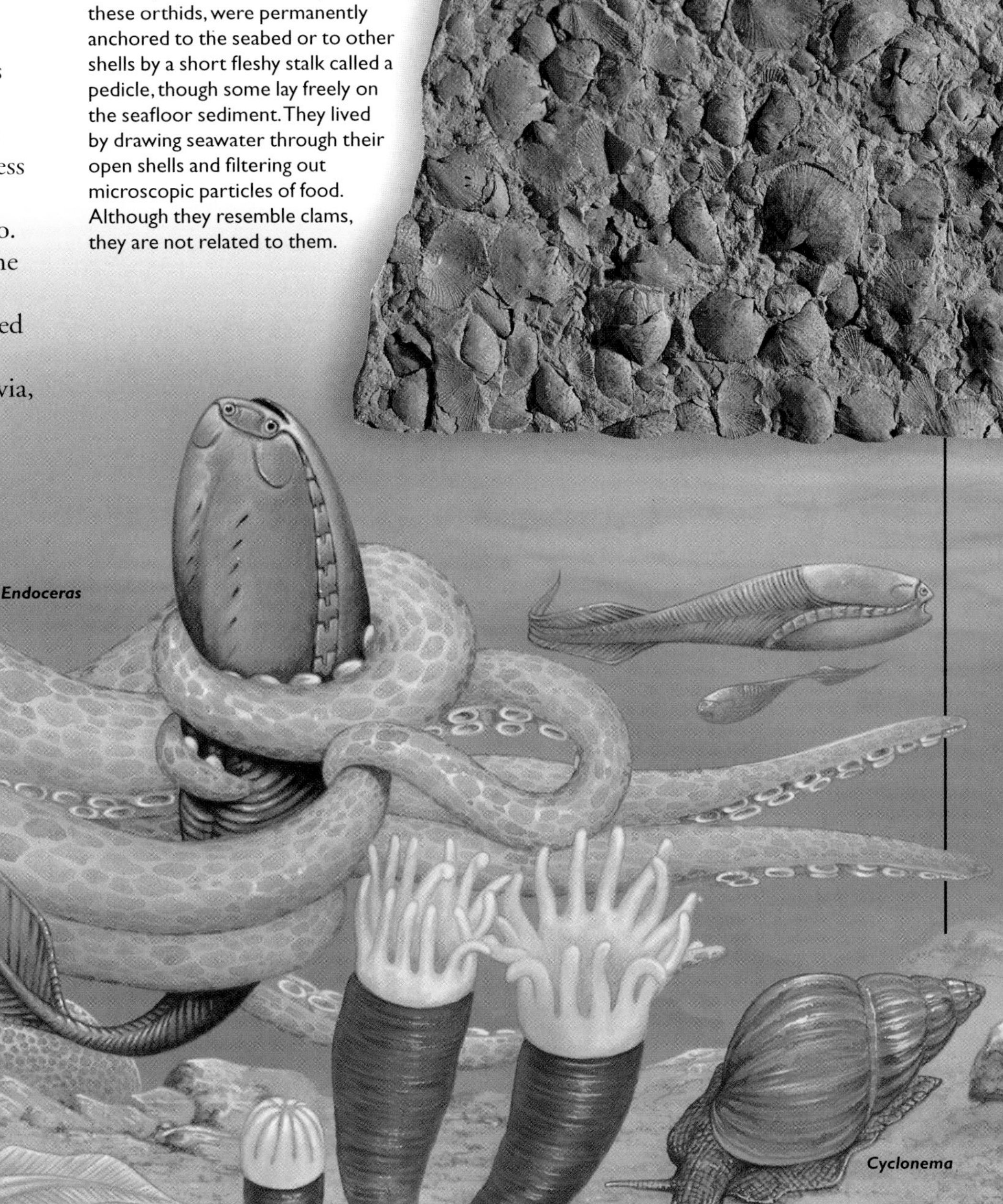

The Silurian Period

IN SILURIAN TIMES LIFE RECOVERED AFTER THE MASS EXTINCTION OF THE ORDOVICIAN PERIOD AND THE LAND WAS COLONIZED BY NEW PLANTS AND ARTHROPODS.

The Silurian age began about 443 million years ago. Although it lasted a mere 26 million years, the strata and fossils from this period in Britain and North America are among the most intensely studied in the world. They were already well known by the mid-nineteenth century, thanks to the efforts of geologists such as Sir Roderick Murchison in Europe and James Hall in North America.

The Silurian period marked a pivotal point in evolution. Following the setback to life caused by the late Ordovician glacial extinction, some animals, including the trilobites, conodonts, and graptolites, never fully recovered. In general, however, there was a major revival as oceans became warmer and sea levels rose. This was the period when plants and invertebrate animals first became solidly established on land, even if the seas remained a far easier environment for life.

SEA CHANGES

In Silurian times, the old Iapetus Ocean gradually closed, as the landmasses of Laurentia (North America), Baltica (northern Britain and Scandinavia), and Avalonia (southern Britain, Nova Scotia, and Newfoundland) approached one another on a collision course. Another ocean then opened up to the south, separating the newly forming northern continent from the southern continent of Gondwana.

The closure of the Iapetus Ocean created a new environment of shallow seas and basins, providing new habitats and ecological niches in which Paleozoic marine life once again flourished and diversified. Vast coral reefs spread throughout the equatorial waters of Laurentia and Baltica.

Many of the shells washed up on a Silurian beach would be generally recognizable to us today.

COLONIAL GRAPTOLITE
Monograptus proteus, was a coiled colony of 118 tiny creatures in a 0.75-inch- (2-centimeter-) wide skeleton. When the colony died, it sank and was buried, becoming flattened as the seabed was compressed to form shale now found in Germany.

SILURIAN AGNATHANS
Birkenia was a 1.5-inch- (4-centimeter-) long agnathan (jawless fish). This example was found in Scotland, but many similar fish have been discovered in the Baltic region of Europe.

HOW THE SILURIAN AGE GOT ITS NAME

The Silurian period was first identified in 1835 by British former army officer and geologist, Sir Roderick Murchison. Together with the Reverend Adam Sedgwick, a young professor at the University of Cambridge, England, Murchison mapped the strata of Wales, thought to be the oldest stratified rocks lying above the first formed igneous rocks. By studying the positions of various fossils within the sedimentary strata, Murchison distinguished strata that he called Silurian lying above Sedgwick's Cambrian. Murchison named the Silurian period for the Silures, a tribe that lived in Wales at the time of Ancient Rome

SPINY TRILOBITE
The large headshield of this very distinctive Silurian trilobite, *Dalmanites myops*, shows evidence of well-developed eyes and long protective ribs extending down the sides of its body. It grew to 2.5 inches (6 centimeters) long and, like many other trilobites, foraged on the seabed for its food. This fine example comes from Dudley in England.

BRACHIOPOD GRAVE
Numerous rhynchonellid brachiopod fossils litter the surface of this Silurian rock slab. When alive, these shellfish were attached to hard surfaces by fleshy stalks. After they died, their shells were swept together by currents running along the seabed. These fossils were found in Wales, close to the border with England.

They were larger than shells from earlier ages, typically up to 1.5 inches (4 centimeters) long. A few were much larger still, such as the conical shells of the squidlike nautiloids, which reached 4 inches (10 centimeters) or more. Brachiopods, clams, snails, echinoderms (such as starfish and sea lilies), and fish continued to diversify.

The shallow seas and basins of the northern continent became progressively shallower and broke up, eventually becoming isolated from one another as lakes. Jawless fish prospered in these warm waters and grew larger than their Ordovician predecessors, reaching a size of up to 8 inches (20 centimeters). New jawed fish and water scorpions preyed upon the jawless fish, which evolved bizarre forms of heavy armor as a defense against this predation.

Most important for the long-term evolution of life on Earth was the spread of plants that were notably more complex than the mosses typical of Ordovician times. Through the mechanism of photosynthesis, they eventually created an oxygen-rich atmosphere that was capable of supporting a complex range of terrestrial animal life.

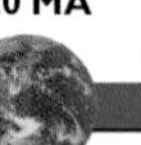

Life on Land and in the Sea

Life on land is tough compared with life in water. Animals and plants need to evolve special equipment to make use of the light mixture of gases we know as air. To survive, they must withstand alternate freezing and boiling, drying out, and solar radiation. Yet in Silurian times the land was increasingly colonized.

Although pioneering bryophyte plants such as mosses had already occupied the land since Ordovician times, they were very limited in form. The Silurian period saw the evolution of the first upright vascular plant that has left a fossil record. Called *Cooksonia*, it featured strengthened stems and tubes for conducting water and nutrients.

Cooksonia was quite unlike modern flowering plants (angiosperms), having no flowers, leaves, or seeds. A *Cooksonia* consisted of tiny upright stems, up to 1.5 inches (4 centimeters) high, which forked into two equal branches, ending in club-shaped reproductive sacs full of spores. The plant's primitive method of reproduction depended on living in wet conditions, so that the male gametes could swim to fertilize the female ones.

The evolution of these upright plants was essential to the formation of a terrestrial food chain. Their photosynthesized tissues provided vegetation for plant-eating animals (herbivores) to eat. Once herbivores had established themselves in numbers, carnivorous animals could then evolve to prey on them.

Digestion of raw plant food is difficult for animals, however. The first herbivores to appear were arthropods that fed on decaying plants. Partly broken down by bacteria, this material was easier to digest. It also incidentally introduced important microorganisms into the herbivore gut that were capable of breaking down plant matter.

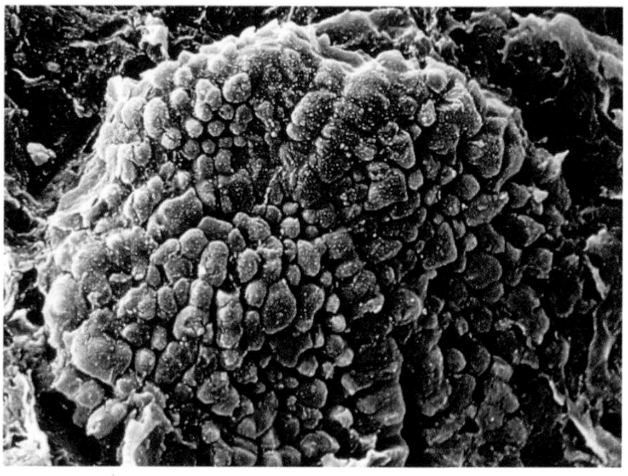

EARLY HERBIVORY
Scattered among the early plant fossils, remains of centipede-like arthropods have been found, along with tiny droppings full of tough plant spores. It is thought that these arthropods did not eat fresh plant material, but rather decaying remains of the primitive *Cooksonia* plants.

CORAL COMMUNITIES
Silurian corals (above and opposite), which formed the first extensive reefs, look similar to ones alive today, but belong to extinct groups.

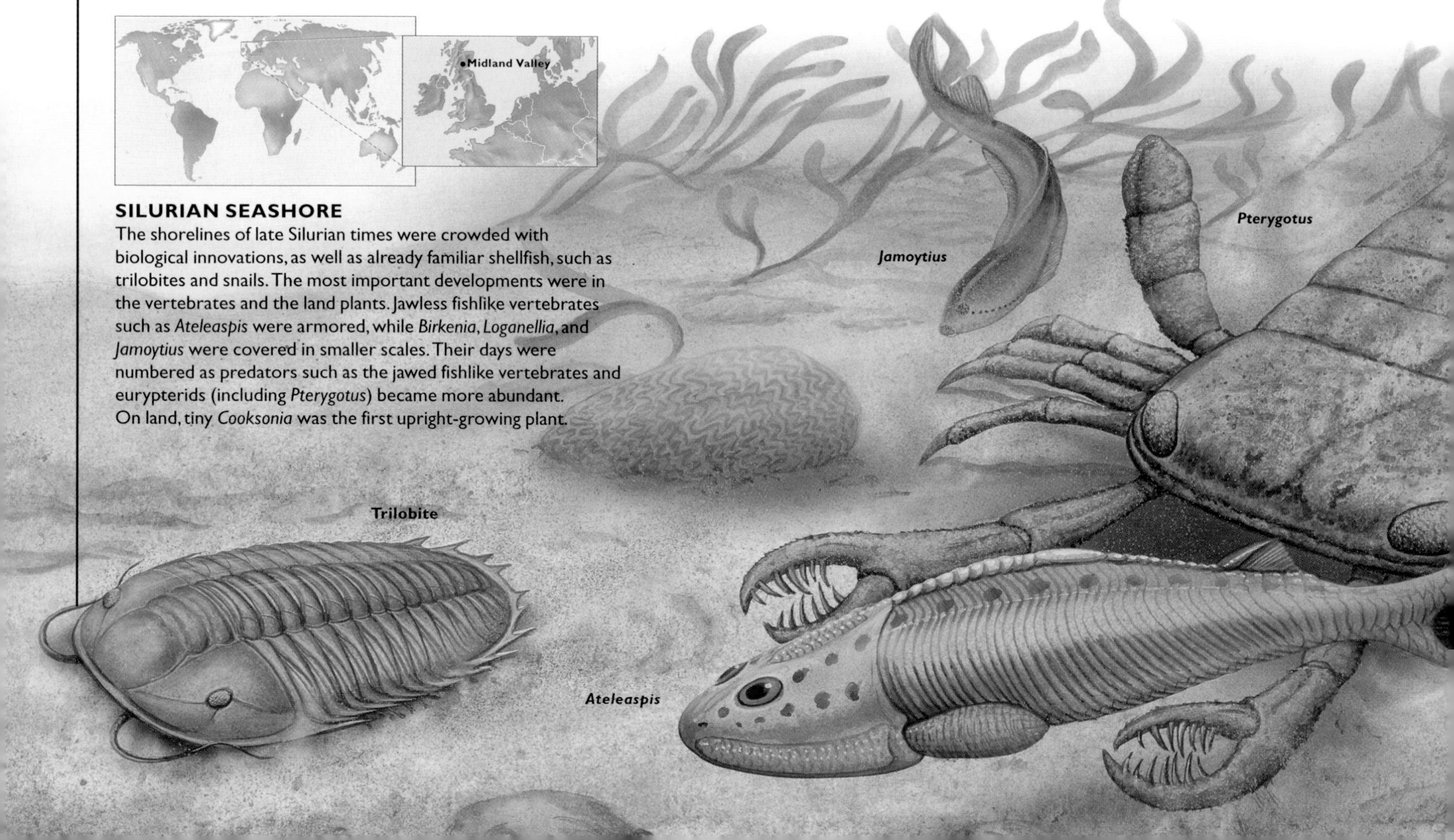

SILURIAN SEASHORE
The shorelines of late Silurian times were crowded with biological innovations, as well as already familiar shellfish, such as trilobites and snails. The most important developments were in the vertebrates and the land plants. Jawless fishlike vertebrates such as *Ateleaspis* were armored, while *Birkenia*, *Loganellia*, and *Jamoytius* were covered in smaller scales. Their days were numbered as predators such as the jawed fishlike vertebrates and eurypterids (including *Pterygotus*) became more abundant. On land, tiny *Cooksonia* was the first upright-growing plant.

SEA SCORPIONS

The first giants of the Earth, living in the Silurian period, were the eurypterids or "sea scorpions," which evolved in Ordovician times and survived until Permian times. They were scorpionlike in shape, and some had large pincers. Their elongated, articulated bodies were covered in a tough exoskeleton, making them one of the best-armored animals of the time. However, because they were arthropods, they had to shed their exoskeleton periodically to allow for growth, a process which left them vulnerable to attack. The eurypterids evolved a variety of lifestyles. Some could swim, some were scavengers, but others were active predators. Eurypterus, *found in the Silurian strata of New York, grew up to 6.5 feet (2 meters) in length. Eurypterids were one of the first animals to make the transition from a marine to a freshwater environment.*

TEEMING WITH LIFE

Many creatures living in Silurian seas would seem unfamiliar today. Some belong to extinct groups such as the Paleozoic corals, mobile trilobite arthropods, graptolites, or free-swimming armored agnathans, eurypterids, conodonts, and straight-coned cephalopods. Others, such as brachiopod shellfish and sea lilies, still exist today but are far less common than they used to be in Ordovician and Silurian times, when they populated the seas of the continental shelf in great numbers and diversity.

THE RISE OF THE VERTEBRATES

The most common vertebrates in Silurian times were the jawless agnathans. They ranged from *Jamoytius*, an eel-shaped, free-swimming creature without scales or body armor, to *Ateleaspis*, a bottom-living creature with its head enclosed in a horseshoe-shaped bony shield. The curious-shaped thelodonts, another type of agnathan, had bodies covered in tiny spiky scales, as sharks have today. There were also more familiar fish-shaped agnathans, such as *Birkenia.*

The biological event that did the most to transform life in the oceans was the evolution of jaws in fishlike vertebrates. The first fishlike jawed vertebrates were the now-extinct acanthodians, which had distinctive spines in front of all their fins. These bony spines are almost all that is fossilized of these small animals, but they are known to have had toothed jaws.

The Devonian Period

OFTEN CALLED THE "AGE OF FISHES," DEVONIAN TIMES FEATURED AN ABUNDANCE OF DIVERSE LIFEFORMS IN RIVERS, INLAND SEAS, AND FRESHWATER LAKES.

The Devonian period lasted for 63 million years, from 417 million to 354 million years ago. During this time, the closure of the Iapetus Ocean was finally completed, as North America and Greenland (Laurentia) collided with the southern British Isles (Avalonia) and Scandinavia (Baltica) to form a single continental mass. A central mountain belt stretched from Scandinavia, through Britain, to Newfoundland and Canada. Meanwhile, the supercontinent of Gondwana moved steadily northward from its polar position.

Global climates remained warm during this period. The formation of new landmasses resulted in ever bigger and drier continental interiors, where vast deserts developed. The continents were traversed by huge rivers flowing into inland seas and lakes that were home to the first extensive freshwater life. By mid-Devonian times, sea levels had risen as the icecaps melted, allowing extensive reefs to develop in Laurentia and Australia.

"WINGED" BRACHIOPODS
The spiriferids were one of the groups of Paleozoic brachiopods. These wing-shaped shells from upstate New York housed a spiral structure used for filtering microscopic food from seawater.

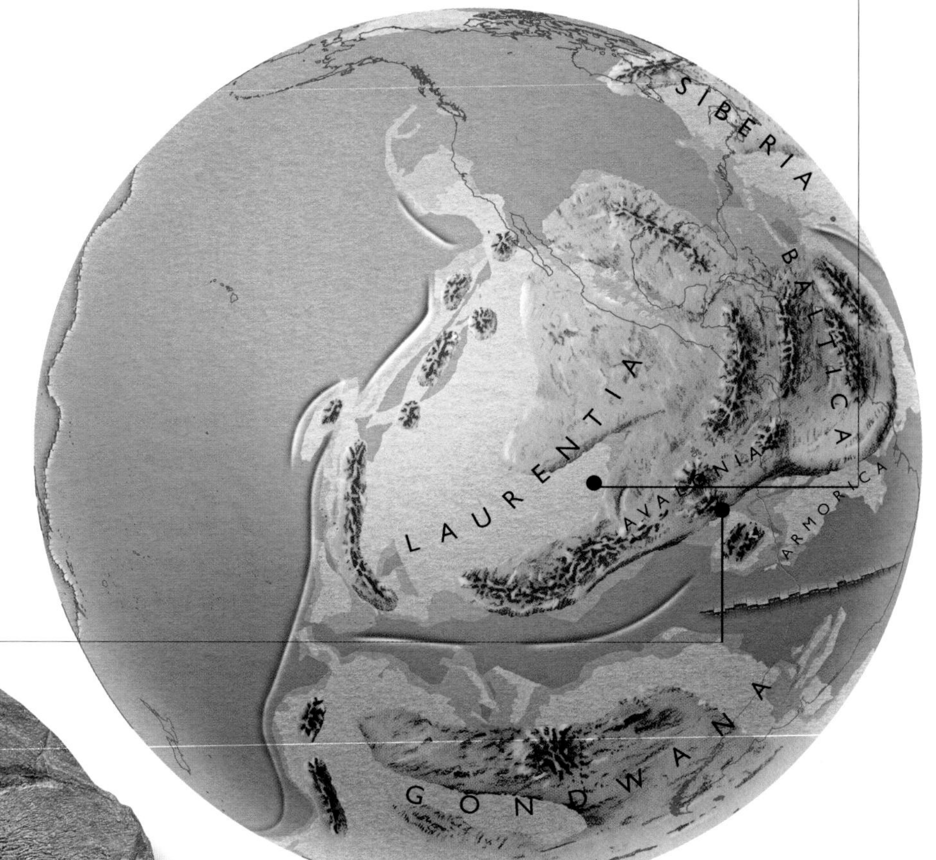

ANCESTORS OF THE FIRST TETRAPODS
The paired fins of this *Eusthenopteron foordi* fish have a single bone and are joined to the body in a similar way to the upper arm or leg bone of a tetrapod (four-legged animal). This fossil was found in Quebec, Canada.

THE "AGE OF FISHES"
The Devonian inland waterways were dominated by predators. The jawless agnathans were the first to invade freshwaters, but they were soon pursued by their jawed predators. By the end of the Devonian period, these predators had wiped out most agnathans. Only the lampreys and the hagfish survived. The jawed group, by contrast, evolved into a new array of groups—placoderms, ray-finned fishes, lobe-fins, true sharks, and lungfishes, some of which were active predators that grew up to 18 feet (6 meters) in size.

SANDSTONE FIGURES
Sandstone typically creates a bare and semi-arid landscape. Originally, storms and flash-floods generated huge rivers that transported and deposited stones into deep sedimentary basins. Erosion of the resulting rock on this Scottish cliff face has created a statuelike sculpture known locally as the Old Man of Hoy.

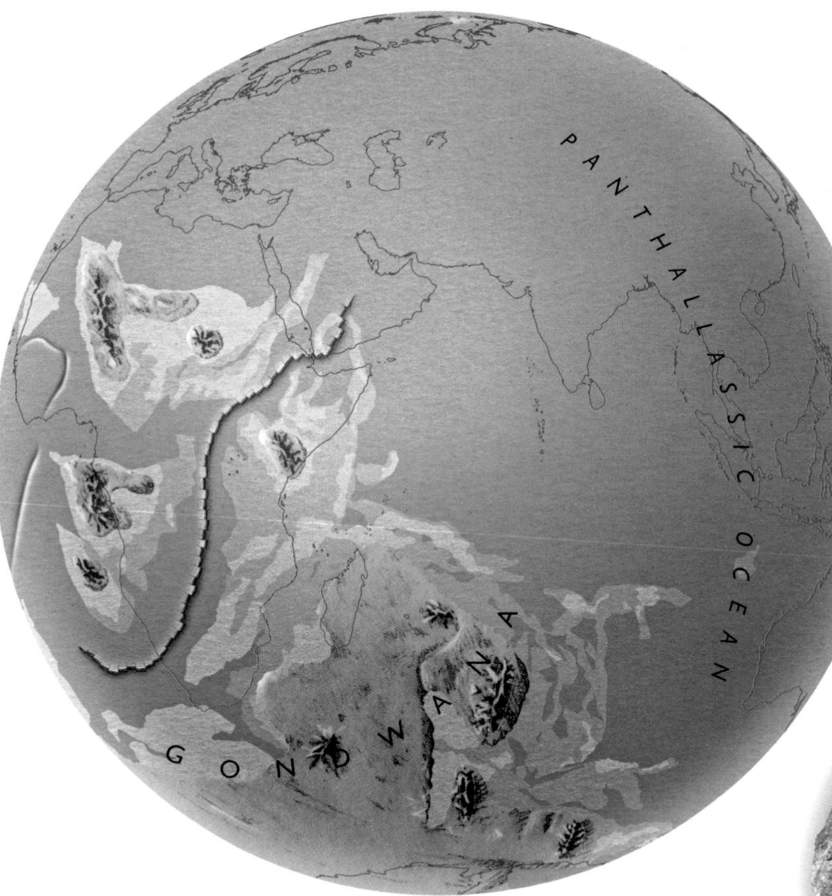

OLD RED SANDSTONE

Periodically, the hot Devonian climate evaporated the waters of inland seas, rivers, and lakes, leaving behind mineral salt deposits that reddened when oxidized by the air. These red and brown strata, known as Old Red Sandstone, are prevalent in Britain and the American Catskills. Old Red Sandstone made excellent building material and was extensively quarried in the 18th and 19th centuries. As quarrymen opened the layers of the strata, they revealed the well-preserved remains of the creatures that had lived in the original rivers and lakes.

MARINE EXPANSION

The remarkable expansion in Devonian vertebrate diversity has become clearer as well-preserved evidence of the period, such as the marine seabed deposits of Gogo in Western Australia, have opened. These deep deposits contain one of the most diverse collection of animals of the age, including over 25 varieties of armored placoderms, ray-finned fishes, lobe-fins, and lungfishes.

The placoderms were primitive jawed forms, growing up to 2 feet (60 centimeters) in length, with a head and trunk enclosed in a boxlike structure of bony plates. Some had long, bony, winglike arms protruding from either side. They evolved in the Silurian age and dominated both the freshwater and marine environments, diversifying into over 200 genera. They looked similar to primitive sharks, but unlike the sharks they died out at the end of the Devonian period.

The lungfishes are a particularly interesting group of primitive air-breathing fish that evolved and flourished in Devonian times. They originally lived in the sea and did not invade freshwaters until the Carboniferous age. Their paired fins and ability to breathe air were thought to link lungfish with landgoing vertebrates, but it is now known that they are not ancestral.

Other creatures in Devonian waters, however, evolved in the direction of terrestrial vertebrates. As plant species continued to develop on land, fish groups such as panderichthyids become almost indistinguishable from the future tetrapods that would eventually leave the water for the land.

FISH FOSSIL
Osteolepis panderi was a mid-Devonian-age fish with muscular paired fins like the lungfish. Mostly small fish that grew to about 8 inches (20 centimeters) long, they were first discovered in the 19th century by quarrymen in the Old Red Sandstone of Scotland.

Equipping Life for Land

When the first tetrapod (four-legged) fossil was found in Upper Devonian lake and river deposits in Greenland, the animal it represented was thought to be a salamander-like amphibian, capable of crawling out of the water and walking. *Ichthyostega*, as the creature was called, seemed to combine limbs and a deep ribcage for air-breathing lungs with its many fishlike features. In effect, *Ichthyostega* appeared to fill the evolutionary gap between fishes and land-going animals.

This original theory has now been revised, however. The limbs of *Ichthyostega* and its contemporary, *Acanthostega*, were better adapted for swimming than walking. Also, these animals retained gills and may have breathed in both air and water. They were gradually adapting toward the final difficult transition from water to land.

Terrestrial vertebrates had to overcome a number of problems in order to survive. Take a fish out of water and it will soon die. It will fall on its side and flap without moving any distance. It will gasp for oxygen but its gills collapse out of water. Having no ears, it will not be able to hear anything and will become blind as the eyes dry out. The skin will lose moisture. Land-living animals also had to be able to move around. Most have evolved legs for this purpose. The first terrestrial creatures, the centipede-like Ordovician arthropods, had inherited many pairs of jointed legs from their aquatic ancestors, but the vertebrates had to make the best of a very different evolutionary heritage. From paired fins, they had to evolve jointed, muscular limbs strong enough to lift the body and propel it forward on land.

The main means of propulsion for fish is the sideways flexing of the body in a series of S-shaped waves. Although this kind of movement works

MUDSKIPPER
The mudskipper is a modern bony fish that can leave the water to find food on exposed mudbanks, using its long, bony pectoral fins to prop itself up and wriggle across soft, wet mud. However, it has to remain wet and cannot stay out of the water for long.

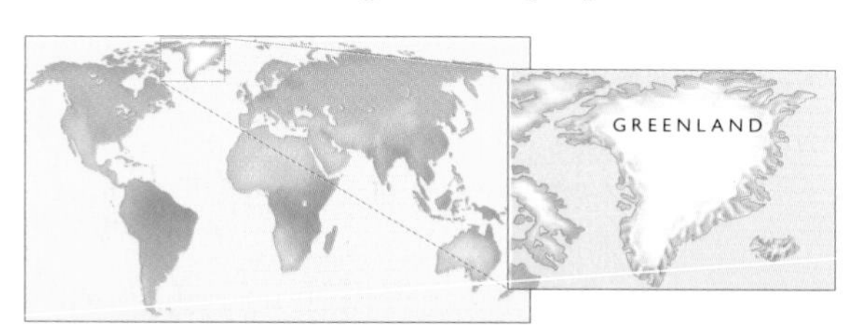

GREENLAND WATERWAYS
The oldest tetrapod fossils, of *Ichthyostega* and *Acanthostega*, have been found in late Devonian river and lake deposits from Greenland. These first four-limbed vertebrates were aquatic creatures. They used their muscular limbs, hands, and feet for additional propulsion, holding on to plants and perhaps digging for shellfish. Growing to about 3 feet (1 meter) long, these early tetrapods were powerful predators, capable of attacking small fish. However, the tetrapod young were probably preyed on by fish, such as the lobe-finned fish, *Holoptychius*, the lungfish, *Dipterus*, and the placoderm *Bothriolepis*, as well as adult tetrapods.

FROM FINS TO LEGS

Terrestrial vertebrates had to evolve legs out of fins. But not all forms of fin are suitable to develop into limbs. The panderichthyids had two pairs of narrow-based fins and, as in the leg structure of most tetrapods, each of these fins was supported by a single bone that joined the shoulder or hip girdle. The girdles in turn are joined to the backbone. At the outer end of each limb bone was a pair of wrist bones and then a number of rays (the spines of the fin). By contrast, today's true fishes have fan-shaped fins that are supported by a number of bones, and a lot of rays. Of the two types of fin, only the former, as found in the panderichthyids, was suitable to develop into a leg strong enough to lift a body.

effectively on land, as demonstrated by snakes, it cannot lift a body off the ground. Many land vertebrates, such as lizards, evolved a compromise solution, where the body still moves in S-shaped waves but is also lifted up onto stiltlike legs. This movement puts new pressure on the backbone, however, so land vertebrates' skeletons had to become stronger and more flexible—an evolutionary process that took a long time.

TETRAPOD ANCESTORS

So what animals did *Acanthostega* and *Ichthyostega* evolve from? Research has revealed that the panderichthyids, a group of fish with paired muscular fins, are anatomically closest to the tetrapods and are their most likely ancestors. *Panderichthys* itself, found at the late Devonian site of Lode, in Latvia, is a remarkable animal. Along with tetrapodlike paired fins at the front and back of the body, it has a skull that is almost indistinguishable from that of the first four-legged animals, with a flat head, closely spaced eyes, and a large mouth. The ribs are also joined to the backbone in the same way. When the remains of *Elpistostege*, one of the panderichthyids, was first discovered, it was thought to be a tetrapod.

ACANTHOSTEGA FOSSIL
By disentangling the jumbled skeletal remains of this early tetrapod fossil, scientists have revised ideas about how backboned animals evolved for life on land. Found high on a remote mountainside in Arctic Greenland and entombed in hard sedimentary rock, the fossil required many days of careful preparation to unveil its secrets. The fossil shows that *Acanthostega* had a flattened skull with eye sockets placed close together on the top surface.

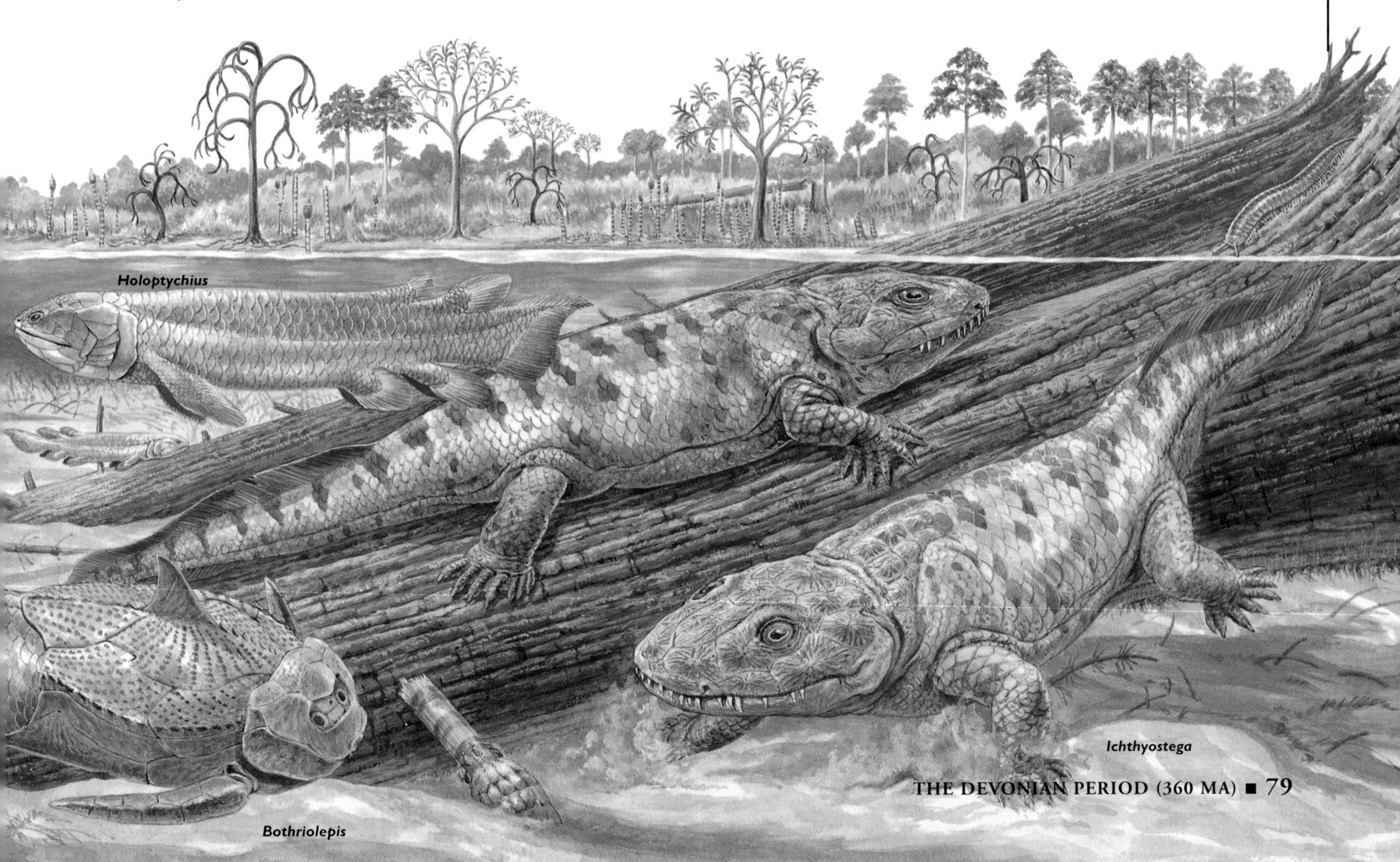

Carboniferous Age

THE AGE OF COAL SAW THE GROWTH OF THE FIRST EXTENSIVE FORESTS ON EARTH. FOUR-LEGGED ANIMALS EMERGED FROM THE WATER, EVOLVING INTO AMPHIBIANS AND REPTILES.

The period from 354 to 290 million years ago is called the Carboniferous, meaning coal-bearing. In this time, the great mass of the southern continents that made up Gondwana rotated clockwise. The eastern part of the super-continent (Australia) moved south and became colder, while the western side (South America) rotated north into warmer latitudes. Laurentia (North America) was assaulted on all sides, folding the Appalachians and forcing up the ancestral Rockies. These impacts among Gondwana, Laurentia, and Baltica marked a major step in the amalgamation of the supercontinent of Pangea.

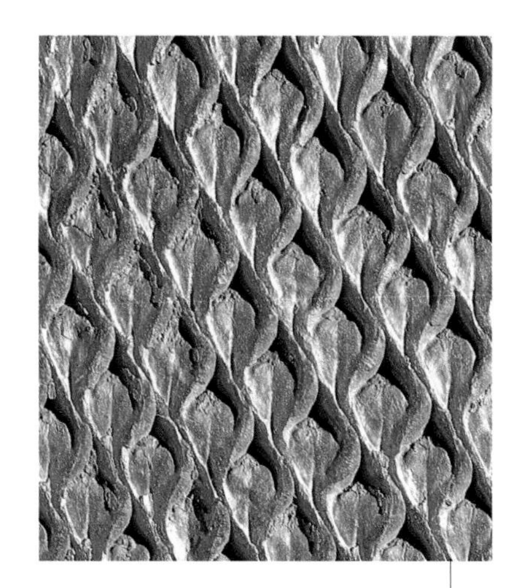

LEPIDODENDRON FOSSIL TRUNK
This fossilized trunk of the clubmoss tree *Lepidodendron*, from a coal forest in Scotland, shows a pattern of diamond-shaped scars and leaf cushions where leaf fronds were attached before being shed during growth.

SEA LEVELS AND CLIMATES

The Carboniferous period is divided into the earlier Mississippian or Lower Carboniferous and the later Pennsylvanian or Upper Carboniferous. In Mississippian times, sea levels rose sharply, further flooding and drowning the old Devonian continents. But in the Pennsylvanian, sea levels fell and landscapes reemerged.

FERN FROND
This fossil fragment of a Carboniferous fern frond from Jerada in Morocco looks similar to living ferns. However, the ferns of the coal forests were more varied in size, with some growing into tree-sized plants. Ferns are still successful today, with over 12,000 living species.

From its hot "global greenhouse" state of the Siluro-Devonian periods (440 to 360 million years ago), the Earth cooled. By mid- to late Carboniferous times, it had become as seasonal as it was during the ice age in the Quaternary (18,000 years ago) and polar icecaps had formed. An extensive glaciation got under way that persisted into the Permian age.

Global rainfall and humidity fluctuated drastically. Climates had become extremely humid by the beginning of the Carboniferous period. They stayed exceptionally wet for a few million

MEASURING OXYGEN LEVELS

The study of plants allows us to measure the relative levels of carbon dioxide and oxygen in the atmosphere in prehistoric times. Plants use pore cells called stomata for gas exchange with the atmosphere. They regulate their intake of carbon dioxide by altering the density of stomata on their leaves. When carbon dioxide levels are high, plants produce fewer stomata. They produce more when levels are low. By comparing the density of stomata on fossil leaves from different ages, scientists can measure how carbon dioxide and, by implication, oxygen levels varied. Devonian plants had lower stomatal densities than Carboniferous plants.

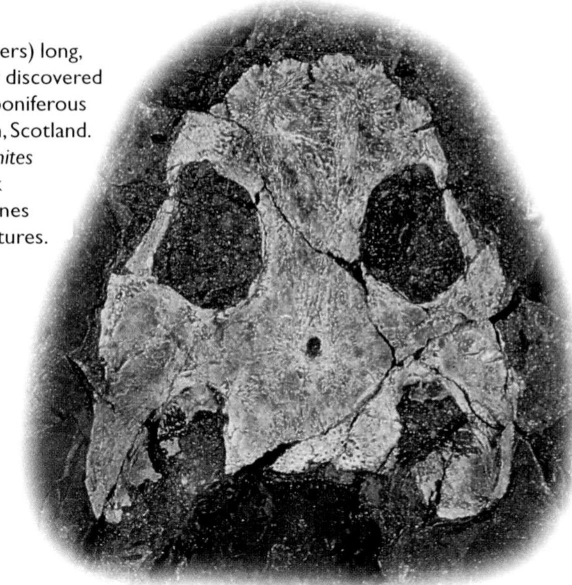

EUCRITTA
Three inches (8 centimeters) long, this is the skull of a newly discovered early tetrapod from Carboniferous limestone at East Kirkton, Scotland. Called *Eucritta melanolimnites* ("creature from the black lagoon"), the fossil combines amphibian and reptile features.

PANTHALASSIC OCEAN

GONDWANA

years. Then, as temperatures dropped and glaciers formed during the late Carboniferous, levels of rainfall and humidity declined.

CREATING A BREATHABLE ATMOSPHERE

Atmospheric oxygen levels increased dramatically thanks to the growth of extensive lowland forests. These huge forests offered new habitats and new sources of food for a thriving animal population, including insects, amphibians, and reptiles. Through photosynthesis, the plants increased the level of oxygen in the atmosphere from a mid-Devonian low of 15 percent to a peak of 35 percent in the late Carboniferous, higher than at any other time in the Earth's history.

The plants also provided the material for the formation of the vast coal deposits of Europe and North America during the Pennsylvanian. Ferns, which flourished at this time, were the most important contributors to this process.

LIFE ON LAND AND SEA

On land, true egg-laying (amniote) tetrapods evolved. Arachnids and insects, which had evolved in Silurian times, increased in size and diversified. The shallow equatorial seas of the Mississippian produced extensive reefs occupied by a wide diversity of marine life. Sharks and bony fishes dominated the seas, though both often took different forms from the ones familiar today. Deposits of shells and other parts of sea creatures formed extensive areas of marine limestone.

FOSSIL TREE ROOTS
These are the fossilized roots of a coal-forest clubmoss tree, *Lepidodendron*, now in Manchester, England. Because the roots are normally found separately from the trunk and foliage of this tree, they have been given a different name—the roots are called *Stigmaria*. Some of these trees grew as high as 130 feet (40 meters).

The First Tetrapods

TREE-FERN
The few living tree-ferns look just like their Carboniferous ancestors. They are crowned with numerous fronds 10 feet (3 meters) in length that would produce an unstable plant but for the growth of massive roots.

Some of the most interesting fossils from the Mississippian (Lower Carboniferous) period found in recent years have come from a limestone quarry in East Kirkton, Scotland. The fossil fauna includes the first of several different early tetrapod groups: amphibians like *Balanerpeton woodi* and *Silvanerpeton*; an animal known as *Eucritta* that combined amphibian and reptilian features; and *Westlothiana lizziae*, an almost true reptile. The tetrapods of East Kirkton formed the world's oldest known vertebrate terrestrial community.

UNDER THE VOLCANO

The limestone of East Kirkton is unusual because it came from freshwater rather than saltwater, originally deposited in a small lake at the foot of volcanically active hills. The mineral-rich soils that formed on the ash and lava promoted the growth of a lush vegetation of clubmosses (lycopsids), horsetails (sphenopsids), ferns (pteridosperms), and seed plants (gymnosperms). The forest provided food and shelter for the variety of terrestrial animals, including vertebrate tetrapods and invertebrate scorpions, myriapods, eurypterids, and harvestmen. Storms, forest fires, and even flooding periodically devastated the area, washing plant fragments and a sample of the animals into the lake where they perished and were quickly covered by a protective layer of sediment, forming well-preserved fossils.

TERRESTRIAL FOOD CHAIN

The terrestrial food chain still relied on arthropod detrivores—animals that fed on rotting vegetation—such as mites and millipedes. But there were many additions to the fauna, including the oldest known harvestman (opilionid arachnid) and the first air-breathing scorpion, *Pulmonoscorpius*, a large, active predator, growing up to 28 inches

TETRAPOD FOSSIL
The salamander-like *Silvanerpeton*, approximately 16 inches (40 centimeters) long, was one of the oldest of the anthracosaurs, an extinct group of tetrapods with a number of reptilian features.

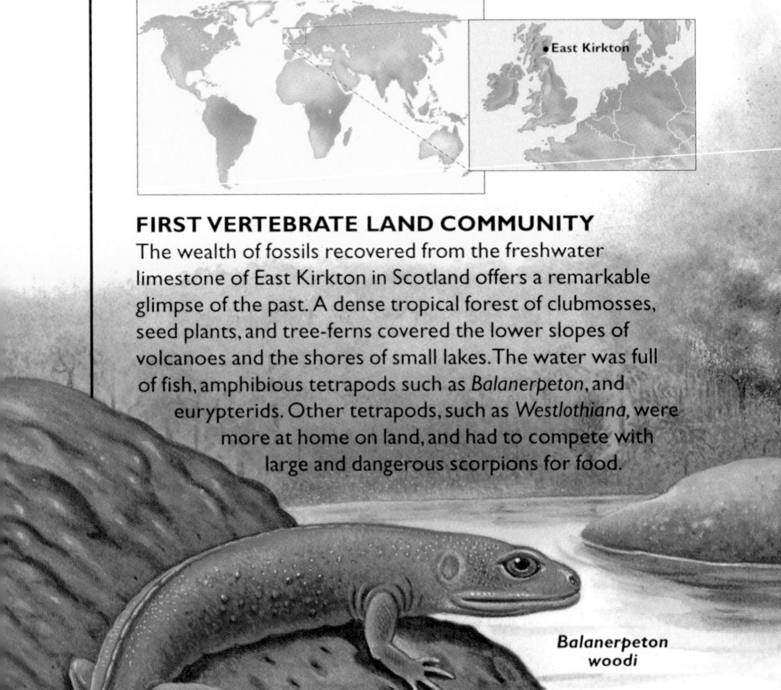

FIRST VERTEBRATE LAND COMMUNITY
The wealth of fossils recovered from the freshwater limestone of East Kirkton in Scotland offers a remarkable glimpse of the past. A dense tropical forest of clubmosses, seed plants, and tree-ferns covered the lower slopes of volcanoes and the shores of small lakes. The water was full of fish, amphibious tetrapods such as *Balanerpeton*, and eurypterids. Other tetrapods, such as *Westlothiana*, were more at home on land, and had to compete with large and dangerous scorpions for food.

AQUATIC LIFE

The waters of the Carboniferous lake in East Kirkton supported a remarkable variety of fish. Six species of bony (actinopterygian) fish were accompanied by two species of spiny (acanthodian) ones, as well as members of two shark families. The most probable explanation for this impressive diversity of life is that the lake was originally linked to a much larger body of water. An infilling of volcanic ash from the surrounding area may have created a natural barrier that cut creatures off from their original habitat, trapping them without the possibility of escape.

(70 centimeters) long. Even this impressive beast was dwarfed by one of the three eurypterids known from the locality. *Hibbertopterus scouleri* looked like a huge, flattened, streamlined lobster. It had a headshield 26 inches (65 centimeters) wide and must have been around 10 feet (3 meters) long. Although it may have been the biggest arthropod ever, it only scavenged small prey.

Westlothiana lizziae, a vertebrate tetrapod that grew to 8 inches (20 centimeters) in length, was once thought to be the world's oldest reptile fossil. It turned out not to be a reptile, however, because it had a number of features, especially in the ankle and palate, more characteristic of primitive tetrapods than true egg-laying (amniote) reptiles.

OTHER KIRKTON FINDS

Several small amphibians growing to around 20 inches (50 centimeters) were among the other vertebrates found at East Kirkton. Some, like *Balanerpeton woodi*, resembled modern salamanders. The structure of the limbs and ankles show that *Balanerpeton* lived mostly on land, but like all amphibians, it was severely constrained by the need to return to water to breed. It also shows crucial changes in skull structure that allowed the development of earbones that detect sound in air. With a mouth full of small sharp teeth, it was an active predator on the lakeshore.

Smaller reptilelike anthracosaurs, which grew to about 12 inches (30 centimeters), were also present. With poorly developed wrists and ankles, these creatures were really better suited to swimming than walking. Other amphibians included the *Ophiderpeton*, an unusual snakelike creature. With 200 vertebrae in its backbone, it probably grew to about 3 feet (1 meter) in length, and was another terrestrial predator.

LAND SCORPION
This well-preserved fossil from East Kirkton is of the oldest known land scorpion, *Pulmonoscorpius kirktonensis*. The scorpion's unusual structures for air-breathing, called "book-lungs," can still be seen.

Coal and Reptiles

It took twenty million years for the low-lying wetland forests and the peat bogs of late Carboniferous times to build up the bulk of the world's coal supplies. Since the Industrial Revolution in the late 18th century, it has taken the human race a mere 200 years to burn up most of these resources. One of the few positive aspects of this rapid exploitation of coal is that it has provided us with an invaluable view of life in the late Carboniferous period. Most important, it has revealed that by that time a group of tetrapods had evolved that could lay shelled eggs—the reptiles had arrived.

THE FORMATION OF COAL

The environmental change from Mississippian (Lower Carboniferous) times, dominated by marine limestone, to Pennsylvanian (Upper Carboniferous) times was marked. After 20 million years of an expanding sea world and diminishing landscapes, sea levels and global temperatures finally peaked and began to fall sharply. Organic deposits, made from plant debris, accumulated in the vast forests, swamps, and bogs that grew over the slowly emerging new land. These accumulations of debris formed the first extensive coal measures (seams), which in places can be hundreds of yards thick.

COAL DEPOSITS OF NOVA SCOTIA

Important information on the life of the coal measures has been provided by the 310-million-year-old coal deposits of Joggins, Nova Scotia. The deposits consist of Pennsylvanian strata, originally deposited in a near-equatorial floodplain environment near the coast.

With a seasonally wet climate, sand and mud sediment was carried down from highlands. Plant fossils found scattered in these sediments show that the floodplains, river banks, and sand bars supported different kinds of plant growth, depending on the nature of the soil. The ground above the floodplains was home to tall, tree-sized gymnosperms called cordaiteans, with strap-shaped leaves and stems up to 20 inches (50 centimeters) in diameter, while the drier parts of the peat swamps had equally high tree-sized clubmosses.

By comparison, only low growth of ferns with an occasional taller *Lepidodendron*, another large clubmoss, could survive on the waterlogged riverside swamps. An abundant growth of *Calamites* (a horsetail) formed on the channel banks and edges of the swamps, which also provided a suitable habitat for the first land snails.

FOSSIL HORSETAIL
This fossil shows the jointed stems and circlets of leaves characteristic of a horsetail. Many of the Carboniferous horsetails grew into tree-sized plants, unlike their small modern survivors.

COAL SWAMPS
Fossils found in the coal deposits at Joggins, Nova Scotia, have given us a picture of the near-equatorial riverside swamp that existed there in Carboniferous times. The dense plant life included horsetails (*Calamites*) at the margins of channels, and tall clubmosses, such as *Sigillaria* and *Lepidodendron*. Large insects provided food for the first reptiles, including *Hylonomus lyelli*. The fossilized remains of reptiles have been found inside hollow trunks.

BODIES IN THE TRUNK

More than 190 fossil skeletons of small amphibians and reptiles have been recovered from about 30 tree-sized stumps of large Carboniferous plants preserved in deposits at Joggins, Nova Scotia. Various explanations have been put forward for the occurrence of the vertebrates in the hollow stumps. It has been suggested that they lived there or that they were natural "bottle traps" into which the animals fell and were trapped and eventually died. Another recent theory is that the animals hid there to escape the fires that swept the swamps.

FOREST DRAGONFLY
Giant dragonflies, like this *Namurotypus* with a 24-inch (60-centimeter) wingspan, inhabited the Carboniferous forests. They were the first creatures to fly and were then, as now, predators on smaller insects.

CARBONIFEROUS REPTILES

One of the most remarkable features of the Joggins site is the presence of numerous tree-sized stumps and trunks of the larger plants preserved in the sediment. Even more surprising is the occurrence inside these stumps of the fossil remains of the oldest known true egg-laying (amniote) reptiles, *Hylonomus lyelli* and *Paleothyris*.

These first reptiles were small—about 8 inches (20 centimeters) long—and looked like modern insectivorous lizards. They probably hatched from a tiny egg, about 0.4 inches (1 centimeter) in diameter. The reptile head was only a fifth of the body length, compared with a third in the earlier tetrapods. The structure of the skull showed an advance on the older amphibians since it allowed more space for larger and stronger jaw muscles.

The reptiles were able to live on land because food—in the form of small arthropods, such as millipedes, spiders, and insects—was abundant. With their small, sharp teeth, the reptiles could pierce these creatures' tough exoskeletons.

A layer of charcoal is often found within the stumps and there are layers of charcoal fragments in the surrounding sediments. The charcoal originated from periodic natural wildfire, suggesting that the animals may have sought shelter in the trunks, only to suffocate and die.

The Permian Age

THE FORMATION OF THE SUPERCONTINENT OF PANGEA PROVIDED AN ENVIRONMENT FOR THE GLOBAL EXPANSION OF TERRESTRIAL LIFE.

EL CAPITAN
Permian reef limestone forms the El Capitan Peak in the Guadelupe Mountains of Texas and New Mexico.

The Permian period started 290 million years ago, when the northern continents of Eurasia and Laurentia joined the southern continent of Gondwana to form Pangea.

This event had a drastic effect on climates and on life, and marked a turning point in the development of global environments. The late Carboniferous icecap that had formed over Gondwana diminished as the continent moved north toward the equator. In the northern part of Pangea, the climate generally became hot and dry within the vast continental interiors, although in the southern part they remained cooler and wetter.

CHANGES IN PLANT LIFE

As temperatures rose, many of the shallow seas and lakes of late Carboniferous times evaporated, leaving extensive deposits of salt minerals across Laurentia. Inevitably, plant life responded to these environmental changes. The humid Carboniferous Coal Measure forests, dependent on damp ground conditions, shrank on a global scale, persisting only in wetter regions, such as China, Siberia, and parts of Gondwana, such as Australia, India, and Antarctica. The lush clubmoss and horsetail trees were replaced by more adaptable seed-bearing plants as the ground dried. In the northern hemisphere, newly evolving conifers, such as *Walchia,* spread rapidly, while as the

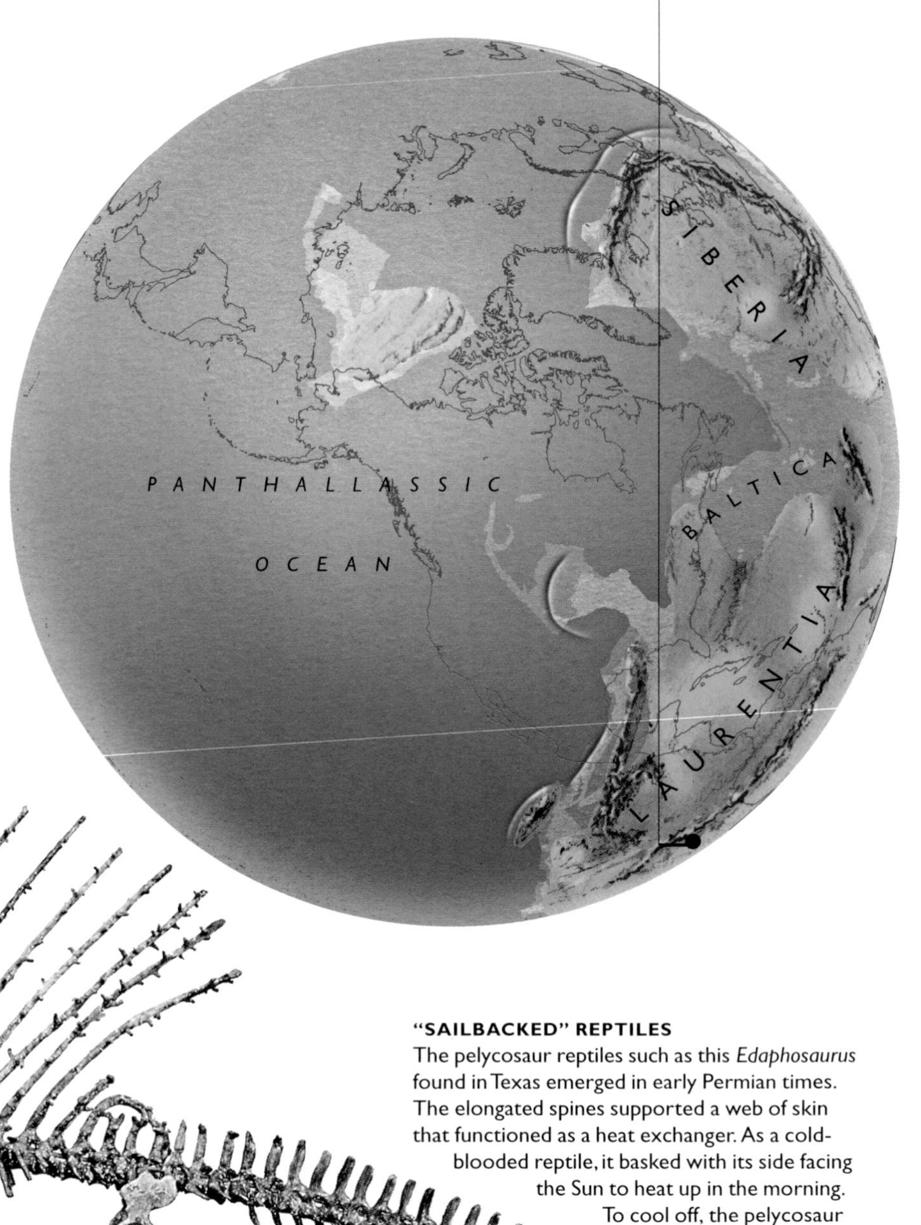

"SAILBACKED" REPTILES
The pelycosaur reptiles such as this *Edaphosaurus* found in Texas emerged in early Permian times. The elongated spines supported a web of skin that functioned as a heat exchanger. As a cold-blooded reptile, it basked with its side facing the Sun to heat up in the morning. To cool off, the pelycosaur turned into the wind.

CONTINENTAL DRIFT

The discovery of fossil flora and fauna of the same type and age in countries that are now widely separated has been used by geologists as evidence that vast landmasses such as Gondwana and Pangea once existed. It is unlikely that life could have spread so successfully on land if the different continents had not at one time been joined together. The first theory that continents move, or "drift," was developed in the early 20th century by the German meteorologist Alfred Wegener, after he recognized that similar late Carboniferous glacial deposits appear on all the continents of today's southern hemisphere.

SEED-FERN LEAVES
The distinctive elongated leaves of this extinct seed-fern called *Glossopteris* have been found in Permian and Triassic strata throughout India, Australia, South Africa, South America, and Antarctica. This distribution has long been seen as evidence that these landmasses were once joined as the supercontinent of Gondwana.

TETHYS OCEAN

GONDWANA

PANTHALLASSIC OCEAN

ice age gradually waned in the cooler southern hemisphere, the seed-fern *Glossopteris* emerged as the dominant flora.

MAMMAL CHARACTERISTICS

A group of tetrapods called the synapsids became more diverse and widespread, moving from the northern to the southern hemisphere by the end of the Permian period. Some species began to evolve characteristics that pointed in the direction of the future evolution of mammals. One of the synapsid groups, called the cynodont therapsids, eventually become warm-blooded, because their lineage includes the first mammals and their living descendants.

Life in the seas was decimated by another extinction event at the end of the period. About 90 percent of the marine invertebrates disappeared, including the brachiopods and trilobites. The reason for this event is unclear, although overspecialization and the resulting inability to cope with environmental change may have been a factor. Life on land generally had greater adaptability and mostly survived.

FILTER-FEEDING SPONGE
This Texan reef-building sponge, *Girtyocoelia*, used its linked pea-sized chambers to filter food from the sea by drawing in water through tiny holes in its sides. The walls of the sponge were made from chalky carbonates present in the seawater.

Ancient Mammal Relatives

Life on land evolved rapidly once the early tetrapods were able to lay eggs that could hatch on land. In Carboniferous times, these amniote tetrapods evolved into two branches—the reptiles, and a group called the synapsids, which eventually gave rise to the mammals. Previously known as "mammal-like reptiles," synapsids were never true reptiles.

PELYCOSAURS

The first synapsids were the pelycosaurs. These were so successful in early Permian times that they made up nearly three-quarters of all tetrapods. An important feature of the pelycosaurs was tooth differentiation, which allowed some to become plant eaters and others carnivores. Two types of pelycosaurs developed a "sail," consisting of long spines covered by a thin web of skin, that stood up from their backs. It may have acted as a heat exchanger, helping to raise the animal's body temperature in the early morning and prevent overheating at noon. Calculations have shown that the sail could have quartered the basking time a large pelycosaur needed before it became active in the morning.

THERAPSIDS OF THE KARROO

The early Permian pelycosaurs became extinct in late Permian times and were replaced by a more advanced group of synapsids, the therapsids.

DICYNODONT EGGS
These fossil eggs, among the oldest known, were found in Permian strata of southern Africa. The eggs are thought to have been laid by reptilelike dicynodont therapsids.

PERMIAN KARROO
The semi-arid scrub of the Karroo desert in South Africa resembles the Permian landscape of over 250 million years ago. Then, the desert was dominated by the forerunners of mammals and reptiles.

PERMIAN LIFEFORMS
The Karroo strata show that during Permian times South Africa was home to many reptilelike forerunners of the mammals, such as the cynodont *Procynosuchus*. Landscapes were dominated by plant-eaters such as the pig-sized *Dicynodon* and the smaller *Robertia*, pursued by carnivores such as *Lycaenops*. Armored amphibians, including *Peltobatrachus*, existed alongside the lizardlike *Milleretta*. Horsetails, ferns such as *Dicroidium*, seed-ferns such as *Glossopteris*, and the first cycads and ginkgos vegetated the land.

EARLY SYNAPSID
This *Dimetrodon* is a sail-backed pelycosaur from North America. It was one of the first backboned land animals that could kill other beasts of its own size.

Fossils of over 100 kinds of therapsids, as well as thousands of reptile, amphibian, fish, and plant fossils have been found in the red sandstone of the late Permian Karroo basin of South Africa since its discovery in the 1840s. They include many varieties of dicynodont therapsid, animals with two large canine teeth. The dicynodonts included the 8-inch- (20-centimeter-) long *Oudenodon*, which lived in corkscrew-shaped vertical burrows, hog-sized animals, such as *Lystrosaurus*, with beaklike bony mouths, and hippo-sized herbivores such as *Kannemeyeria*.

CYNODONTS

More interesting, from the evolutionary point of view, are the cynodont therapsids, which evolved at the end of the Permian age and gave rise to the first mammals in late Triassic times. These cynodonts, such as *Procynosuchus*, evolved shorter tails, elbows that flexed backward, knees that flexed forward, more powerful jaws, and diversified teeth, which shows their close relationship to the mammals. The cynodonts survived through a large part of the Jurassic, living alongside the dinosaurs, and then became extinct.

TEETH

Early tetrapods had simple undifferentiated teeth. Food could not be chewed, it was just torn off and swallowed. The stomach extracted nutrients from the unchewed food. But therapsids began to differentiate incisor, canine, and molarlike teeth, suggesting a varied diet of food that may have been chewed and pre-digested in the animal's mouth before being swallowed.

MASS EXTINCTIONS

THE HISTORY OF LIFE ON EARTH HAS BEEN punctuated by a series of extinction events. Perhaps the best known is the one that occurred at the end of the Cretaceous, about 65 million years ago, marking the end of the reign of the dinosaurs. Life on Earth suffered its greatest setback, however, at the end of the Permian, around 248 million years ago, when organisms were struck down on a massive scale, both on land and in the seas. Although the organization and evolution of marine organisms had been drastically altered before, this was the first time that life on land had known such devastation.

Terrestrial vertebrates were severely hit. Some 21 families of therapsid reptiles (63 percent of the total number of tetrapod families) and 33 percent of amphibian families disappeared. But hardest hit of all were sea-dwelling creatures. Marine diversity was reduced from about a quarter of a million species to less than 10,000. Altogether some 60 percent of marine families became extinct. Casualties included some important Paleozoic fossil groups such as the trilobites.

Several different mechanisms have been proposed for why mass extinctions occur. The first and most spectacular is the impact of a large asteroid or a comet with the Earth. In addition to the lifeforms killed by the impact itself and the earthquakes and tidal waves it would trigger, such an impact would throw huge amounts of dust and debris high into the atmosphere, blocking out the Sun's radiation and creating cold,

RUGOSE HORN CORAL
Aulophyllum (left) is just one of many Carboniferous corals that made up the vast reefs of the tropical seas of the time. All the rugose and tabulate corals were replaced in mid-Triassic times by a new group of corals (the scleractinians).

RECORD OF EXTINCTIONS

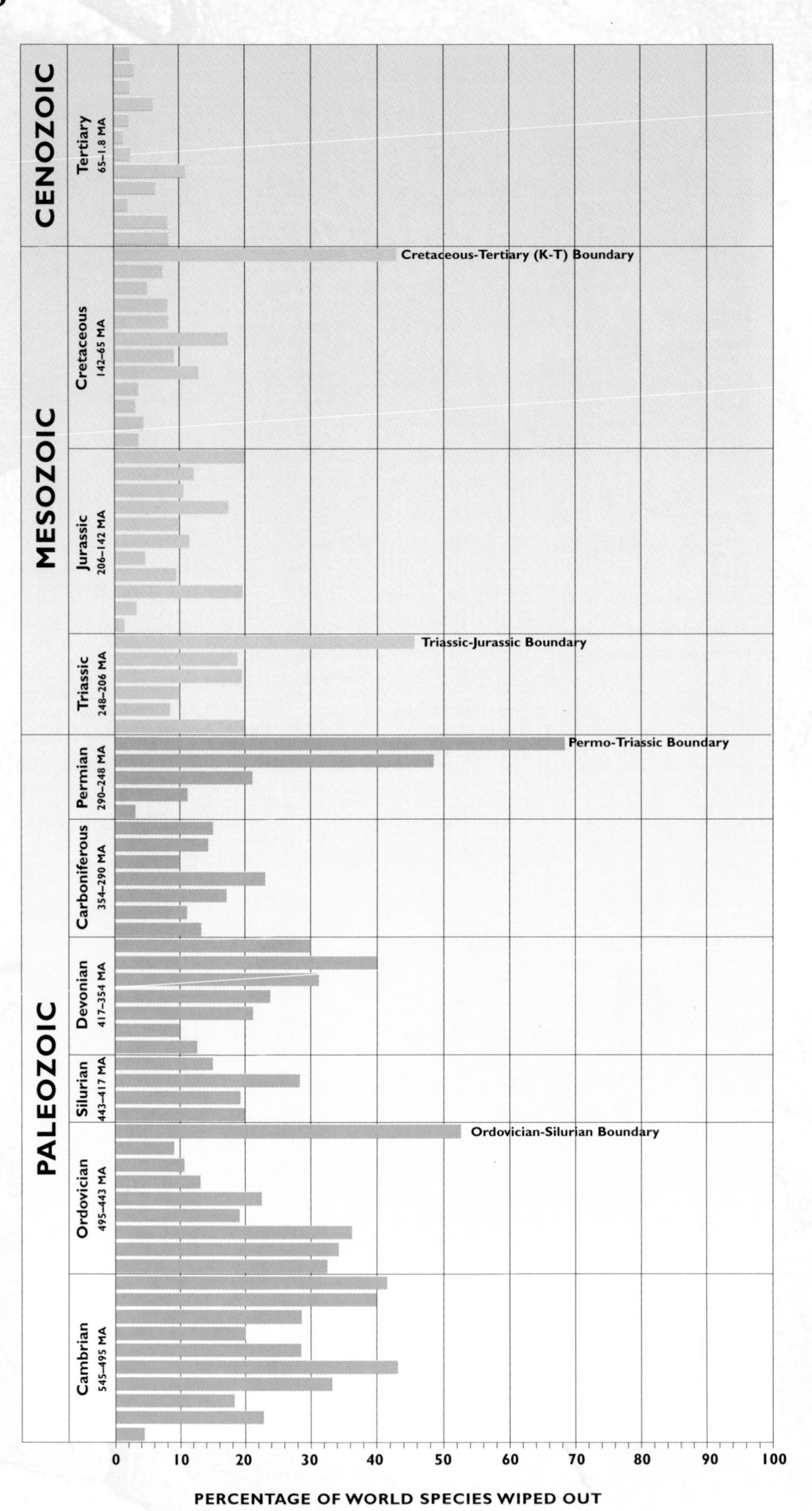

CAUSES OF THE EXTINCTIONS
This chart shows that mass extinctions often mark the major divisions in geological history and coincide with significant meteorite impacts, volcanic eruptions, or sea-level changes. The largest extinction, at the Permo-Triassic boundary, occurred at the same time as a fall in sea levels, which killed off much of shallow marine life, and volcanic eruptions in Siberia, leading to global climate change. The Cretaceous-Tertiary boundary is associated with sea-level change, volcanic eruptions, and a layer of iridium (a rare metallic element) in rocks that is clearly linked to a meteorite impact.

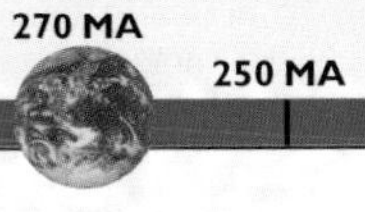

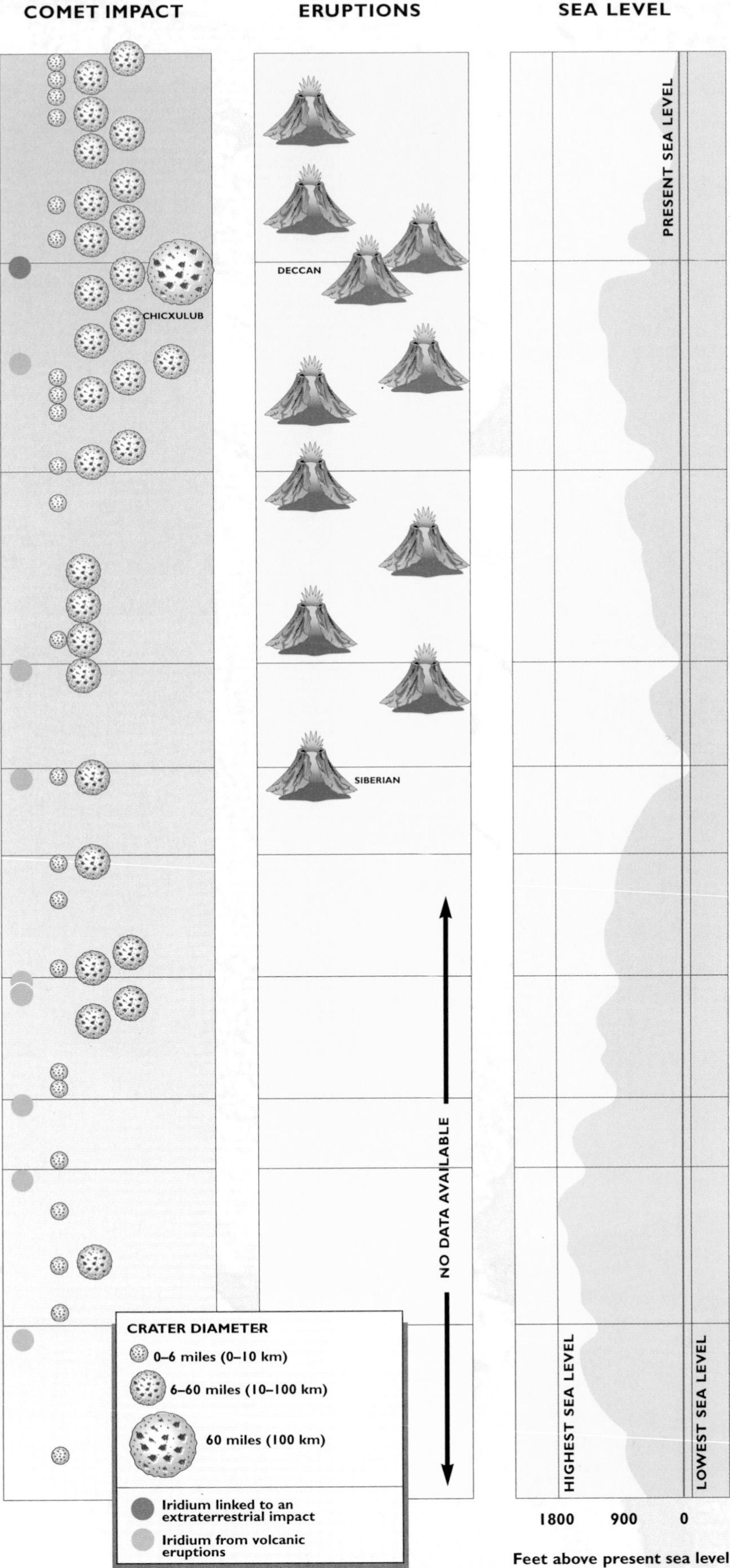

THERAPSID SKULL
Titanophoneus was one of the therapsids that replaced the sailbacked pelycosaurs in late Permian times, only to become extinct themselves at the end of the Permian period.

dark conditions. If the impact was big enough, living conditions would become so severe that few species would survive.

Another possible cause for mass extinction is an episode of massive volcanic eruptions. Flood basalts are layers of volcanic rock laid down by volcanic eruptions much bigger than any seen in modern times. Eruptions can alter global climates in dramatic ways and since eruption episodes can happen repeatedly, adverse conditions can persist long enough to affect animal and plant species.

The third mechanism for a mass extinction is sea-level change, caused by climate change and movements of the Earth's crustal plates. Throughout Permian times sea levels had been steadily falling. But in the early Triassic they dropped to an all-time low in the last 545 million years. Communities such as coral reefs, which thrive in warm, shallow coastal waters, become stranded and die off when sea levels fall.

The final mechanism for a mass extinction is global climate change. Although they are more gradual than the rapid changes in climate brought about by eruptions or impacts, the Earth's weather patterns can undergo major changes in very short times in geological terms.

Recently scientists have begun assessing the causes of the great extinction events of prehistory. A huge meteorite impact in Mexico's Yucatan peninsula, for example, is certainly implicated in the late Cretaceous extinctions. But there was also volcanic eruption, climate change, and a fall in sea level. No major meteorite impact has been found that correlates to the dramatic loss of species at the end of the Permian period. In most extinctions, the story does not appear to have been simple. Rather it seems that such extinctions are precipitated by a combination of factors.

The Triassic Period

AS LIFE SLOWLY RECOVERED FROM THE PERMIAN EXTINCTION, REPTILES, INCLUDING THE FIRST DINOSAURS, BECAME THE DOMINANT ANIMALS.

The Triassic period lasted for over 40 million years, from 248 to 206 million years ago. At first, as the supercontinent of Pangea crept northward to straddle the equator, much of its vast landmass became increasingly warm and arid. By the end of the period, however, Pangea was beginning to break up and global climates had become cooler and wetter.

During the early Triassic, there was a marked recovery in the percentage of oxygen in the atmosphere, but later oxygen levels declined. Sea levels also fluctuated. They plunged to a new low in the early Triassic, then rose again around the middle of the period, only to fall once more toward the end of the age.

LIFE ON LAND AND IN THE SEA

These environmental changes signaled major developments in the vertebrates (backboned animals). The mammalian relatives that had dominated the land in Permian times declined (although one group, the cynodonts, spread and diversified). Instead, a new wave of reptiles, the archosaurs, emerged. Later, at the end of Triassic times, some famous archosaur descendants, the dinosaurs, came to the fore.

Terrestrial ecosystems became more complex and diverse, with the rise of the first gliding and flying reptiles, the first turtles, and the first frogs. Plant life also changed significantly. Forests of primitive conifers clothed the dry hillsides. Savanna-like open spaces supported smaller conifers, such as *Woodworthia*, tree-ferns, cycads, and cycadophytes. The ancient treelike glossopterids went into final decline, as modern-looking horsetails flourished.

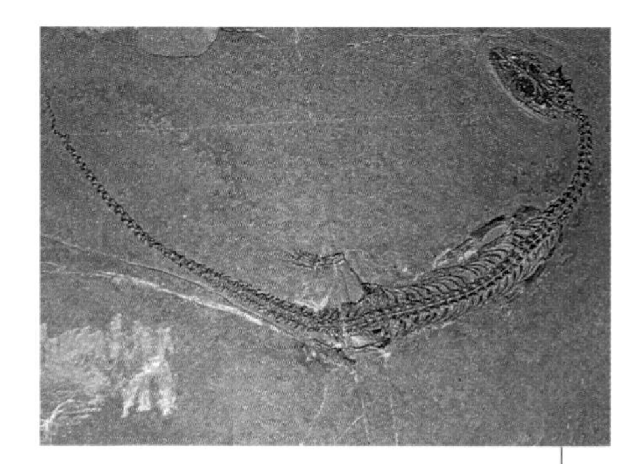

FISH-HUNTERS
The nothosaurs were marine predators that evolved from land-based reptiles during Triassic times. They had a long slim body, tail, and neck and preyed exclusively upon fish. This fossil is from Switzerland.

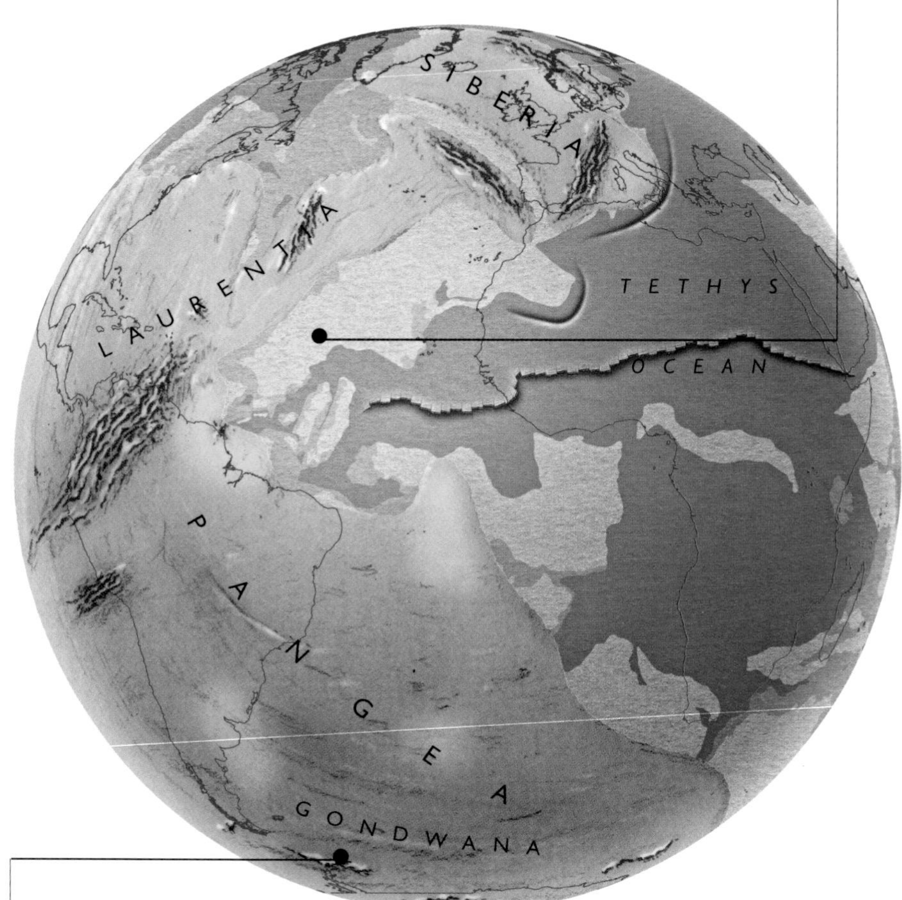

CYNODONT SKULL
The cynodont *Cynognathus* from South Africa was a predator of the early to mid-Triassic. It had a mammal-like posture, possibly a covering of hair, and differentiated teeth: incisors, canines, and ridged cheek teeth for fast chewing.

BIOZONES

The rapid evolution of Triassic ammonoid shellfish resulted in constant changes in the details of their shells. Experts have used these changes to identify levels called biozones within marine fossil-bearing strata. Deposits on land are similarly zoned using pollen, plant spores, and terrestrial vertebrate remains. Detailed pictures of life within biozones have been built up and correlated from different parts of the world.

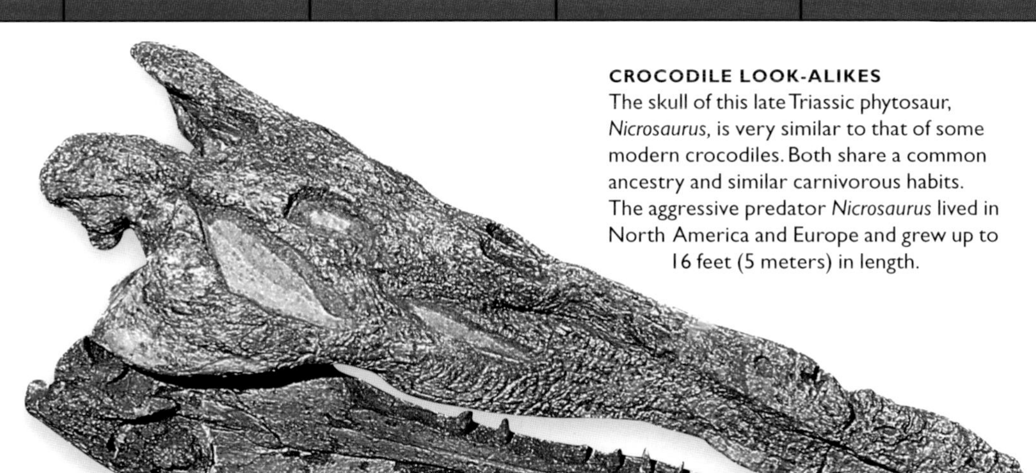

CROCODILE LOOK-ALIKES
The skull of this late Triassic phytosaur, *Nicrosaurus*, is very similar to that of some modern crocodiles. Both share a common ancestry and similar carnivorous habits. The aggressive predator *Nicrosaurus* lived in North America and Europe and grew up to 16 feet (5 meters) in length.

The ecosystems in the sea were also transformed. The Triassic period saw the rise of groups of bony fish, that although more modern-looking, still differed greatly from sea life today. Some common living marine animals such as crab- and lobsterlike crustaceans did not evolve until Jurassic times. Ammonoids (coiled shellfish) flourished after the devastation wreaked by the late Permian extinction. From only a few survivors, such as *Ophiceras*, there were soon 100 genera. They, and their distant relatives the belemnite cephalopods, played an increasing role in the seas as swimming predators. The Triassic also saw the arrival of modern-looking corals, an extremely diverse and successful group of colonial organisms that form the largest living structures known—coral reefs. All living corals, known as hexacorals, are structurally different from the Paleozoic corals that existed before the extinction event at the end of the Permian period. Modern corals appear to have evolved from survivors of that mass extinction. The first reefs built in Triassic times were small compared with today's, however. Constructed by no more than 20 different types of coral, they grew about 3 feet (1 meter) above the seafloor. Large reefs were not established until the end of the Triassic period.

Mollusk bivalves and gastropods were able to exploit an enormous range of niches in the Triassic seas. Some were permanently attached to the seabed, others were burrowers and free-swimmers. They also invaded freshwater and, in the case of snails, eventually took to the land as well. By comparison, the superficially similar but more limited brachiopods were already in decline and would eventually be largely eclipsed.

EARLY PTEROSAUR
This fossil of one of the oldest flying reptiles, the fish-eating *Eudimorphodon*, displays two types of teeth: plain conical spikes at the front and three-pointed ones at the back. It was discovered in late Triassic strata of northern Italy.

Dawn of the Dinosaurs

One of the richest dinosaur deposits ever found was at the evocatively named Ghost Ranch in the New Mexican desert. It was discovered in 1947 by American paleontologists George Whitaker and Edwin H. Colbert, from the American Museum of Natural History. Over a thousand 220-million-year-old skeletons of small two-footed dinosaurs, many of them complete, were huddled together within a narrow band of sandstone. The Ghost Ranch skeletons are all of the same kind of animal but include specimens of different sizes, from hatchlings less than 3 feet (1 meter) in size to older individuals up to a maximum size of 10 feet (3 meters).

Fast-moving hunter

Named *Coelophysis*, the Ghost Ranch dinosaur had all the hallmarks of a fast-moving, hunting meat-eater. It had a slender, muscular body, with hollow, light bones and long legs, and its narrow skull was armed with numerous dagger-shaped teeth with sharp cutting edges.

What were such a large number of predatory meat-eaters doing together? *Coelophysis* was probably a pack hunter, roaming the upland forests, lakes, and rivers of the late Triassic world, preying on small reptiles and, possibly, shrewlike mammals. Today, most big vertebrates that move around in large numbers are plant-eaters, which herd together for safety. There are no living pack hunters that operate in such large groups. But all of our modern-day examples are mammals—for reptilian dinosaurs it was presumably different.

Details of the mass of skeletons made it clear that the dinosaurs must have died together, overwhelmed by some catastrophe. The most

DINOSAUR BADLANDS The rocky ridges around Ghost Ranch, New Mexico, expose a sequence of fossil-rich strata, from the Triassic red hills in the foreground, through Jurassic yellow cliffs, to the Cretaceous Dakota sediments of the skyline.

TRIASSIC NEW MEXICO The plant-eating reptile *Desmatosuchus* was 16 feet (5 meters) in length with heavy armor, including 18-inch spines projecting from its shoulders, but it would have been no match for large carnivores such as the crocodile-like *Rutiodon* and the land-living archosaur *Postosuchus*. *Coelophysis* pack hunters ate anything they could catch and kill. Plant-eating *Placerias* was a shy animal living in upland woods. *Metoposaurus* was a large amphibian that fed on fish, as did the flying reptile *Eudimorphodon*.

likely cause is a flash-flood which may have swept along a river valley, carrying many of the herd away and drowning them. Even today, herds of wildebeest can be similarly overcome in Africa.

PREY AND PREDATORS

Coelophysis was far from being the only predator in this environment. In the streams and rivers, *Rutiodon*, a crocodile-like representative of a new reptile group, the phytosaurs, was top predator. The land was dominated by a large archosaur reptile, *Postosuchus*, with a long skull similar to the later tyrannosaurs. It was probably too slow to catch the swift *Coelophysis* and preyed instead on plant-eating reptiles, such as *Desmatosuchus*, *Typothorax*, and *Calyptosuchus*. These were slow-moving but heavily armored. They moved on all fours, with sturdy legs to support the weight of their body plates and neck and tail spikes. Another plant-eater was the ox-sized *Placerias*, a dicynodont with a short tail, a large broad skull, a pair of sharp tusks, and pointed beaklike jaws covered in horny sheaths. The skies may have been home to the first true flying pterosaur reptile, *Eudimorphodon*, and in the forests the gliding lizardlike *Icarosaurus* swooped from tree to tree. Last but not least, *Dinnetherium*, a small shrewlike descendant of the cynodonts (reptiles with doglike teeth), was living a nocturnal life, feeding off insects. This seemingly insignificant creature was, it is now thought, a possible direct ancestor of humans.

DINOSAUR CANNIBALS

Some of the Coelophysis skeletons found at Ghost Ranch, New Mexico, were discovered to have smaller dinosaurs of the same species within their body cavity. At first scientists thought that these must have been unborn young, showing that Coelophysis gave birth to live offspring, rather than laying eggs like most reptiles. It is now known, however, that the dinosaur's hip bones were too narrow for live birth—it simply must have laid eggs. Experts believe it is more likely that Coelophysis practised cannibalism. One theory is that dominant males may have killed and eaten offspring sired by other displaced males. Similar behavior has been observed in such modern-day meat-eaters as lions.

DEATH THROES
The heads of these *Coelophysis* skeletons were pulled back by contraction of the neck muscles after death. The posture indicates some delay before the corpses were buried.

Reptilian Domination

The global development and spread of the reptiles during the Mesozoic era was astonishing. As much of the world's climate became hotter and drier, the reptiles, who could lay their eggs on land, took advantage of the new niches available to them, venturing into new territories and returning to old ones. For the first time they took to the air, and they also returned to the water from where their tetrapod ancestors had originated.

GLIDING LIZARD
This late Triassic, long-legged reptile, *Kuehneosaurus*, could glide through the air using a membrane-covered wing that spanned more than 12 inches (30 centimeters) and was supported by elongated ribs. A similar technique is used by the living lizard *Draco volans*, and both can fold the wing when at rest.

FLYING REPTILES

The remarkable adaptability of the reptiles is highlighted by the repeated evolution of species that took to the air. The first of these, *Coelurosauravus*, whose remains have been found in Europe and Madagascar, was Permian in age. Closely resembling the living flying lizard *Draco volans* of Southeast Asia, *Coelurosauravus* was a highly effective glider and an excellent example of convergent evolution (in which similar patterns of evolution are seen in unrelated species). It grew to a length of 16 inches (40 centimeters) and had greatly elongated ribs that extended sideways from the body to provide an overall wingspan of 12 inches (30 centimeters). A web of skin that stretched over the ribs formed a fixed wing structure. The reptile's light skeleton and skull reduced overall weight and there was an aerodynamic frill at the back of its skull.

Like *Draco volans*, *Coelurosauravus* and the unrelated but similar *Kuehneosaurus* from the late Triassic probably lived in trees and used the novel trick of gliding to escape predators. *Draco volans* can glide for 200 feet (60 meters) and lose only about 6 feet (1.8 meters) in altitude.

By late Triassic and early Jurassic times, other winged reptiles called pterosaurs were evolving. Unlike *Coelurosauravus*, these had wings stretched between the limbs and body rather than attached to ribs. They had well-developed powers of sight and wing control and light but strong skeletons.

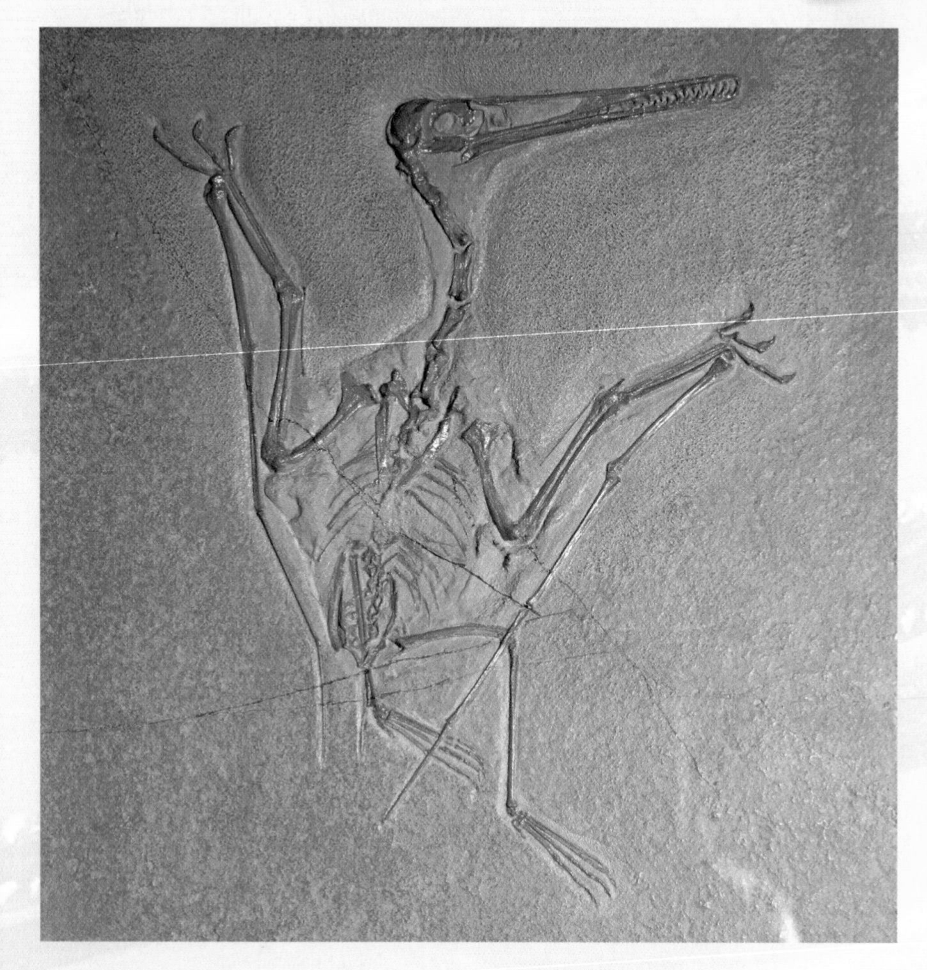

FLYING REPTILE
A well-preserved specimen of the pterosaur *Pterodactylus kochi* (left) from the Jurassic Solenhofen limestone strata of Bavaria still retains an imprint of the wing membrane.

FOSSIL ICHTHYOSAUR
Ichthyosaurs made many adaptations to aquatic life, including giving birth to live young underwater. This fossil of a species of *Stenopterygius* is 6 feet (2 meters) long. Its elongated jaws, flippers, backbone, and vertical tail are all clearly visible.

MARINE REPTILES

During the Mesozoic, several reptile groups reverted to their ancestral habitat—water. The placodonts, resembling large iguanas, grew to 6½ feet (2 meters) long and featured broad, armored bodies. They fed on shellfish from the seafloor, grubbing up clams with their forelimbs or pulling them from the rocks with peglike front teeth.

The dolphinlike ichthyosaurs were highly specialized marine reptiles able to swim at speeds of up to 25 miles per hour (40 kilometers per hour). The first ones were about 3 to 6 feet (1 to 1.8 meters) long. Their diet consisted of fish and belemnites (swimming mollusks, a bit like cuttlefish), as we know from their stomach contents and coprolites (fossilized feces). The prey was snatched and swallowed whole.

Shonisaurus of the late Triassic, from Nevada in North America, is the largest known ichthyosaur. It grew to a length of 50 feet (15 meters), with the head and neck, the body, and the tail divided approximately into equal lengths. The backbone bent downward into the lower lobe of the fishlike tail—a feature of later ichthyosaurs. It must have swum in schools, because one deposit contained several dozen specimens. This particular group did not survive the end of the Triassic, but ichthyosaurs as a whole went on to even greater success in the Jurassic.

CONVERGENT EVOLUTION

Ichthyosaurs are a classic example of convergent evolution, the process by which two lines of evolutionary development bring about superficially similar end-points. When different groups of organisms are subjected to the same environmental selection pressures, they tend to evolve similar design features. The streamlined body form of the reptilian ichthyosaurs is similar to that of living mammalian dolphins. Like dolphins, ichthyosaurs had powerful muscular bodies and keen eyesight. However, dolphins have a horizontal tail and a bigger brain.

SPOTTED DOLPHINS
The reduced limbs have been specially adapted for steering.

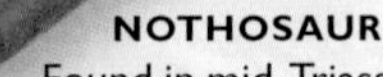

NOTHOSAUR
Found in mid-Triassic strata throughout Asia, Europe, and North Africa, *Nothosaurus* grew to 10 feet (3 meters) in length. With webbed feet and a long, flexible neck and tail, they probably lived like seals, fishing at sea and resting up on land.

The Jurassic Period

ALTHOUGH POPULARLY KNOWN AS THE "AGE OF THE DINOSAURS," THIS WAS ALSO A TIME WHEN MARINE LIFE FLOURISHED AND FLOWERING PLANTS EVOLVED.

SEED CONE
The reproductive seed cones of conifers are often fossilized, after being carried by streams far from the parent plant. This cone fell from a monkey-puzzle-like conifer in Patagonia, South America.

The 64-million-year period in the Earth's history from 206 to 142 million years ago is known as the Jurassic. It is named for rock formations found in the Jura Mountains in western Europe. Although some forms of life had suffered in the extinction event at the end of the preceding age, the Triassic, the diversity of plants and animals had recovered to its previous level by mid-Jurassic times. This recovery marked the start of a long period of growth, which continued through the remainder of the Mesozoic era.

GLOBAL CHANGES

During the Jurassic period, the global super-continent of Pangea began to break up. Gondwana moved back south, opening a westward extension of the Tethys Ocean through the Panama region. Laurasia (North America and Eurasia) was separated from Gondwana and the land link between North and South America was broken. These changes had far-reaching effects on the development of differing environments and the evolution of animals and plants in the northern and southern hemispheres.

LARGE PREDATOR
The enormous dagger-shaped teeth, and scissor cut of the jaw made the *Allosaurus* a very effective predator. Remains of the dinosaur, which grew to a length of 40 feet (12 meters), are found in late Jurassic strata of the American Midwest.

At the start of the period, global temperatures and humidity levels fell. After early Jurassic times, however, the trend reversed, with the rapid development of a much warmer "greenhouse" global climate by the end of the period. Sea levels rose and fell, but gradually rose to maintain overall higher levels than during the Triassic period. This activity drowned the coastal regions of continents, and as these new waters flooded inland, widespread shallow shelf seas developed. These warm, sunlight-filled bodies of water were ideal breeding grounds for increasingly diverse

JURASSIC SNAKESTONES

Jurassic limestone and shale sweep in gentle hills and vales across much of western Europe, from the Alps to western Scotland. They have been quarried for building materials since medieval times, giving up fossils that entered folklore as "snakestones," "thunderbolts," or "devil's toenails." Not until the early 19th century, however, was it realized that the fossils could be used to identify the Jurassic strata as representing a distinct geological period.

PLATED DINOSAUR
Stegosaurus, from the late Jurassic of western North America, was the largest of the plant-eating stegosaurids. A double row of diamond-shaped plates ran along the neck and back, and the tail had two pairs of spikes.

and complex marine life. From early Jurassic times, large reefs were re-established in the shallow seas. Phytoplankton, the microscopic, plantlike organisms that still form the basis of most food chains, enjoyed a new lease on life with the evolution of many of the groups that still dominate the microlife of the oceans today—the dinoflagellates and the nanoplankton.

By the end of the period, bony fishes (teleosts) had become increasingly similar in appearance to the fish we are familiar with today. They were hunted down by the spectacular "sea monsters" of the Jurassic seas, the predatory ichthyosaurs (fish-lizards) and plesiosaurs (near-lizards).

THRIVING FLORA AND FAUNA

On land, several groups of Triassic reptiles had died out. Mammals thrived, albeit in the shadows, but synapsids (ancient relatives of the mammals) became extinct during this age.

The airways became increasingly busy as more and more flying reptiles (pterosaurs) evolved and diversified to fill different ecological niches. In late Jurassic times these pterosaurs were joined by dinosaurs that had feathers, and some of these could fly—the birds were beginning to evolve.

Landscapes were gradually transformed and colored by the evolution of new plant life. A key event of the Jurassic age was the growth and diversification of sophisticated flowering plants, the angiosperms, which eventually came to dominate the terrestrial vegetation.

AMBER TOMB
Some species of pine trees have produced amber resin since Jurassic times. Insects accidentally trapped in the amber resin become preserved, like this specimen from the Baltic Sea in Europe.

Reptiles of the Jurassic Seas

The discovery of fossil skeletons of marine reptiles at Lyme Regis, in southwest England, in the early 19th century, was one of the key events that helped promote the novel idea that creatures which existed in the past might have become extinct. The fossil skeletons were once ichthyosaurs (fish-lizards) and plesiosaurs (near-lizards) that were unlike any living creatures known to the scientists of the time. They had evidently lived in the seas of the distant past, since they were found alongside the shells of typically marine clams, starfish, ammonites, and other squidlike cephalopods. Presented by early popularizers of paleontology as "sea dragons" and "denizens of the abysmal slime," these large marine reptiles immediately took a permanent hold on the popular imagination.

MARINE STRATA
The early Jurassic strata of the cliffs around Lyme Regis in southwest England are full of fossilized marine shells, such as ammonites, clams, cephalopods, fish, and some rare reptiles.

MONSTERS OF THE DEEP

The ichthyosaurs grew up to 50 feet (15 meters) long. Some specimens had a large skull and a distinctive dolphinlike jaw set with a fearsome array of typically reptilian teeth. These small, sharp, cone-shaped teeth were probably ideal for snatching and holding fish before swallowing them whole. Fossilized stomach contents reveal fish scales and large numbers of tentacle hooks.

The ichthyosaurs were adapted for deep diving, with large, light-gathering eyes for hunting in dark waters. Rings of bones around the eyes protected against the pressure deep underwater. With their streamlined bodies, many ichthyosaurs looked like living dolphins, and they were clearly adapted for high speed cruising and the pursuit of small, fast-swimming fish.

It was initially thought that these magnificent marine reptiles went ashore to lay their eggs. It was only when a specimen was found with juveniles within the body cavity that scientists realized that like mammals, these reptiles retained fertilized eggs within the body, until the embryos were sufficiently well developed to be born directly into the sea.

Plesiosaurs ranged in size from 6 to 45 feet (2 to 14 meters) and were very well adapted for swimming, with four large, paddle-shaped limbs and long, flexible necks. Most large plesiosaurs possessed small skulls and long snouts, and had to

JURASSIC MARINE PARK
In Jurassic times, life under water was just as "nasty, brutish, and short" as life on land. The seas were populated with swimming cephalopods, and fish, including coelacanths, which were preyed upon by large marine reptiles. These predators were beaked ichthyosaurs (*Ichthyosaurus*), long-necked plesiosaurs (*Plesiosaurus*), and short-necked pliosaurs (*Rhomaleosaurus*). The coiled, shelled ammonites also preyed on small fish.

FINDING SEA MONSTERS

Some of the most important fossil finds of the early 19th century were made by a self-educated woman, Mary Anning, and her family, from the coastal cliffs of Lyme Regis, England. The Annings eked out a precarious existence scouring the cliffs for fossils to sell to genteel tourists. Between 1811 and 1830, they uncovered complete flattened skeletons of early marine "monsters." These ichthyosaur and plesiosaur discoveries helped revolutionize our view of life in the prehistoric past.

come to the surface to breathe. Their jaws were full of closely interlocking crocodile-like teeth, helpful for catching and holding slippery fish. Given their huge size and slow swimming speed, the plesiosaurs may have been ambush hunters, using their long necks to snatch fish from passing shoals.

There is also a separate group of short-necked plesiosaurs, known as pliosaurs. The pliosaurs had relatively massive skulls, armed with long, sharp teeth that often stuck out from the jaws. They were faster-moving predators than the other, long-necked plesiosaurs. Since some grew to around 40 feet (12 meters) long, they probably hunted such large prey as ichthyosaurs and other smaller plesiosaurs as well as fish.

GRACEFUL HUNTER
A fast-swimming marine reptile up to 6 feet (2 meters) long, *Ichthyosaurus* hunted fish and squidlike cephalopods. The beaklike jaws and sharp, conical teeth were used for snatching and holding prey.

JURASSIC FISH

The marine reptiles shared the seas with a great diversity of fish. Like Jurassic fish, most living fish are called teleosts. In Jurassic times, the teleosts had begun to evolve, but were still overshadowed by an older group of fish, the holosteans, which had deep bodies and heavy, bony scales. Many holosteans became extinct in the Cretaceous age, but some, including the garpike, still thrive today.

Another ancient group of bony fish were the chondrosteans, of which sturgeons are survivors. Sharks and rays, such as *Squaloraja*, also gradually increased in number and diversity.

Discovering Extinction and Deep Time

Modern, science-based understanding of the fossil record is little more than 200 years old. During the European Renaissance, in the 1400s and 1500s, the collection and illustration of fossils became an accepted pastime for wealthy patrons and collectors. But it was not until the middle of the 17th century that fossils began to be recognized as the remains of dead creatures, rather than objects formed by some force or fluid within the ground.

DRAGONS
Dragons were familiar in the mythology of pre-modern cultures from China to Western Europe. Their ferocious image was based on features drawn from snakes and lizards. Not surprisingly, perhaps, the image of the dragon formed the basis for the original reconstructions of the first fossil reptilian "serpent" such as the *Iguanodon*.

QUESTIONING THE BIBLE

The study of fossils could be justified as a worthy one in Christian Europe because, within the Christian tradition, the natural world was seen as the prime example of everything glorious created by God. But the pursuit was acceptable only so long as it did not conflict with the biblical story of the Creation. It was generally held that all the creatures on Earth had been created in a few days, in their current form. They had neither changed through time nor become extinct. In 1650, the date of this creation was estimated as 4004BC by James Ussher, the Protestant Archbishop of Armagh in Ireland.

The discovery of fossils resembling sea creatures far inland and high up on mountains, if anything, confirmed the traditional Christian view of the past. The story of the Flood allowed these fossils to be passed off as the bodies of creatures that had either been drowned in the deluge or stranded on land once the waters receded.

By the early 1800s, however, great thicknesses of fossiliferous strata were discovered. It became clear that they could not all have been produced by a single flood, however catastrophic. Furthermore, the duration of the Earth's early prehistoric development could no longer be confined to a duration of a few thousand years.

BEFORE THE FLOOD
Animals line up two-by-two to enter Noah's Ark in this engraving by an unknown artist. The influence of this Old Testament story was so great that early 19th-century geologists thought fossils might be the remains of creatures drowned by the deluge. The idea was abandoned as fossils were found in more and more geological strata.

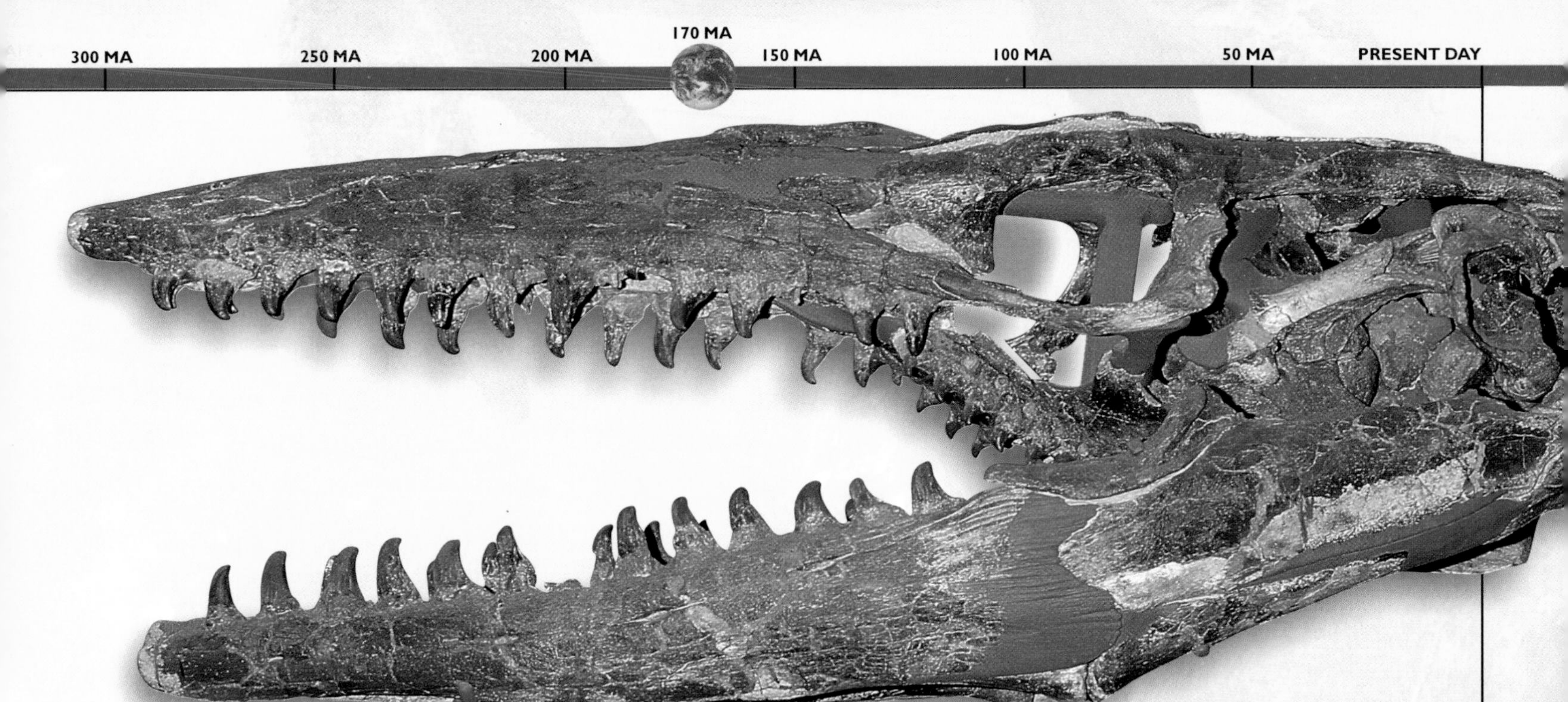

As an understanding of the slowness of the rates of many geological processes such as erosion and sedimentation developed, the age of the Earth had to be extended into millions, rather than just thousands, of years. What became clear was that during this long history there had been continual burial of organic remains within several layers of sediment, and that the types of fossils found varied throughout the different rock strata.

A NEW VIEW OF THE WORLD

By the late 18th century, fossil finds of large and often unrecognizable animals were being made in different parts of the world. Elephant-like bones were found on the banks of the Ohio River in North America (1739, named *Mastodon* in 1806). In 1796, fossil remains from Paraguay were described as those of a giant sloth. A giant marine reptile, the "Beast of Maastricht," was found in 1786 (see page 120). With the discovery of the "sea-dragons" *Ichthyosaurus* and *Plesiosaurus* at Lyme Regis in England in the early 19th century, naturalists had to face up to the idea that animals that had once existed had become extinct.

Evidence was also growing that individual species and groups of animals and plants appeared in the geological record at different times but with progressive modifications, which raised questions over just how fixed in form species were.

From the mid-19th century, a bitter debate was engaged between defenders of the traditional Christian view of the Creation and proponents of a new scientific view of the world that focused on the slow evolution of life and shifts in the surface of the Earth over almost unimaginable periods of time. In the 20th century, it was finally recognized that the Earth's age had to be measured in billions of years—a concept referred to as "deep time."

DRAGON LOOK-ALIKE
The awesomely toothed skull of this magnificent Cretaceous mosasaur, *Tylosaurus proriger*, resembles that of the mythical dragon. The reason is that the image of the dragon's head is based on folk knowledge of lizards, and mosasaurs are extinct marine lizards. Their jaws were nearly 3 feet (1 meter) long, and their total body length was about 32 feet (10 meters).

VALUABLE CATCH

The coelacanth is an animal that, until recently, was known only from the fossil record. It was common from Devonian to Jurassic times (370 to 150 million years ago) but was thought to have died out in Cretaceous times. In 1939, a scientist came across a specimen by chance off the South African coast, but he failed to preserve the fish properly and it disintegrated. Thirteen years later in 1952 a second specimen was identified in the Comoros Islands, off the east coast of Africa. Unknown to scientists, fishermen from the Comoros had for a long time regularly seen coelacanth in their catches. Since the fish were inedible, they had no value and were simply discarded. The islanders were unimpressed by the excitement about the coelacanth, but glad that the fish they called "Kombessa" had now become a valuable catch.

LIVING FOSSIL FISH
Coelacanths belong to an ancient group of creatures that were related to four-legged animals. First found in rocks of Devonian age, they were thought to be extinct until a specimen of *Latimeria chalumnae* was identified in the Indian Ocean in 1939. Scientists have now been able to observe them in their living habitats.

Life Takes to the Air

In late Jurassic times, a large lagoon, dotted with low-lying islands and sheltered from the Tethys Ocean by a reef, occupied an area of what is now Bavaria in southern Germany. The fine-grained limestone deposited on the bed of this Solenhofen lagoon proved an excellent medium for the preservation of fossils. The bodies of land animals and plants were washed into the water, settled on the lagoon bed, and covered with chalky mud. Solenhofen limestone holds the delicate remains of insects, such as dragonflies, flying pterosaurs, small dinosaurs, and, most famous of all, *Archaeopteryx*.

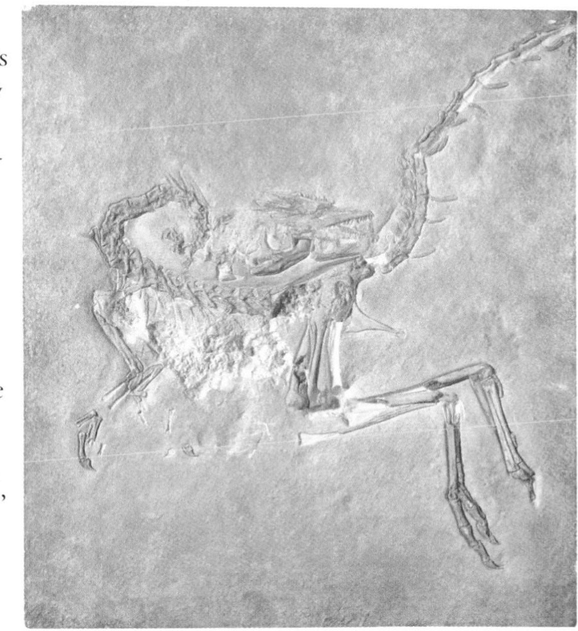

FAST RUNNER
Compsognathus was only 28 inches (70 centimeters) long. It had distinctive two-clawed hands and was a fast-running predator or scavenger. Its skeleton is very similar to *Archaeopteryx*.

EARLY BIRD

In 1861, when the debate over Charles Darwin's new theory of evolution by natural selection was at its most intense, the fossil skeleton of *Archaeopteryx* was discovered. This feathered fossil was classified as the first bird, although it actually showed some reptilian characteristics as well. The connection between *Archaeopteryx* and reptiles was reinforced by the discovery later in the decade of a small bipedal (walking on hind legs only) dinosaur, *Compsognathus*, found in the same deposits. *Compsognathus*, one of the tiniest of predatory dinosaurs, bore a remarkably close physical resemblance to *Archaeopteryx*, although without the feathers.

SENSES AND CLAWS

Archaeopteryx was a medium-sized bird, like a magpie, about 20 inches (50 centimeters) long from the tip of its snout to the end of its long tail, and stood approximately 10 inches (25 centimeters) high. The bird's skull housed large eyes and well-developed optic lobes in the brain, showing that sight was a key sense. The pointed, beaklike jaws were armed with widely spaced sharp teeth and the forelimbs had three greatly elongated fingers, each ending in a curved claw. The hind limbs were particularly birdlike, with the inner toe situated at the rear of the foot as in living birds. There has been much debate about the living

SOLENHOFEN LAGOON
The waters and shorelines of a shallow, late Jurassic lagoon in southern Germany were vegetated with horsetails, small conifers, and palmlike cycads. The area was a good hunting ground for small reptiles such as *Compsognathus*. There were numerous flying pterosaurs, including the long-toothed, fish-eating *Rhamphorhynchus* and the smaller *Pterodactylus*, an agile flyer that may have caught insects on the wing. Most famous of all is the early bird *Archaeopteryx* which, with its long tail, was probably a fairly slow and cumbersome flyer.

habits and flying ability of *Archaeopteryx*. Traditionally, it has been portrayed as climbing trees and then gliding from tree to tree to find food. Gliding could then have evolved over time into wing-powered flight. But, in fact, birds evolved from swift little predatory dinosaurs, so flight could well have begun from the ground up.

It is now known that the lagoon environment in which the bird lived did not include many tall trees, and thus was not the ideal place for a glider to prosper. Nevertheless, the asymmetric arrangement of the primary wing feathers suggests that *Archaeopteryx* could indeed fly. Flightless birds do not have this arrangement.

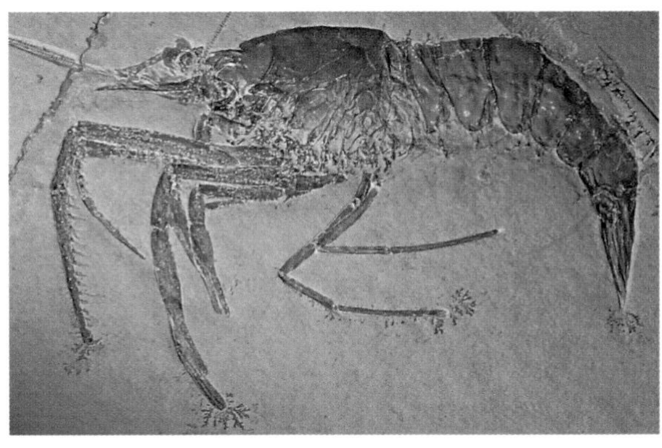

JURASSIC SHRIMP
With its long antennae and five pairs of walking legs this *Aeger*, 8 inches (20 centimeters) long, is clearly a shrimp (decapod crustacean). It is preserved in fine-grained limestone of late Jurassic age.

FLYING REPTILES

Archaeopteryx shared the Jurassic airways with flying reptiles, the pterosaurs. The earliest pterosaurs appeared during the late Triassic age, and they evolved throughout the Jurassic period. Their hollow, light skeleton was ideal for flight, but their most striking feature was an extra-long fourth finger on their forelimbs, which was the spar of the wing. Three shorter fingers were retained on the wing's front edge.

Originally, the pterosaurs had long tails that provided stability during flight at the expense of maneuverability. During the late Jurassic age, pterosaur tails became considerably shorter, making the creatures more agile hunters. The smaller species of these later pterosaurs had wingspans of up to 16 inches (40 centimeters) and were probably able to feed on insects while on the wing. The larger species were fish-eaters, diving to scoop their prey out of the sea. The wingspan of some pterosaurs grew as large as 35 to 40 feet (11 to 12 meters).

ARCHAEOPTERYX
One of the world's most famous fossils, *Archaeopteryx* has many of the features of a small dinosaur, with a long bony tail and toothed jaws. Wings and flight feathers suggest, however, that it was a bird and could fly.

Early Mammals

Today's mammals are easy to recognize, with their shared traits of hair, warm blood, and live-born young that suckle. These familiar features, however, did not evolve simultaneously, but rather over a long period of time. It is difficult to know when each manifested, since they are soft-tissue features not preserved in the fossil record.

The first mammal-like characteristics were seen in small, late Carboniferous, lizardlike reptiles. They showed the beginnings of tooth differentiation (a range of different teeth for different purposes) and skull modifications that were part of the mammalian trend.

By mid-Triassic times, mammal relatives called cynodonts ("dog teeth") had mouths that were filled with teeth with many cutting edges. They also had a bony roof plate (secondary palate) in the mouth that allowed them to continue breathing while chewing food. Changes to their jaw allowed a larger brain case, as well as the development of an ear that allowed them to distinguish sounds in a more complex way than reptiles. The small cynodonts were able to burrow, and this life in dark places led to the evolution of whiskerlike structures around the head, designed for feeling a way through tunnels.

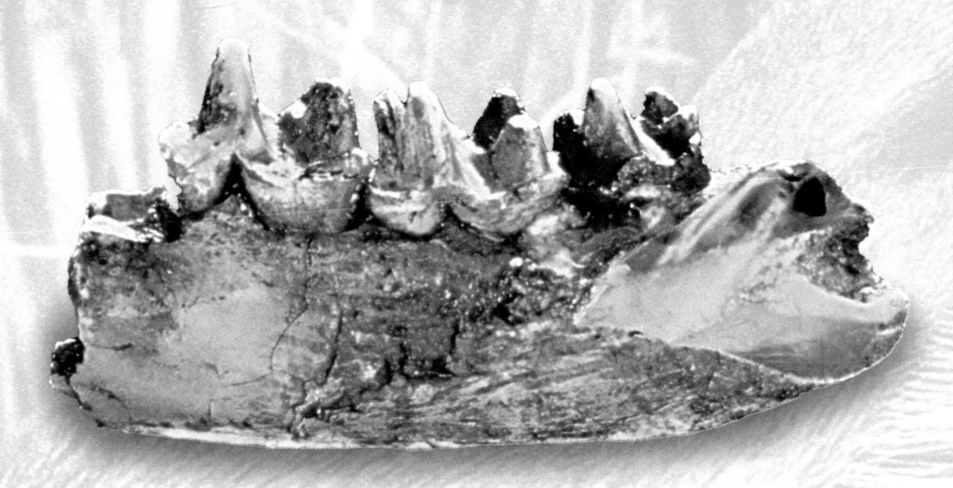

OPAL TEETH
This fossil is a jaw fragment of an early Cretaceous mammal from Australia. The teeth have features that link the creature to egg-laying mammals (monotremes) such as the living echidnas. After burial in sediment, the original bone material was dissolved away and the cavity infilled with opal, a silica mineral similar in composition to flint.

FIRST TRUE MAMMALS

Although early cynodonts such as *Adelobasileus* from North America or *Sinoconodon* from China may not be the direct ancestors of today's mammals, they tell us a lot about early mammalian history. However, the fossil remains of the American and Chinese specimens are incomplete, so scientists have used more recent mammals to deduce the probable lifestyle of these animals. *Megazostrodon,* found in southern Africa, was the size and shape of a shrew, small enough to curl up in a matchbox. Its body was long and low, with a flexible backbone and long limbs, which were held out to the side in a primitive squatting posture that is still assumed by some small mammals today.

SOUTH AFRICAN INSECT-EATER
Megazostrodon, from late Triassic strata in southern Africa, was 5 inches (12 centimeters) long. This insect-eating, shrewlike animal may have been nocturnal.

RATLIKE MAMMAL
Ptilodus was a primitive rodentlike mammal that lived in early Tertiary times in North America. It belonged to an extinct group of mammals called the multituberculates and probably ate nuts and seeds.

IDENTIFYING EARLY MAMMALS

Land is an inhospitable environment for the preservation of animal remains. Small vertebrates with delicate bones, such as the early mammals, were likely to have been eaten whole by scavengers. However, the fecal remains (coprolites) left by the scavengers sometimes contain undigested fragments of the animals they ate, especially teeth. The fossil record of small mammals is thus mostly made up of their teeth and bits of their jawbones. Fortunately, the pattern of cusps, ridges, and furrows on the surface of mammalian cheek teeth changed rapidly over time and is distinctive for each species. Consequently, even though there is an almost complete lack of skeletal remains of these early mammals, it is possible to identify the different species on the basis of their teeth alone.

DENTAL RECONSTRUCTION
A single tooth is all that remains of this earliest mammalian primate, *Purgatorius*. Found in late Cretaceous rocks in Montana, the tooth belonged to an insect-eater, about 4 inches (10 centimeters) long. The reconstruction above is based on an understanding of other primitive primates.

The skeleton of another animal, *Morganucodon*, also showed how the first true mammals lived. *Morganucodon* grew to a length of 6 inches (15 centimeters) and was found in early Jurassic strata in both England and China. It reflected all the mammalian traits of *Adelobasileus* but had a more advanced ear structure.

The teeth of *Morganucodon*, in particular, were typically mammalian. The juvenile milk teeth were followed by a single set for adult life, unlike reptiles whose teeth are replaced several times in a lifetime. The cheek teeth were also developed into premolars and molars, as in all later mammals. Chewing involved a triangular movement of the lower jaw rather than the simpler up and down, back and forth movement of the advanced cynodonts. The teeth suggest that *Morganucodon* was carnivorous, probably feeding on insects and worms at night, when predatory lizards were less active.

The morganucodonts were agile animals capable of fast movement but not sustained running. Their nocturnal habits required them to generate body heat internally. This was achieved by means of their teeth and jaws, which worked to break down food before it reached the stomach, allowing the rapid release of energy from a high-protein diet. To conserve body heat during the night, they would have needed a covering of hair, but so far the fossil record has not revealed this critical soft-tissue evidence. As a group, these small mammals survived for 40 million years.

Altogether within the Mesozoic era, while the dinosaurs dominated the land, 20 or more families of mammals evolved to live in a hidden coexistence with the massive reptiles.

MONGOLIAN PLACENTAL MAMMAL
One of the earliest placental mammals (which could bear well-developed live young) was *Zalambdalestes* (above). This shrewlike animal lived in Mongolia in late Cretaceous times and, like the living elephant shrew, had long back legs.

ELEPHANT SHREW
The fossil record of *Elephantulus* (right) and other elephant shrews extends back to early Tertiary times. They used to be regarded as primitive insectivores, but surprisingly they are closer related to the elephants.

Early Cretaceous Period

THE BREAK-UP OF THE SUPERCONTINENT OF PANGEA LED TO DIVERGENT ANIMAL AND PLANT DEVELOPMENT ON LANDMASSES SEPARATED BY BROAD SEAS.

By 130 million years ago, the North Atlantic had started to open up, breaking North America and Europe apart, although a link was probably maintained in northerly regions for another 25 million years. As Pangea fragmented, Africa and South America also began to pull apart, starting the formation of the Central and South Atlantic. The Tethys Ocean extended westward until an east-west tropical marine corridor divided North America and Eurasia in the north from Gondwana in the south, shutting down the exchange of animals and plants.

CHALK CLIFFS
The cliffs of southern England and northern France are formed from Cretaceous limestone, made of tiny skeletons of planktonic organisms called coccoliths.

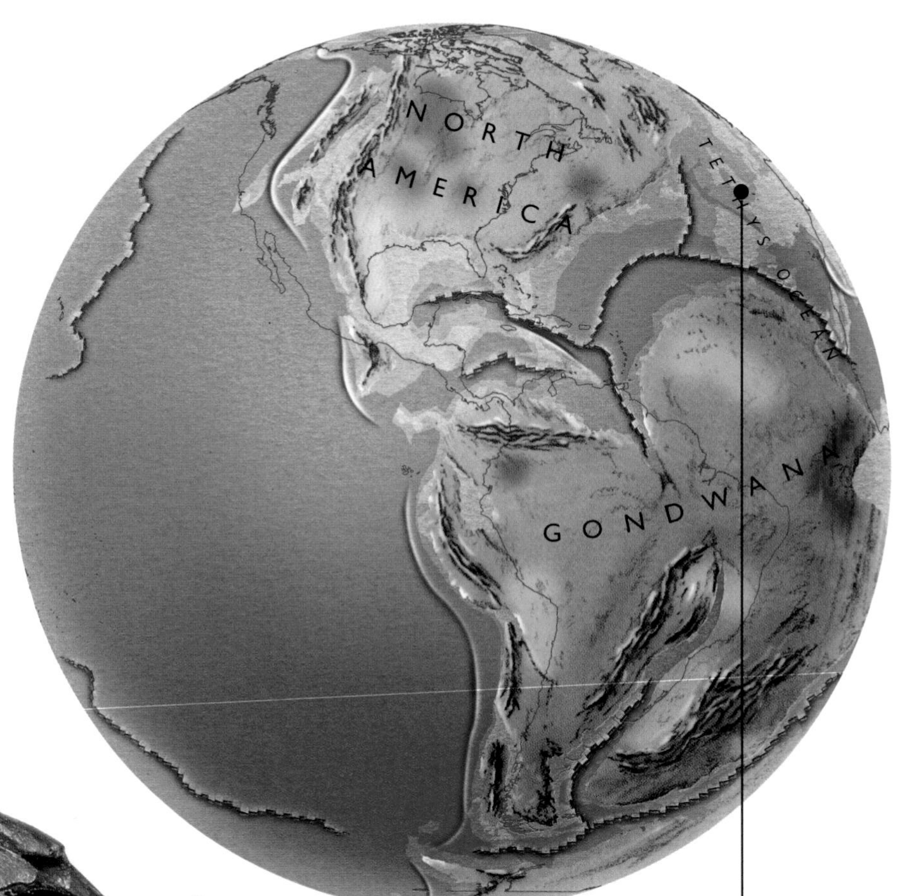

RING OF FIRE

Along the western margin of the Americas a great volcanic mountain chain developed, extending from Chile to Alaska. It survives today as the eastern flank of the Pacific Ring of Fire. During early Cretaceous times, these mountains formed a fertile ground for the evolution of terrestrial life.

The level of carbon dioxide in the Earth's atmosphere was high, producing warm, dry global climates in a greenhouse effect. Sea levels, which had been falling from a late Jurassic high, rose rapidly as temperatures increased and the polar icecaps melted, flooding great areas of the continents with shallow seas, especially in North America, southern Europe, and Antarctica. These shelf seas abounded with marine life, including reefs with rich populations of fish, preyed upon by large marine reptiles and sharks. Vegetation was gradually changing. As early Mesozoic ferns declined, more modern types of ferns became dominant. Seed-ferns, cycads, ginkgos, and the older groups of conifers were in decline, being replaced by cedars and redwoods. Most important for the future was the appearance

IGUANODON SKULL
The beaklike snout and long rows of similar-shaped cheek teeth show that this early Cretaceous ornithopod dinosaur, *Iguanodon*, was a plant-eater. This iguanodon lived on what is now the Isle of Wight, in southern England, when sea levels were lower than those shown in these maps.

NEW LIFEFORMS

Recent fossil finds show that the Cretaceous was a period of remarkable biological innovation. While the reptiles continued to dominate, other fauna developed new forms. Fossils from China, Mongolia, and Spain have shown that several groups of toothed birds evolved in the early Cretaceous age. Small, primitive mammals also diversified. Most of the birds and many of the mammals were wiped out in the mass extinction at the end of the Cretaceous period, along with the dinosaurs. But enough survived to provide the basis for the evolution of modern terrestrial life.

PARROT-JAW DINOSAUR
The parrotlike, toothless beak and jaws of *Psittacosaurus*, a ceratopsian dinosaur from early Cretaceous strata in Mongolia, were adapted for eating tough plant material. A bony ridge on top of the rear of the skull subsequently evolved into the bony frill that protected the neck of later ceratopsians.

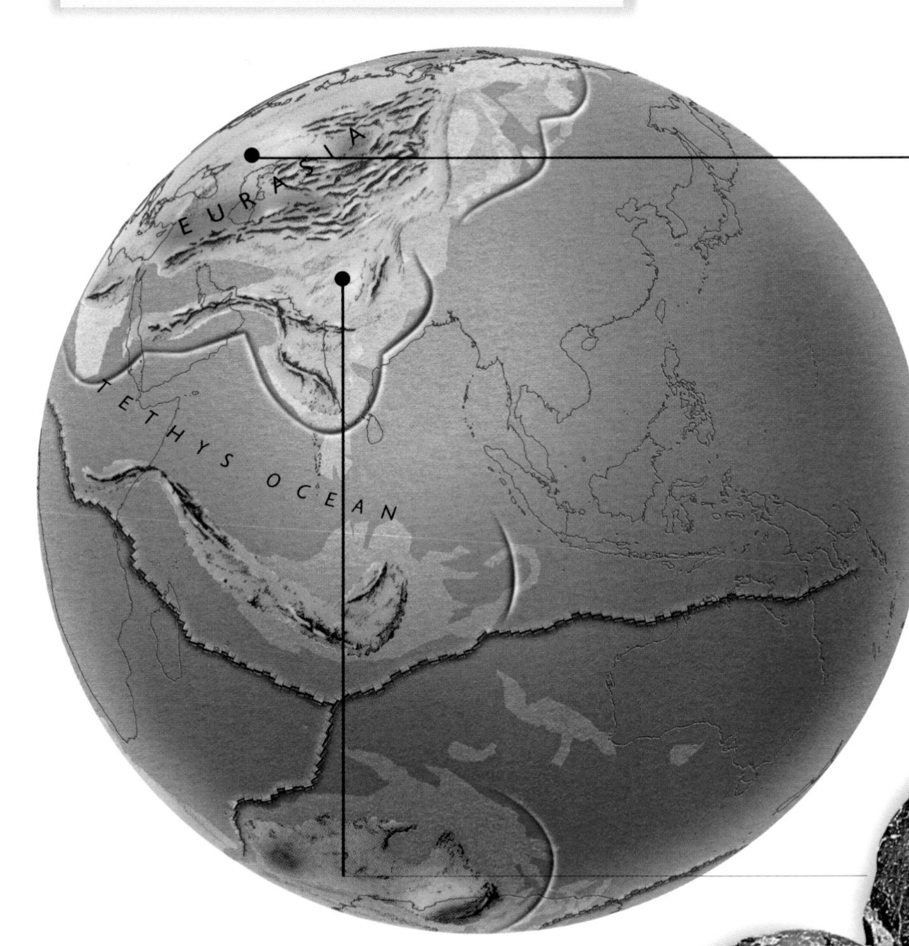

of angiosperms, the flowering plants that dominate and color modern landscapes. The air was buzzing with flying reptiles, birds, and ever-growing numbers of insects. The insects and the angiosperm plants benefited mutually from the development of flowers and pollen.

The dinosaurs continued to dominate the land while small mammals became increasingly diverse and numerous. Dinosaurs such as *Iguanodon* and some hypsilophodonts (a group of swift, bipedal, plant-eaters) were able to migrate from Europe to North America in earliest Cretaceous times. But as the link between the continents was broken, by mid-Cretaceous times, the dinosaur groups diverged. In North America, a massive hypsilophodont called *Tenontosaurus* became dominant among the ornithopods (plant-eating dinosaurs that predominantly walked on two legs). In Europe, the ornithopod group called iguanodonts continued to thrive.

NORTH-SOUTH DIVIDE

Tetrapod faunas in the northern and southern hemispheres also began to show marked differences. In the north, the number of species of sauropods (giant plant-eating dinosaurs) and stegosaurs declined. Concurrently, the armored ankylosaurs and the iguanodonts increased in diversity and numbers, and the first ceratopsian dinosaurs, such as *Psittacosaurus*, appeared. By contrast, in the southern hemisphere the sauropods remained the dominant plant-eaters.

DINOSAUR EGGS
The tough mineralized shells of some dinosaur eggs, like these Cretaceous eggs from China, have been preserved in nest clutches similar to those laid by turtles and crocodiles today. These eggs are 5 inches (13 centimeters) in diameter.

The World of the Iguanodon Dinosaur

One of the world's most exciting fossil finds was made by two Belgian coalminers in 1878. Working in the Sainte-Barbe pit near Bernissart, southwest Belgium, they found complete skeletons of large plant-eating dinosaurs. The skeletons all belonged to *Iguanodon*, a dinosaur that had already been named on the basis of fragmentary remains.

FAST-MOVING HERBIVORE
The bipedal *Hypsilophodon* was a small 5-foot- (1.5-meter-) long fast-running, gazellelike herbivore. In the early Cretaceous, it lived in Europe and North America.

RECONSTRUCTING IGUANODON

Excavation of the find was handed over to the scientists of the Royal Museum of Natural History in Brussels, led by Louis De Pauw and Louis Dollo. The problem the Belgian scientists faced was how to rebuild the skeletons in their original life positions. The structure of the hip bones and hind legs was distinctly birdlike, so Dollo and De Pauw used an emu skeleton as a model. But they also realized that *Iguanodon* had important differences from birds, especially in its long muscular tail, strong forearms, wrists, and hands. To account for these features, they also used a kangaroo as a model. They ended up with a cross between a kangaroo and a flightless bird—an upright bipedal dinosaur with a birdlike neck and a tail resting on the ground. This model has been radically revised in the late 20th century. Evidence suggests that *Iguanodon* was primarily four-legged. Although its forearms were significantly shorter than its hind limbs, they were powerful, with strong wrists. The middle three fingers of the large hands could be splayed into a weight-supporting foot for walking. The tail bones of *Iguanodon* were actually strapped together by bonelike ligaments that would have made the tail stiff—it could not have been flexed as the kangaroo-based model devised by Dollo

THUMB SPIKE

On the end of its thumb, Iguanodon *had a sharp, bony spike that might have formed a very effective weapon against predators. In the earliest reconstructions of* Iguanodon, *the thumb spike was mistakenly seen as a rhinoceros-like nose horn.*

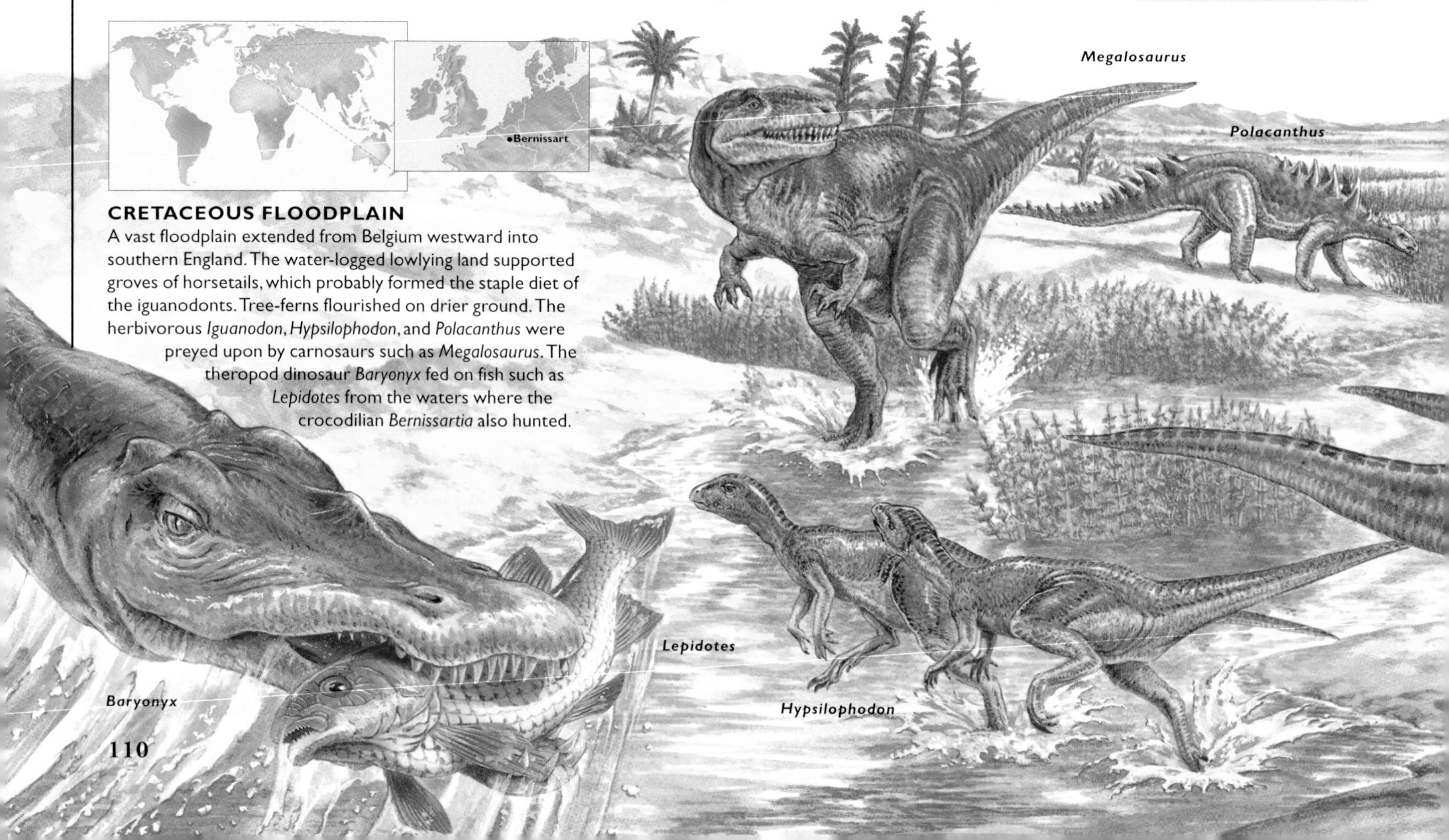

CRETACEOUS FLOODPLAIN
A vast floodplain extended from Belgium westward into southern England. The water-logged lowlying land supported groves of horsetails, which probably formed the staple diet of the iguanodonts. Tree-ferns flourished on drier ground. The herbivorous *Iguanodon*, *Hypsilophodon*, and *Polacanthus* were preyed upon by carnosaurs such as *Megalosaurus*. The theropod dinosaur *Baryonyx* fed on fish such as *Lepidotes* from the waters where the crocodilian *Bernissartia* also hunted.

and De Pauw required. Young *Iguanodons* were probably more likely to stand on two legs, while the much heavier adults usually walked on four legs, only raising themselves on their hind legs for feeding, fighting, and mating.

Iguanodon was large, about 2 tons in weight, and needed to be an efficient feeder. A herbivore, its food consisted of cycads, horsetails, and conifers, plants tough to chew and low in nutrition. To break down the coarse cellulose fibers for digestion, herbivores need powerful jaw muscles and strong cheek teeth to grind the plant material up as much as possible before swallowing it. The front of *Iguanodon*'s jaws lacked teeth but were covered with a turtlelike horny beak, ideally suited for cropping vegetation. Cheek teeth formed parallel, interlocking rows of about 100 leaf-shaped teeth with serrated edges. Using its flexible mouth, *Iguanodon* could grind its upper teeth from side to side against its lower ones.

TRIASSIC SURVIVOR
Crocodylus, the modern crocodile, is a survivor of a reptile group that originated in the late Triassic age. Dinosaur reconstructions were orginally based on crocodiles, until it was determined that many dinosaurs were either two-legged, or simply too big to maintain a lizardlike posture.

LIVING ALONGSIDE IGUANODON

Hypsilophodon, another plant-eating, "bird-footed" (ornithopod) dinosaur, existed alongside *Iguanodon* in early Cretaceous times. Surprisingly, this small bipedal animal was highly successful. It used to be thought that *Hypsilophodon* lived in trees because one specimen had a foot that appeared to have a birdlike, "perching" toe on the back of the foot. This reconstruction was later found to be incorrect, and other features show that *Hypsilophodon* was built for speed and agility. It was the dinosaur equivalent of today's gazelle. Another herbivore was the four-legged *Polacanthus,* which used armor for defense.

The top predators of the time were carnosaurs (meat-eating dinosaurs), although not much is known about them. British strata of this age have also produced evidence of a large fish-eating theropod dinosaur, *Baryonyx*. The lakes and rivers of the locality were populated with turtles (*Plesiochelys*) and crocodiles (*Bernissartia*), as well as fish, clams, and snails.

Inventing and Picturing the Dinosaurs

Dinosaurs have taken the place of the dragons and monsters of myth and legend, playing an enduring role in the modern imagination. These terrible lizards were a 19th-century invention of the newly emerging science of paleontology. As icons of popular science, they have gone through a number of transformations over the years, before ending up as the fleet-footed, colorful creatures depicted in dinosaur books and movies today.

The story starts some time before 1818, when part of a fossil jawbone with large, bladelike teeth was found in the mid-Jurassic strata of Oxfordshire, England. It was estimated that *Megalosaurus*, as the dinosaur was named, would have stood about 8 feet (2.5 meters) high. Further puzzling fossil bones were unearthed in 1825 in lower Cretaceous limestone. Naturalists of the time, such as Gideon Mantell, were puzzled by these fossils and had little idea about the real shape of the animal. It was clear from the size of the fossil remains that they were dealing with a gigantic land reptile, but living lizards, such as the iguana and crocodiles, were the only models that these early investigators had. Mantell imagined *Iguanodon*, as he called it, as a four-legged and lizardlike creature with a very long tail.

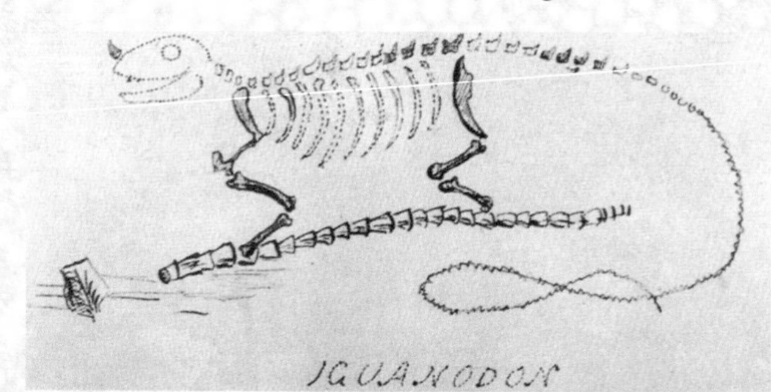

FIRST DRAFT
This unpublished sketch of 1833 (above) by Gideon Mantell was the first attempt to reconstruct the dinosaurs. Mantell had only a very incomplete jumble of bones of his new *Iguanodon* fossil and mistakenly positioned the thumb spike as a rhinoceros-like horn.

IGUANID ROLE MODEL
The living iguana lizard (left) provided the model for the first attempts to reconstruct a dinosaur. But growing to only a few feet long, it is not possible that the iguanas are just a miniature version of much larger dinosaurs, such as *Iguanodon*.

JURASSIC PARK

Michael Crichton's novel and Steven Spielberg's film of Jurassic Park *have played an important part in changing the popular perception of dinosaurs. Their reputation as dim-witted, cold-blooded, and slow-moving creatures has now been reassessed, with studies of their living habits and behavior showing that they were as diverse as mammals.*

In the film, the predatory, carnivorous velociraptors are portrayed as aggressive fast-running creatures, capable of intelligent thought and displaying acute senses. In a frightening chase scene, a Tyrannosaurus rex *nearly outruns a jeep. Quite a few of the dinosaurs featured in the film are, however, actually Cretaceous, rather than Jurassic, in age.*

CELLULOID STEGOSAURS
In an early scene from the film *Jurassic Park: The Lost World*, two enormous, plated stegosaurs make their first appearance crossing a dry river bed.

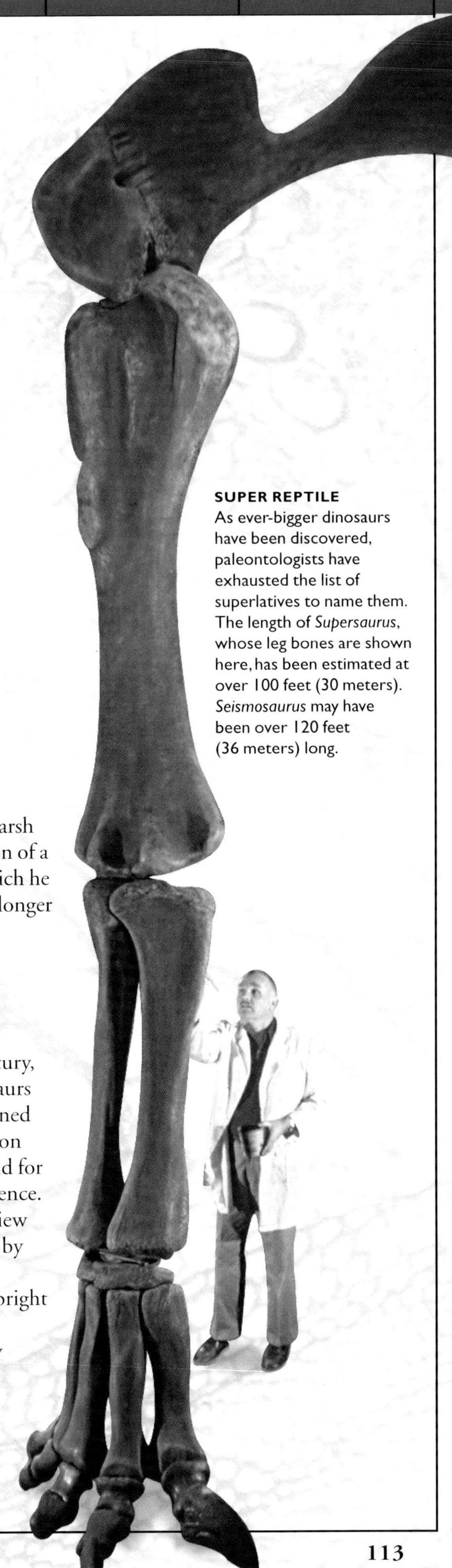

SUPER REPTILE
As ever-bigger dinosaurs have been discovered, paleontologists have exhausted the list of superlatives to name them. The length of *Supersaurus*, whose leg bones are shown here, has been estimated at over 100 feet (30 meters). *Seismosaurus* may have been over 120 feet (36 meters) long.

DINOSAURS ARE NAMED

The name dinosaur was first coined in 1842 by a British professor of anatomy, Richard Owen. He advocated the creation of a whole new division of animals—the class Dinosauria—to distinguish anatomically between recently discovered fossil reptiles and known living reptiles.

Owen's vision of the dinosaurs was a huge popular success, and by the 1860s dinosaur research had taken off in a big way in the United States. America had already been the site of a major discovery. In 1802, some fossil footprints were uncovered on a farm in Massachusetts. Edward Hitchcock, a local naturalist, claimed that the curious three-toed footprints must have been made by giant birds. In fact, they had been made by a dinosaur. The discovery was the first evidence that some dinosaurs walked on two rather than four legs, although the right connection was not finally made until 70 years later.

In the 1870s, the United States was the scene of the "dinosaur wars"—a bitter rivalry between two experts, Professor Othniel Charles Marsh of Yale University and Edward Drinker Cope of Philadelphia. Their competing expeditions led to the discovery and description of some 130 new species of dinosaur. In 1883, Marsh produced the first reconstruction of a giant plant-eating dinosaur, which he called *Brontosaurus* (a name no longer used). The image of these huge sauropods captured public imagination the world over.

REVAMPING THE IMAGE

In the first half of the 20th century, the popular image of the dinosaurs was as slow-moving, small-brained creatures, a byword for extinction through the failure to adapt, and for lumbering size without intelligence. In the 1960s, however, a new view of the dinosaurs was promoted by Dr. Robert Bakker and others. Intelligent, diverse, arrayed in bright colors and patterns, the new dinosaurs were shown as highly successful creatures whose extinction is still interestingly problematic. These new dinosaurs have proved even more popular than the old.

Later Cretaceous Period

OCEANIC CHANGES DURING THE MID- AND LATE CRETACEOUS LED TO A HOTHOUSE ENVIRONMENT IN WHICH LIFE CONTINUED TO DIVERSIFY RAPIDLY.

Approximately 100 million years ago, during the mid-Cretaceous, the movement of the Earth's crust was being driven by the opening up of new oceans in the southern hemisphere, such as the Southern Ocean and South Atlantic Ocean. These oceans and the formation of new ocean floor were in turn driven by changing convection patterns within the Earth's mantle.

Gondwana continued to break up. Madagascar split away from India, which then moved northward. New Zealand rifted from Australia as the Tasman Sea opened. In the Far East, the final collision of landmasses such as Tibet and Southeast Asia formed new mountain belts and completed the eastern margin of Eurasia. In Europe, the northward rifting of the Atlantic opened the Bay of Biscay and split Britain, Labrador, and Newfoundland, followed by the separation of Norway and Greenland.

OCEANIC CHANGES

Geological evidence points toward an unusually high rate of volcanic activity during the mid-Cretaceous, especially at mid-ocean ridges. Ridge systems rose high above the old ocean depths and lifted the neighboring deep ocean floors with them. As a result, sea levels rose worldwide up to 650 feet (200 meters) higher than present levels, causing worldwide flooding. Sea levels had fallen again by the end of the Cretaceous.

Ocean water temperatures saw a sharp rise, fall, and partial rise again before falling toward the end of the period. These changes were prompted by fluctuating patterns of ocean circulation as the continents moved apart. Periods of rapid ocean warming (and oxygen depletion) appear to have caused extinctions among marine life.

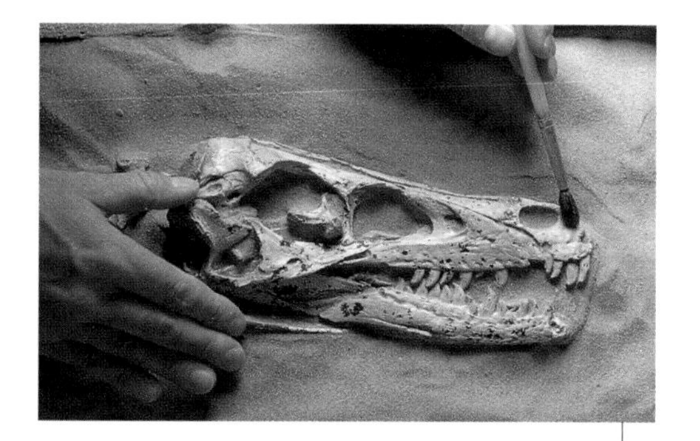

VELOCIRAPTOR SKULL
A small late Cretaceous dinosaur whose remains have been found in Mongolia, *Velociraptor*'s large eye sockets and sharp curved teeth are typical of a highly active carnivore.

TYRANNOSAURUS REX
Tyrannosaurids such as *T. rex* were at large in North America and Central Asia during the late Cretaceous. This photograph of a *T. rex* skull amply depicts the curved and serrated bladelike teeth.

300 MA | 250 MA | 200 MA | 150 MA | 95 MA | 50 MA | PRESENT DAY

MAIASAURA
This fossil of a hadrosaur hatchling was found in Montana. It is so small that, for survival, its parents must have cared for it just as adult birds look after their chicks. Parental care is reflected in the dinosaur's name which means "good mother."

HOTHOUSE SHIFT

Extensive submarine volcanic activity during the mid-Cretaceous period released massive amounts of carbon dioxide into the ocean and atmosphere. This caused warming due to the greenhouse effect. In fact, the mid-Cretaceous was perhaps the warmest episode of Earth's entire history. As global warming peaked, temperate forest vegetation spread to high latitudes, shifting more than 1,250 miles (2,000 kilometers) from the equator toward the poles.

PACIFIC OCEAN

AUSTRALIA

ANTARCTICA

SOUTH AMERICA

INDIA

AFRICA

LIFE DURING THE MID- TO LATE CRETACEOUS

Dinosaurs continued to diversify and dominate the land. Theropods of the mid- and late Cretaceous ranged from the huge tyrannosaurids such as *T. rex* and smaller predators such as *Deinonychus* and *Velociraptor* to the ostrichlike ornithomimosaurs. Also in evidence were duck-billed hadrosaurs such as *Maiasaura*, ankylosaurs, and ceratopsians such as *Triceratops.*

The organisms that dominate our modern terrestrial ecosystems, the flowering plants, birds, and mammals, underwent explosive growth in species diversity in the mid-Cretaceous hothouse. Mammals ranged from shrew- to cat-sized, and were mainly nocturnal. The earliest angiosperms (flowering plants) were very probably shrubby weeds. In time they increased in range and variety, filling in as smaller trees beneath the forest canopy of conifers. Flora of the late Cretaceous included figs, willows, poplars, magnolias, and plane trees. Insects diversified rapidly worldwide in parallel with the spread of the angiosperms.

In the water, the top predators were a group of massive, flippered lizards known as mosasaurs. Plesiosaurs and the giant turtle *Archelon* roamed the oceans, and the first teleost fishes (today's dominant fish group) appeared. Ammonites, bivalves such as clams, and gastropods became widespread. Marine planktonic microorganisms flourished and the accumulation of their remains in seabed sediments laid down the hydrocarbon basis for much of the world's present oil supply.

CLAM FOSSILS
Trigoniid clams were common in the warm waters of the Tethys Ocean in Mesozoic times. Their strong, ribbed shells protected them against battering waves. One tropical group of trigoniids has survived to the present day.

The Mammals and Dinosaurs of Mongolia

The remote deserts of Mongolia, in the heart of central Asia, have produced some of the most exciting fossil finds of the 20th century. In Cretaceous times, Mongolia was often swept by desert dust storms that buried the remains of hundreds of lizards, mammals, and dinosaurs in the sandstone hills. The fossil skeletons are often complete, with even the smallest, most delicate bones preserved. They provide fascinating, if often controversial, evidence about life around 90 million years ago.

During the latter part of Cretaceous times, two groups of bird-hipped (ornithischian) dinosaurs, the hadrosaurids and the ceratopsians, evolved new species and spread across the globe. This is reflected in the wide range of dinosaur fossils found in Mongolia, which also include many reptile-hipped (saurischian) dinosaurs, such as theropods, dromaeosaurs, and oviraptors.

MONGOLIAN MORTUARY
The arid deserts of Mongolia have revealed some of the richest dinosaur-bearing strata known. Thousands of specimens have been recovered from these Mesozoic deposits over the last 80 years.

"EGG-STEALER" DINOSAUR

The most famous reptile-hipped dinosaur fossil discovered in Mongolia is *Oviraptor philoceratops*, identified and named in the 1920s by Roy Chapman Andrews. A lightly built, two-legged dinosaur, it was originally thought to prey on the eggs of the ceratopsian dinosaur *Protoceratops*—hence its name, *Oviraptor*, or "egg-stealer." Since the remains of an *Oviraptor philoceratops* was found within what was believed to be a *Protoceratops* nest, Andrews jumped to the conclusion that it had died while feeding on the eggs. Recent research has shown, however, that the *Oviraptor* does not live up to its name. Using new techniques to examine the fossilized embryos inside the eggs, experts have revealed that the embryos belonged to the *Oviraptor*. In other words, the *Oviraptor* died sitting on its own nest.

MONGOLIAN DUST STORM
Predators such as *Velociraptor* and the large tyrannosaurid *Tarbosaurus* would attack other dinosaurs, including plant-eaters such as *Oviraptor* and *Gallimimus*. The ceratopsian *Protoceratops* laid eggs on the ground in mud-mound nests. The peculiar one-fingered dinosaur *Mononykus* had powerful, short forelimbs. At the time, small mammals, such as *Zalambdalestes*, *Kennalestes*, and *Kamptobaatar* seemed insignificant, but their descendants would take over after the dinosaurs had gone.

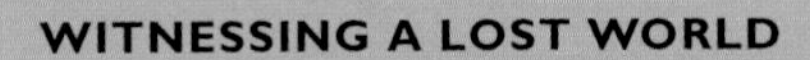

WITNESSING A LOST WORLD

Excavating Mongolia's fossil riches has been an exciting experience for paleontologists. In 1994, an expedition from the American Museum of Natural History found the well-preserved remains of more than 500 Cretaceous animals in the hills of Ukhaa Tolgod. The expedition's leader, Professor Michael Novacek, has written: "It was almost as if we had stumbled upon a giant graveyard where, just a few moments before, these animals had given their last gasp. It was as close as we will ever come to stepping back in time, walking into that world, and seeing a community of extinct animals..."

LIVING IN THE DINOSAURS' SHADOW

Although the dinosaurs still dominated the land in late Cretaceous times, small mammals were increasing in number and diversity. There were four types of mammal: placentals (whose young are born reasonably mature), marsupials (the young are born immature and nourished in a pouch), monotremes (egg-layers), and a group that is now extinct, multituberculates.

The multituberculates were at the time by far the most abundant type of mammal. They were probably plant-eaters, in contrast to placentals, marsupials, and monotremes, who were insect-eaters. It was once thought that multituberculates were tree-climbers, but Mongolian forms, such as *Nemegtbaatar*, have an anatomy close to that of living gerbils. It is now believed that they were nocturnal animals, adapted for running and burrowing rather than tree-climbing.

Examination of a well-preserved pelvis of another of the Mongolian multituberculates, *Kryptobaatar*, has proved that these creatures gave birth to live young, rather than laying eggs like the monotremes. The young must have been very undeveloped at birth, like those of the marsupials, because the creature's birth canal was very small. Looking after such helpless young would have been a further reason for living in a burrow, which could be used as a nursery.

The multituberculates died out only about 35 million years ago, in the late Eocene age. The placental mammals, represented in late Cretaceous times by creatures such as the shrewlike, insect-eating *Kennalestes*, and the slightly larger *Zalambdalestes*, survived. A few marsupials and monotremes have also survived up to the present day, but the placentals have proved by a long way the most successful mammals. This probably reflects the advantages to be gained by giving birth to far more developed young.

CAREFUL HANDLING
Part of *Protoceratops*, a ceratopsian dinosaur, is carefully cleaned before being extracted from the rock matrix. Even large dinosaur bones need gentle handling to preserve them for the future.

Hadrosaurs and Carnosaurs

More than 300 dinosaur skeletons have been unearthed along the Red Deer River in Alberta, Canada, now the site of the Dinosaur Provincial Park. Upper Cretaceous sediment, around 75 million years old, was exposed by the erosive power of meltwaters pouring out of the retreating glaciers some 13,000 years ago. No other rocky landscape of similar size on Earth has produced as many individual skeletons of different dinosaurs, including a wealth of late Cretaceous hadrosaurs (herbivores with a ducklike beak and webbed feet) and carnosaurs (bipedal carnivores).

The original discovery was made in 1909 when a rancher from Alberta, Canada, told the famous dinosaur collector, Barnum Brown of the American Museum of Natural History, that some bones discovered on his ranch were similar to those on display in the museum. Brown wasted no time and immediately established a camp alongside the Red Deer River. He worked the area from 1910 to 1915, recovering a spectacular variety of unusually complete skeletons with skulls. The sedimentary strata in Dinosaur Provincial Park represent a rich variety of environments, from offshore through foreshore, barrier, lagoon, swamp, and delta to river channel and floodplain. And the fossils from within these strata reflect the diversity of Cretaceous life. The total number of fossils found includes an astonishing 300 articulated large skeletons, representing 36 species of dinosaur and another 84 species of other vertebrates, including fish, amphibians (salamanders and frogs), reptiles (turtles, lizards, crocodiles, and pterosaurs), birds, and mammals. These specimens are currently exhibited in museums around the world.

UNEARTHING A GIANT
The rare find of a complete tyrannosaurid skull and some bones is painstakingly excavated by a team of paleontologists.

THE DINOSAUR ROLL CALL

A plentiful water supply produced lush vegetation in the area in Cretaceous times, allowing plant-eating hadrosaurs to flourish, including *Corythosaurus* and *Lambeosaurus,* with their characteristic crested skulls. There are thin layers of chewed-up plant debris in the Cretaceous strata that have been

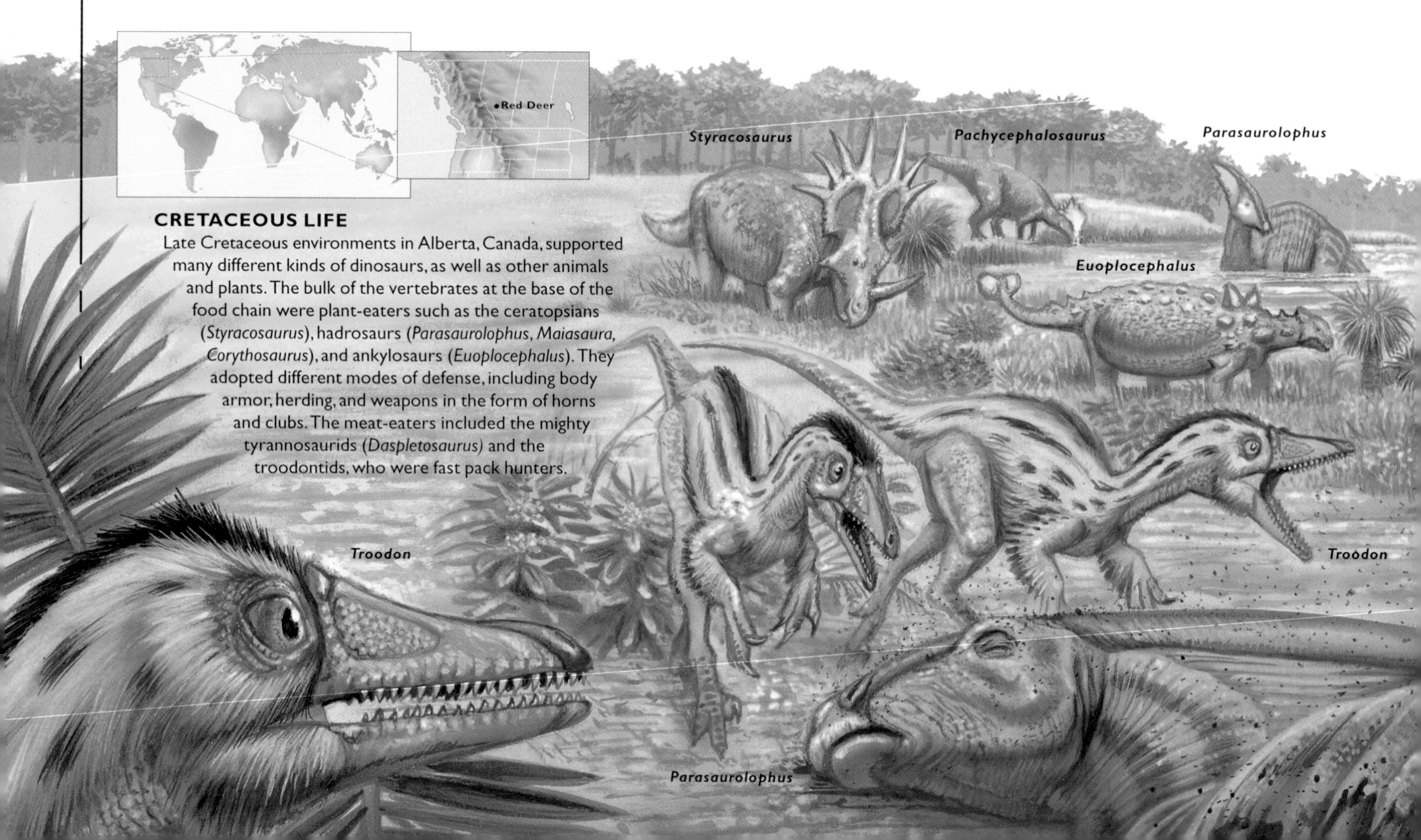

CRETACEOUS LIFE
Late Cretaceous environments in Alberta, Canada, supported many different kinds of dinosaurs, as well as other animals and plants. The bulk of the vertebrates at the base of the food chain were plant-eaters such as the ceratopsians (*Styracosaurus*), hadrosaurs (*Parasaurolophus, Maiasaura, Corythosaurus*), and ankylosaurs (*Euoplocephalus*). They adopted different modes of defense, including body armor, herding, and weapons in the form of horns and clubs. The meat-eaters included the mighty tyrannosaurids (*Daspletosaurus*) and the troodontids, who were fast pack hunters.

interpreted as dung from the herds of large herbivores. Most of the hadrosaurs and other ornithopod ("bird-footed") dinosaurs weighed over 2,200 pounds (1,000 kilograms), but the fauna also included some smaller dinosaurs, such as the ankylosaurs (armored dinosaurs), pachycephalosaurs (thick-headed dinosaurs), and hypsilophodonts.The latter were so small, at 22 to 220 pounds (10 to 100 kilograms), that they probably had high metabolic rates and needed high-energy, specialized plant diets. Likewise, the small mammals of the time must have consumed high-energy food such as fruits and seeds.

GIANT FLESH-EATERS

The most numerous of the carnivorous residents of the Red Deer area in Cretaceous times were *Troodon formosus,* a birdlike theropod, the dromaeosaur *Saurornitholestes langstoni*, and the tyrannosaurid *Gorgosaurus libratus*. The tyrannosaurids, "tyrant lizards," were the largest of the theropods, growing up to 46 feet (14 meters) long and standing over 18 feet (5.5 meters) high. These awesome creatures had enormous heads on short muscular necks, and stiff tails balanced on top of long, powerful legs. The tiny arms, with short, two-fingered hands, are puzzling as they seem to have been almost useless. They could not even reach as far as the mouth.

Tyrannosaurids have popularly been portrayed as fast runners, but recent discoveries suggest that they were not so speedy after all. English biologist Robin McNeil Alexander calculated from body weight, leg length, and gait, that *Tyrannosaurus rex* had a maximum speed of 19 miles (30 kilometers) per hour. Another specialist, the American Jim Farlow, has pointed out that if an animal of this height and weight tripped, its head would hit the ground hard enough to smash its skull. So large tyrannosaurids could not have run fast because of the risk of a fatal fall.

ARMORED DINOSAUR
Euoplocephalus was one of the largest ankylosaurs. Its skull was protected by bony plates and even its eyelids were armored. Bony spines and plates protected the back of the head, neck, and shoulders.

SCAVENGERS

Although the popular image of Tyrannosaurus rex *is as an actively hunting predator, this huge carnivore may in fact have been a scavenger that fed on carrion. Such a lifestyle would have required much less speed and involved less risk of injury. However, this is still an unsettled issue.*

The Beast of Maastricht

CHALK DEPOSITS, FORMED BY THE TINY calcareous skeletons of planktonic microorganisms, are particular features of the late Cretaceous period, especially in Europe. People have quarried this soft limestone rock for thousands of years in search of flints, and more recently the chalk has been worked for lime. All this mining activity has uncovered many spectacular fossils—none more impressive, however, than the "Beast of Maastricht," named for the town in Holland where it was found.

DISCOVERY
This engraving shows the discovery of a set of massive *M. hoffmani* jaws within a chalk mine in St. Pieter's Mount, Maastricht, in 1786. The find was to become a scientific sensation throughout Europe.

THE TERROR OF THE CRETACEOUS SEAS

The creature, *Mosasaurus hoffmani*, was one of the last and most advanced of the mosasaur marine reptiles. It was also the largest. The mosasaurs were a group of carnivorous lizards that had left land and returned to the sea, filling a niche left by the decline of the earlier predatory marine reptiles, the ichthyosaurs.

Mosasaurus hoffmani grew to over 50 feet (15 meters) in length and had enormous jaws. Its skull was stronger and more rigid than that of its ancestors. Its eyes were quite large, indicating relatively good sight, although its binocular vision was limited, so depth perception would have been poor. There are also indications that the animal's sense of smell was not particularly good.

The creature's jaws, which were lined with numerous large, curved, and serrated cone-shaped teeth, were powerful and effective. The jawbones had a flexible joint that helped absorb the impact and stress of biting large prey. The teeth's cutting edges were the most advanced of any marine reptile—each tooth crown had numerous cutting and crushing facets. The fearsome jaws and the huge size of the animal meant that most marine animals of the time were potential prey.

To add to these capabilities, *Mosasaurus hoffmani* was a fast swimmer. Propulsion was produced by side-to-side undulations of the tail, while the shape of the paddlelike limbs indicates that they were used as rudders to steer the massive body through the water.

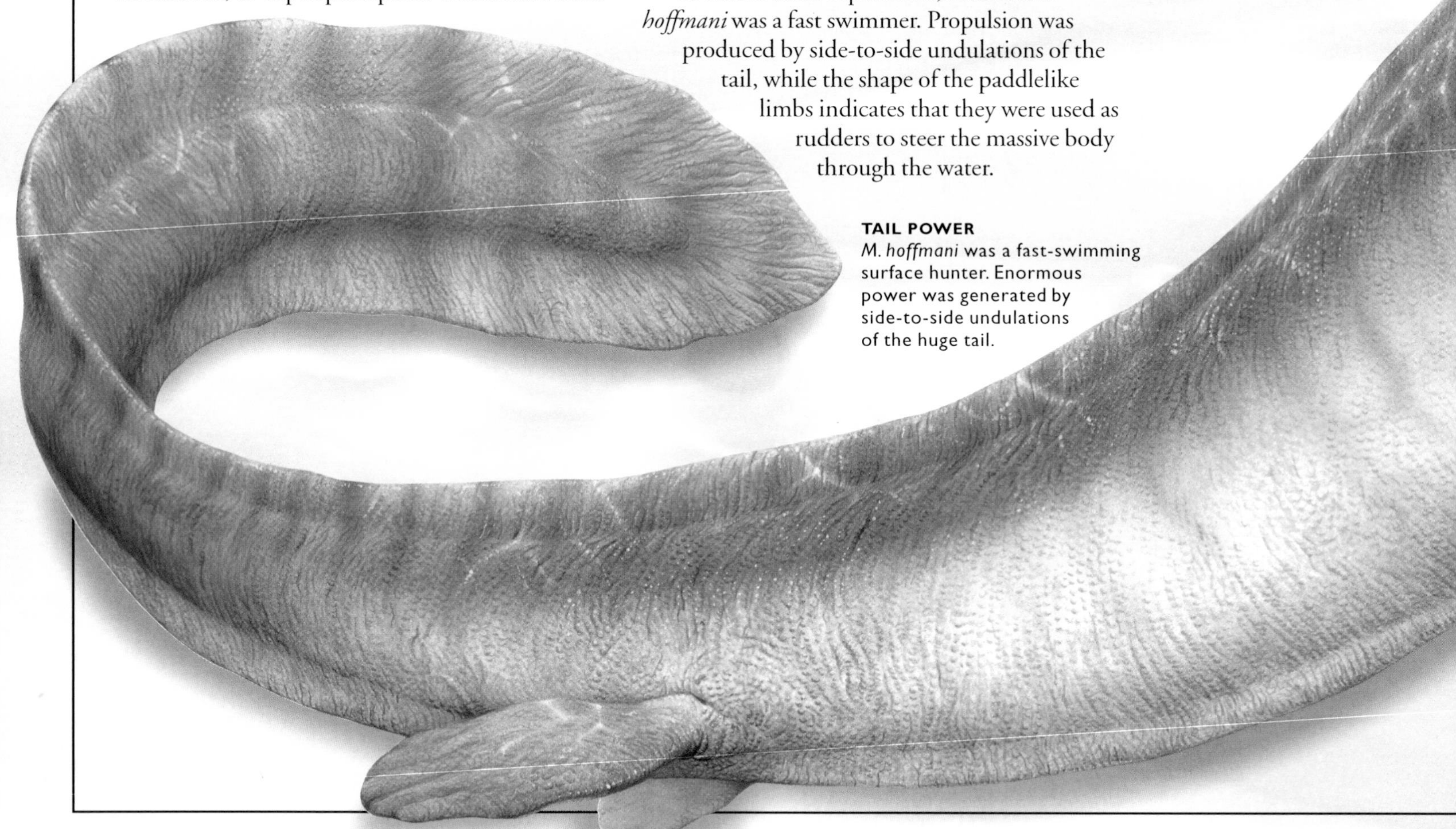

TAIL POWER
M. hoffmani was a fast-swimming surface hunter. Enormous power was generated by side-to-side undulations of the huge tail.

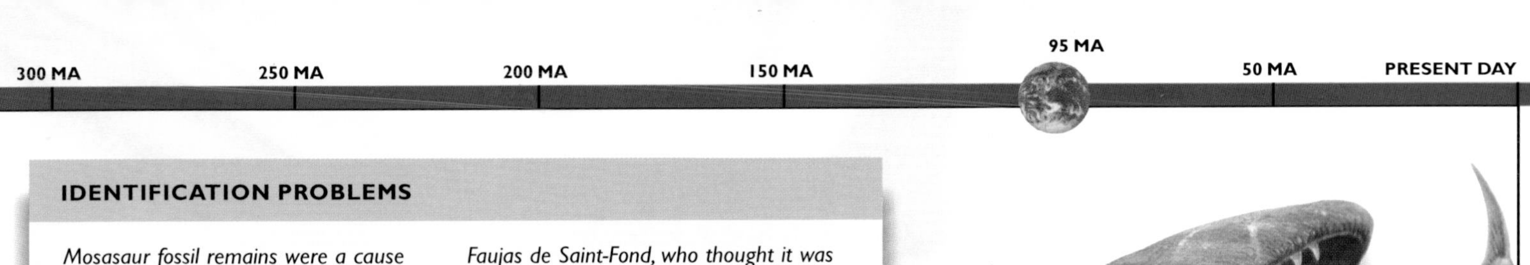

IDENTIFICATION PROBLEMS

Mosasaur fossil remains were a cause for some concern in the pre-Darwinian era, at a time when people had no idea that animals could become extinct. The initial concern, however, was over the animal's identity. Dutch naturalist Pieter Camper concluded in 1786 that it was a whale. His theory provoked further debate, especially with French scholar Faujas de Saint-Fond, who thought it was a crocodile. But in 1800, Camper's son, Adriaan, claimed that it was a giant lizard. He communicated his ideas to the French paleontologist Baron Georges Cuvier, who named the fossil Mosasaurus, *or "lizard from the River Meuse."*

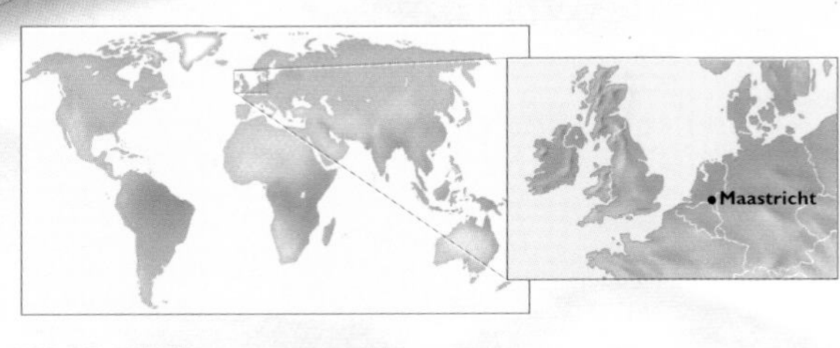

MORE JAWS
Although the "Grand Beast of Maastricht" referred to the single specimen discovered in 1786, with jaws more than 3 feet (1 meter) long, other large fossil jawbones had been discovered previously in the area. Since then, mosasaur jaws up to 5 feet (1.6 meters) in length have been found.

SHORT-LIVED PREDATOR

Tooth marks on a fossilized shell of the giant turtle *Allopleuron hoffmani* and healed jawbone fractures in a number of mosasaur fossil specimens show that they were indiscriminate predators. It has also been suggested that they engaged in potentially fatal male-to-male combat with other members of their own species. The fact that some of them survived jaw fractures shows they had an ability to recuperate rapidly, in much the same way that crocodiles do today.

As a group, these awesome animals spread successfully throughout the oceans of the late Cretaceous world, producing some gigantic forms and evolving into 20 different genera with some 70 species worldwide. But they had an extraordinarily brief existence of only about 25 million years, becoming extinct before the end of the Cretaceous age, about 65 million years ago. Their place in the world's oceans was soon taken up, during Tertiary times, by marine mammals.

WAR BOOTY
The actual jaws of the Maastricht beast, broken up by the process of fossilization, are held in the Natural History Museum in Paris. They were brought there in 1795 by Napoleon's troops.

The K-T Boundary

THE END OF THE CRETACEOUS HERALDED DRAMATIC CHANGES ON A GLOBAL SCALE, CULMINATING IN THE EXTINCTION OF MANY LIFEFORMS ON LAND AND SEA.

No dinosaur remains have been discovered in rocks younger than 65 million years old, the boundary between the Cretaceous and Tertiary periods. Along with their distant reptilian relatives the marine plesiosaurs, the mosasaurs, and the flying pterosaurs, dinosaurs had become extinct by the end of the Cretaceous, as had the most numerous fossil group of the Mesozoic era, the ammonites. By contrast, mammals and birds increased in abundance during Tertiary times. This dramatic turnover of animals was first recognized by scientists more than 100 years ago. The change in time periods is referred to as the K-T Boundary, K for Kreide (the German word for chalk) and T for Tertiary.

CLUES TO EXTINCTION

The cause of the K-T Boundary extinction was for many years a mystery. Then in the 1970s, an American geologist, Walter Alvarez, found significant traces of the element iridium in a thin clay layer that marks the exact boundary between sediments of Cretaceous and Tertiary times. This layer can be detected in many parts of Europe and North America. Iridium, one of the platinum metals, is found in meteorites and meteoric

BOUNDARY LAYER
The thin clay layer in this sequence of strata from Colorado marks the Cretaceous-Tertiary boundary. The clay is enriched with iridium from atmospheric fallout from the Chicxulub meteorite.

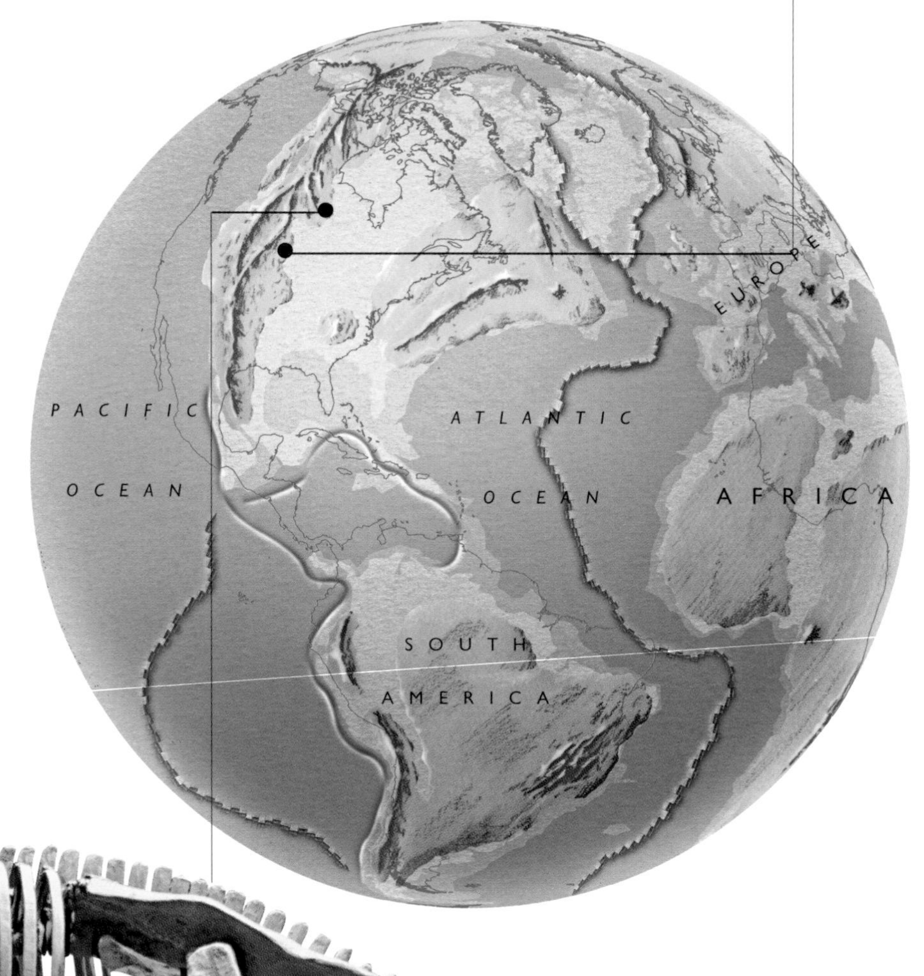

CHASMOSAURUS
This ceratopsian, from the Red Deer River in Alberta, had a bony extension to the back of the skull that was covered in skin. It may have been used for sexual display in males and for defense against predators. *Chasmosaurus* disappeared toward the end of the Cretaceous period.

TSUNAMI DEPOSIT

K-T Boundary sediments at Brazos River, Texas, contain an unusual hard sandy layer that is exactly at the boundary and clearly distinct from the softer sediments above and below. Some scientists think that the sand layer was deposited by a tsunami, a huge wave, set in motion by the Chicxulub impact 65 million years ago.

SHOCKED QUARTZ
Viewed in polarized light under a microscope, the crystal lattice of this quartz grain from Montana, has been distorted by pressure shock waves. Mineral grains of this kind are found in strata immediately above the K-T Boundary. They were shocked by the K-T impact and scattered over a wide area, along with molten glass drops called tektites, as part of the ejecta from the impact.

dust. Alvarez suggested that many changes occurring at the K-T Boundary had been precipitated by the impact of a large meteorite—an asteroid or comet.

Some scientists have suggested that the impact of such a collision could have had a catastrophic effect on the Earth's climate, throwing up dust and debris into the atmosphere that would have blotted out sunlight for several years and may have caused mass extinction. A buried crater that could have been the site of the K-T meteorite impact was eventually pinpointed at Chicxulub, in Yucatan, Mexico, extending many miles into the Gulf of Mexico.

MASSIVE VOLCANISM

Despite the coincidence of the meteorite impact with the K-T Boundary, it was not necessarily the primary cause of the extinctions. Plants do not show massive extinctions at the K-T Boundary, dinosaurs were declining gradually, and many environmentally sensitive animals, such as amphibians and turtles, survived with few losses.

There were also large-scale volcanic eruptions at the time, accompanied by the emission of huge quantities of carbon dioxide. This would have boosted global warming and promoted the extinction of plants and animals, especially on land. So this volcanic event may have caused a background wave of extinctions, with the meteorite impact then delivering the final blow.

THE DECCAN TRAPS
A river gorge cut into the Panna Hills in India exposes the plateau lava of the Deccan Traps. A deep "hot spot" in the Earth's mantle produced the outpouring of this basaltic lava during late Cretaceous times as India rifted from Madagascar. The accompanying volcanic fumes and emissions may have contributed to climatic change and mass extinctions.

The Last of the Dinosaurs

The end of the Cretaceous period was a critical time in the history of life, the point at which the dinosaurs and a wide range of other creatures disappeared forever. Many different theories have been put forward to explain the extinction of the dinosaurs ranging from disease to the effect of a large meteorite impact 65 million years ago. But there are no great fossil graveyards piled with bones to be found at the K-T Boundary between the Cretaceous and the Tertiary periods. When the fossil record of these times is examined in detail, the changeover is not as clear-cut as might be expected if extinction had been caused by a single catastrophic event.

DINOSAURS IN DECLINE

Several of the main dinosaur groups, such as the large herbivorous sauropods, ankylosaurs, and hypsilophodonts, were in decline before the end of the Cretaceous period. This can be clearly seen by comparing the fossil record of two sites in western North America, the 75-million-year-old Judith River sediments of southern Alberta, Canada, and the 65-million-year-old sediments of Hell Creek in northeastern Montana. The older Judith River sediments preserve 32 different kinds (genera) of dinosaur; the Hell Creek sediments, from the very end of the Cretaceous, preserve only 19 different kinds. This decrease in diversity suggests that dinosaurs were already in decline before the impact event.

The last dinosaurs found in North America included large herbivores such as the rhinoceros-like ceratopsians. But *Triceratops* (30 feet/9 meters long and up

TIMESCALE

Although the age of the dinosaurs ended abruptly, in geological timescales "abrupt" can mean as long as 100,000 years. It is not possible to tell from rocks whether the events causing the extinction took place over a few years or a much longer time period. Although a meteorite impact now seems to have played a major role, other factors also played their part in the extinction event.

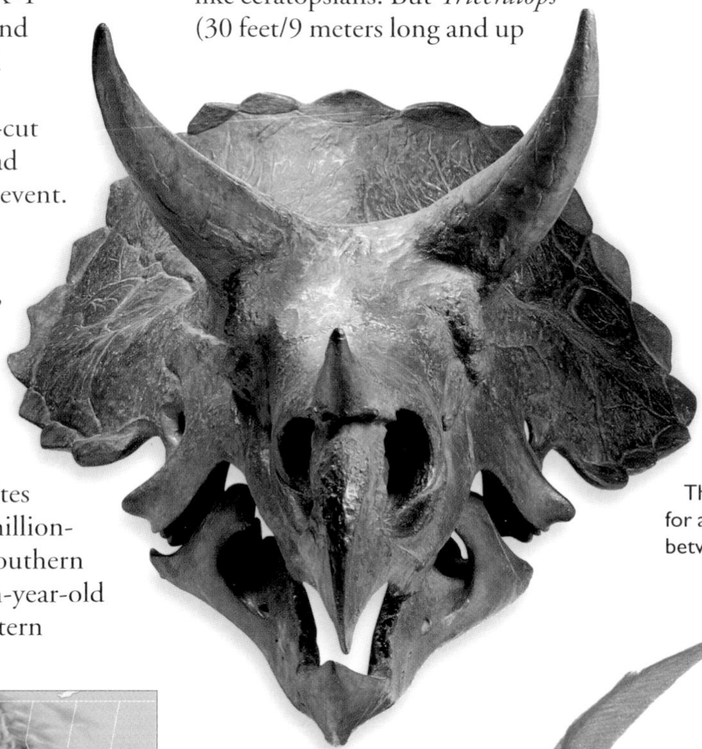

HORNED HERBIVORE

Triceratops, whose name means "three-horned face," roamed in herds across the west of North America. The horns and large neck frill were used for attack and defense in fights, most often between rival males for herd dominance.

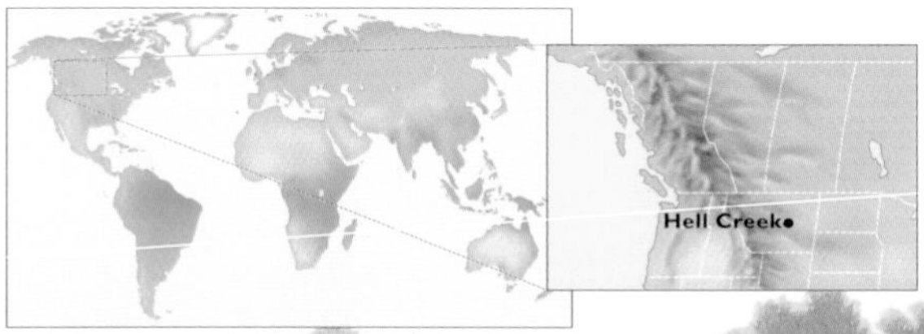

Hell Creek

LATE CRETACEOUS LIFE

The final stages of the Cretaceous in North America saw a great variety of animals living in a lush landscape of rivers and swamp. The horned *Triceratops*, the armored *Ankylosaurus*, and hadrosaurs such as *Edmontosaurus*, *Lambeosaurus*, and *Parasaurolophus* were all herbivores. The giant pterosaur *Quetzalcoatlus* had a wingspan of 40 feet (12 meters). None of these animals survived into Tertiary times, but many mammals did, including the primitive marsupial *Palaeoryctes*.

Quetzalcoatlus

Albertosaurus

Triceratops

Palaeoryctes

to 9 tons in weight) and *Torosaurus* (25 feet/7.6 meters long) were the only two out of five ceratopsians that persisted to the end of Cretaceous times. Likewise, there were only two "duck-billed" hadrosaurids (large bipedal/ quadrupedal plant-eaters with large, flat heads), *Anatotitan* and *Edmontosaurus*, at Hell Creek, compared with seven in the earlier Judith River strata.

The last of the smaller plant-eating dinosaurs included the spiny-skinned *Ankylosaurus*. This creature was armored, with heavy nodes and spikes of bone set in its leathery skin, and wielded a massive, bony club at the end of its tail. It was accompanied by *Stegoceras*, a thick-skulled, head-butting pachycephalosaurid ("thick-headed lizard") that grew to just over 6 feet (2 meters) long.

These were all bird-hipped (ornithischian) dinosaurs. The other major dinosaur group, the reptile-hipped saurischians, included the giant plant-eating sauropods and the predatory theropods. Sauropods had disappeared from most of North America by late Cretaceous times, although a few survivors existed elsewhere—for example, *Nemegtosaurus* in Mongolia. The theropods, by contrast, were flourishing, especially the tyrannosaurids. Not all of them were as large as *Tyrannosaurus rex*, which weighed in at up to 8 tons (elephants weigh up to 5 tons). *Albertosaurus* was about 2 tons and the smaller *Aublysodon* a mere 450 pounds (200 kilograms), which is similar to a modern-day adult male lion.

HELL CREEK
When the last dinosaurs roamed its landscape some 65 million years ago, Hell Creek (part of modern Montana) was situated on a coastal plain to the east of the Rockies.

Some theropod groups did decline in numbers and diversity during the last few million years of the Cretaceous period, notably the fleet-footed, ostrichlike ornithomimids, which grew to 13 feet (4 meters) long, including their long stiff tails. Only one of three ornithomimid genera persisted near to the end. Other small theropod dinosaurs, such as the active, fast-running predatory dromaeosaurids, *Dromaeosaurus* and *Velociraptor*, had disappeared by the end of the Cretaceous period.

Looking beyond the dinosaurs, flying reptiles were in steep decline by the late Cretaceous, and so were marine reptiles. The ichthyosaurs and plesiosaurs died out long before K-T times. A change was already well under way when Earth was struck by a meteorite 65 million years ago.

Impact from Outer Space

At the end of the Cretaceous period, 65 million years ago, a massive object crashed into Earth with devastating effect. It was not the first such extraterrestrial collision, nor will it be the last. There have been five hundred or so major impacts from outer space over the last 500 million years. But the meteorite that impacted close to what is now the village of Chicxulub on the coast of Mexico's Yucatan peninsula was to mark a turning point in the history of life. Before the cataclysmic impact, dinosaurs and their reptile relatives ruled the land, seas, and skies. Their subsequent extinction left the way clear for the mammals and birds to take over.

DOOMSDAY
One estimate is that the impact at Chicxulub released energy equivalent to the explosion of 100 million hydrogen bombs. The rock excavated by the impact was blasted back through the atmosphere as a huge mushroom cloud.

ZERO HOUR AT CHICXULUB

The meteorite, measuring about 6 miles (10 kilometers) wide, blasted a hole 60 miles (100 kilometers) across and 7.5 miles (12 kilometers) deep, and must have immediately annihilated all life for many thousands of square miles around the impact site. About 12,000 cubic miles (50,000 cubic kilometers) of pulverized limestone rock were blasted into the atmosphere as dust, droplets of molten rock, and microdiamonds. Tiny grains of Chicxulub rock have been found in K-T Boundary sediments thousands of miles away. The impact also threw hundreds of millions

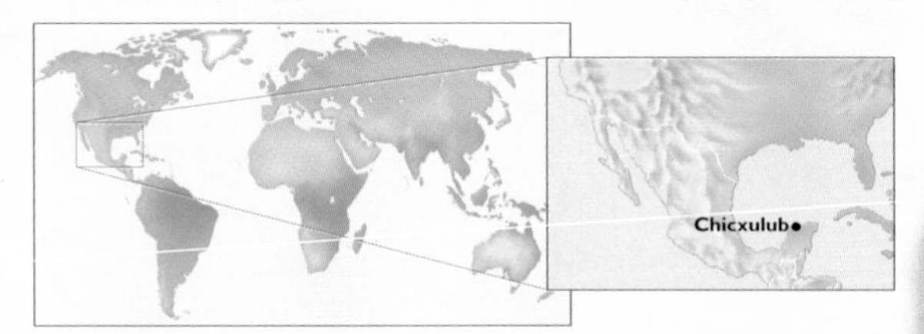

CHICXULUB SITE
The search for the site of the K-T Boundary impact took many years. Eventually the distribution of shocked (physically distorted) grains of quartz and deposits from tsunamis (giant waves) around the Caribbean helped to confirm the site at Chicxulub.

PATH TO DESTRUCTION
Geophysical analysis shows the meteorite, traveling at about 19 miles (30 kilometers) a second, approached at a low angle from the southeast (right). In late Cretaceous times, South America was still separate from North America.

Earthquakes

Wildfires

Worldwide darkness

SHORT- AND LONG-TERM EFFECTS
It has been calculated that the impact caused earthquakes of magnitude 10 on the Richter scale and huge tsunamis. Other short-term effects (days to weeks) probably included fires that poured soot into the atmosphere. It is speculated that longer-term effects included global darkness and acid rain.

CRATER CROSS SECTION
The impact pushed up a mountainous rim 5 miles (8 kilometers) high around the crater. The unstable rim collapsed soon after and fell back into the crater, creating massive earthquakes and further crater collapse rings up to 90 miles (150 kilometers) from the epicenter.

of tons of sulfur into the atmosphere. Mixing with water droplets, this would have generated vast quantities of acid rain (dilute sulfuric acid).

One scenario envisages that ten minutes after the impact, a searing blast of heat from the explosion swept across the Americas. Forests would have spontaneously ignited, blackening the sky with smoke and soot—so much vegetation was burned that particles of charcoal were blown around the world and are found as layers of soot in rock strata. The combination of dust from the impact and smoke from the fires would have darkened skies, causing temperatures to fall. Ten hours after the impact, giant waves called tsunamis would have approached the eastern coastlines of the Americas and pushed far inland, drowning animals that had survived the initial blast.

WAVE OF EXTINCTIONS

Some scientists claim that within a week of the impact, the most vulnerable animals in North America had become extinct. These included the remaining giant sauropods and top carnivores—species that were already on the endangered list, with relatively few members. Plants may also have started dying off from acid rain and lack of light. But the final extinction of the dinosaurs probably did not come until about 100,000 years after the catastrophe, and the last ammonites (shelled creatures that had been abundant in the seas of the Mesozoic era) survived for a further 200,000 years after that. Global environments, with fully re-established climate, ocean circulation, and normal interactions between animals and plants, probably did not get back to normal for 2.5 million years.

IDENTIFYING THE CRATER

The Chicxulub crater was first discovered in the 1970s but subsequently forgotten, partly because it is hidden under a deep layer of sediments, the result of being underwater for most of its existence. In the 1990s, it was investigated once again and its date of formation was found to correspond very closely to the date of the K-T Boundary. The image of the crater (right) was computer-generated from seismic data and then color-enhanced. The blue area at the bottom represents a furrow that was excavated by the meteorite on approach.

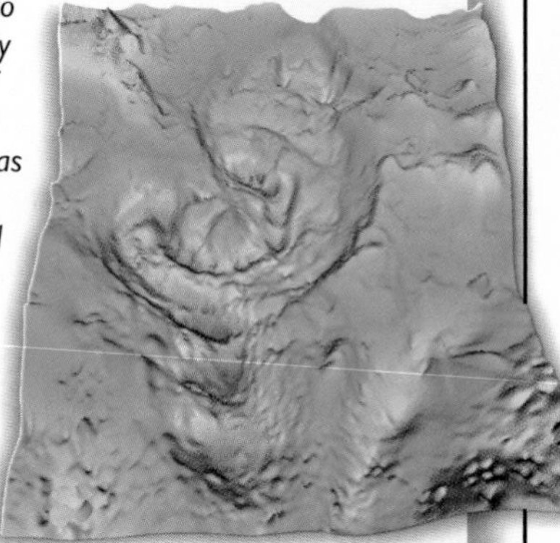

Victims and Survivors

Within hours of the Chicxulub impact, the skies over the immediate region were filled with dust. The situation worsened as forest fires spread, which added smoke and soot to the dust. Within weeks this pollution darkened skies all over the globe, blocking out the Sun and preventing plants in the oceans and on land from photosynthesizing normally.

Plants underpin all life on Earth. They are the food store for herbivores, which in turn constitute food for carnivores. Any major disturbance of the Earth's chemical and physical environments, such as a drastic reduction in light or temperature within the oceans or the atmosphere, immediately affects plant life. The repercussions then cascade throughout the whole of the ecosystem.

After the meteorite impact, the microscopic plants of the oceans were probably the first to die, thereby upsetting the marine ecosystem. The meteorite only accelerated their demise, however, as there is evidence to suggest that they had started to decline before the impact, probably as

SHELLED VICTIMS
Marine animal extinctions were far more numerous at the end of the Cretaceous period than those of the terrestrial animals. Marine animals to die out included the ammonites, which had lived in the oceans for about 300 million years.

EXTINCT HERBIVORE
This plant-eating dinosaur, *Triceratops*, was common in Cretaceous times. By the end of the period, they were still abundant and successful animals. But then, like all the other dinosaurs, they disappeared from the fossil record.

THE "FERN SPIKE"

Fossil evidence shows that, before the K-T extinction, North American landscapes were covered by broad-leaved evergreens and some conifers. In Tertiary strata, the rocks reveal a "fern spike" (sudden preponderance of ferns) immediately after the K-T Boundary. This spike of fossil fern pollen shows that ferns similar to the living fern Stenochlana *were tough survivors and unaffected by the impact. Other fossil plants gradually start reappearing in the rock strata over time. When landscapes are devastated by volcanic eruptions today, ferns are the first plants to return, and they dominate the vegetation before other flora grow back. The similarity between this observation and the events of 65 million years ago suggests that plants at the end of the Cretaceous suffered some trauma.*

a result of a major change in ocean circulation. It is speculated that on land, the impact not only blotted out the sunlight but may also have caused widespread fires and acid rain, which would have adversely affected land plants.

The record from the rocks in Hell Creek, Montana, shows that over 75 percent of plant species in the North American interior became extinct. The overall pattern indicates that the newly evolving flowering plants (angiosperms) were among the worst hit, along with some of the common Mesozoic plants, such as the ginkgos and cycads. In the short term, the ferns survived quite well and, in the longer term, the conifers also thrived. Strangely, land plants in the southern hemisphere were barely affected by the extinction event, suggesting that the impact was not as disastrous as some scientists claim.

When global vegetation began to grow back as the effect of the devastating impact receded, the flowering plants were best able to take advantage of the situation. Eventually, they took over most of the landscapes of the world, evolving into an enormous variety of plants, from small weeds and grasses to giant trees.

THE END OF THE DINOSAURS

Although the plants recovered, many animal groups did not—most famously, the dinosaurs and the flying pterosaurs. The giant marine reptiles, such as the mosasaurs and plesiosaurs, also died out. There is still much debate over why the dinosaurs became extinct, when many other vertebrates—bony fish (12% extinct), frogs (0%), salamanders (0%), lizards (6%), and placental mammals (14%)—were almost unaffected.

Apart from dinosaurs, the reptiles of the late Cretaceous period, before the mass extinction, included 45 families of turtles, crocodiles, lizards, and snakes. The turtles and crocodiles were most affected, but, like the plants, the survivors adapted rapidly to a new environment. Today, there are still more reptile species than mammals.

The initial decline of the reptiles allowed for the rapid expansion of the mammals, although these also suffered in the mass extinction. About 20 percent of all the early mammal families of the Cretaceous period became extinct. The marsupial mammals were particularly affected.

About 75 percent of all animal species became extinct at the K-T Boundary. Many were rare species and at risk of extinction anyway, but there is no obvious explanation why some species died out and others survived. Some scientists believe that survival was really only a matter of luck.

SHELLED SURVIVOR
Turtles and tortoises belong to the same group of reptiles, the Testudines. Over time they have diversified as both plant- and meat-eaters and have become very successful on land and in water. However, they all retain a similar shelled form, which may have helped them survive the K-T extinction event.

Early Tertiary Age

THIS PERIOD OF RAPID CONTINENTAL MOVEMENT ALSO MARKED THE TIME WHEN MODERN ANIMALS, FROM MAMMALS TO SONGBIRDS, BECAME DOMINANT.

The Tertiary period lasted from 65 million years ago almost to the present day. Its first 30 million years are conventionally divided into two epochs, the Paleocene (65 to 55 million years ago) and the Eocene (55 to 34 million years ago).

The early Tertiary was a time of dramatic mountain building and rearrangement of the global jigsaw of oceans and continents. Africa and India moved relentlessly northward, gradually closing the Tethys Ocean. As these fragments of the old supercontinent of Gondwana crashed into the southern flank of Eurasia, they began to compress sedimentary strata, initiating a process of mountain building along a broad front from the Alps to the Himalayas. Farther west, Iberia (Spain and Portugal) collided with France, pushing up the Pyrenees in the process.

OCEAN FISSURES

The Atlantic Ocean continued to rip open northward during early Tertiary times. The continental crust under the ocean was domed up by a deep-seated mantle "hot spot." As it stretched apart and fractured, great outpourings of lavas emerged from the fissures. A line of huge volcanoes ran from Dingle in southwest Ireland to Skaergaard in eastern Greenland. Iceland was created and Greenland split from Scandinavia.

Sea levels continued to fall from the high point reached during mid-Cretaceous times, but in detail, they fluctuated throughout the Tertiary period. Global climates became increasingly

GIANT'S CAUSEWAY
These basalt lavas in Northern Ireland poured out of fissures and volcanoes as the crust rifted with the opening of the North Atlantic in early Tertiary times.

PRISCACARA
This common bony fish is one of two species found in the freshwater Eocene-age deposits of the Green River Formation of Wyoming. It is related to the living perch and grew to 15 inches (38 centimeters). The spiny needles on its back helped protect it from being swallowed whole by larger fish.

MAMMALS DIVERSIFY

The early Tertiary period saw an extraordinarily rapid diversification of mammals. During the entire course of the Tertiary period, which lasted for some 63 million years, nearly 4,000 mammal species evolved. A large proportion of these evolved during the first 10 million years, the Paleocene epoch, including at least 15 new lineages—groups of closely related organisms. The diversification of mammals, many of them plant-eaters, was partly stimulated by the appearance of new angiosperms (flowering plants) at this time. Mammals may also have had the intelligence and adaptability to flourish during a period of rapidly changing environments.

TRIONYX
Growing to 24 inches (60 centimeters) long, this was the largest known Eocene-age freshwater turtle. The shell was covered by a thick skin. The turtle survived dry periods by burrowing into the mud. This example was found in Germany.

KANGAROO RAT
This extinct mammal from Messel in Germany was 30 inches (75 centimeters) long. With its long hind legs and short arms, balanced by a long tail, it looks as if it would have hopped, but the structure of the ankle shows that it actually ran as it preyed on small creatures.

humid in early Tertiary times. This allowed tropical and subtropical climates to spread into high latitudes. But from the end of the Eocene epoch, global climates became drier and generally cooler. This had a significant effect on the overall development of marine and terrestrial life.

MODERN LIFE ASSEMBLES

Flora and fauna changed and diversified radically as life recovered from the extinction event at the end of the Cretaceous period. In the marine environment, life rebounded quickly and creatures began to take on a more present-day appearance. Bony fish (called teleosts) and sharks became dominant, and were joined by the first marine mammals, such as early whales.

However, the most rapid exponential growth was seen on land. Many non-dinosaurian reptiles, such as snakes and lizards, survived from Cretaceous times but failed to capitalize on the demise of the dinosaurs. Instead, the birds, mammals, insects, and flowering plants (angiosperms) quickly came to dominate the land.

Plants and Animals of Messel

One of the most important fossil sites in the world for early Tertiary life is a quarry in Messel, near Frankfurt in Germany. Some 50 million years ago, the site was a lake that held the remains of plants, vertebrates, and invertebrates. Together, the fossils represent an almost complete ecosystem.

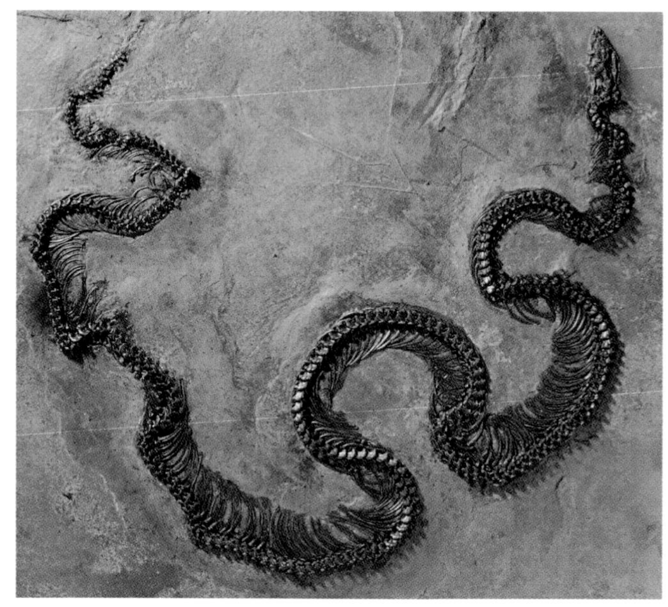

CONSTRICTORS
Early Tertiary pythons and boas were constrictors, which strangled their prey. The *Palaeopython* grew to 6.5 feet (2 meters) long and fed on small reptiles, birds, and mammals. Poisonous snakes did not evolve until Miocene times.

VARIED MAMMALS

Although the mammal fossils form only a small proportion (2 or 3 percent) of the total vertebrate animal life at Messel, 35 different species have nevertheless been found, belonging to 13 orders. These orders all have living representatives, and although the Messel mammals are different in size to modern mammals, they would still look familiar to us today. Marsupial opossums grew to 10 inches (25 centimeters) long, and bats and rodents, such as the 3-foot- (1-meter-) long *Ailuravus*, had started to become very successful. As well as these, tree-climbing, lemurlike primates were found, such as *Europolemur*, 20 inches (50 centimeters) long. The primates have fingernails instead of claws and an opposing first finger and thumb that enable them to grip, and later, use tools. Lemurs, monkeys, humans, and other apes are all primates.

The ancestors of horses were then about the size of a large dog, and there were small, rabbit-sized, cud-chewing ancestors of cattle and deer. Other mammals included an anteater, as well as examples of some extinct early mammal groups such as the cat-sized, hooved, meat-eating mammal, *Paroodectes*.

MESSEL POND LIFE

The 65 species of plants that form the basis of the ecosystem were distinctly modern, with now-tropical citrus trees (*Toddalia*), palms (*Phoenicites*), vines (*Vitis*), and laurels (*Laurophyllum*) thriving. Oaks, beeches, and rare conifers, now typical of more temperate environments, also grew. Freshwater ponds and lakes were filled with water

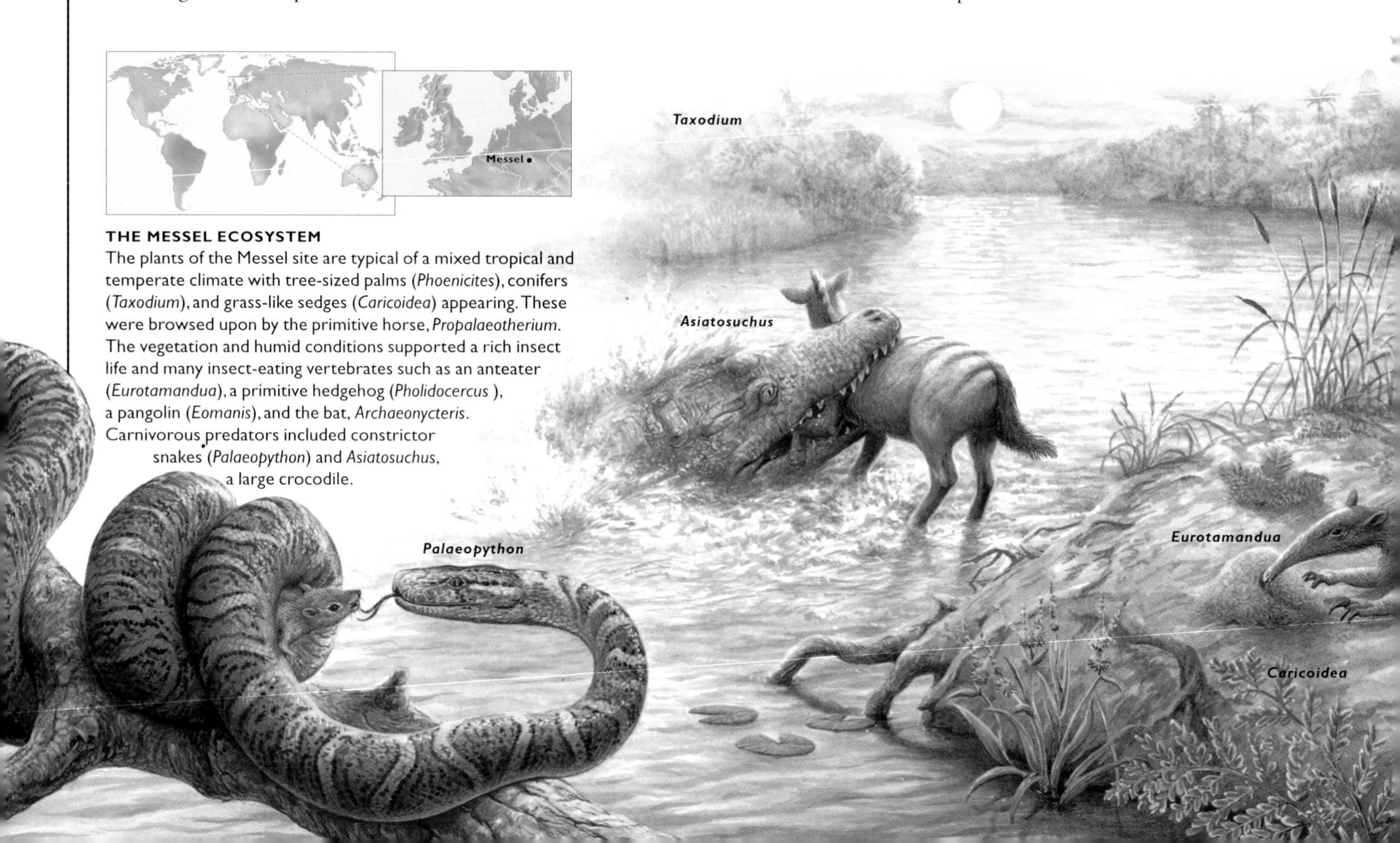

THE MESSEL ECOSYSTEM
The plants of the Messel site are typical of a mixed tropical and temperate climate with tree-sized palms (*Phoenicites*), conifers (*Taxodium*), and grass-like sedges (*Caricoidea*) appearing. These were browsed upon by the primitive horse, *Propalaeotherium*. The vegetation and humid conditions supported a rich insect life and many insect-eating vertebrates such as an anteater (*Eurotamandua*), a primitive hedgehog (*Pholidocercus*), a pangolin (*Eomanis*), and the bat, *Archaeonycteris*. Carnivorous predators included constrictor snakes (*Palaeopython*) and *Asiatosuchus*, a large crocodile.

lilies and populated with snails and insects, such as waterfleas, skaters, and boatmen.

These insects were preyed upon by frogs, toads, and a salamander (*Chelotriton*). Shoals of predatory fish, aquatic reptiles (such as freshwater turtles), and carnivorous crocodiles up to 9 feet (3 meters) long patrolled the lake.

SNAKES AND LIZARDS

The Messel reptiles include snakes and some large lizards. *Xestops*, an armored lizard, fed on snails alongside a tree-climbing predatory monitor lizard, an iguana, and a snakelike limbless lizard. They all grew to between 8 and 20 inches (20 and 50 centimeters) long.

The first fossil snakes appeared in the late Cretaceous period and although their ancestry is as yet unknown, the group included constrictors, pipe snakes, and digging snakes. The constrictors, over 6 feet (2 meters) long, fed on small animals; one specimen was found with a small alligator in its stomach.

Birds were also very modern in appearance and ranged from the *Aenigmavis*, a flightless bird, to hawks, fowls, ibises, cranes, flamingos, owls, and an ostrichlike bird, *Palaeotis*. This assemblage combines modern European, North American, South American, and southern Asian forms.

CROSSROADS

The discovery of Eurotamandua, *the anteater, and* Eomanis, *the pangolin, in this European setting is important, since they were thought to be respectively South American and Southeast Asian. Europe may therefore have been a migratory crossroads for Eocene mammals.*

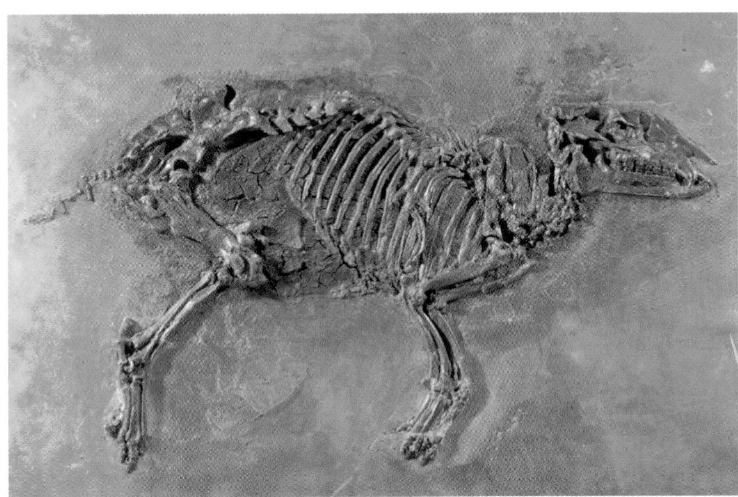

PRIMITIVE HORSES
Over 70 fossil horses were found at Messel, including foals and pregnant mares. This *Propalaeotherium* horse, with its four-toed hoof on each front leg and three-toed hoof on each back leg, stood only 24 inches (60 centimeters) high at the shoulder.

Opening the North Atlantic

During the early Triassic period, about 245 million years ago, the Americas, Europe, and Africa were joined together in the Pangean supercontinent. By 200 million years ago, there were signs of stress, heralding the supercontinent's subsequent break-up. New England and the eastern seaboard developed rifts in the continental crust, through which lava poured out, creating basalt rocks such as the Palisades on the Hudson River in New Jersey. But it was not until mid-Jurassic times, around 180 million years ago, that rift ruptures opened a narrow seaway between the continents and began the formation of the North Atlantic.

TERTIARY VOLCANICS

At first, the widening of the North Atlantic was extremely slow. By the beginning of the Tertiary period, 65 million years ago, Greenland and the British Isles were still joined and Iceland did not exist. But between 63 and 52 million years ago, the region was the site of intense volcanic activity. Vast outpourings of lava, originating from a series of southwest-northeast oriented fissures, inundated the landscape. These eruptions were probably due to the flare-up of a hot spot—an upward flow of hot molten magma from the Earth's interior.

THE FORMATION OF AN OCEAN

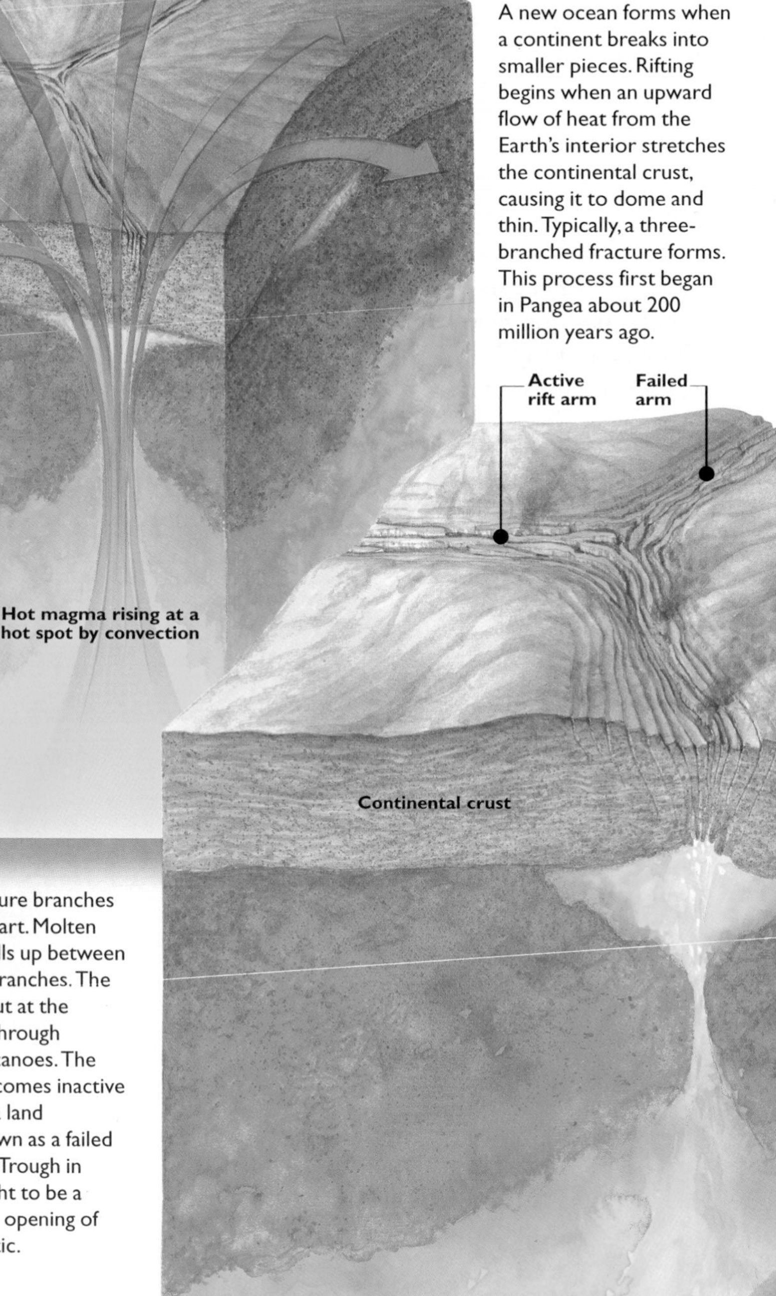

STAGE ONE

A new ocean forms when a continent breaks into smaller pieces. Rifting begins when an upward flow of heat from the Earth's interior stretches the continental crust, causing it to dome and thin. Typically, a three-branched fracture forms. This process first began in Pangea about 200 million years ago.

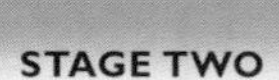

STAGE TWO

Two of the fracture branches move farther apart. Molten rock magma wells up between the separating branches. The magma pours out at the surface as lava, through fissures and volcanoes. The third branch becomes inactive and remains as a land depression, known as a failed arm. The Benue Trough in Nigeria is thought to be a failed arm in the opening of the South Atlantic.

COLUMNAR BASALT OF FINGAL'S CAVE

Cooling lava formed the columns that support a sea cave, named for a mythical giant, on the island of Staffa off Scotland's west coast. The lava, part of a 1.2 mile- (2 kilometer-) thick sequence, poured out of a volcano on the nearby island of Mull in Tertiary times, between 60 and 57 million years ago.

STAGES IN THE SPLIT

The opening of the Atlantic over the last 100 million years has been most significant in the separation of Africa from North and South America and Northern Europe from Labrador.

100 MA

50 MA

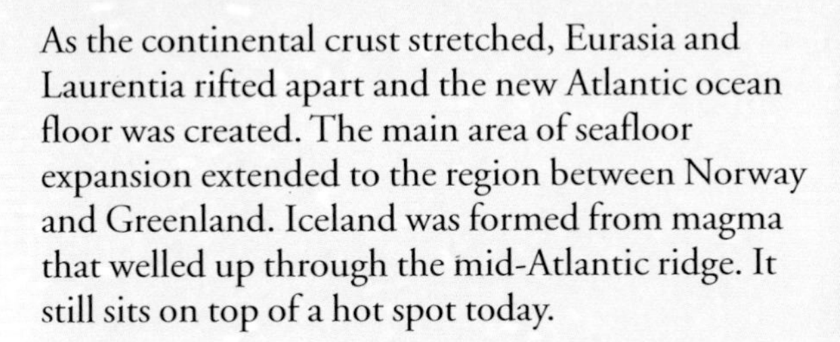

As the continental crust stretched, Eurasia and Laurentia rifted apart and the new Atlantic ocean floor was created. The main area of seafloor expansion extended to the region between Norway and Greenland. Iceland was formed from magma that welled up through the mid-Atlantic ridge. It still sits on top of a hot spot today.

ICELANDIC FIRE
The hot spot in the Earth's surface that started the rifting of Greenland from the British Isles some 60 million years ago still exists under Iceland. Volcanic eruptions on Iceland give scientists an opportunity to find out how ocean floor rocks are formed.

THE LAVAS

In Northern Ireland and the inner Hebrides of Scotland great masses of basalt lava, with flows 48 feet (15 meters) thick on average, erupted from fissures and volcanoes. The remains of some of the fissures can still be seen. Over 1,500 square miles (3,800 square kilometers) of lava are still preserved in Northern Ireland. The Giant's Causeway, a stepping-stone formation of huge columnar rocks in County Antrim, is one of many visible remnants of the eruptions.

The second phase of igneous activity was the formation of a string of volcanoes from Ireland to the west coast of Scotland. Despite the hardness of the rocks, these now extinct volcanoes were deeply eroded by glaciers during the last ice age (18,000 years ago), making it easier for scientists to study them.

Examination of the region's igneous rocks has provided vital clues to their formation. The magma from which the rocks were formed underwent cycles of change in composition. Crystals of different minerals sedimenting out of the magma at different times caused some of the rocks to become layered. A layered formation discovered on the island of Rum off Scotland confirms that the rocks created in the Tertiary period were caused by a mantle hot spot. This formation contains abundant platinum group minerals, associated with the high temperatures occurring during mantle plume activity.

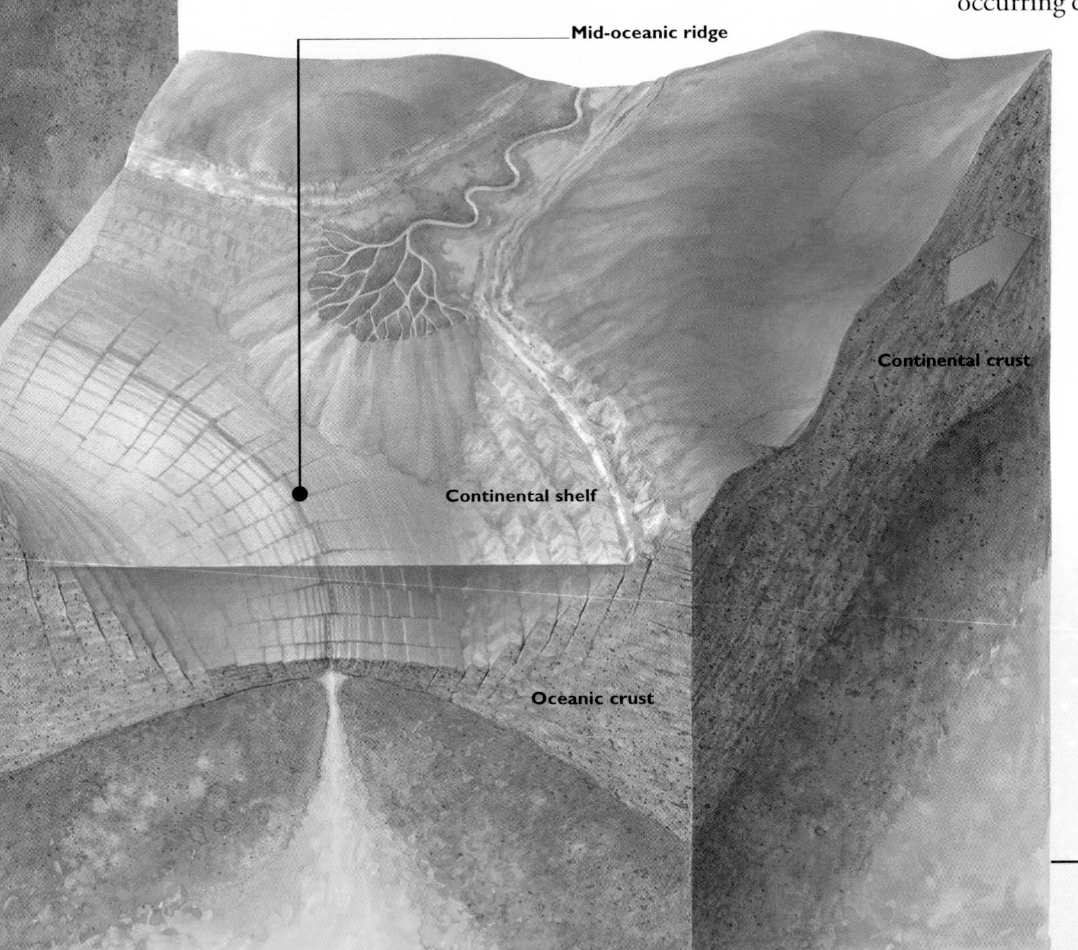

STAGE THREE
Continued rifting separates blocks of continental crust, and the one-time edges become the foundations for continental shelves. The active rift arms develop into a mid-oceanic spreading ridge with the formation of new ocean floor.

FOSSILIZED LAKE

At Ardtun on the Hebridean island of Mull, the first lavas to erupt flowed into a small lake, burying a variety of plants that had been carried into the lake from the surrounding hills and preserving them as fossils. These provide a rare insight into the life of the time. The flora includes trees such as plane, hazel, oak, and the maidenhair tree (ginkgo), all typical of a temperate climate. Insect remains have also been found, including a beetle and a weevil.

The Evolution of Plants and Flowers

Much of our knowledge of the early evolution of land plants comes from a site at Rhynie in Scotland. The 390-million-year-old Rhynie sediments have fossilized 22 species of plants, including the first primitive plants with veins for circulating water (vascular plants) known as rhyniophytes. These upright plants were bog-dwellers, and grew no more than 8 to 12 inches (20 to 30 centimeters) high.

Some 15 million years later, about 375 million years ago, the first forestlike growth of terrestrial plants appear, as seen from the Gilboa strata in New York's Catskill Mountains. The tree-ferns and clubmosses (lycopsids) were the first plants to grow to 10 feet (3 meters) or more, the size of small modern trees. The evolution of rootlike structures enabled them to grow to this height, and provided access to groundwater. There were also internal structural changes to the stems, which produced the first strengthened, woodlike tissues.

Another major advance was the evolution, from the late Devonian onward, of seed-bearing plants (gymnosperms), which included conifers, ginkgos, palmlike cycads, and pteridosperms (seed-ferns). Through the Mesozoic era, from 248 to 65 million years ago, these plants, together with ferns and horsetails, dominated landscapes worldwide. Many plants reproduced through wind-borne seeds; some may even have depended on insects for the fertilization process.

EARLY COLONIZERS
Tiny plants called bryophytes, like this living *Marchantia* liverwort from Australia, may have been the first plants to colonize the land in Ordovician times. These plants are incapable, however, of growing far above the ground. Only plants with strengthened stems (vascular plants) can do that. Vascular plants first appeared in Silurian times.

FLOWERING PLANTS

Angiosperms, the flowering plants, first emerged around 140 million years ago. Plant scientists have regarded magnolias as the most primitive living angiosperms, but a new fossil plant from northeast China, called *Archaefructus*, is now considered to be the oldest flowering plant.

By mid-Cretaceous times, the flowering plants had diversified widely and rapidly into the basic

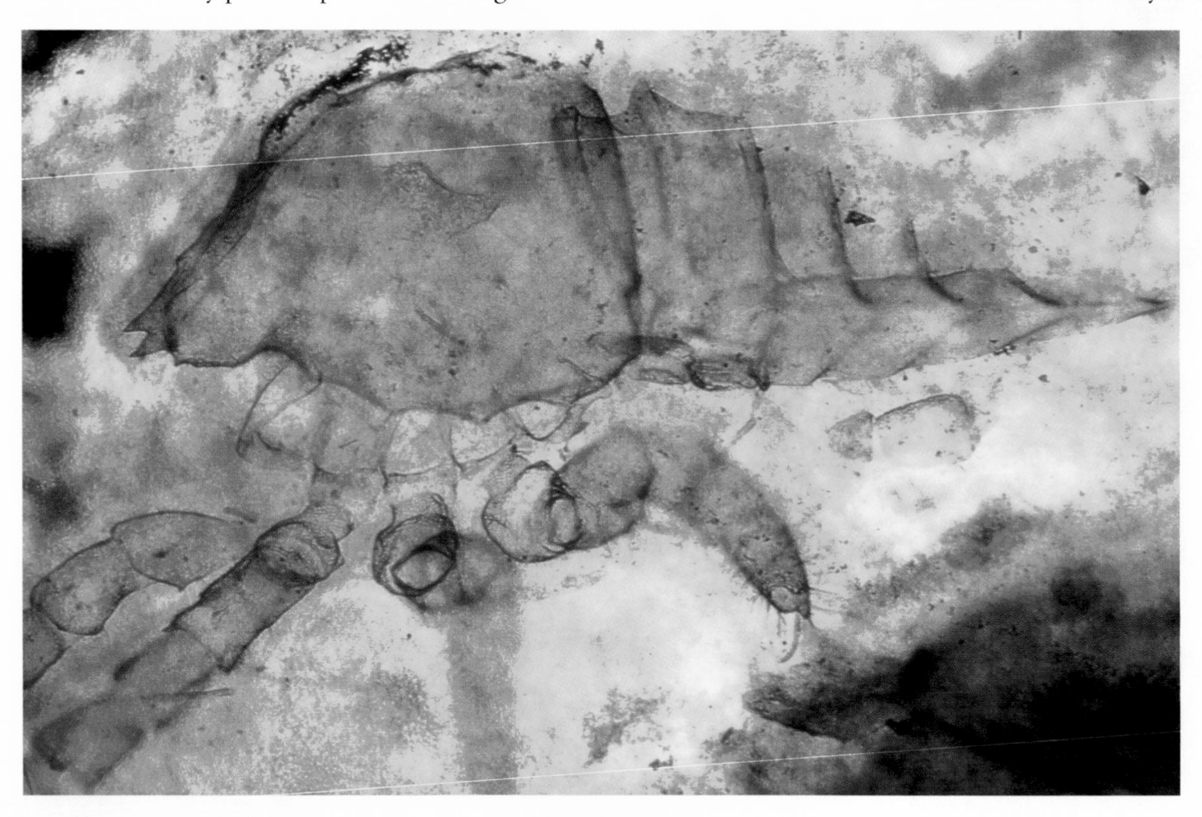

TINY PREDATOR
One of the earliest known land-living predators, *Palaeocharinus*, was found in late Silurian strata in Scotland. It was only 0.02 inches (0.5 millimeters) long, but it preyed on mites that were smaller than itself. These in turn fed on abundant rotting plant vegetation. Their presence shows that simple terrestrial ecosystems already existed 420 million years ago.

FLOWERING PLANT
This 140 million-year-old fossil plant *Archaefructus* comes from early Cretaceous strata in northeast China. It has the critical features of a flowering plant, with fruits enclosed in a female reproductive structure that has developed from a flower. This fossil is the oldest known flowering plant.

family divisions that are still familiar to us today. They can be grouped into monocots (such as palms and lilies) and dicots (such as broad-leaved trees, shrubs, and many herbaceous plants). The angiosperms replaced the ginkgophytes, cycads, and pteridosperms, which were all declining in diversity. The pteridosperms were extinct by Cretaceous times, and the ginkgophytes and cycads were devastated by the extinction event that occurred at the end of the Cretaceous period; they barely survived and very few species (just one ginkgophyte) have persisted to the present day. In contrast, the ferns and conifers fared better after the extinction event and are still common today.

After the mass extinctions at the end of the Cretaceous period, the flowering plants dominated in all their incredible diversity. An increase in global humidity promoted the development of tropical rain forests, which were filled with large-leaved trees. These large leaves had developed distinctive "drip tips" to help shed rainwater. High global temperatures allowed these forests to grow as far north as 60 degrees latitude in some places. In higher latitudes, extensive deciduous woodland replaced the previous broad-leaved evergreens, many of which are now extinct.

All the major groups of flowering plants, including the precursors of the grasses (such as the basic grains—rice, wheat, and corn), had evolved by the beginning of the Tertiary period, which started 65 million years ago. The major types of fruit had also evolved, so that by early Tertiary times there was a wide variety of capsules, nuts, drupes (plumlike fruits), berries, and pods. The world's landscapes have had this familiar modern-looking vegetation ever since.

EARLY FLOWER
This flower, *Silvianthemum suecicum*, was found preserved in late Cretaceous strata in Sweden. It is a typical insect-pollinated flower with petals and reproductive parts, both male (the pollen-bearing stamen) and female (the style, which leads to the ovary).

FOSSIL FLOWERS

Flowers are delicate structures, so the chances of finding a fossilized specimen are small. However, pollen, fruits, and seeds, all part of a flowering plant's reproductive cycle, are much tougher and are often fossilized, although they are usually scattered far and wide. The challenge is to match the pollen, seed, and fruit fossils found in rock strata to a particular plant without the guidance of any flower remains.

BEELIKE INSECTS
Although the first true bees appear in mid-Tertiary strata in France, beelike insects are also found in older, late Cretaceous amber from North America.

Mid-Tertiary Period

GLOBAL COOLING, CONTINENTAL COLLISIONS, AND INCREASED ARIDITY ENCOURAGED THE GROWTH OF OPEN GRASSLANDS AND LARGER PLANT-EATERS.

Continents and oceans were close to their present global positions 20 million years ago. There were, however, small, but significant, differences. Australia was still moving north, as were Africa and India, which were heading toward Europe and Asia. The subsequent collisions built the Alps in Europe and the Himalayas in Asia and created the Tibetan plateau, the "roof of the world," 3 miles (5 kilometers) above sea level. The Himalayas are one of Earth's most dramatic features, rising over 4.5 miles (7 kilometers) above sea level to form a 1,800-mile (3,000-kilometer) barrier between India and central Asia.

In North America, terranes (fragments of continental crust) welded onto the west coast, but the connection with South America, broken in mid-Jurassic times, had yet to be re-established. Finally, Greenland separated from Scandinavia.

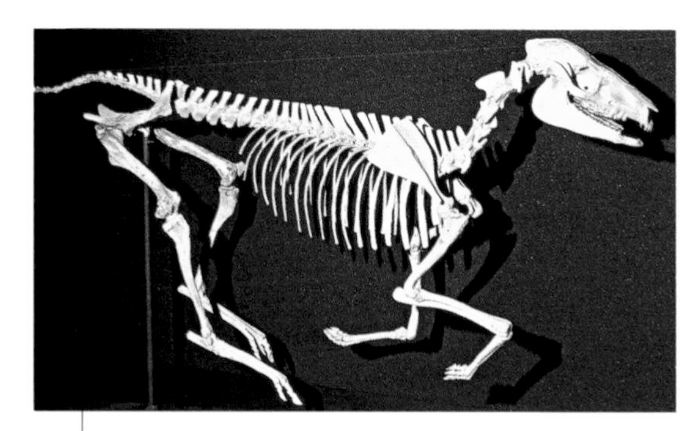

THREE-TOED HORSE
Mesohippus was a primitive horse from North America, the first to have three, rather than four, toes on each foot, making it closer to the single-toed modern horse.

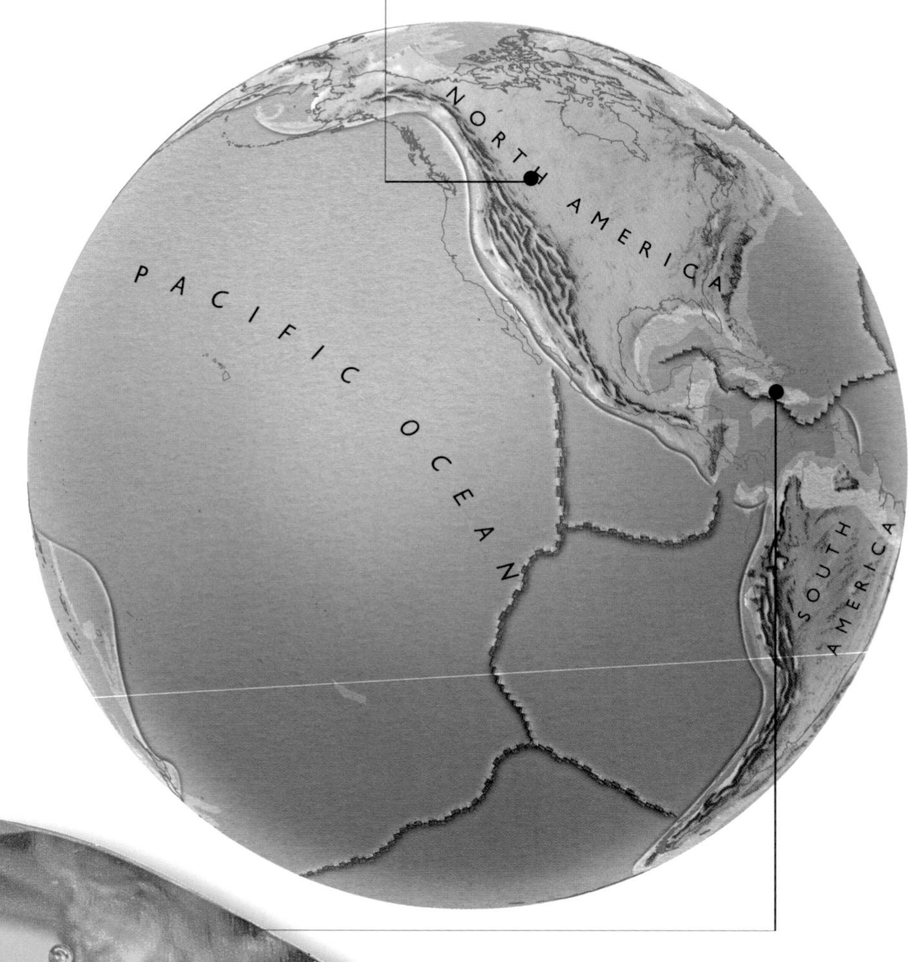

GLOBAL CLIMATES AND MONSOONS

The global climates of early Tertiary times were still warm and humid. But by about 25 million years ago, the Earth cooled and the Antarctic icecap began to develop. Overall, much drier conditions prevailed. Although there was some fluctuation between colder and warmer phases, the Earth was heading toward the ice ages of the later Quaternary period. The building of the

AMBER FROG
Many different kinds of organisms have been trapped in amber resin, but frogs are very rare. Perhaps a bird caught this frog, flew to a resin-producing tree to eat its prey, but dropped it into a patch of sticky resin. This specimen formed in the Dominican Republic at a time of higher sea levels than shown in the maps.

THE SEASONS

A major feature of the cooling of the climate in the mid-Tertiary period is the development of the seasons. These took the form of winter and summer months, and dry and monsoon periods, particularly in Asia. Seasonality requires plants to adopt once- or twice-yearly reproductive phases, with seeds that can survive bad weather while lying in a dormant state. The grasses were particularly successful at doing this, resulting in open savanna grasslands.

BALTIC FLY
The vast majority of creatures trapped in amber are insects, such as this 35-million-year-old fly from the Baltic region of Europe. The almost perfect preservation that amber provides allows creatures to be accurately identified. Despite claims, however, that the genetic blueprint, or DNA, of amber insects can be recovered, modern research shows that this is not yet possible.

ASIA
AFRICA
INDIAN OCEAN

Himalayas and the Tibetan plateau changed the climate of Asia by establishing the monsoon. This occurs because the vast, high Himalayan region is quickly warmed by the summer sun, heating the air and causing it to rise. This draws in moist air from the sea and the moisture falls as rain.

Sea levels fluctuated during Tertiary times but fell overall, putting an end to the continental shelf seas. At the end of the Cretaceous period, about 60 percent of modern North America was under water. By mid-Tertiary times it had fallen to 5 percent, and the seas have not returned since.

FLORA AND FAUNA CHANGES

From early Tertiary times, most plant-eating mammals were small, and many of the flowering plants were large forest trees. Consequently, the plant-eaters were browsers that ate leaves, fallen fruits, and seeds. But as the climate cooled and became drier, the lush forests grew smaller, and were replaced by the open savanna grasslands of North America, Africa, and Asia. These savannas favored grazing plant-eaters and led to a marked increase in the size of the animals. Of the early Tertiary plant-eating mammals, only the horses (which by mid-Tertiary had grown to the size of large modern dogs) and rhinos took full advantage of the change. However, they had to compete with the new cud-chewing plant-eaters such as deer, camels, and later, cowlike bovids and hippos.

Other vertebrate groups promoted by the climate change were the songbirds and primates. The reduction of the forests forced the primates out into the open to obtain food. Movement across large open spaces in turn promoted the use of two legs instead of four, and the use of arms and hands for purposes other than climbing.

KANGAROO JAW
The Tertiary age rocks of Riversleigh in northwest Queensland, Australia, are rich in fossil remains. Most of the fossils, like this kangaroo jawbone, are well-preserved bones of vertebrates that lived and died in and around the lake. Their corpses sank into the soft mud at the bottom of the lake, which is now hard limestone.

Riversleigh Marsupials

By late Eocene times, Australia had become isolated from the rest of the world, taking its primitive mammals with it—in particular, the marsupials. These mammals, which give birth to underdeveloped young that are then cared for in a pouch, evolved in mid-Cretaceous times in North America and spread to South America and Australia.

Unlike their South American cousins, which were overthrown by the invasion of more modern placental mammals from North America, the Australian marsupials survived as a dominant group because of their geographic isolation.

RIVERSLEIGH FOSSIL SITE

Evidence for Australian marsupials ranging from 23 million to less than 20,000 years old comes from a remote outback ranch at Riversleigh in northwestern Queensland. Fossil records for the area date from 1900, but the real breakthrough in fossil discovery came in 1983, when a few blocks of weathered Riversleigh limestone were found to be literally bristling with bones. Within an hour or so, the investigating team had found 30 fossil mammals new to science.

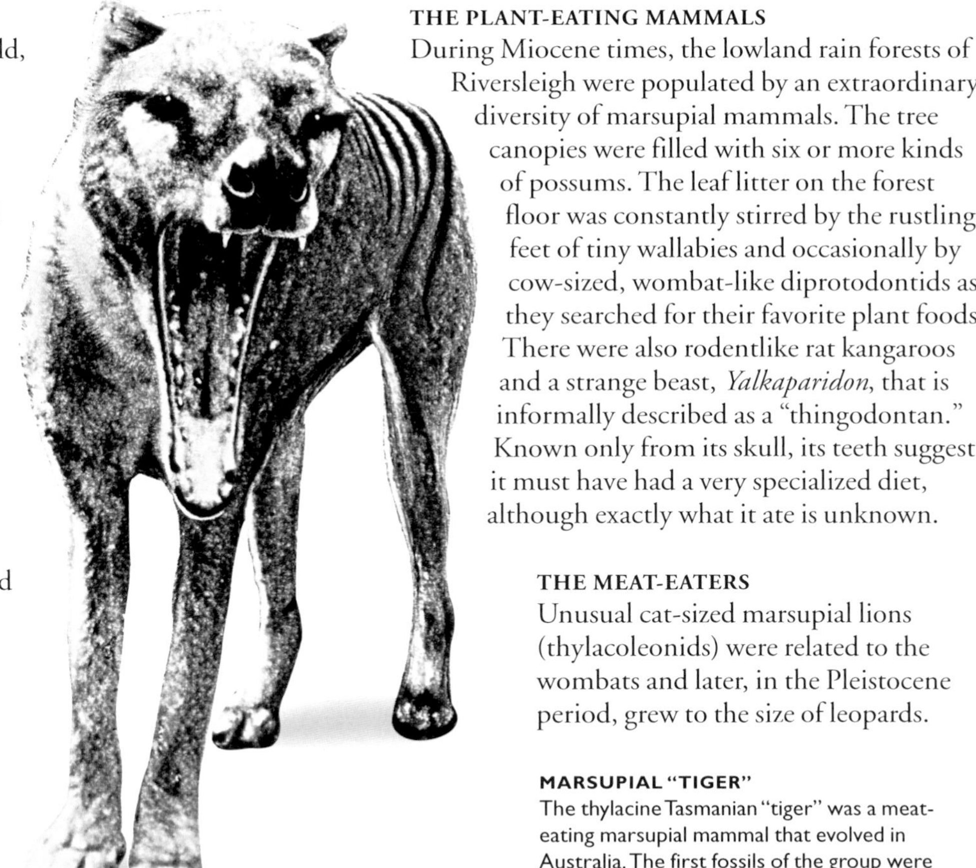

THE PLANT-EATING MAMMALS

During Miocene times, the lowland rain forests of Riversleigh were populated by an extraordinary diversity of marsupial mammals. The tree canopies were filled with six or more kinds of possums. The leaf litter on the forest floor was constantly stirred by the rustling feet of tiny wallabies and occasionally by cow-sized, wombat-like diprotodontids as they searched for their favorite plant foods. There were also rodentlike rat kangaroos and a strange beast, *Yalkaparidon*, that is informally described as a "thingodontan." Known only from its skull, its teeth suggest it must have had a very specialized diet, although exactly what it ate is unknown.

THE MEAT-EATERS

Unusual cat-sized marsupial lions (thylacoleonids) were related to the wombats and later, in the Pleistocene period, grew to the size of leopards.

MARSUPIAL "TIGER"

The thylacine Tasmanian "tiger" was a meat-eating marsupial mammal that evolved in Australia. The first fossils of the group were found at Riversleigh. The species survived until 1933, when the last thylacine died in captivity.

RIVERSLEIGH LIFE

Riversleigh was a lowland rain forest teeming with life. Although plant fossils are rare, the remains of plant-eaters, such as the cow-sized *Neohelos*, plant-eating rat kangaroos (*Hypsiprimnodon*), and possums (*Burramys*), show that there was a lot of vegetation. Predators were few but there was a cat-sized marsupial "lion" (*Priscileo*) and a flesh-eating kangaroo (*Ekaltadeta*). The relative lack of predators allowed flightless birds such as *Bullockornis* to develop.

Flesh-eating kangaroos preyed on a range of small mammals, birds, and invertebrates. Marsupial moles burrowed through the soil and leaf litter after their invertebrate prey. The night skies were filled with a variety of bats competing from their cave homes for the abundant insects. The only other predators were crocodiles that patrolled the lakesides and snakes that slithered along the forest floor, climbed the trees, and swam in the rivers.

THE WATER-DWELLERS

Apart from the large reptilian vertebrates, the freshwaters of the lakes and rivers were inhabited by turtles, frogs, and lungfish, perhaps as much as 13 feet (4 meters) long, eels and catfish, most of which were able to breathe oxygen directly from the atmosphere. The invertebrate prey for these fish included abundant water fleas and snails.

THE BIRDS

By far the most conspicuous of Riversleigh's bird fossils were the so-called thunder birds, a group of large flightless ostrichlike animals that became extinct only some 26,000 years ago and were known to the first aboriginal inhabitants of Australia. They were distantly related to the other bird groups such as the emulike flightless birds. Songbirds (passerines), which comprise more than half of all living species of birds, were also abundant but have yet to be identified.

The only problem with recreating the Riversleigh environment is the lack of plant fossils. In the warm climate of the area, the limestone that forms the rock sediment does not readily preserve plants, which are attacked by microbes and soil-dwelling detritivores such as millipedes, also part of the fossil remains.

ROCKY RECORD

Riversleigh holds the record for density of new fossil finds. In 1983, 70 cubic feet (2 cubic meters) of rock from the area yielded 58 new mammals. This is because the area lay in a limestone terrain with plenty of surface water. These were ideal conditions for bone preservation.

BAT BONES
One of the most common fossils found at Riversleigh are bats. Leaf-nosed bats lived in limestone caves in huge numbers. Their bones and droppings accumulated on the floors of the caves and were fossilized.

The Himalayas and the Tibetan Plateau

The story of how the Himalayas and the Tibetan plateau were created begins about 55 million years ago. At the time, India, which was a separate landmass, was crashing into the continent of Asia. The point of collision formed the Himalayas, the highest and youngest mountain range in the world. It also formed the Tibetan plateau, the largest upland region on Earth, which is on average 3 miles (5 kilometers) above sea level. For this reason it is known as the "roof of the world." The rock (called the continental crust) beneath Tibet is an astonishing 46 miles (74 kilometers) thick, about twice the average crustal thickness.

THE FORMATION OF THE HIMALAYAS

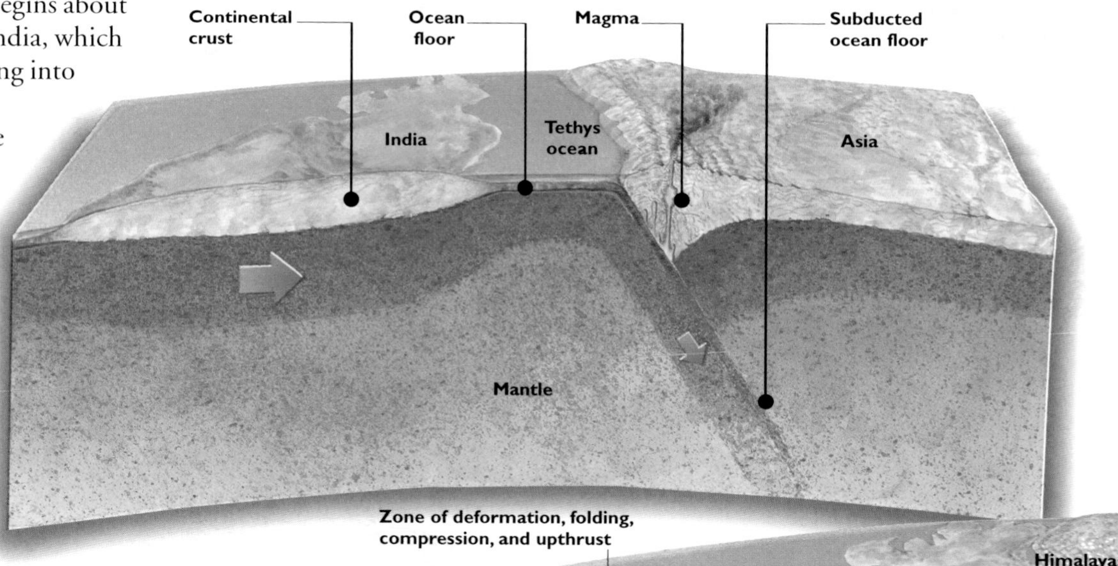

Zone of deformation, folding, compression, and upthrust

Himalayas

India

55 MILLION YEARS AGO
The Himalayas were created when India collided with Asia. As India approached Asia, the ocean floor in between the two landmasses was pushed down (subducted) under Asia. The rocks melted, and either cooled to form granite or escaped as magma through volcanoes.

MOUNTAIN-BUILDING MECHANICS

The mechanism by which mountains are formed has long been understood. As two continents collide, enormous forces are exerted on the rock at the point of impact, crumpling, folding, compressing, deforming, and altering its chemical composition. Some of the rock is pushed skyward to form the peaks of the mountains, while other rock is pushed deep down into the Earth's mantle to form the "roots" of the mountains. A mountain range such as the Himalayas is, in effect, the thickening of the crust caused by rocks being pushed both upward and downward.

In addition, the rock of the deep mantle is denser than the rock of the crust above it. As the crust thickens, the mantle effectively buoys up the line of mountains. As the mountains get bigger, this mantle support increases and the entire mountain range is pushed skyward. This elevation

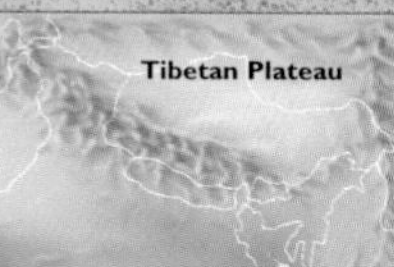

MOUNTAIN PEAKS
Annapurna is just one of many peaks in the Himalayas that rise over 5 miles (8 kilometers) above sea level. These peaks are still being uplifted by some 4 inches (10 centimeters) a century and eroded at the same rate, with the debris carried away by great rivers, such as the Ganges.

DEFYING GRAVITY

The Tibetan plateau covers some 2 million square miles (5 million square kilometers) of Asia, and the remarkable uniformity of its elevation, at about 3 miles (5 kilometers) above sea level, suggests that this may be the maximum possible height at which rocks in the Earth's crust can be supported over such a large surface area. Any further thickening would put such pressure on the rocks deep in the base of the plateau that they would melt and shift.

is counterbalanced, however, by the erosive action of the weather, which continuously strips off the top layer of the mountain peaks.

BUILDING THE TIBETAN PLATEAU

While this model explains the origin of most mountain ranges, it does not explain why the Tibetan plateau, the edge of which is over 190 miles (300 kilometers) away from the Himalayas, is also elevated. It appears that as India approached Asia, the ocean plate in between the two landmasses was pushed under Asia, in a process called subduction. As the two continents collided, part of the landmass of India was also subducted, following the ocean crust down into the mantle. The edge of Asia was pushed over the top of India.

The rock from both continents was folded, deformed, and compressed during the collision, and parts of both continents and the ocean plate were pushed up to form the Himalayas. However, crucially, the Indian crust did not totally subduct. Its rock was less dense than the rock of the Earth's mantle below it, so instead of being pushed downward, it started to move horizontally, effectively pushing a wedge under Asia. The effect was to lift the Tibetan plateau up in one piece, thickening the crust dramatically as it did so.

ROOF OF THE WORLD
A view of the floodplain of the Ganges River (left), the snow-covered Himalayas, and the Tibetan plateau (right), as seen from a NASA Space Shuttle.

Asia

25 MILLION YEARS AGO
As India pushed into Asia, the rocks were crumpled together, and pushed down as a deep root or upthrust as a mountain belt. The intervening crust was shortened by some 1,500 miles (2,500 kilometers) and a huge slab, around 180 miles (290 kilometers) wide, was probably pushed under Tibet.

TODAY
In the roots of the mountain chain, the high pressures chemically alter the composition of the rocks. As the mountains are elevated from beneath, their peaks are worn down by erosion. The subduction of India under Asia continues at a rate of 2 inches (5 centimeters) a year.

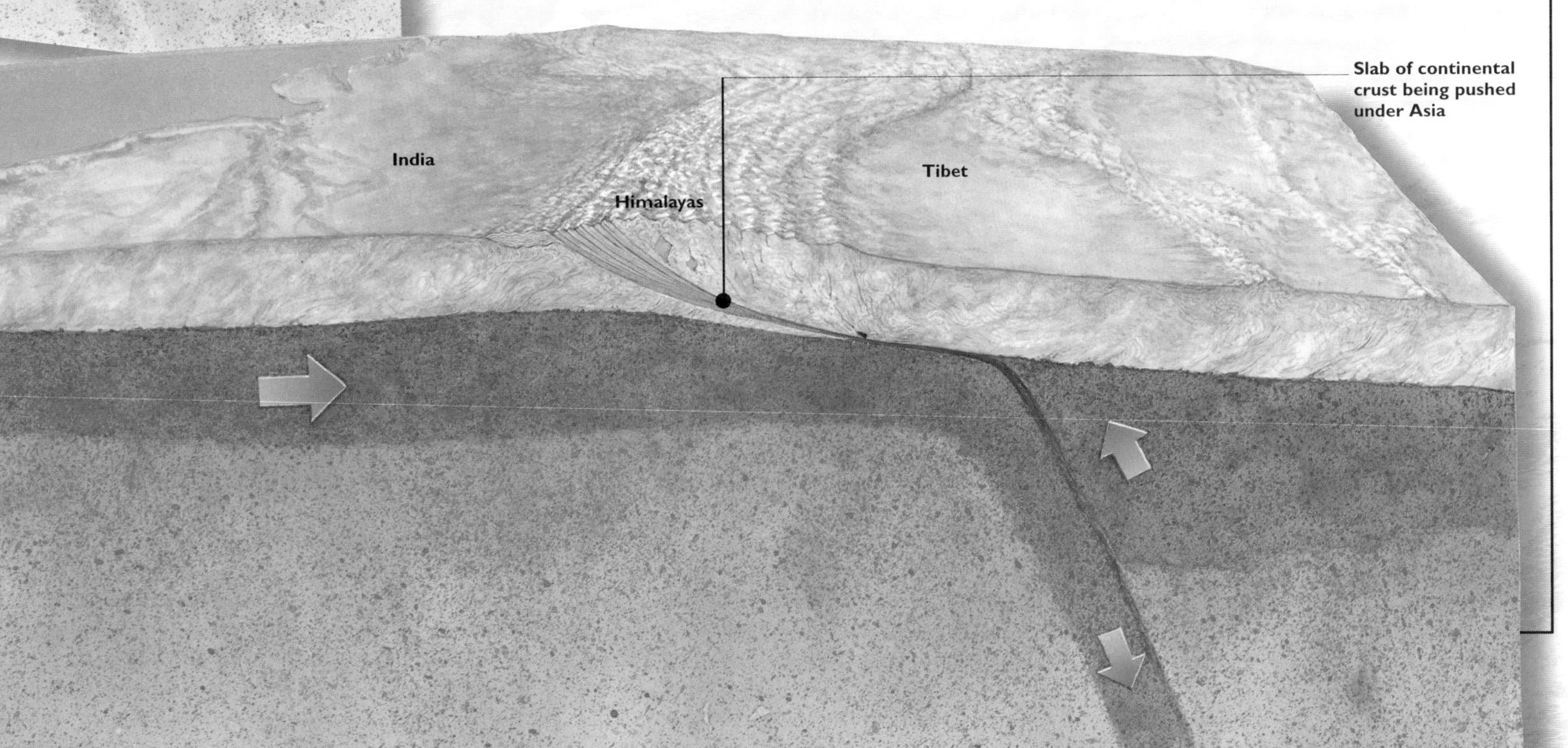

Late Tertiary Period

THE DIRECT ANCESTORS OF MODERN HUMANS EMERGED IN AFRICA BETWEEN FIVE AND TWO MILLION YEARS AGO, AS THE EARTH BEGAN TO COOL TOWARD THE END OF TERTIARY TIMES.

In late Tertiary times (Pliocene), the global distribution of continents and oceans was very similar to that today, and the same inexorable geological forces were at work. At any one time, the outward expansion of ocean floors from mid-ocean ridges averaged about 1 inch (2.5 centimeters) a year. Even at this slow rate some 15½ miles (25 kilometers) of new ocean floor would have been created every million years with the same amount lost by being dragged down into ocean trenches or forced under the landmasses of the continents in areas called subduction zones.

This dynamic activity of the Earth's crust generated constant earthquakes, volcanoes, and plate movement. India continued to push north into Asia, Africa pushed into southern Europe, and East Africa began to break apart. The Red Sea and the Gulf of Aden opened up. The isolation of the two American continents was eventually ended when the Panamanian isthmus reconnected South and North America about 3 million years ago. Subsequently North America and Asia were also connected. These new land bridges allowed the exchange of animals and plants and, eventually, the migration of humans all over the world.

Climate in the late Tertiary period was characterized by fluctuating temperatures and humidity. Sea levels rose and fell several times as water first became locked up, and then released, by the polar icecaps. But these fluctuations were only temporary. Glaciation began in earnest in the northern hemisphere about 2.5 million years ago.

LENGAI VOLCANO, TANZANIA
A series of volcanoes mark where the crustal rocks of East Africa were rifted some 2 to 5 million years ago. Lava and ashfall blanketed the layers of sediment in the valleys, preserving a treasure trove of fossils for future researchers.

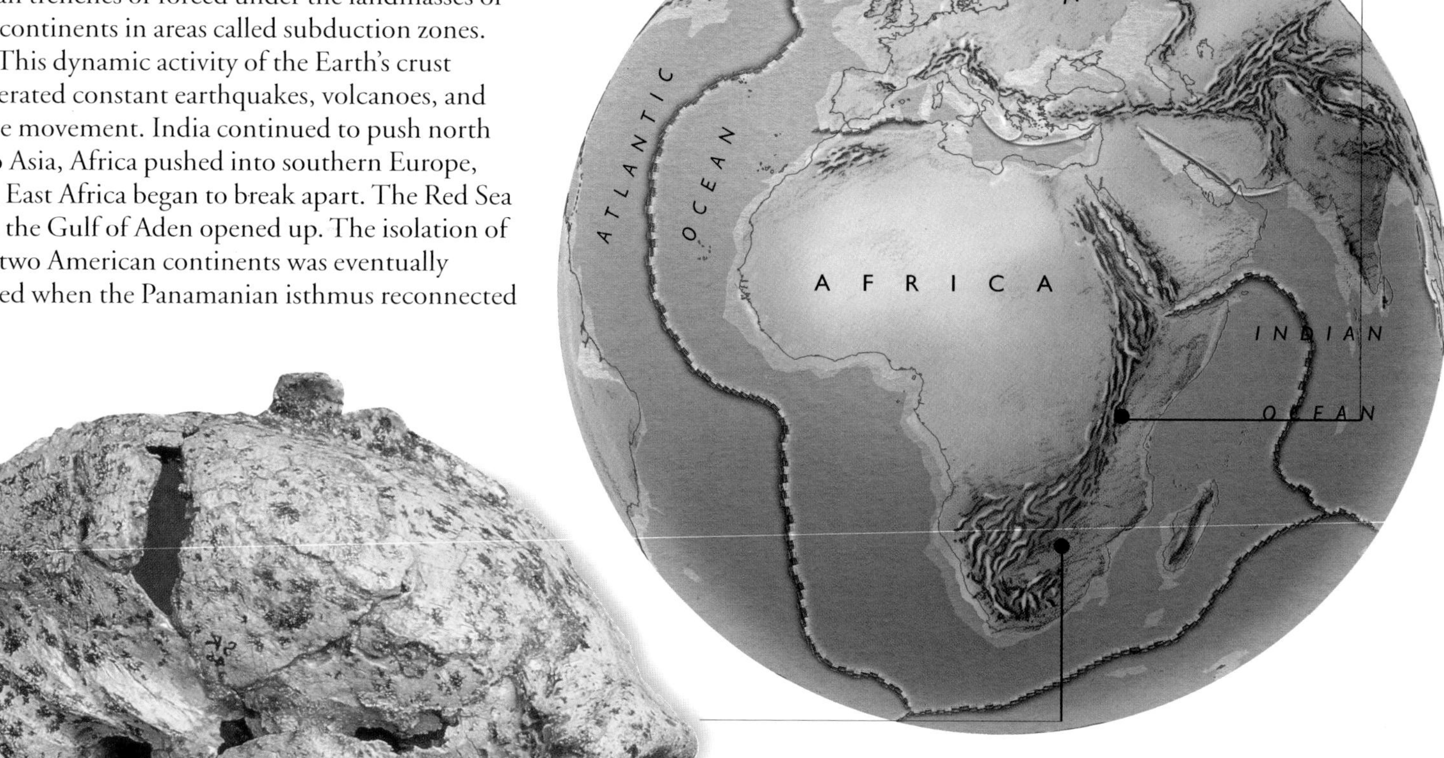

SKULL
Australopithecus robustus lived between 1 and 2.2 million years ago in Africa (this skull was found in South Africa). With a massive muscular jaw and large teeth, it lived mainly on plant food. Adult males grew to 5 feet 4 inches (1.6 meters) tall and were powerfully built.

THE HOMINIDS

Late Tertiary times marked a key stage in the evolution of humankind. This was the period, between 5 and 1.5 million years ago, when the genus Homo *evolved from an australopithecine (meaning "southern ape") ancestor in Africa. From the 4.5-million-year-old hominid* Ardipithecus ramidus, *a succession of southern apes evolved until they became extinct around 1 million years ago. By this time, several different species of* Homo *had evolved, including two different species of* Homo habilis, *that belonged to the same group as modern humans, and subsequently,* Homo erectus, *the first human to migrate from Africa.*

FOSSIL FOOTPRINT
About 3.6 million years ago, three of our hominid ancestors, *Australopithecus afarensis*, walked away from a volcanic eruption in the Rift Valley in Tanzania. Their footprints are among the first evidence of hominids walking fully upright. Two of the group walked side by side and the third dogged their steps, treading in the prints of the largest individual.

THE EMERGENCE OF HOMINIDS

During the 1990s, it became clear that the 3-million-year-old *Australopithecus afarensis* (first found in the Afar region of northern Ethiopia) is the most likely ancestor of the human lineage, which starts with the 2-million-year-old *Homo habilis,* an inhabitant of East and southern Africa. The vital million-year gap in the fossil record between the two was filled in the late 1990s with the discovery of a new australopithecine, *A. garhi,* also from Afar. These 2.5-million-year-old hominids lived in open grasslands around a lake with abundant game. Stone tools from the Afar region, along with cut and hammered bones of bovids and horses, provide some early evidence that hominids killed and butchered large game. This represents a shift from a predominantly vegetarian hominid diet to one that included nutritious meat and bone marrow. The onset of meat-eating seems to coincide with the emergence in East and southern Africa of the genus *Homo* and has major behavioral and social implications since it requires collaborative hunting and the development of skills such as tool-making.

MATTERHORN
The pyramid-shaped horn of this alpine peak in Switzerland has clearly been sculpted by a glacier. Although glaciers are still present in the European Alps, they are only a remnant of the much deeper and more extensive ice sheets that started to develop in late Pliocene times over 2 million years ago.

Hominids and Other Mammals

THE LAKESHORE AND RIVER deposits surrounding Lake Turkana in Kenya, East Africa, contain the richest fossil record of early hominids in the world, preserved in strata known as the Koobi Fora Formation.

HUMAN ANCESTORS

The most famous remains from the area are skulls of *Homo habilis*, one of the first representatives of the human genus *Homo* and the ancestor of modern humans. The skulls, dated 1.9 million years old, show the face of *Homo habilis* as having been long, broad, and flat with prominent cheekbones, like that of much older hominids, the australopithecines. But *Homo habilis* was clearly distinguished from its contemporaries, the australopithecines, by the size of its brain case, with a brain capacity of 25 fluid ounces (750 milliliters), compared with less than 17 fluid ounces (500 milliliters) for the australopithecines.

Slightly younger hominid fossils at the same site, dated to 1.8 million years ago, have been distinguished as *Homo erectus*, a species that survived in Africa for more than a million years. It was the most advanced of the Lake Turkana hominids and the first to venture beyond Africa. Indeed, fossils of *Homo erectus*, along with stone tools (Acheulian hand axes), have been discovered throughout Europe and as far afield as China (so-called Peking Man) and Java (Java Man).

One of the most complete *Homo erectus* fossils was found near Lake Turkana in 1984. It is the skeleton of a robustly built boy with long legs and narrow hips. Aged about 11 and standing 5 feet 6 inches (168 centimeters) tall, he had a long, low skull with prominent brow ridges and a slightly more pronounced nose.

The brain size of *Homo erectus* increased over time. By a million years ago, its brain had reached a capacity of about 33 fluid ounces (1,000 milliliters), rising 500,000 years later to about 43 fluid ounces (1,300 milliliters). In comparison, *Homo sapiens* has a brain capacity of 58 fluid ounces (1,750 milliliters).

RIFT VALLEY LAKE
The region around Lake Turkana has experienced countless volcanic eruptions over the last tens of millions of years. The outpourings of lava and ash have helped bury and preserve sediments containing the fossil remains of our human ancestors.

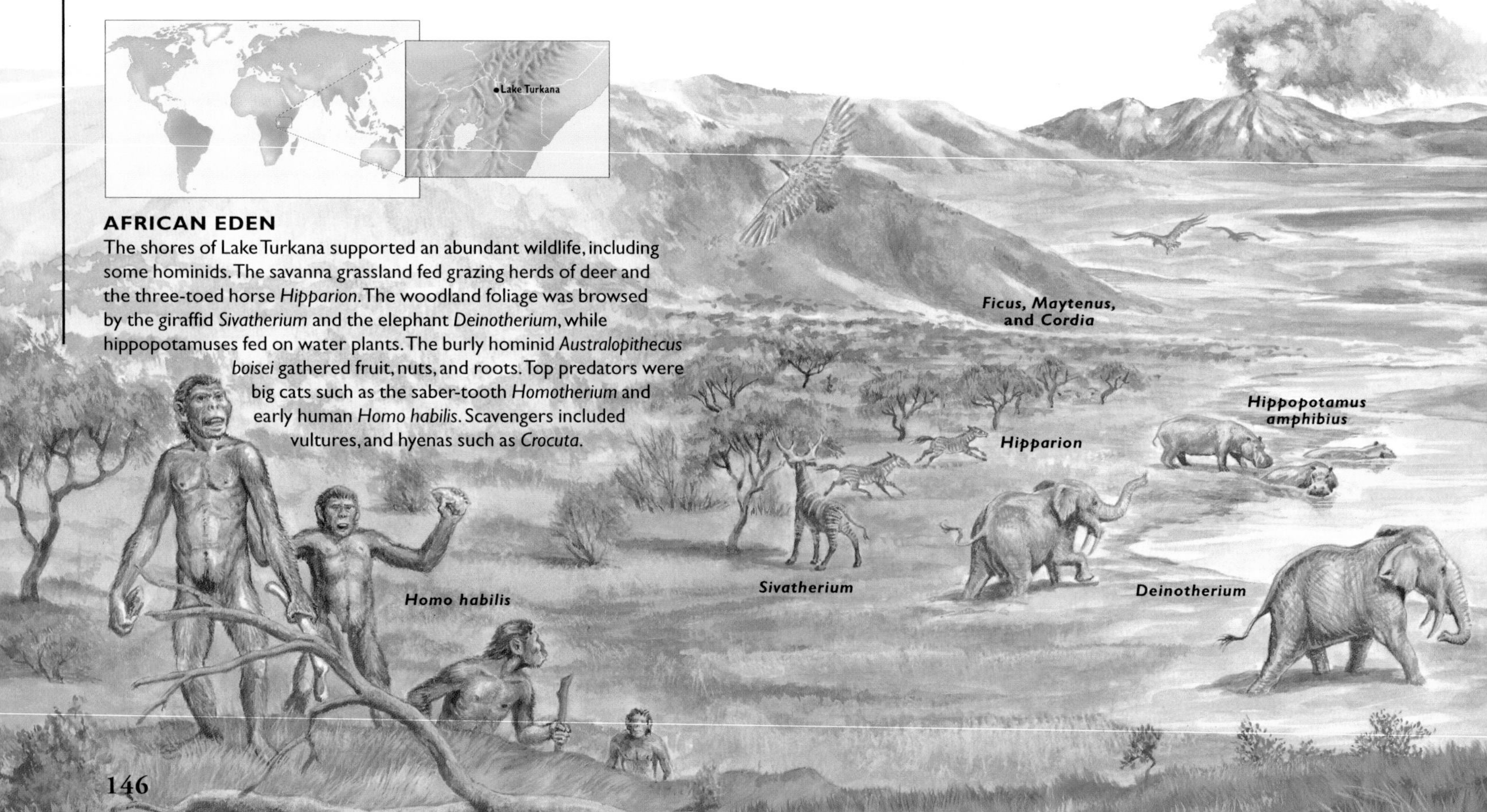

AFRICAN EDEN
The shores of Lake Turkana supported an abundant wildlife, including some hominids. The savanna grassland fed grazing herds of deer and the three-toed horse *Hipparion*. The woodland foliage was browsed by the giraffid *Sivatherium* and the elephant *Deinotherium*, while hippopotamuses fed on water plants. The burly hominid *Australopithecus boisei* gathered fruit, nuts, and roots. Top predators were big cats such as the saber-tooth *Homotherium* and early human *Homo habilis*. Scavengers included vultures, and hyenas such as *Crocuta*.

The variety of hominids decreased, so that by 800,000 years ago, *Homo erectus* was one of only two hominids left to carry forward the human lineage. The other is known as *Homo ergaster.*

OTHER TURKANA MAMMALS

There is a wealth of other animal and plant fossils in the surroundings of Lake Turkana, many of them of animals and plants that are familiar to us today. Baboons (*Theropithecus*) and monkeys (*Rhinocolobus*) were as common at this time in the Lake Turkana region as they are today. They generally lived in the riverside forests, although some species preferred more open, drier woodland. They were hunted by the same large carnivores that live in modern-day savanna communities, such as large lions, pack-hunting hyenas (*Crocuta*), and dogs (canid *Lycaon*).

Elephant-like proboscideans were the largest of the big plant-eaters and lived both on the open savannas and in forested habitats. Early horses (*Hipparion*) were common, but were replaced by the modern savanna-grazing *Equus* around 2.3 million years ago. Camel and giraffe remains have also been found, along with 40 different kinds of bovines. These cowlike creatures eventually inhabited wet grasslands.

Analysis of the plants locked away in the Turkana deposits shows a gradual dominance of grasses over trees and shrubs. Initially, the grasses made up 20 to 40 percent of the vegetation, but over time, this figure increased to 65 percent.

MODERN MEGAHERBIVORES
The African savanna developed in Miocene times (23 to 5 million years ago), as the climate became cooler and drier. Plant-eating mammals emerged from the forests and switched over from browsing foliage to grazing grass.

CONNECTIONS

Twenty-one different types of fossil fish have been found in the Lake Turkana strata, compared to 34 types of fish living in the lake today. These fossils include a freshwater stingray (Dasyatis africana) *that must have originally migrated into the lake from the Indian Ocean. Other fish include the African lungfish,* Polypterus, *and other species that show an early link with the Nile River in Egypt to the north.*

Mammals of the Americas

For most of the past two hundred million years, South and North America have not been connected. The isolation of South America as an island for long periods of time, combined with migrations of animals both south and north via temporary land bridges, has had a profound effect on the mammal populations of the two continents at different times in the past.

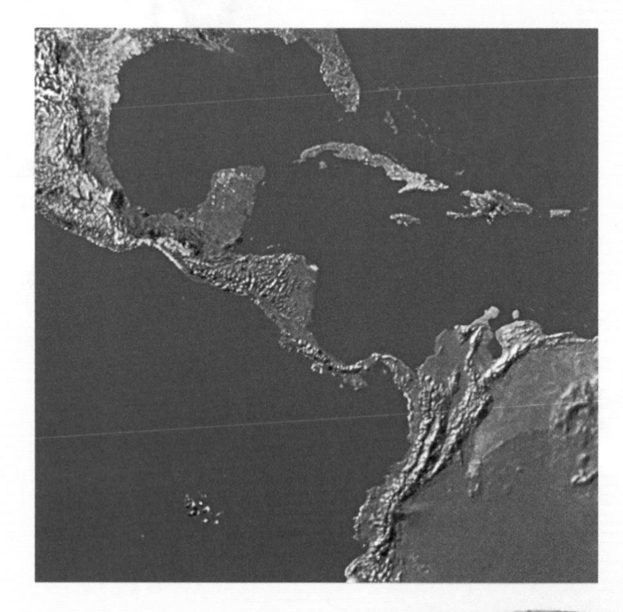

BRIDGING THE GAP
The current land bridge between North and South America is a narrow strip of land comprising the countries of Panama and Costa Rica. This bridge was established about 3 million years ago. Before that, occasional falls in sea level may have turned some seabeds into land, allowing animals to migrate across chains of islands in the West Indies and what is now Central America.

AN INVASION DURING THE CRETACEOUS

During Cretaceous times, a population of small, primitive mammals lived alongside the dinosaurs in South America. In North America, a mammalian group called the therians (made up of placental mammals and marsupials) dominated. Toward the end of the Cretaceous, a connection was temporarily established between North and South as a result of a change in sea levels. Some therians migrated south, where they evolved into some highly unusual and singular forms.

About 15 marsupial families became established in South America during Tertiary times, including a group of saber-toothed marsupial meat-eaters. But the most distinctive animals to develop were a group of placental mammals, the xenarthrans (meaning "strange joints"), including sloths, armadillos, and anteaters. The most spectacular of these were the armadillo-like glyptodonts, which grew to the size of a large automobile. Superficially they resembled ankylosaurs since they had a protective bony shell and a spiked club on the end of the tail. The tail itself was powerful and flexible, supporting the animal like a tripod when it reared up on its hind legs in defense or for reproduction. The massive skull had powerful jaws and teeth that were used for chewing the tough prairie grasses.

ARMORED PLANT-EATER
Doedicurus, a glyptodont, grew to 23 feet (4 meters) in length and lived in Patagonia about 1 to 2 million years ago. It bore a bony club at the end of its tail; the club was covered in spikes and used as a defensive weapon.

The sloths were also plant-eaters. They first appeared some 30 million years ago and included tree sloths and ground sloths. *Megatherium*, the largest known ground sloth, grew to 19 feet (6 meters) long. Ground sloths were a highly successful group and later

GIANT GROUND SLOTH
Megatherium inhabited an area that now includes Bolivia and Peru. Although as large as a modern elephant, it could rear up on its hind legs, supported by its thick tail. In this position, it browsed near the treetops, hooking down branches with its clawed forefeet.

spread into North America across a newly formed land bridge. They survived until 11,000 years ago when they became extinct along with many other large plant-eaters.

PAMPAS BROWSER
Toxodon was a 9-foot- (2.7-meter-) long rhinoceros-like plant-eater. A browser and grazer, it fed on the grasses and shrubs of the central Argentinian Pampas region about 2 million years ago.

THE AMERICAS "SWAP" ANIMALS

These distinctive mammals of South America have now almost died out. Their extinction has been explained by the opening of a new land bridge with North America about 3 million years ago, and the subsequent invasion of the southern half of the continent by North American mammals. While North American horses, deer, bears, and pumas moved south, opossums and some xenarthrans moved into North America. This interchange was an extraordinary two-way traffic across the Central American animal "freeway." About 50 percent of South America's present mammals are derived from North America and 20 percent of North America's mammals originated in the south.

Although it may seem like northern domination, the total mammal population increased in the south and the levels of extinction in the two continents were similar. The major extinctions in South America affected the hoofed animals and xenarthrans but many were already declining before the northern invaders arrived.

HOOFED MAMMALS

The hoof-bearing (ungulate) and plant-eating mammals of Tertiary times are familiar today. They include pigs, horses, cows, rhinos, elephants, and deer. In South America, they evolved into some unique rabbit-, horse-, and camel-like forms. These included the 10-foot- (3-meter-) long *Macrauchenia*, which had a long neck, substantial trunk, and nostrils placed high on the skull between the eyes. One of the largest hoofed mammals, *Toxodon*, had a barrel-shaped body on short, stocky legs, a broad head, and small 3-toed hoofs. Charles Darwin, who collected *Toxodon* fossils in Argentina, described it as "one of the strangest animals ever discovered."

EARLY EQUID
Widespread in North America, Asia, and Europe 50 million years ago, *Hyracotherium* (left) was about the size of a labrador dog. It is thought to be the ancestor of all horses.

MERYCHIPPUS
Herds of *Merychippus* roamed the North American prairies 5 to 10 million years ago. It was one of the first horses to feed almost entirely on grass. As an adaptation to this diet, its teeth were taller and higher-crowned than those of its ancestors.

HORSES EXTINCT IN NORTH AMERICA

Along with many other large mammals, horses became extinct in North America about 11,000 years ago, possibly as the result of an epidemic or human activity. But the genus Equus *survived in Europe, Africa, and Asia as zebras, asses, and wild horses. It is thought that horses were first domesticated in eastern Asia between 3,000 and 4,000 years ago. The horse was reintroduced to the Americas in the 16th century by Spanish explorers.*

WILD HORSES
The mustangs of the 19th-century American plains were descended from domesticated horses introduced 300 years earlier by the Spanish.

Divergence of Apes and Hominids

Humans are members of a large group of primates called the catarrhines, which includes the apes and the Old World monkeys of Africa, Asia, and Europe. The history of this group can be traced back to a common ancestor that lived around 28 million years ago. By 22 million years ago, the Old World monkeys had diverged on to a separate evolutionary path. Only 4.5 million years ago, the hominid ancestors of humans diverged from the other African apes. The difference between the DNA (genetic material) of humans and their closest relatives, the chimpanzees, is less than 2 percent.

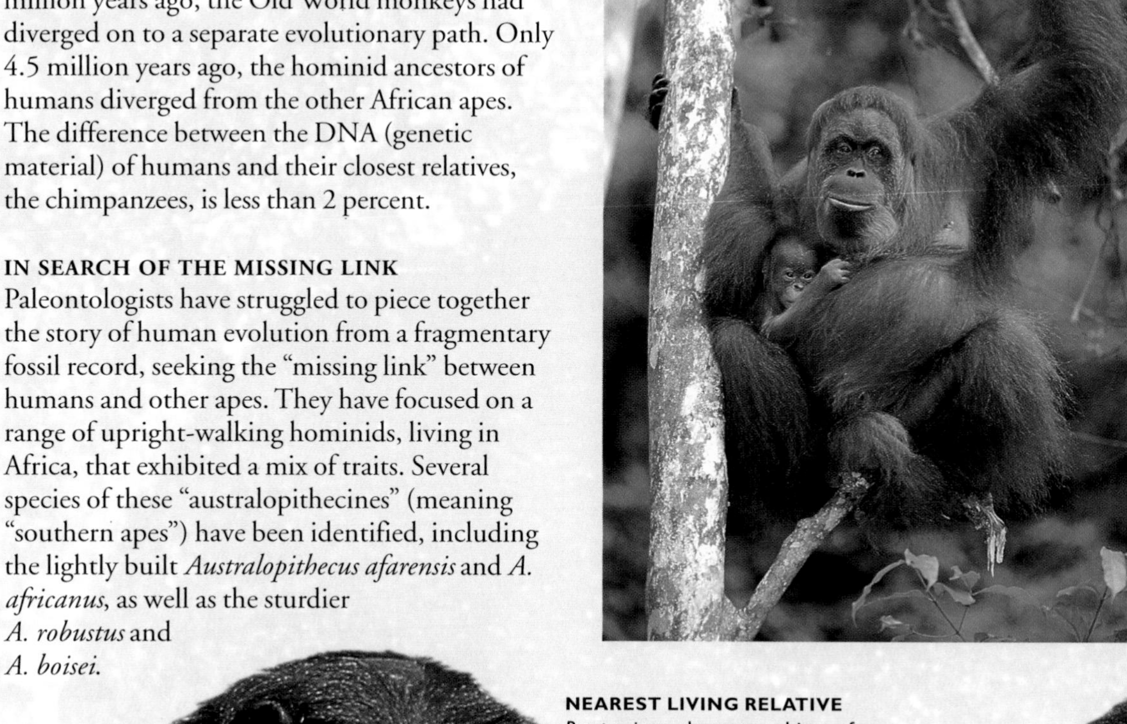

DISTANT RELATIVE
The orangutan, a native of Southeast Asia, was once thought to be our closest ape relative. With its large brain and considerable intelligence, it was thought to belong to the same group of apes as the African chimpanzee and gorilla. It is now known, however, that the African apes are more closely related to humans.

IN SEARCH OF THE MISSING LINK

Paleontologists have struggled to piece together the story of human evolution from a fragmentary fossil record, seeking the "missing link" between humans and other apes. They have focused on a range of upright-walking hominids, living in Africa, that exhibited a mix of traits. Several species of these "australopithecines" (meaning "southern apes") have been identified, including the lightly built *Australopithecus afarensis* and *A. africanus*, as well as the sturdier *A. robustus* and *A. boisei*.

NEAREST LIVING RELATIVE
Pan paniscus, the pygmy chimp of Central Africa (also known as the bonobo), is our nearest living relative. Its DNA is a few tenths of one percent closer to ours than that of the common chimp, *Pan troglodytes*.

THE SKULL OF "MRS. PLES"
This skull of *Australopithecus africanus* was nicknamed "Mrs. Ples" by scientist Robert Broom in 1935. Later, Broom was able to show that this 2.5 to 3.0 million-year-old hominid grew to just over 4 feet (1.4 meters), could stand fully upright, and walk like a human.

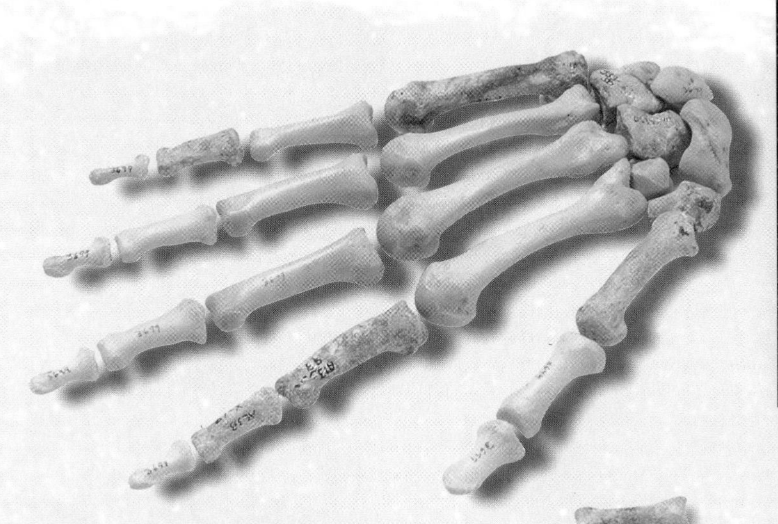

DOWN FROM THE TREES

As more and more research is conducted, the age of these possible human ancestors has been gradually pushed back. In the 1960s, scientists were startled to find that a skull of *A. boisei* from the Olduvai Gorge, Tanzania, was 2 million years old. But in 1994, an australopithecine found in Ethiopia, *Ardipithecus ramidus*, was dated to 4.5 million years ago. The most primitive hominid yet discovered, it bore many similarities to living chimpanzees. However, it did not knuckle-walk like the chimpanzees, but instead walked upright.

A fully grown male *Ardipithecus ramidus* was about 4.5 feet (1.3 meters) tall and weighed around 60 pounds (27 kilograms). Females were considerably smaller and lighter. This species lived in a woodland habitat, sleeping in trees, but active on the ground during the day. Walking upright freed its hands for carrying food and kept the hot sun off its unprotected back. Its dietary habits probably distinguished it from other apes, with the addition of scavenged meat to its staple meals of fruit and plant roots. It may also have banded together to hunt small animals.

It is unlikely that *Ardipithecus ramidus* made tools, since no evidence of these items has been found dating earlier than 2.6 million years ago.

ANCIENT HANDS
The hands of this 3.3 milllion-year-old *Australopithecus afarensis* from Ethiopia are close to, but not the same as, those of modern humans. They show the characteristics of both a tree-climber and a ground-based tool-maker.

However, the early australopithecines probably used sticks, twigs, and bones as tools in the way that chimpanzees do today.

Since the discovery of *Ardipithecus ramidus*, the heritage of the australopithecines has finally been pieced together. *A. anamensis*, found in 1995, is dated at 4.2 to 3.9 million years ago. It has an apelike jaw, but with more advanced teeth. The oldest *A. afarensis* is dated to about 3.8 million years ago. *A. africanus* emerged around 800,000 years later. The latest discovery, *A. garhi*, is around 2.5 million years old, and seems to be the best candidate for direct ancestor of genus *Homo*, while *A. robustus* and *A. boisei* survived alongside *Homo* species for over a million years.

AFRICAN DISCOVERIES

The first evidence for the existence of the man-ape australopithecines was a child's skull found in a cave at Taung, South Africa, in 1924. This "Taung boy" was an A. africanus. *In 1959, a skull of the larger* A. boisei *was found in the Olduvai Gorge, Tanzania. Dated to 2 million years ago, the skull convinced many researchers that australopithecines were the ancestors of modern humans. "Lucy," a famous example of* A. afarensis, *was found at Hadar, Ethiopia, in 1979.*

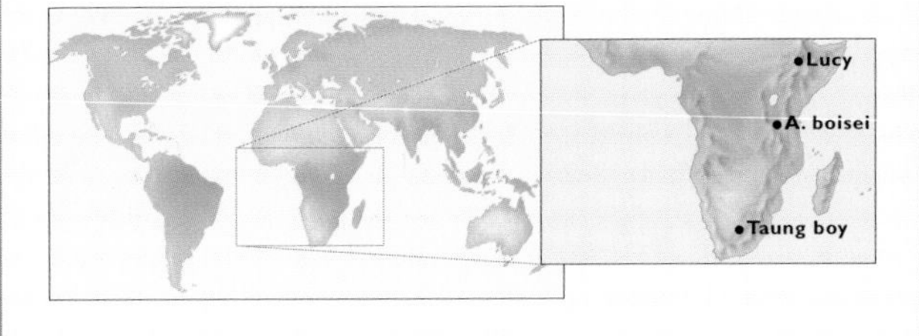

The Quaternary Age

A VIEW OF THE EARTH 18 THOUSAND YEARS AGO SHOWS A FROZEN WORLD. ICE SHEETS, IN PLACES TWO MILES THICK, COVERED VAST TRACTS OF THE NORTHERN CONTINENTS.

The Quaternary age is the most recent period of geological time, lasting from 1.8 million years ago up to the present day. In geological terms, the Earth 18,000 years ago was almost the same as it is today. Continents, mountains, ocean ridges, and subduction zones were all in nearly identical positions. The face of our planet, however, greatly differed from today, for the Earth was in the grip of an ice age. It was the most recent of many ice ages to have punctuated Earth's history. Huge ice sheets spread southward from the North Pole, and glaciers all over the world were larger than their present sizes.

Despite their name, ice ages are not always unrelentingly cold. During the last ice age, the climate swung between glacials, cold periods when the ice sheets grew, and interglacials, when the ice shrank back. Each glaciation has lasted for about 100,000 years, with periods of warmer interglaciation lasting 10,000 years in between. The Earth is still in the grip of this last ice age, although it is experiencing an interglacial period.

At the peak of the last ice age, ice and frozen ground spread far south of the Arctic circle. So much water became frozen—about 5 percent of all the water on Earth (including 90 percent of the freshwater)—that sea levels fell by 330 feet (100 meters). The drop in sea level meant that shallow

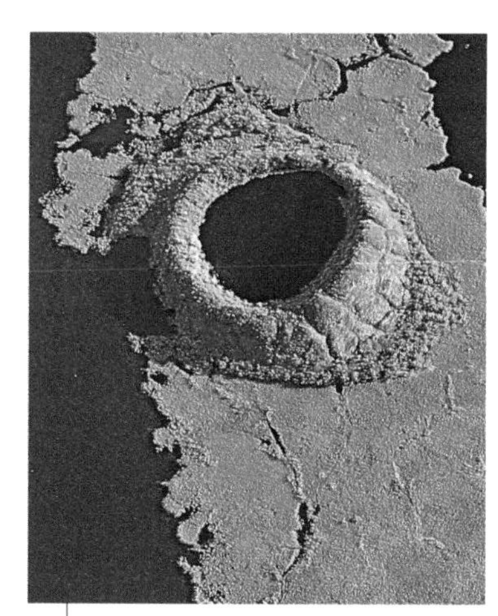

PINGOS
In the Canadian Arctic, the growth of underground ice pushes up mounds called pingos. As the ice core melts, the mound collapses to form a crater. Fossil pingos in Ireland and England show where permafrost once existed during the last ice age.

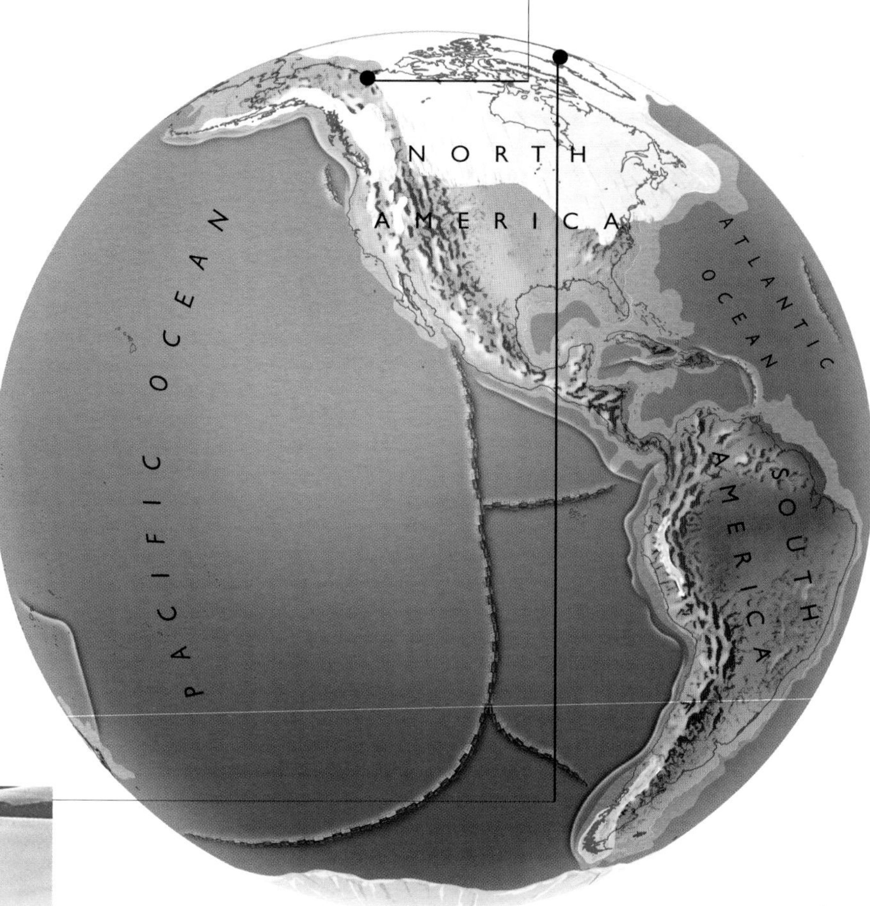

ICE POWER
Ice sheets build up over years. The growing pile of snow compresses the bottom layers into ice. Any slope in the ground makes the pile unstable so that it begins to slide slowly and flow down the hill under its own weight, as if it were a liquid. Here the Greenland ice sheet overflows through a gap in a mountain ridge.

NORTH AND SOUTH

Large-scale glaciation can develop only where there are extensive polar landmasses because land freezes more easily than the sea. During the last glaciation, ice sheets were more widely developed in the northern hemisphere because of the cluster of continents around the Arctic Ocean. The surface waters of the Arctic Ocean did eventually freeze and carry ice as far south as the British Isles.

seas suddenly became dry plains, connecting previously isolated islands and continents. The opening up of these land bridges was to have a dramatic effect on the distribution of animals and plants. Humans also took advantage, passing from Asia into the Americas via the Bering Strait and from Europe into the British Isles.

WHY DID THE ICE ADVANCE?

Fossil records show us that the global climate has been cooling slowly for the past 40 million years. Three million years ago, the cooling quickened and the polar icecaps and mountain glaciers of the northern continents began to grow. These changing weather patterns were influenced by the configuration of the continents. The gradual rifting of Antarctica from other southern continents led to the formation of a circular current, the Westerly Drift, which cut off the flow of warm air and water, and resulted in the cooling of the South Polar region. A polar icecap formed and sea temperatures dropped, precipitating an overall cooling of the Earth's climate.

About three million years ago, North and South America became joined by a land bridge, the Isthmus of Panama, so warm Atlantic water was no longer able to flow around the equator, but was instead diverted northward. This led to increased precipitation in eastern Canada, Greenland, and Scandinavia—three of the main areas of ice accumulation, where parts of the ice sheets were 10,000 feet (3,000 meters) thick. The warm ocean currents pulled moist air along with them, so that the amount of rain and snow falling on northern lands increased. In turn, the rivers poured more freshwater into the Arctic Ocean. Because freshwater freezes more readily than seawater, the Arctic sea-ice grew quickly.

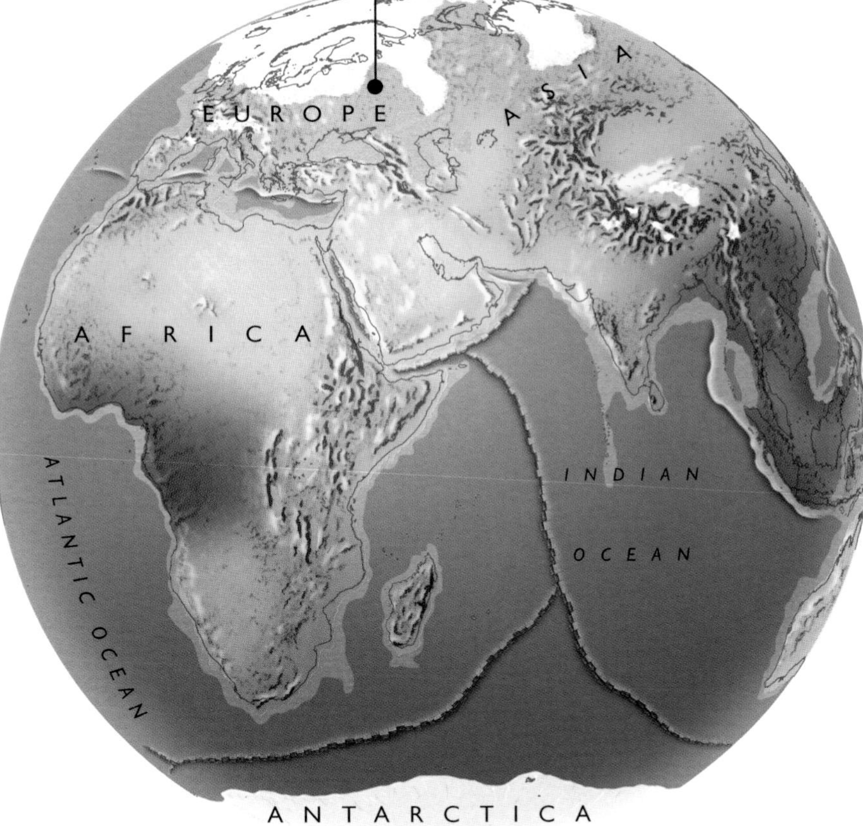

MAMMOTH MOLARS
Woolly mammoths were common across Europe and Asia during the last ice age. Their cheek teeth (above) were massive and heavily ridged to break up the coarse grass and shrubs of the steppe tundra.

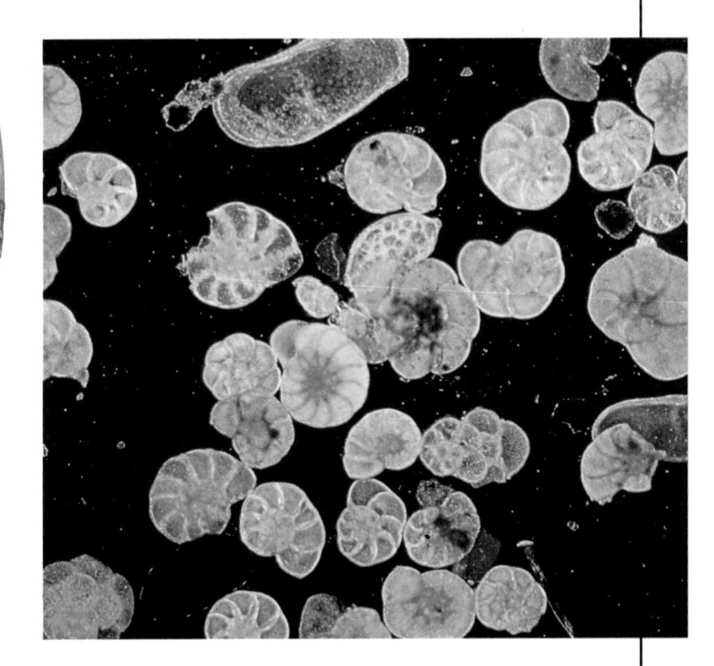

FOSSIL PROOF
From the shell composition of single-celled creatures (above) trapped in seafloor sediment, geologists can chart past changes in the temperature of seawater. Because sea and air temperatures are closely linked, changes in past climates can also be worked out.

The Russian Mammoth Steppe

The freezing conditions of a glacial, the coldest phase in an ice age, make it very difficult for plants and animals to survive. For plants, the extreme cold is a very difficult environment to survive in as there is often an absence of water and pollen-carrying insects. Permanently frozen ground also makes it almost impossible for seeds to take root. In turn, animal life cannot be supported, because there is no vegetation for plant-eaters to feed on. To complete the cycle, no meat-eaters can survive, since there are no plant-eaters to prey on.

However, many animals and plants survived the frozen wastelands of the last glacial, in areas beyond the ice. They occupied slightly warmer windswept lands with a summer thaw, deep in the southern parts of the North American and Asian continents. Animals that lived in these areas at the time included the woolly mammoth and rhino, who, like today's polar creatures, were animals that could survive intense cold. Their heavy fur acted as insulation, as did layers of body fat, which also provided a source of energy during the harsh winter months. The cave bear also conserved energy by hibernating.

One of the richest places for fossils of these animals is on the mammoth steppe, what is now eastern Russia. At the time, the steppe must have resembled a frozen variation on the hot African grasslands of today. Where modern Africa has elephants, rhinos, and lions, the steppe had mammoths, woolly rhinos, and large predatory cats. In effect, the area was home to woollier versions of species that we are familiar with today.

The mammoth steppe was devoid of trees, but during a brief spring and summer, colorful swathes of flowering herbs and grasses burst into

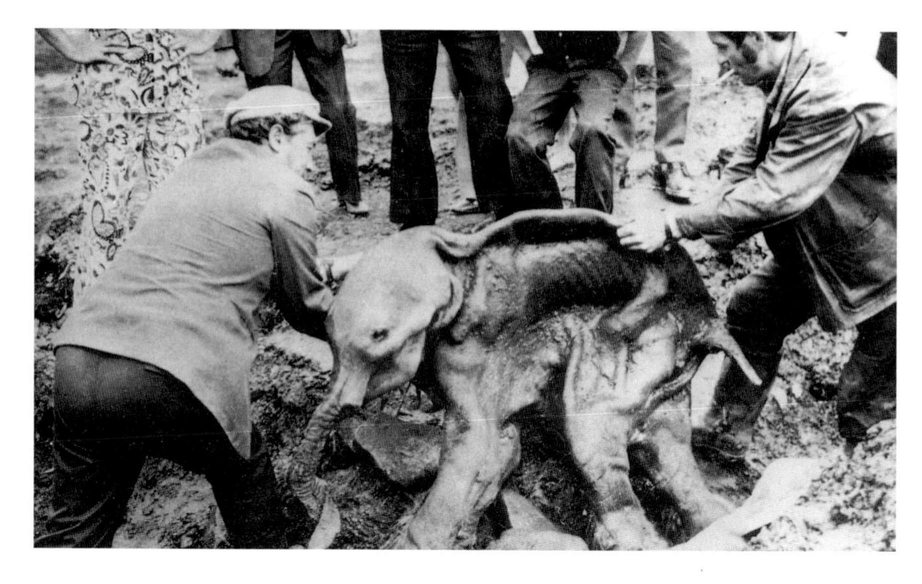

40,000-YEAR-OLD BABY
In June 1977, Dima was discovered in Siberia under 6 feet (2 meters) of frozen silt. Dima was a sickly mammoth, 6 to 12 months old, that had died 40,000 years before when he fell into a pool or bog which froze and preserved his body tissue.

LIFE ON THE MAMMOTH STEPPE
The Russian mammoth steppe was a mostly grassy habitat that stood between the northern ice sheet and wooded habitats farther south. It was home to many large herbivores, including woolly mammoths and rhinos, giant deer, horses, and the ancestors of most domesticated cattle. These were prey to hunters, such as large lion-type cats and humans.

The plants of the mammoth steppe are still seen today. They include a variety of hardy grasses and buttercups, and plants that flower in the Arctic tundra, such as purple and yellow saxifrage.

life. This annual greening provided food for herds of migratory mammals, which were closely followed by hungry predators. One predator, *Homo sapiens*, humankind, was so successful at exploiting this valuable food resource that many species were soon extinct.

CHANGING GLOBAL CIRCUMSTANCES

As the last glacial period came to an end and the climate warmed, the icecaps started to melt, leading to a radical change in the environment. The amount of habitable land increased as the ice retreated. The rise in temperature suited the growth of trees, so the vast grasslands, which were suited to colder conditions, began to disappear and were replaced by forest. Herds found their migration paths blocked by the new forests and broke up into smaller, more vulnerable groups. The leaves and shrubs that the animals now fed on were much less nutritious than the grasses, and their numbers declined ever more quickly as humans and other predators hunted them. In a few thousand years, the mammoths, woolly rhinos, giant deer, and cave bears were all extinct.

In isolated parts of Eurasia and North America, however, some species survived the most recent ice age, and are still in evidence today. Unfortunately, some, such as the bison, bear, wolf, lynx, arctic fox, and condor, are now endangered. Other survivors fared better, particularly humans.

RECLAIMING THE LAND

At the end of the last glacial phase, the ice sheets began to retreat, and plants were able to colonize the newly exposed land. The first vegetation to become re-established had to be very hardy. The pioneers, like the first plants ever to colonize the land over 450 million years ago, were lichens and mosses. Slowly, enough soil and organic matter gathered to allow other species to thrive. The mosses and lichens were joined by low-lying, tough shrubs and trees such as juniper, dwarf willow, and birch. Sedge grasses, bog cotton, and saxifrages also took root. These species can all be found in today's Arctic tundra.

ARCTIC BLOOM
Blooms of purple saxifrage such as these once colored the mammoth steppe.

CAVE DWELLERS
This stylized image of a mammoth was painted in the cave of La Baume Latrone in France by hunters who lived during the last ice age. The animal's body, 4 feet (1.2 meters) long, is shown in profile, while the tusks are depicted as if seen from the front.

The Human Journey

The story of human evolution is complex.It can be pieced together only tentatively using fragmentary fossil evidence from around the world. The earliest fossils that we can label *Homo* (human) are roughly 2.4 million years old, come from Eastern and Southern Africa, and belong to *Homo habilis*. Around 1.9 million years ago a type of human more advanced than *Homo habilis* is thought to have evolved in Africa. *Homo erectus*, "upright human," was taller and had a bigger brain than its predecessor and possessed a skeleton similar to that of a modern human. This new type of human was particularly successful and spread relatively rapidly. By 1.8 million years ago humans of this type had reached the Caucasus Mountains in Asia Minor and between one and half a million years ago they had become established in Europe.

By 500,000 years ago, it is now believed that two separate branches of *Homo* were beginning to emerge, one of which eventually gave rise to the Neanderthals, *Homo neanderthalensis*, and the other to modern humans, *Homo sapiens*, meaning wise or knowing human.

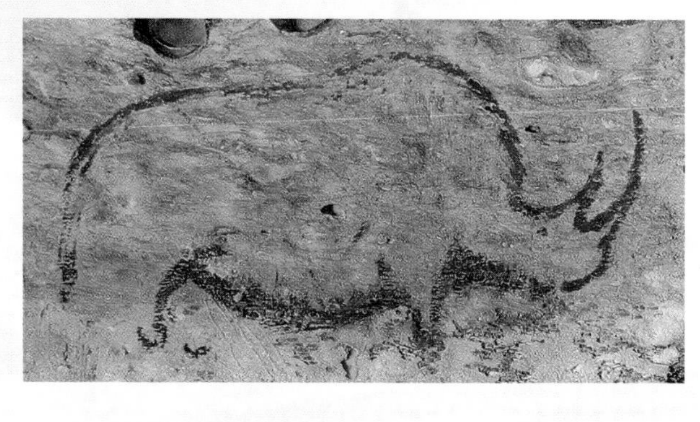

ANCIENT ARTS
The culture of Cro-Magnon people was highly developed and even artistic. They left many paintings and sculptures in caves around Europe. This rhinoceros painting was found in a cave in Rouffignac, France.

NEANDERTHALS

The remains of the Neanderthals, *Homo neanderthalensis*, are found only in Europe and the Middle East. Their fossils range in age from 120,000 years to 35,000 years old. Neanderthals have an undeserved reputation for being primitive and stupid when in fact they were culturally advanced. For example they buried their dead and made a variety of tools and weapons.

The remains of the Neanderthals show that they were thicker set and generally stronger than modern people. They also had heavy brow ridges on their skulls and a sloping forehead, and, on average, they actually had larger brains than modern humans. But the Neanderthals all seem to have died out by about 35,000 years ago.

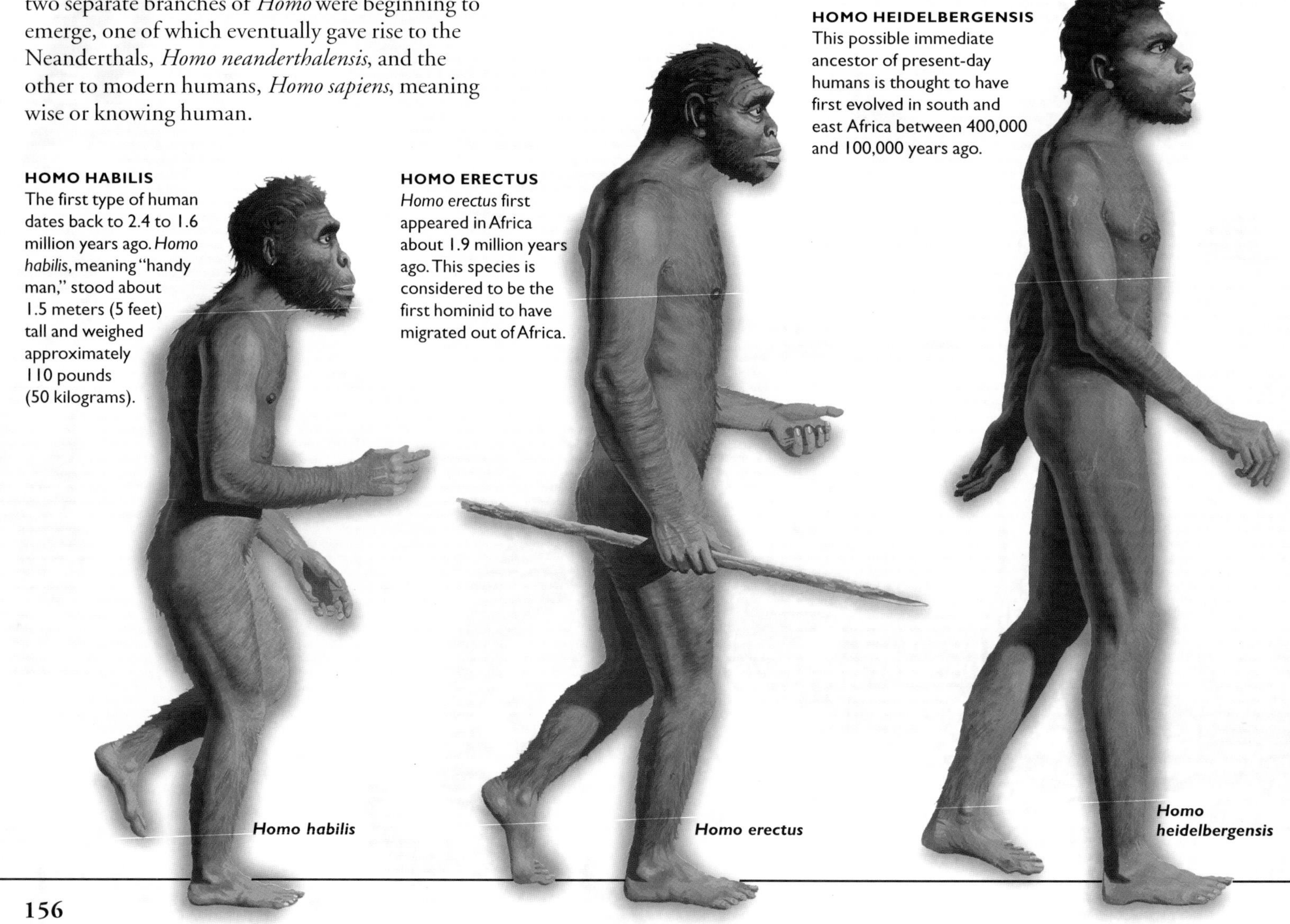

HOMO HABILIS
The first type of human dates back to 2.4 to 1.6 million years ago. *Homo habilis*, meaning "handy man," stood about 1.5 meters (5 feet) tall and weighed approximately 110 pounds (50 kilograms).

HOMO ERECTUS
Homo erectus first appeared in Africa about 1.9 million years ago. This species is considered to be the first hominid to have migrated out of Africa.

HOMO HEIDELBERGENSIS
This possible immediate ancestor of present-day humans is thought to have first evolved in south and east Africa between 400,000 and 100,000 years ago.

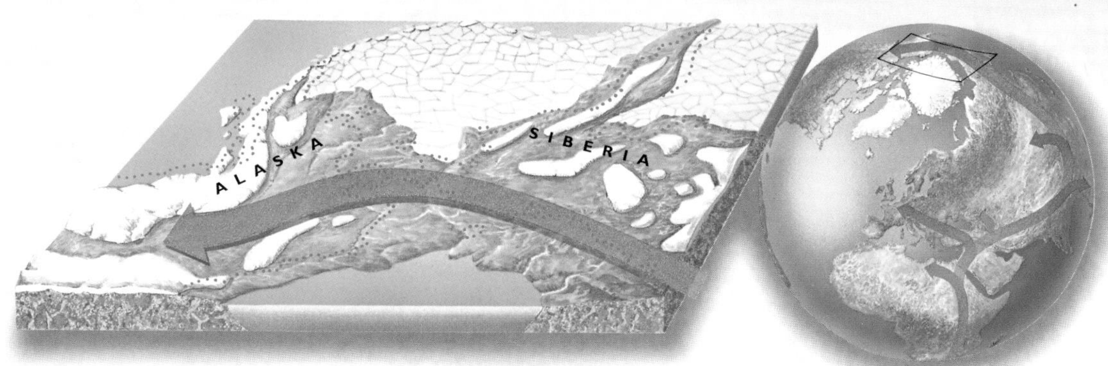

PEOPLING AMERICA
The Bering land bridge, formed during an ice age as a result of depressed sea levels, connected northeastern Russia with Alaska and provided a crossing point for animals and humans. It is generally thought that fully modern humans first crossed from Asia into North America via the land bridge some 30,000 years ago.

MODERN HUMANS

Homo sapiens probably evolved from an African group descended from the *Homo erectus* lineage; *Homo heidelbergensis* is a possible intermediate form. The earliest definite remains of our species have been found in Africa and are between 100,000 and 120,000 years old. Similar finds in Israel, from around 90,000 years ago, show that modern people reached the region before the Neanderthals. This refutes the theory that modern people are descended from the Neanderthals. It is currently thought that the Neanderthals were a now-extinct branch of the human family, a view supported by DNA analysis of their bones.

By 40,000 years ago, fully modern humans were alive in areas as far apart as Borneo and Europe. Most evidence now suggests that modern humans evolved in Africa and spread to the other continents. They may, however, have interbred with older groups in different areas and have probably evolved locally to a small extent to produce the various peoples of the world today.

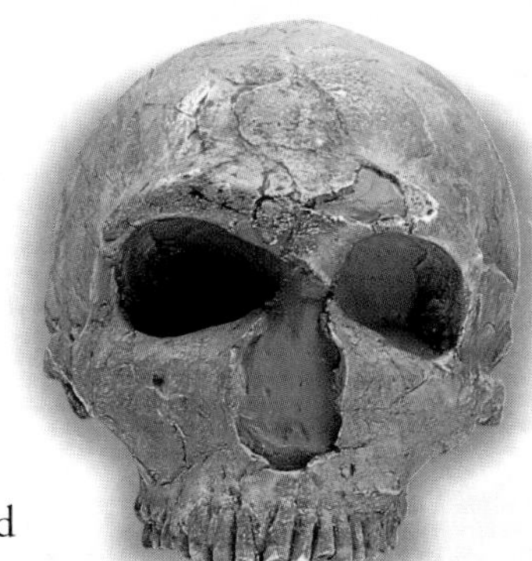

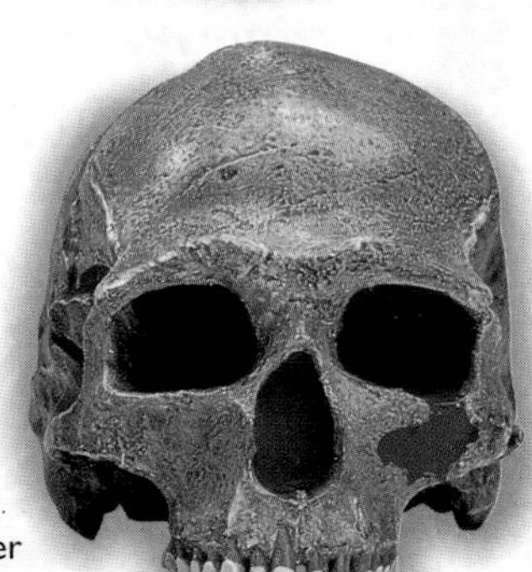

SKULLS
The skull of a Cro-Magnon (top) and a modern human skull (bottom) show only minor differences. Cro-Magnons had more rounded brain cases and slightly larger jaws and noses.

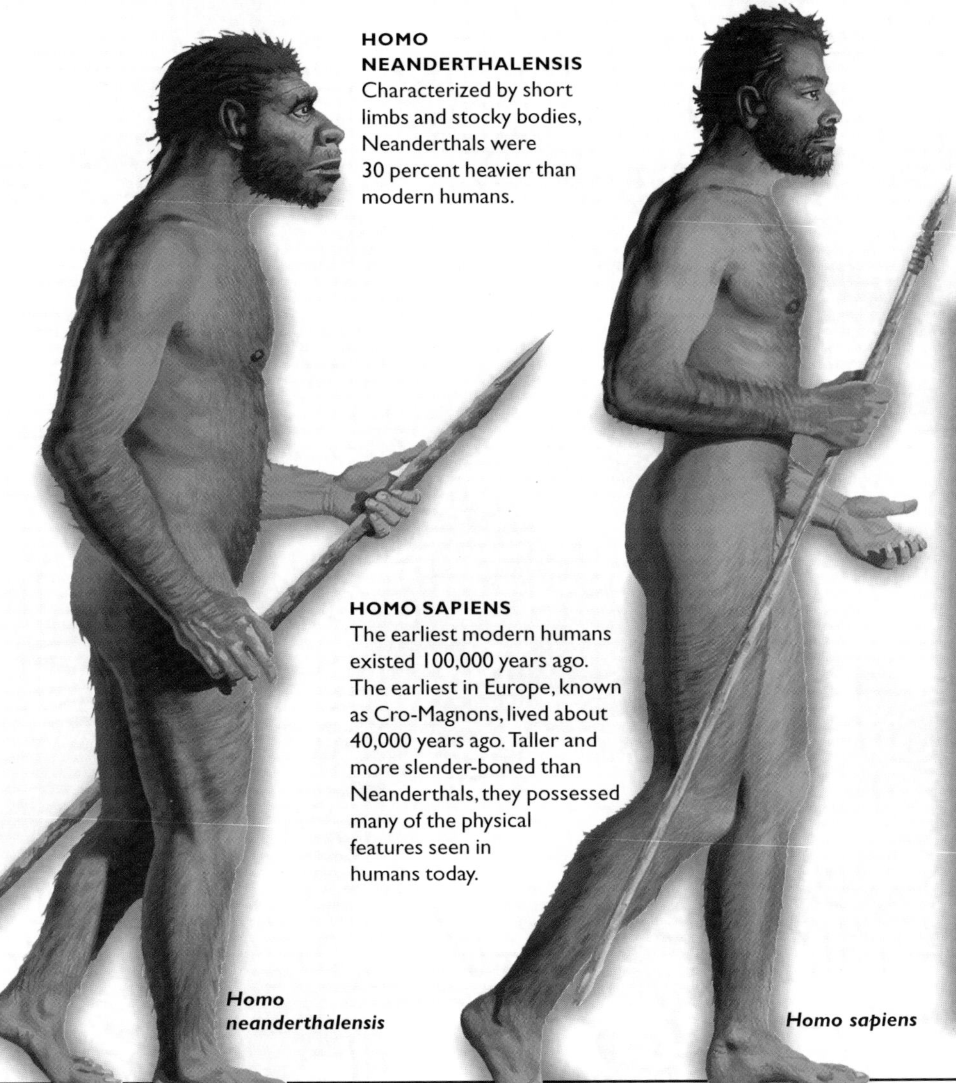

HOMO NEANDERTHALENSIS
Characterized by short limbs and stocky bodies, Neanderthals were 30 percent heavier than modern humans.

HOMO SAPIENS
The earliest modern humans existed 100,000 years ago. The earliest in Europe, known as Cro-Magnons, lived about 40,000 years ago. Taller and more slender-boned than Neanderthals, they possessed many of the physical features seen in humans today.

Homo neanderthalensis

Homo sapiens

EARLY AMERICAN HUMANS

The Clovis culture, marked by its distinctive style of stone technology, is accepted as the earliest in the Americas, and is about 11,500 years old. The site of Monte Verde, in southern Chile, however, is providing convincing support for much older occupation. Wedged between the Andes and the Pacific Ocean, the site has been dated at 12,500 years old. It is argued that for people to have traveled this far south, some 10,000 miles (16,000 kilometers) from the Bering land bridge, they must have arrived in North America much earlier than 11,500 years ago.

WEAPON MAKERS
The Clovis point is a razor-sharp spearhead made of stone. Many of these points have been found wedged between mammoth bones.

Beyond the Ice Age

TEN THOUSAND YEARS AGO, A cold glacial period in the Earth's most recent ice age came to an end. Global temperatures climbed quickly, and the great ice sheets began to melt and retreat. Just as advancing glaciers can scar and sculpt the landscape, creating deep valleys and smoothed-off hills, so the retreat of an ice sheet also leaves its mark.

As the ice melted, great lakes of meltwater began to form. Some lakes were created where rock and ice remnants of the retreating glaciers formed natural dams. When the ice dams finally melted, too, cataclysmic floods followed, such as those that scoured the land to form the remarkable Channeled Scablands in Washington State.

The meltwater also added greatly to ocean volume. Rising seas drowned land bridges such as that joining Alaska to eastern Siberia opening the Bering Strait and isolating the animal and plant life of Northern America from Asia.

In other places, the melting of the ice sheets caused shorelines to be lifted clear of the sea. The ice sheets were extremely heavy and weighed down the continental crust below them, pushing it down into the flexible mantle of the Earth. When the weight of the ice was removed, the land rebounded, inch by inch. Each upward movement created a new coastline and raised the land that was previously on the coast.

HIGH AND DRY
Raised beaches occur where land that was once pressed down by the weight of an ice sheet "springs back," lifting sections of shoreline, as here on the Isle of Mull, Scotland, clear of the sea (above).

THE GOOD TIMES

Temperatures on Earth have been relatively stable for the last 10,000 years, a time during which human civilization has flourished. But this success of humans as a species is having a considerable impact on global temperatures. Since the beginning of the Industrial Revolution, human activity has had an increasingly damaging effect on the Earth's atmosphere. "Greenhouse" gases released by burning fossil fuels such as coal, gas, and oil trap more of the Sun's energy than is normal, warming the global climate. Some scientists think that the average rise in temperature over the next 50 years may be as much as 9°F (5°C). Ultimately, if this trend continues, the icecaps will melt, and sea levels will rise by about 23 feet (7 meters), enough to flood almost all the world's rivers and coastlines and the cities built on them.

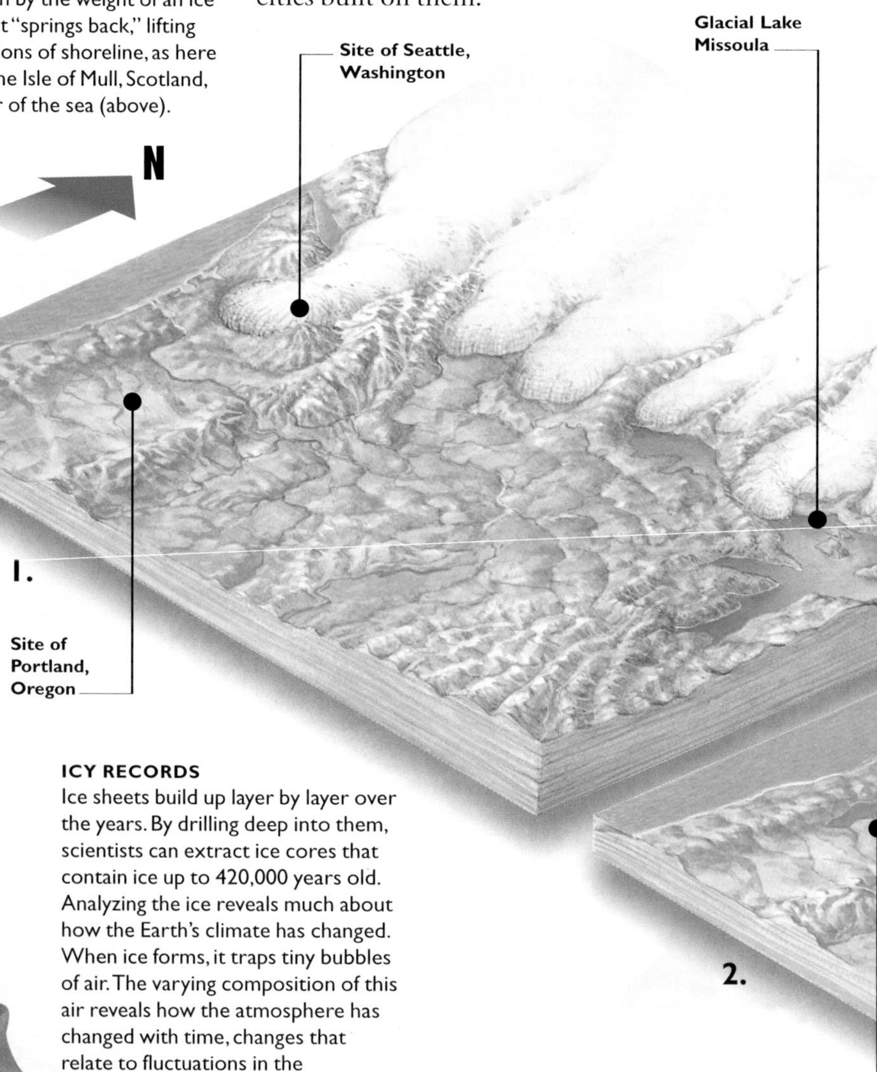

ICY RECORDS
Ice sheets build up layer by layer over the years. By drilling deep into them, scientists can extract ice cores that contain ice up to 420,000 years old. Analyzing the ice reveals much about how the Earth's climate has changed. When ice forms, it traps tiny bubbles of air. The varying composition of this air reveals how the atmosphere has changed with time, changes that relate to fluctuations in the temperature of the Earth.

THE POWER OF FLOOD

A sudden flood of meltwater from a glacier can have spectacular consequences. The prehistoric floods that gouged out the Channeled Scablands of eastern Washington State must have also wiped out much of the life in the area as they swept past. Catastrophic floods like this are caused when glacial ice melts rapidly. Often, the heat to melt the ice is supplied by an erupting volcano situated underneath the glacier. Part of the glacier itself can even flow down the slope of the volcano. A dramatic example of this occurred in Iceland in 1996 when a volcano erupted underneath the Vatnajökull glacier. The hot lava and gas quickly melted the glacial ice and precipitated a flood known as a "Jökulhaup." As much as 1.6 million cubic feet (45,000 cubic meters) of water poured down the valley each second, destroying two bridges and sweeping away a six mile section of road.

FIRE AND ICE
As a volcano erupts under the Vatnajökull glacier in Iceland, the ice can be seen cracking as it melts (top left of picture).

UNLIKELY CATCH
Mammoths lived on the dry land between Europe and Britain during the last glacial when sea levels were low. Their fossil teeth and bones are sometimes trawled from what is now the bed of the North Sea.

THE NEXT ICE AGE

Despite global warming, the most recent ice age may not be over. We may be living through a long, warm interglacial period. Evidence shows that previous interglacials have been both longer and warmer. Some scientists think that the present phase of rising temperatures is merely delaying the onset of the next cold period, which could start in 5,000 years' time and last for 15,000 years.

Such predictions are very difficult to make because global warming shows us how small changes in the atmosphere can trigger major effects in the global climate. So far we cannot predict accurately how the warming effect of greenhouse gases will balance other influences that tend to make the climate cooler, and so we cannot be certain when the next ice age will begin.

Site of Seattle, Washington

Lake Missoula overflows

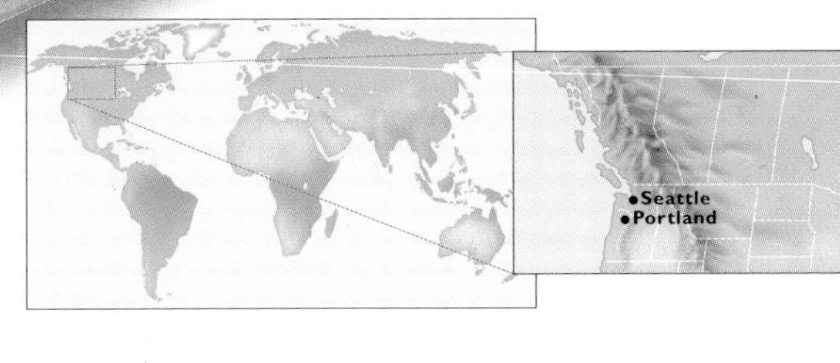

SCABBING THE LAND
1. Lake Missoula formed when a finger of ice trapped meltwater from the North American ice sheet 13,000 years ago. The lake filled to more than 1,000 feet (300 meters) deep.
2. Eventually, the lake overflowed. More than 720 million cubic feet (20 million cubic meters) of water flooded toward the sea per second, cutting into the bedrock and depositing piles of rock debris as huge sand ripples.

Earth Fact File

Earth's history is all around us, recorded in the rocks beneath our feet. Interpretation of the evidence is rarely easy at first glance. However, advancements during the past 200 years have allowed scientists to learn more about the dynamic forces that sculpted the land and fostered life. This section explores the history of the Earth sciences, as well as revealing the nature of the forces, from the formation of rocks to the movement of continents, that have literally shaped the planet's past.

Earth History: The Geological Timescale

The scientists who pieced together the Earth's history began without any geological "calendar" or "clock." Their task was like constructing a family tree from a mass of anonymous photographs; family likenesses, hairstyles, and fashions all point to relationships and chronology, but those limited clues can be misleading. The discovery of the Earth's distant past and the establishment of its broad chronology have been achieved only in the last 200 years. Now, thanks largely to radiometric dating, we can accurately date the formation of some rocks. We know with some certainty that the Earth is 4.6 billion years old.

English naturalist Charles Darwin's (1809–82) theory of evolution took little account of the fossil record because of its imperfections and lack of a timescale. His calculation of 300 million years for Tertiary times was a considerable overestimate, it lasted 65 million years.

A 6,000-YEAR-OLD EARTH

During the 17th and 18th centuries, attempts to determine the age of the Earth used the only dating techniques then available—historical documents, calendar systems, and astronomy. Even the greatest natural philosophers and mathematicians, such as Isaac Newton, believed that human history had prevailed through the same period in time as the history of the Earth. In 1650, James Ussher, Archbishop of Armagh in Ireland, calculated the date of the Earth's origin, according to biblical chronology, as 4004 BC. This age was generally accepted for nearly 200 years.

LAYING DOWN STRATA

Most early work on establishing a geological timescale focused on examining sedimentary strata—layers of rock formed by the deposition, or sedimentation, of mineral particles carried to the sedimentation site by water or wind. As early as 1669, the Danish natural philosopher and physician, Nicolaus Steno, formulated the "law of superposition." This stated that, in a given sequence of sedimentary strata, the bottom layers were laid down first, and layers become progressively younger toward the top. As a result of early investigations of superimposed strata, undertaken between 1780 and 1830, geologists gradually recognized that Earth processes, such as weathering, erosion, and transportation of sediment were incredibly slow. The accumulation of the great thicknesses of strata making up the layers of the Earth must, therefore, have taken a great length of time, much longer than the 6,000-year span allowed for by Christian theologists.

THE PRINCIPLES OF STRATIGRAPHY

Stratigraphy is a means of interpreting the history of the Earth's changing landscapes and seascapes. Past environments and their lifeforms are revealed by examining successive rock layers. These strata record deposition and erosion on land and at sea. It has taken 200 years to sequence, subdivide, match, and interpret these strata. The story of the last 600 million years is now known, but the history of the Earth's first 4 billion years is still uncertain.

PROBLEMS WITH STRATIGRAPHY

Stratigraphic layers do not always appear in chronological order. Many factors can cause older layers to appear above newer ones. The action of plate tectonics and mountain building can turn rock strata completely upside down (inversion).

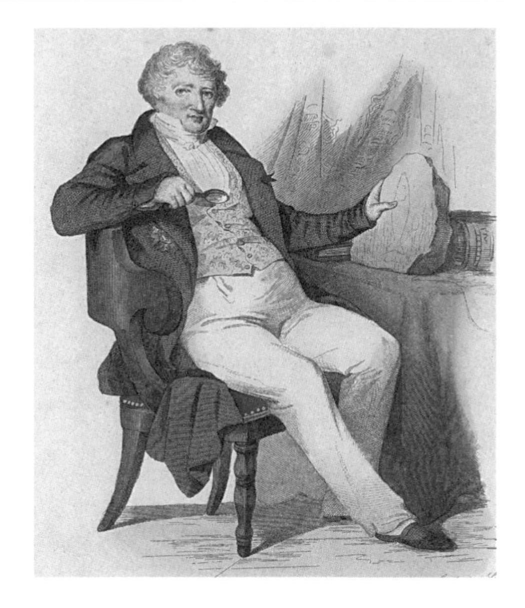

From left to right: Georges Cuvier, Roderick Murchison, and Adam Sedgwick, early 19th-century pioneers of "biostratigraphy," a method of using fossils to identify successive rock strata.

In addition, volcanic igneous rock may intrude into sedimentary strata and other rock. When this happens, the igneous rock forms a relatively young layer between two older layers. This is an example of a cross-cutting relationship.

CROSS-CUTTING RELATIONSHIPS

A specific kind of cross-cutting relationship is called an angular unconformity. An unconformity represents a period during which no sediment is being deposited in an area. Folding, faulting, and erosion disrupt and displace the surface of the non-depositional area. When deposition is resumed, it cross-cuts the original surface to form an angular unconformity. The entire process can take millions of years, so unconformities represent major time gaps in the stratigraphic record. The most famous example of an angular unconformity, at Siccar Point in Berwickshire, Scotland, is known as Hutton's unconformity. Here, vertically inclined gray sandstone is overlain by gently inclined red sandstone.

THE FOSSIL RECORD

By the end of the 18th century, fossils were generally accepted as the remains of past, frequently extinct, forms of life. In the early 19th century, William Smith in England and Georges Cuvier and Alexandre Brongniart in France, discovered that successive layers of sediment contained fossils that were characteristic of certain chronological periods.

FOSSILS AND STRATIGRAPHY

The discovery of the relationship between fossils and certain geological time periods opened up the possibility of using fossil discoveries to establish a relative sequence of rock deposition through time. In addition, the fossil deposits within sedimentary layers from different localities could be used to match and compare rock from diverse regions. When parts of separate sequences of strata were matched a general stratigraphic history gradually emerged.

THE FIRST BIOSTRATIGRAPHIES

William Smith was a practising engineer engaged in building canals in southern and central England, in the early 19th century. The economics of canal cutting required the accurate prediction of the nature of the underlying rock. From his practical experience Smith found that he could identify particular strata by their fossils. By measuring the inclination of strata he could also predict the next layers in the sequence. By a combination of taking vertical sections and identifying rock outcrops at the surface and noting their geographical distribution, he was able to map out the three-dimensional form of strata over large areas of countryside.

THE FIRST GEOLOGICAL MAPS

Smith extended his geological mapping across southern England, where most of the Secondary strata (now called Mesozoic) are gently inclined. Like the younger Tertiary strata of the Paris Basin (mapped by Georges Cuvier and Alexandre Brongniart in 1811), they have a relatively simple geological structure of folds and faults.

THE STRATIGRAPHIC COLUMN

By 1815, Smith published his remarkable map of the geology of England and Wales, one of the earliest of such large-scale maps in the world. He also produced a generalized stratigraphic column, extending from the youngest Diluvium strata (now known to be Holocene and Pleistocene) at the top, down to the oldest undifferentiated Grauwacke strata of Wales. The geological complications of these older strata, almost completely unknown at the time, were unraveled by Roderick Murchison and Adam Sedgwick in the 1820s. As Murchison wrote, they were only able to do so by employing Smithian principles—identifying successive strata by their fossils.

ESTIMATING THE AGE OF THE EARTH

Attempts were made in the mid-19th century to calculate the age of the Earth using sedimentation and erosion rates. The British geologist, Charles Lyell, estimated the age of the Earth at about 100 million years. Charles Darwin, using similar methods, dated the length of time that had passed since the Cretaceous era at about 300 million years—a considerable overestimate.

THE RADIOACTIVE BREAKTHROUGH

By the 1890s, the main divisions of geological history, such as the Cambrian and Carboniferous periods, had been named and generally agreed upon internationally. But there was still no means of putting accurate dates on the geological calendar of the Earth. By the start of the 20th century, the radioactive decay of certain chemical elements was recognized as a natural and continuing process within the minerals of the Earth. Radioactive decay could be used to calculate absolute ages of rocks and minerals—and, therefore, of the Earth.

The Geological Timescale

By 1850, enough was known about the rocks of the Earth's surface to show that the total thickness of strata amounted to many miles. Fossils were found throughout many rock layers, even in some of the deepest and oldest strata. It had become clear that the Earth was much older than previously thought. In order to understand the complex history of the Earth's rocks and their record of past life, it was necessary to divide the rock record into recognizable phases. By the end of the 19th century, the basic divisions of "deep" time had been established around the world.

THE THREE GREAT ERAS

In the 19th century the periods of geological time thought to contain prehistoric life were grouped into three formal eras: the Paleozoic, (from the Greek *palaios,* ancient); Mesozoic (*meso,* middle); and Cainozoic (*caino,* recent). By 1860, John Phillips, professor of geology at Oxford, showed that distinctive plant and animal life (biotas) was associated with each great era.

FORMALIZED TIME

The divisions of the geological timescale are based on changes in fossils; boundaries between eras are marked by major extinction events. During the early 19th century, the entire geological time span was carved up into 16 periods, from the Cambrian to the Quaternary. Beneath the oldest fossil-bearing rocks of the Cambrian lay an earlier phase of Earth history. Since it was thought to have been devoid of life, it was called the Azoic ("without life," in Latin).

THE PRECAMBRIAN MYSTERY

By the end of the 19th century there was fossil evidence that primitive life may have evolved before Cambrian times. The discovery and use of radioactive dating in the early 20th century showed that the Precambrian era was much longer than had previously been thought. But without common fossils, the subdivision and correlation of Precambrian sequences of strata seemed impossible.

THE PRECAMBRIAN ERAS

In the last few decades there has been a remarkable change in understanding of the 4 billion years of Precambrian history. Three eras of Precambrian time are now recognized: the Hadean (4.6–3.8 billion years ago, or byr); the Archean (3.8–2.5 byr); and the Proterozoic (2.5–0.545 byr). Little is known about the early formation of the Earth as so few rocks of this age are preserved at the Earth's surface.

THE EARLIEST FOSSIL REMAINS

Archean times are now known to have the oldest known sedimentary rock and the first fossil remains, which are 3.7-byr chemical traces of organisms from Greenland. By 3 billion years ago stromatolitic organisms (blue-green algae) populated shallow seas.

THE PROTEROZOIC ERA

The youngest part of the Proterozoic era (Neoproterozoic 1000–545 million years ago, or MA) is divided into two well defined periods, the Riphean (1000–680 MA) and Vendian (680–545 MA). The Riphean saw the radiation of the eukaryotes, the build-up of atmospheric oxygen, and possibly the first multicellular organisms. Vendian times were marked by a major ice age with widespread glaciation (around 630 MA). This was followed by the diversification of multicelled organisms and the evolution of widespread and abundant marine, soft-bodied lifeforms, called Ediacarans. The extinction of these lifeforms and the arrival of the first shelly marine animals marked the beginning of Cambrian times and the Phanerozoic era.

THE PALEOZOIC ERA

The six periods of the Paleozoic, from the Cambrian to the Permian, span nearly 300 million years (545–248 MA). At first, distinctive Paleozoic lifeforms were largely confined to the marine realm. Early Paleozoic marine invertebrates were initially very small, but by mid-Cambrian times some predatory arthropods grew to about 3 feet (0.9 meters) in size. Gradually, a marine "arms race" developed. By the Silurian period predators equipped with teeth had evolved, and life was

The boundaries between each of the four great eras is marked by a drastic change in lifeforms preserved as fossils, signifying that great extinctions occurred at the end of each era.

EON	ERA	PERIOD	EPOCH	START OF INTERVAL	LIFEFORMS
Phanerozoic	Cenozoic	Quaternary	Holocene	0.01MA	Spread of modern humans
			Pleistocene	1.8	Appearance of first humans (*Homo*)
		Tertiary	Pliocene	5	Earliest-known hominids appear
			Miocene	24	Apes and whales; large browsing mammals;
			Oligocene	34	
			Eocene	55	Grasslands begin to appear; ancestors of horse and camel appear
			Paleocene	65	First large mammals (dinosaurs die out)
	Mesozoic	Cretaceous	Upper		
			Lower	142	First flowering plants; placental mammals appear
		Jurassic		206	First birds and mammals Rise of dinosaurs
		Triassic		248	First flying reptiles and dinosaurs appear
	Paleozoic	Permian		290	First tetrapods with mammal-like features
		Carboniferous	Pennsylvanian	323	First reptiles
			Mississippian	354	Winged insects appear First forests appear
		Devonian		417	First tetrapods First tree ferns
		Silurian		443	First land plants and insects
		Ordovician		495	First freshwater animals First corals
		Cambrian		545	First fish; early shelled organisms
Precambrian	Proterozoic			2500	First colonial algae and jellyfish (soft-bodied invertebrates)
	Archean			3800	First multicelled organisms First life: algae and bacteria
	Hadean			4600	

forced to protect itself with shelly armor or escape down into the sediment.

PALEOZOIC LIFE

Distinctive Paleozoic groups included ancient arthropods, such as the trilobites and eurypterids. There were also plantlike graptolites, which were, in fact, colonial animals, and numerous straight and coiled cone cephalopods. There were also representatives of the more familiar snails, clams, sea urchins, starfish, and shrimplike arthropods.

THE FIRST VERTEBRATES

By 460 million years ago, the first vertebrate animals appeared—bizarrely shaped jawless fishlike animals (modern equivalents are lampreys and hagfish). By Silurian times the first jawed fish had evolved, intensifying the aquatic arms race.

LAND INVADERS

The Silurian period also heralded one of the major developments in the history of life—the invasion of the land, first by tiny plants only a few inches high. Altogether, life took over 3.4 billion years to conquer the land. Within 100 million years of the first arrival of life on land, extensive forests of tree ferns and clubmosses provided shelter for a diversity of animals.

THE FIRST COAL DEPOSITS

Early four-limbed vertebrates (tetrapods) included the ancestors of the amphibians, reptiles, and mammals. They preyed on abundant invertebrates—arthropods, such as the early millipedes, cockroaches, scorpions, and the dragonflies, the first flyers. Their fossil remains, buried in swamps and bogs, became the first coal deposits of the Carboniferous age (*carbo* being Latin for charcoal).

PALEOZOIC EXTINCTIONS

A number of extinction events occurred during the Paleozoic, but the Permo-Triassic extinction, which marked the end of the era, 248 million years ago, was the biggest extinction event of all time. Calculations suggest that nearly 70 percent of all marine species were wiped out at this time. The probable cause was a fall in sea level, which exposed the continental shelves, destroying shallow-water marine habitats.

THE MESOZOIC ERA

The Mesozoic era lasted some 183 million years (248–65 MA), from Triassic to Cretaceous times. Following the Permo-Triassic extinction event, life took a long time to recover its diversity. The marine realm had been particularly devastated but gradually new mollusks and arthropods replaced the extinct forms. Bivalves replaced the brachiopods and new kinds of corals evolved. Marine reptiles, such as the ichthyosaurs and plesiosaurs, became the top predators in the oceans, feeding off abundant fish and cephalopods. The latter evolved new distinctive forms, the ammonites and belemnites. On land, cycads, gingkophytes, and conifers dominated the vegetation, providing the basis of the food chain.

GIANT PREY AND PREDATORS

Mesozoic forests fed the largest terrestrial herbivores ever—the giant sauropod dinosaurs and other reptilian herbivores. Many of these, in turn, fed the reptilian carnivores, especially the theropods, which ranged in size from the Triassic *Coelophysis* (5 feet/1.5 meters long) to the famously large tyrannosaurs of late Cretaceous times (up to 49 feet/15 meters long).

MESOZOIC INNOVATIONS

From Triassic times, the air was invaded by flying reptiles and then by a group of feathered dinosaurs. The extinct pterosaurs were the most successful of the flying reptiles, but then the more versatile birds took over. The birds from the late Jurassic age onward radically changed the nature of life on Earth. The emergence of small, warm-blooded, shrewlike mammals in the late Triassic and then the flowering plants (angiosperms) at the end of Jurassic times were both important developments. The birds, mammals, and angiosperms were to make their mark later when the ruling reptiles had gone.

EXTINCTION

The end of the Mesozoic was marked by another extinction event, which is particularly famous for a dramatic meteorite impact that coincided with the demise of the dinosaurs. The collision of the 6-mile (10-kilometer) meteorite with the Yucatan area of Mexico is thought to have increased the magnitude of the extinction event, although the importance of this impact is still being debated.

CLIMATE CHANGE

At the same time, a volcanic eruption caused a vast outpouring of basalt in the Deccan area of India that would also have produced a dramatic and long-lasting climate change. Certainly the dinosaurs and a number of reptiles became extinct at the end of the Cretaceous period. The marine ecosystem was also seriously disturbed at this time, with the extinction of a significant proportion of planktonic microorganisms and the cephalopod ammonites.

THE CENOZOIC ERA

The Cenozoic era comprises the most recent 65 million years of geological time and extends from the Paleocene through to the present. The main, internationally recognized periods of Cenozoic time are the Paleogene, Neogene, and Quaternary, with further subdivision into seven epochs, from the Paleocene to the Holocene.

CENOZOIC MAMMALS

Although a large percentage of Cenozoic organisms are still in existence today, a visit to a Cenozoic landscape of 50 million years ago would have revealed many unfamiliar mammals, some resembling dogs or bears, others being pig- or hippolike. Some of these mammals took to the seas and were the ancestors of today's whales, seals, and dolphins. Mammal populations of the isolated continents of Australia and South America included many dog- and catlike marsupials, which evolved in parallel with the more advanced and modern placental mammals.

***Anahoplites*, a Cretaceous ammonite and extinct fossil relative of the squid.**

A FAMILIAR LANDSCAPE

Recognizable flowering plants, from herbs to trees, grew during the Cenozoic. Song birds evolved, and horses and deer grazed the extensive grasslands. The big planteaters were, in turn, hunted by carnivores, such as big cats, wild dogs, hyenas, and the newly emerging hominids. During ice ages, caused by changing climates toward the end of the Cenozoic era, cold-adapted species evolved, such as the woolly mammoth and rhinoceros. At the end of the last ice age, however, extinctions were caused by climate change and hunting by humans.

Methods of Dating: Innovations and Discoveries

Throughout the 19th century, there was no means of dating the geological past absolutely, therefore the age of the Earth was still a matter of speculation. The discovery of the radiometric "clock" at the beginning of the 20th century revolutionized our understanding of the deep history of the Earth, confirming what geologists had been claiming for decades—that it extended back over many hundreds of millions of years. Nevertheless, new, accurate dating methods posed further problems for the geologists; dates obtained by new techniques now had to be matched to the established, and widely accepted, divisions of geological time that had evolved in the 19th century.

Irish physicist Lord Kelvin (1824–1907) used physico-chemical principles to calculate the age of the Earth.

British physicist Ernest Rutherford (1871–1937), discovered the atomic nucleus and used radioactive decay to calculate the age of rocks.

FOSSIL CHRONOLOGY

Once the relationship between sequences of strata and successions of characteristic fossils had been established at the beginning of the 19th century, geologists soon discovered that there were very broad changes in the overall fossil content of strata. The three great geological eras, the Paleozoic, Mesozoic, and Cenozoic, could each be characterized by distinctive groups of fossils. Some fossils were so restricted in their distribution through time that they could be used to subdivide divisions of time more discretely.

ZONE FOSSILS

In the mid-19th century, Albert Oppel showed that detailed successive changes in ammonites could be used to recognize subdivisions (biozones) within sequences of Jurassic strata all over Europe. Oppel's method was enthusiastically taken up by other paleontologists. Charles Lapworth discovered that graptolites could be used to subdivide early Palaeozoic marine strata in the same way. Some ammonite and graptolite biozones can be recognized with durations of only one or two million years—a very short period in the context of the unimaginably long geological timescale.

ZONING TODAY

The biozonal method is still widely used, for instance in the subdivision of modern marine sediment and terrestrial deposits of the recent past. Foraminiferan microfossils, taken from deep-sea sediment cores, are one of the most useful ways of subdividing and matching oceanic deposits. On land, pollen and insect remains, such as beetle wingcases, are used for dating deposits from the last ice age.

KELVIN'S THEORY

In 1897, Lord Kelvin, the great Irish physicist, was one of the first scientists to use physico-chemical principles in calculating the age of the Earth at between 20 and 40 million years. He assumed that the mass of the Earth had cooled from an initial molten state. This estimate was far lower than geologists had expected, but Kelvin's prestige was high, and his figures were widely quoted. His calculations, however, had not taken into account the effects of both the convection of the Earth's mantle and of radioactivity, neither of which were known about at the time.

RADIOACTIVE DECAY

In the early 20th century, Ernest Rutherford and Arthur Holmes in England and Bertrand Boltwood in the U.S., realized that radioactive decay could be used to date minerals and rocks. In 1905, Rutherford used the decay of uranium to calculate a mineral's age at 500 million years old. This dating method depends on the fact that radioactive decay is random and unaffected by physical or chemical processes such as surface temperature or pressure variations.

RADIOMETRIC DATING

Radiometric dating is based on the amount of time it takes certain radioactive substances to decay. Atoms with identical chemical properties, but different weights, are known as isotopes of the same element. Most elements are mixtures of isotopes. Radiometric dating measures the proportions of certain chemical isotopes within minerals. Every isotope decays at a known rate, making it possible to calculate the age of rock formations. Radiometric dating allows each rock to be positioned more or less exactly at its correct time of formation in Earth history.

RADIOMETRIC DATES AND STRATIGRAPHY

Radiometric dating could originally be applied only to igneous rock, that is, rock formed as the result of crystallization of minerals from a molten material (magma) as it cooled. Until recently, sedimentary rock was not suitable for radiometric dating. This is because the age of a specific grain in a sedimentary rock, such as a sandstone, is the age at which the mineral formed in its original igneous setting and not when it was locked into the sedimentary deposit. The problem has been to relate radiometric dates from igneous rock to the stratigraphic record, with consists of sedimentary rock.

PROBLEMS WITH RADIOMETRIC DATING

Dating a zircon (a type of mineral) grain from a sediment illustrates the problems with radiometric dating. Zircon, a robust mineral, may have survived several cycles of erosion and many millions of years before being included in the sediment. But a new radiometric method can date tiny crystals that grow on zircon grains after deposition. As a result, it is now possible to date sedimentary rock, even if it does not contain fossils, such as Precambrian sandstone.

RADIOMETRIC ACCURACY

Volcanically extruded lava is one of the most useful rocks for radiometric dating. It is often interbedded with sedimentary deposits. The age of the lava is closely related to the time at which the sediment above and below it was deposited. This provides an accurate match between the radiometric dates and the dates taken from the stratigraphic timescale.

THE OLDEST MINERAL

The oldest known mineral on Earth, dated by the radiometric method, is a zircon, dated at 3,962 $\pm$ 3 million years, found in Archean granites from the Slave Province in northwestern Canada.

RADIOCARBON DATING

The decay of carbon isotopes within living organisms can be used to date organic materials such as charcoal, shell, and bone. Unfortunately, the radioactive isotope Carbon-14 decays relatively quickly (its half-life is only 5,730 years) so that the method is only of use for archeological or "sub-fossil" materials.

MAGNETOSTRATIGRAPHY

Many rocks, particularly igneous ones, but also a range of iron-rich sediments, contain magnetic minerals. These can be aligned with the Earth's magnetic field and become fixed in that magnetic orientation when the rock is formed. In an igneous rock, the magnetic minerals are locked in their magnetic orientation as the molten rock cools below temperatures of around 6,000°C.

MAGNETIC REVERSAL TIMESCALES

The Earth's magnetic field reverses sporadically. This gives rise to sequences of rocks that have "normal" polarity (their magnetic North is in the same direction as present-day magnetic North) and rocks with "reversed" polarity. Changes in the Earth's magnetic field, which occur roughly every half million years, generate a characteristic pattern over time. A particular reversal pattern in a rock sample may be matched, like a barcode, with the timescale of Earth's magnetic reversals to determine relative age. The magnetic reversal timescale is calibrated by radiometric dating.

MAGNETIC POLARITY OF SEDIMENT

As sediment is formed, tiny particles of magnetized iron within the grains of the sediment become aligned with the direction of the Earth's magnetic field. As the sediment solidifies into rock, this alignment is preserved. The establishment of the magnetic polarity of sediment has proved particularly useful in dating certain environments. It has helped to give age estimates for the important Miocene terrestrial sediments of the Siwalik region of northern Pakistan. A wide range of mammal fossils have been found there, including hominoids, but the age of the sediment was not known. Thirteen paleomagnetic reversals have been identified that help to place the sequence somewhere between 6.5 and 8.6 million years ago.

FISSION TRACK DATING

A number of new dating methods can be used in very specific situations. Fission track dating is based on the spontaneous fission (breaking apart) of the radioactive isotope Uranium-238, which produces trails of damage, a few microns long, near the site of the uranium atom within a mineral such as zircon. The number of trails increases over time, at a rate that is dependent on the uranium content of the mineral. The age of the mineral can be computed by measuring the density of fission tracks in a mineral and the uranium content. Fission track dating is used to verify radiometric dates. It has been particularly useful in dating the volcanic ashes interbedded in the hominid fossil-bearing strata of East Africa.

ATOMIC CLOCKS

Two innovative dating methods, electron spin resonance and thermoluminescence, both measure the number of electrons caught up in defects within minerals' atomic structure. These methods have proved particularly useful for dating a variety of inorganic materials, especially those in anthropological settings, such as burnt flints found in ancient hearths.

AMINO ACID RACEMISATION

Certain organic (carbon-based) chemicals exist in right- and left-handed forms, which are mirror images of each other. Amino acid racemisation, a new and sophisticated technique, depends on the slow chemical conversion of the left-handed amino acids naturally present in living organisms to their right-handed amino acid counterparts. This process is sensitive to environmental conditions, especially temperature. The method has proved particularly useful for dating some archeological materials, such as shells and bones, which are not suitable for dating by radiocarbon methods. This form of dating, however, can only extend back a few hundred thousand years.

OPPORTUNISTIC DATING

A useful, but rarely available, method of dating uses ash from volcanic eruptions, because it can be distributed over extremely wide areas instantaneously. Asteroid and meteorite impact events can spread tektites (glassy fragments formed from rock melted by the heat of the impact) over wide areas in a geological instant.

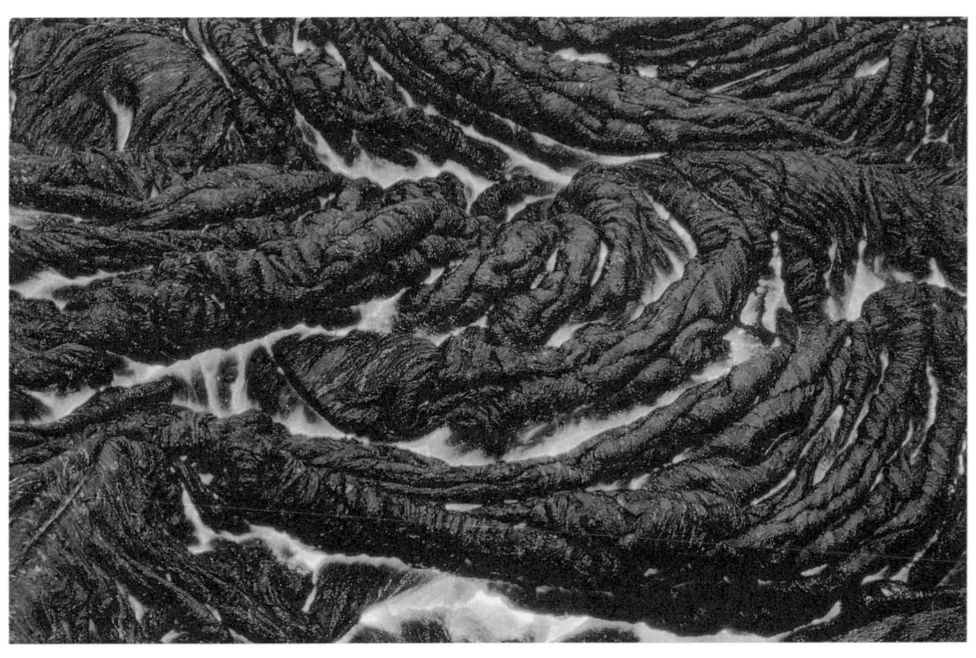

Lava, the result of volcanic eruptions, is a useful dating tool for geologists. Since it is igneous, it can be dated radiometrically, providing a useful chronological context for adjacent sedimentary rock.

Geological Controversies

Among the sciences, geology has a deserved reputation for controversy. Arguments have constantly arisen over interpretation of data, the quality of the information, and whether ideas can be tested adequately. Sampling of geological material is often difficult and sample sizes can be very small. When interpreting fossils, for example, entire species have been described on the basis of single specimens.

Abraham Gottlob Werner (1749–1817). He emphasized the importance of field and laboratory observations in geology.

GEOLOGICAL INFERENCE

Many geological features and processes are not directly observable, especially those taking place within the Earth. They can only be inferred by interpretation of data from special kinds of exploration and analysis, such as geophysical methods of gravity or seismic measurement.

THE TIME FACTOR

For most sciences, testing theories in laboratory conditions is a crucial research tool. However, most of the major geological processes, such as mountain building and the folding of rocks, take place over many millions of years and it is not possible to replicate them in the laboratory using the same materials. Current geological challenges include the accurate prediction of earthquakes and volcanic eruptions. Since these complex, multifactor processes cannot be replicated by conventional scientific means, they require sophisticated mathematical modeling.

OBSERVING ROCKS

In the 18th century, most geological theories were based on arguments about previous ideas and lacked rigorous assessment of the quality of the information. Gradually, field studies of rock were accepted as necessary for understanding the geology of the Earth. One of the earliest attempts to relate direct observation of rock and strata to theory was attempted by Giovanni Arduino (1713–95), an 18th-century Italian professor of mineralogy at Padua. He divided the rock found in northern Italy into four groups: Primitive, Secondary, Tertiary, and Volcanic.

WERNER'S THEORY

Arduino's findings were incorporated into other Earth theories such as the one proposed by the German mineralogist Abraham Gottlob Werner, who claimed that the oldest (Primitive) rock was formed by precipitation from a universal ocean that had enveloped the Earth. Werner was a very successful teacher who attracted students from all over Europe. But he was very dogmatic, particularly as he grew older, and he became incapable of accepting new information and ideas.

THE NEPTUNIST THEORY

Werner's school of thought was characterized as Neptunist because of his reliance on the idea of a primitive ocean. He argued that "Primitive" deposits, including rocks such as granite, did not, therefore, contain fossils or sedimentary particles (clastic material). As the fluid level lowered due to the formation of this rock, continents emerged and became colonized. Rock formed in the liquid during this period was called Transition rock and included limestone and slate. The final and youngest "Floetz rock" was composed mainly of sediment, such as mudstone and sandstone.

THE PLUTONIST SCHOOL

Other observers came increasingly to support a different view, characterized as the Plutonist school, which looked to cooling magma, solidifying beneath the Earth's surface, as the main cause of rock formation. They supported the French geologist Nicolas Desmarest, who made a detailed study of the Auvergne volcanoes in central France in the mid-18th century. From field observations Desmarest suggested that basalt was igneous and came from volcanoes.

THE GEOLOGICAL CYCLE

Generally, the prevailing 18th-century view of nature and the Earth was centered on humans (anthropocentric). According to Werner's theory, continents were continually being eroded. There

The volcanoes of the Auvergne in central France were studied by French geologist Nicolas Desmarest. His discovery that basalt was igneous led to his refutation of prevailing 18th-century theories.

was no renewal because the fluid from which the rocks had solidified had gone. Humans, therefore, were confronted with the threat of disappearing continents. This concern stimulated the Scottish natural philosopher James Hutton to present a new theory in 1785, which viewed geological processes as cyclical. Eroded material from the continents is deposited in the oceans, forming new sedimentary strata. When old continents are eventually worn down, the elevation of new rocks from the seabed forms new continents.

HUTTON'S UNIFORMITARIANISM

In direct opposition to the Neptunists, Hutton proposed that granite was formed from the solidification of molten igneous (volcanic) material and was younger than the adjacent strata. He also suggested that old continental rocks could be submerged and covered in new rocks, only to be elevated again. He believed that such processes were slow and repeated many times; the Earth was, therefore, very old. Hutton's theories came under attack in the first half of the 19th century. The development of stratigraphic rock sequences suggested that Earth history was not cyclical, as suggested by Hutton, but linear.

THE PROBLEMS OF CONTINENTAL DRIFT

One of the major arguments in the early 20th century within Earth Sciences concerned the question of how the continents could have moved around the surface of the Earth. Until very recently, there was no known physical process by which masses of rock and sediment the size of continents could have been moved over distances of thousands of miles. Yet a disturbing number of geological observations seemed to suggest that this had indeed happened in the distant past. It took a series of unsuccessful theories over the course of half a century before one theory emerged that could successfully explain these observations.

18th-century studies of the rock of the Giant's Causeway in Northern Ireland revealed that they were similar to erupted volcanic lava.

James Hutton (1726–97) is regarded as the founder of modern geology. He proposed that cyclical processes characterized Earth history.

WEGENER'S THEORY

Alfred Wegener, a German meteorologist, suggested in 1915 that all the continents had once, in late Paleozoic times, been united as a supercontinent, which he called Pangea. He reconstructed the subsequent breakup of Pangea and the movement of the continents into their present positions in a remarkable series of maps. Wegener put forward a number of circumstantial arguments to support his theory: the shape of the coast on either side of the North Atlantic fits so closely together that it cannot be just a matter of accident; similar fossils are found in different continents now separated by large masses of water; evidence of a past ice age is found in India, southern Africa, South America, and Australia—this would be very unlikely in their present-day positions.

THE WEGENER DEBATE

Wegener's ideas were met with fierce opposition and ridicule from many geophysicists and geologists. The famous British geophysicist Harold Jeffreys argued that oceanic basalt was too strong to allow continents to move through it. Some geologists, however, were prepared to go along with the idea. In 1928, Arthur Holmes proposed that mantle convection could drive continental movement. His idea was all but ignored. In 1937, the South African geologist Alexander Du Toit published a detailed article supporting the idea of continental drift and the conglomeration of the southern continents as one supercontinent, called Gondwana.

PALEOMAGNETIC REVELATIONS

In the early 1950s, opinions began to change. Paleomagnetic measurements on continental rocks of various ages showed that magnetic North had moved over time. In addition, measurements from separate continents mapped out different polar "wandering" paths for magnetic North. These findings suggested that the continents had been moving independently. Irregular magnetic patterns (anomalies) on the ocean floor were shown to be displaced by hundreds of miles—the observation demonstrated that large movements were indeed possible. In 1963 Fred Vine and Drummond Matthews showed that ocean-floor, magnetic anomalies were attributable to reversals in the Earth's magnetic field over time.

THE ACCEPTANCE OF PLATE TECTONICS

In 1962, Harry Hess suggested that continents do not move through the oceans but are attached to the ocean floors, and that both continents and ocean floor move over the Earth's mantle, driven by heat convection processes. He postulated that mid-ocean ridges are sites where the hot mantle rises to form new ocean crust in discrete, roughly linear zones. This fitted in well with the previous observations of symmetrical magnetic stripes on the ocean floor. The location and distribution of earthquakes and volcanoes on the Earth's surface was subsequently found to mark the boundaries where the various pieces of the Earth's surface layer, called plates, meet. At this point, in the face of overwhelming evidence, the theory of plate tectonics was born, 50 years after Wegener's formulation of continental drift.

ONGOING ARGUMENTS

It has been proposed that heat convection from the Earth's hot core through the mantle to the crust provides a driving mechanism for plate tectonics. However, there is good evidence that the mantle is layered into upper, transition, and lower zones and that the pattern of heat convection may be more complicated than previously thought.

Rock

Volcanoes, earthquakes, and glaciers are a constant reminder of the Earth's power to create rock. Igneous rock, cooled and crystallized from molten magma, may be ejected onto the surface through volcanoes, or cool farther deep within the Earth's crust. Metamorphic rock is transformed by high pressure and temperatures deep within mountains. Sedimentary rock is formed by long-term processes of weathering, erosion, and deposition.

In c. AD 125, the Romans built Hadrian's Wall across northern England, a distance of over 75 miles (120 kilometers). They built on top of a natural prominence formed by the Whin Sill, a horizontal intrusion of hard basalt, the result of volcanic activity during the Tertiary era.

IGNEOUS ROCK

Rock that cools and crystallizes from a magma, either on the surface (extrusive volcanic rock), or within the Earth's crust (intrusive), is known as igneous rock (from *ignis*, Latin for fire). The Earth's heat flows from the core through the mantle as rising convection currents. This heat flow drives plate tectonics and promotes melting at the base of the crust, a process known as igneous activity. The molten material generated in the crust by this process is known as magma.

AN IGNEOUS EARTH

Most of the Earth's surface is composed of igneous rock material that has been molten at some time during Earth's 4.6-billion-year history, especially during the early formation of the Earth over 4 billion years ago. Igneous rock forms the Earth's hot core and mantle, over 3,900 miles (6,300 kilometers) thick.

INTRUSIVE IGNEOUS ROCK

Intrusive igneous rock is formed from magma deep within the Earth's crust. Vast domes of granite, thousands of cubic miles in size, have invaded the roots of mountain chains. Walls and sheets of basalt have squeezed through cracks only a few yards wide and yet run for hundreds of miles through the crust of the Earth. Both granite and basalt are intrusive igneous rock but each has a very different mode of formation.

GRANITE

Granite is generally a light gray, cream, or pink rock, made of large crystals of minerals such as feldspar, muscovite, and quartz. They have crystallized slowly from molten rock at depths of several miles within the root zones of mountain belts. The composition of granite can be changed by the incorporation and melting of the surrounding rock that it is intruding.

BASALT

Sheets of basalt rock are formed by volcanic activity and intrude the crust. Basalt is typically dark gray or greenish gray and is made up of very small crystals of silicate minerals such as feldspar, pyroxene, and biotite.

SOLIDIFIED LAVA

Sometimes lava does not reach the Earth's surface. Instead it solidifies (freezes or crystallizes) underground, and so is technically an intrusive rock. Vertical wall-like sheets of solidified lava are called dykes, horizontal sheets are called sills. Some dykes and sills are the channels through which lava flows onto the surface. Fissures like these are important in forming the mid-ocean spreading ridges, through which lava flows to form new ocean floor.

THE WHIN SILL
The famous wall across the north of England was built by Emperor Hadrian in c. AD 125 on top of a prominent basalt intrusion, the Whin Sill. The Romans used the Sill's blocky basalt rock in their construction. The Tertiary intrusion is related to volcanic activity in northwest Scotland.

EXTRUSIVE IGNEOUS ROCK
The intensity of surface volcanic activity has decreased enormously since the early evolution of the Earth's surface some 3.5 billion years ago. Nevertheless, rock that cools or crystallizes from volcanic lava is still the most common of all surface rock. Most lava is not visible because it forms the floor of the oceans, and the oceans make up some three-fifths of the Earth's surface.

PLATEAU BASALT
Volcanic rock is not confined to the ocean floor. Mantle plumes of heat flow also occur under the continents and produce outpourings of lava called plateau basalt; examples include the late Permian Siberian Traps in Russia, the late Cretaceous Deccan Traps in India, the early Tertiary Antrim lavas in northern Ireland and northwest Scotland, and the late Tertiary Columbia River Basalts in the U.S. Such large-scale outpourings of lava, ash, and gas have been linked with climate change and mass extinctions.

SEDIMENTARY ROCK
All the Earth's rock materials are brought to the surface by the processes of mountain building and are broken down into sediment by a cycle of weathering and erosion. The build-up of layers of sediment buries the deposits and compresses soft and loose sediment into sedimentary rock. Familiar sedimentary rock includes sandstone and limestone, used as building materials.

From top to bottom: igneous gneiss dyke intruded as a magma into metamorphic rocks. Feldspar, muscovite, and quartz are igneous minerals crystallized from molten magmas within continental crust rocks. Marble is a limestone that has been heated and compressed to form a metamorphic rock.

METAMORPHIC ROCK
Rock that is carried down into the depths of the Earth by geological processes is increasingly superheated and compressed the deeper it goes. As temperature and pressure increase with depth many rocks change their form (recrystallize) and, depending on their original composition, may be chemically reconstituted. The end-product of this process is metamorphic rock.

USES OF METAMORPHIC ROCK
Marble is metamorphosed limestone and is one of the most beautiful rock materials. It has been used by sculptors since classical Greek and Roman times. Slate is metamorphosed mud. It has been used as a natural roofing material for hundreds of years. Both rocks are the product of processes of heating and compressing during mountain building.

ROCK OF THE OCEAN FLOOR
The volcanic rock and deep-sea sediments of the ocean floor have been constantly recycled throughout Earth history. No ocean floor is much older than 180 million years—comparatively recent in geological terms.

PLATE TECTONICS AND ROCK FORMATION
The collision of the Earth's crustal plates not only pushes rock to the surface (mountain building) but also down into the Earth, where it is heated and compressed. At depth, rock may even melt to form new igneous rock.

IGNEOUS ROCK AND VOLCANIC ACTIVITY
All around the Pacific Ocean, the notorious "Ring of Fire" is a chain of volcanoes generated by the subduction of the ocean floor below the continental crustal plates. It stretches from New Zealand, through Japan and Alaska, and down the length of the west coast of the Americas. This dangerously explosive type of volcanic activity is generated by partial melting of rock at the base of the continental crust.

REVEALING EARTH'S MYSTERIES
The continental crust still preserves some of the oldest rock on Earth (dated at about 3,962 MA), most of which is metamorphosed igneous and sedimentary rock. In addition, a variety of younger sedimentary, volcanic, and igneous rock has been added to the older continental rock through time by geological processes. Over the last 300 years, geologists have dated and matched these rocks, slowly pasting together the history of Earth's environments and life.

Metamorphic and Sedimentary Rock

When the crustal plates that form the Earth's surface collide, they create mountains. The crust is wrinkled and thickened by the impact of the collision and rock is forced down as far as 40 miles (68 kilometers) deep into the Earth's crust where they are compressed by heat and transformed, a process called metamorphism. The Earth's crust is in constant slow motion and metamorphism is continually occurring, producing an infinite variety of altered rock, which geologists can use to decipher the conditions within the Earth. Sedimentary rock, on the other hand, is created by cyclical processes on the Earth's surface, such as weathering, erosion, and deposition.

Eroded material, carried by rivers and deposited at the river mouth, accumulates to create deltas. In the past, large-scale build up of plant material around fertile deltas has formed coal and peat deposits.

CONTACT METAMORPHISM

The process of metamorphism can take place on a very large scale, involving tens of thousands of cubic miles of rock. It can also take place on a relatively small scale. In either case, the process is ultimately driven by heat energy within the Earth. Localized heating at the base of the crust produces molten rock, or magma, which then rises up, or intrudes, the rock above. Sometimes the magma cools below the Earth's surface to form pods of igneous rock, known as plutons. Crustal rock intruded by igneous plutons is baked by the hot magma. The heating causes metamorphic changes to the minerals and appearance of the surrounding rock, a process known as contact metamorphism. The zone of altered rock is relatively narrow, from as little as a few inches to as much as a mile or so.

HOT-WATER METAMORPHISM

Hot fluids can also act as agents for metamorphism. At mid-ocean ridges, where oceanic crustal plates are moving apart (about 2 miles/3 kilometers underwater), molten rock is continually rising between the two plates and solidifying to form new seafloor (ocean crust). High temperature drives seawater through the brittle and fractured lava, a system known as hydrothermal circulation. Vast amounts of water (410 million tons per day) pass constantly through this global network of fractures and the hot 572°F (300°C) salty seawater reacts with the new ocean crust, changing or metamorphosing it. This metamorphism is often associated with the production of ore minerals such as iron sulfide.

METAMORPHIC VARIETY

Any type of rock—igneous, sedimentary, or even metamorphic—may be metamorphosed. The mineralogy and appearance of the end product depend on the original composition of the rock, and the conditions (temperature and depth) of the metamorphism. For example, a mudstone that is buried up to 6 miles (10 kilometers) deep is metamorphically compressed into a slate. The same mudstone buried to a depth of 12 miles (20 kilometers) and heated to 932°F (500°C) will become a silvery-colored rock with very pronounced layering known as a schist. This rock will contain aluminum-rich minerals such as muscovite, biotite, and garnet.

SEDIMENTARY ROCK

Sedimentary rock is created by processes that occur on the Earth's surface. Sedimentary material includes rocks created by the weathering of existing rock (sandstone), by ice (tillites), wind (eolian deposits) and rain, rock consisting of the organic remains of animals (limestones) and plants (coals), and rock deposited as a result of chemical reactions or evaporation (salt) at the Earth's surface.

THE RECYCLING PROCESS

Sedimentary rock, created by the reformation of existing rock, is the most common deposit. The parent rock, which may be igneous, metamorphic, or sedimentary, must first be broken down. The destruction of this rock may be a gentle dissolution by slightly acid rainfall, cracking by the expansion of freezing water, or vicious grinding by traveling glaciers. Rock particles, once created, are generally carried to another location before sedimentation and this transport may be by water, wind, ice, or snow.

THE POWER OF WATER

Water is the most common mode of transport for sedimentary particles. Boulders weighing several tons may be carried by mountain streams in flood, while slower-moving rivers running through flatter countryside carry smaller mud and silt particles, frequently in vast quantities. Flooding sometimes spreads this fine-grained sediment over the surrounding land. Eventually, rivers transport the particles to the sea where they are deposited in estuaries and deltas.

RIVER AND DELTA DEPOSITS

Terrestrial river sediment may build up to form great thicknesses of deposits. Over time, the sediment is squeezed and dried out by the weight of overlying deposits to form hard sedimentary rock, a process known as lithification. Such sedimentary rock preserves the story of how it was transported and where it was deposited. River deposits typically have winding channels filled with rippled sandstone. They are surrounded by thin layers of alternating siltstone and mudstone, which frequently contain fossil roots from the plants that colonized the river and delta floodplains.

Sand dunes are the result of the deposition of sand and fine rock particles by desert winds. Some dunes stand over 150 feet (45 meters) high, and extend for hundreds of miles.

DESERT SANDSTONE

Rock grains carried by wind generally finish their journey trapped in a river or stream, but if no water is available they may settle in a desert sand dune. The dry interiors of the great continents have little rain or plant cover, so loose rock particles are easily blown away by any strong wind, exposing fresh rock to weathering and further erosion by sand-laden wind. Blown sand builds up into dunes whose size depends on the strength and persistence of the wind.

MARINE SEDIMENTARY ROCK

Transportation by waves and currents redistributes land sediment along coasts and farther out to sea. The shallow water shelves that fringe the continents are the final resting place of most land-derived sediment. Over millions of years the continental shelves accumulate wedges of sediment several miles thick and extending for tens if not hundreds of miles into ocean basins. When continental shelf deposits solidify into rock, they typically form extensive sheets of sandstone, siltstone, and mudstone. These are often full of marine fossils, the remains of the great abundance of marine life and some land fossils brought down by rivers.

LIVING ROCK

In tropical environments, the abundance of life may be sufficient to build up reefs, which are made up of corals or other organisms such as stony sponges, moss animals (bryozoans), and calcareous algae. The surface of the living structure is then colonized by other organisms, which help strengthen and build it up. Because reefs are mostly made of limy minerals, such as calcium carbonate, which crystallize at normal atmospheric pressures and temperatures, they can form massive sedimentary deposits that soon solidify into limestone rock.

SHALLOW SEAS

In past times of high sea level, shallow seas have flooded deep inland and produced vast continent-wide limestone deposits, such as the Silurian and lower Carboniferous (Mississippian) limestone of North America. Chalk rock is another form of limestone, which developed during Cretaceous times and forms the spectacular white cliffs of southern England and northwestern France. This carbonate rock is formed of millions of skeletons of single-celled microorganisms called coccoliths. The creatures lived in the plankton and, over a few million years, their skeletons piled up on the seabed to form carbonate mud, which is now limestone up to 1,000 feet (300 meters) thick.

SALTY DEPOSITS

The great salt mines of Siberia, which are 550 million years old, were formed by a process of evaporation. This process occurs when shallow marine basins or lagoons are intermittently connected to the sea. With a combination of high air temperatures and little input of freshwater from rivers or rainfall, evaporation rates are high. When the seawater evaporates, it leaves behind crystals of the minerals that make up seawater, especially sodium chloride (common salt).

DEEP SEA DEPOSITS

The deep sea is beyond the reach of most sand-sized sediment, except when a special type of current carries it there. Periodic turbidity currents, triggered by small earthquakes, transport great volumes of sand and mud from the edge of the continental shelves, down into submarine valleys which are cut into the shelf slope. The valleys confine and channel the flow, like an avalanche, until it reaches the deep sea floor. The flows then spread out over thousands of square miles and deposit sheets of muddy sand up to a yard or so thick over time. These deposits can build up into piles of sediment many hundreds of yards thick in marginal ocean basins.

FROM DEEP SEA TO LAND

Since ocean floor crust is constantly recycled by the subduction process of plate tectonics, deep sea deposits are generally lost to the rock record. However, deposits formed by turbidity currents may be scraped off the ocean floor in great wedges and spliced onto the edges of the continents. Turbidite sandstone of deep-sea origin from the Tertiary era is found onshore in California as a result of this process.

INTERPRETING ANCIENT DEPOSITS

Any fossil content within a sedimentary rock will indicate its age and the type of environment in which it was deposited. Sedimentary rock often contains organic and inorganic materials. For example, early Jurassic black mudstone, found in the cliffs of Lyme Regis in southern England, contains organic material in the form of fish teeth and ichthyosaur bones. The mud itself is made of small inorganic rock particles, but its black color suggests a high carbon content, the result of decomposition of the soft body parts of animals.

THE CYCLE CONTINUES

Most sediment is deposited underwater, and is then buried farther before it becomes rock. The exposure of sediment above sea level is due either to tectonic processes, such as earthquakes or volcanic eruptions, or to a general decrease in sea levels. Once sedimentary rock is exposed, weathering begins, particles are transported, and the cycle begins again.

The largest biological structure in the world, Australia's Great Barrier Reef is an expanse of living rock 1,260 miles (2,027 kilometers) long.

Earth Processes: Plate Tectonics

Two hundred million years ago it would have been possible to walk on dry land from Australia to North America—many dinosaurs and other land-living vertebrates did just that. A map showing the distribution of continents and oceans at that time is almost unrecognizable today. The changes in locations and characteristics of the continents are a result of the geological processes known as continental drift and plate tectonics. The continents, which lie embedded in larger plates of ocean crust, have moved over the surface of the globe over geological time, and continue to do so.

The San Andreas Fault is where the edge of the North American continent slides past the plate that makes up the Pacific Ocean floor. The plates move relative to each other at a rate of 0.4 inches (1 centimeter) a year. Their irregular movements are the main cause of the large number of earthquakes in the region.

THE CONTINENTAL JIGSAW

One of the first observations leading to the remarkable theory of plate tectonics was made in 1756 by German priest Theodor Lilienthal, who noted that the facing coasts of many countries, for example the southern parts of the Americas and Africa, fitted together like pieces of a jigsaw puzzle, even though they were separated by oceans thousands of miles wide. This continental relationship continued to provoke a good deal of speculation, but it was not until the second half of the 20th century that progress was made.

SUBMARINE RELIEF

With the advance of ocean exploration, great lines of submarine volcanic mountains, called mid-ocean ridges, were discovered in the middle of all the major oceans. The mountain ranges rise nearly two miles (3.2 kilometers) from the ocean floor and link up to form the longest mountain chain on Earth, some 31,000 miles (50,000 kilometers) long. Chasmlike submarine trenches, up to 5 miles (8 kilometers) deep, border continental margins and island arcs. These topographic discoveries led H.H. Hess, an American geologist, to propose that the ocean floor was created at the mid-ocean ridges, then carried away from the ridges on top of convecting mantle currents. Eventually this conveyor belt process takes ocean floor to a deep-sea trench where it sinks, or is subducted, back into the Earth's mantle.

THE OCEAN FLOOR

The final proof for this process was provided when the study of ocean floor magnetism revealed that young ocean floor was always found close to the ridge volcanoes and old ocean floor near the coasts of the continents. The age of ocean floor increases away from the ridge, on either side. Scientists discovered that the entire ocean floor is less than 180 million years old.

PLATE TECTONICS

The theory of plate tectonics explains that the Earth's crust is divided into rigid pieces, called plates, that are moved around the surface by currents in the underlying mantle. The continents are embedded in ocean crust, and thus move along with the ocean floor. Many features of the Earth's geography and geology can be explained by plate tectonics. Earthquakes and volcanoes are more frequent around the rim of the Pacific Ocean (the Ring of Fire) and along mid-ocean

A sequence of continental movements from 250 million years ago shows the supercontinent Pangea and its gradual break-up, resulting in the formation of the Atlantic Ocean.

ridges. The Ring of Fire marks plate boundaries, and seismic and volcanic activity is explained by the movements and collisions of the plates.

SUBDUCTING PLATES

When oceanic crust collides with continental crust at a plate boundary, the denser oceanic crust will sink (subduct) down into the mantle, and eventually melt. Deep trenches in the seafloor, such as the 6-mile- (10-kilometer-) deep Marianas Trench, are found where plates are subducting. Volcanoes and earthquakes are caused by this process.

FOLDING AND FAULTING

When two continents collide the crust "wrinkles" and thickens, folding and fracturing as the plates move toward each other. Wrinkling produces massive mountain belts like the Himalayas. Plates may also move horizontally, adjacent to each other, without colliding. As they slide past one another their contact is marked by a fault. Fault movement creates earthquakes, but few volcanoes.

OCEAN-FLOOR SPREADING

As oceanic crust is destroyed by subduction, it is replaced by mid-ocean ridge volcanoes. If this did not happen, the Earth would shrink. As the mid-ocean ridge is pulled apart, magma wells up and pours out as lava onto the ocean floor, where it hardens to form new ocean crust. New seafloor can spread from a mid-ocean ridge at up to 7.8 inches (20 centimeters) per year.

BUILDING SUPERCONTINENTS

Reconstruction of crustal plate movement shows that many, if not all Earth's crustal plates have joined to form supercontinents only to break up again. Break-up was almost certainly caused by rising mantle plumes, that have domed (forced up into a dome shape), stretched, and rifted the supercontinents apart. This happened in the case of Pangea, formed by the coming together of the ancient continents of Gondwana and Laurasia around 240 million years ago. A rising mantle plume caused doming and rifting along the join between the present-day continents of Africa and North America. Magma broke through the rift, forming new ocean floor lavas, eventually leading to the formation of the Atlantic Ocean.

Earthquakes and Tsunamis

Earthquakes are one of the most devastating of Earth's natural phenomena. On average, two major earthquakes, causing virtually total loss of property and heavy loss of life, occur each year. Part of the Earth's geological history, they are most frequently caused by the build-up of forces within the crust, the result of the inexorable movement of crustal plates. Earthquakes can also be triggered by the movement of molten rock below a volcano, or large-scale subsidence of strata deep within the Earth. Tsunamis, or giant waves, are most often the side-effects of earthquakes and can be equally devastating.

EARTHQUAKES AND FAULT LINES

Earthquakes are mainly generated by the breaking apart of the brittle rock in the Earth's crust. Stresses and strains are built up in the crust over hundreds to thousands of years by forces within the Earth, generated by the movement of crustal plates. The rock of the crust eventually breaks along fault lines. Faults can extend for hundreds of miles, both horizontally and deep into the crust. Frictional movement along the fault planes causes the rock to "judder" with such intensity that earthquakes are produced.

EARTHQUAKES AND SUBDUCTION

A different type of earthquake occurs when plates move toward each other. When a plate of oceanic crust collides with one consisting of continental crust, the higher density oceanic crustal plate sinks below the continental plate in what is known as a subduction zone. As the rigid ocean crust sinks through the mantle it sets off earthquakes that may originate up to 435 miles (700 kilometers) below the Earth's surface. The Pacific Ring of Fire is a string of subduction zones surrounding the Pacific Ocean.

SHAKING VOLCANOES

Not all earthquakes can be attributed to plate motion. When molten rock (magma) builds up or moves below the ground, or beneath a volcano, the Earth's surface stretches to accommodate the new material. This stretching induces earthquakes. Quake frequency is used in attempts to predict the date of the next volcanic eruption.

MEASUREMENT AND DAMAGE

Traditionally, the size of an earthquake has been measured on the Richter sliding scale of 1 to 10, which quantifies the energy released. Recently, the more practical and descriptive Mercalli scale, of 1 to 12 has been introduced. Most scientists still use the Richter scale—typically, a magnitude 3 quake involves fault movement of less than half an inch, and will be felt by some people sitting indoors, but causes no damage. Approximately 100,000 earthquakes of this size occur every year. A major earthquake of magnitude 8 releases 10 million times more energy than one of magnitude 3. Movements along fault planes are in the order of yards, causing widespread damage and loss of life.

EARTHQUAKE-PRONE AREAS

Some areas of the world rarely experience earthquakes. In Britain, for example, they are unusual occurrences, always of low magnitude, and cause little or no damage. Yet regions such as Japan or the west coast of California in the USA are regularly racked by small quakes, with large, catastrophic earth movements occurring every two centuries or so. This unequal global distribution of earthquakes can be explained by the location of the boundaries of the Earth's crustal plates. There is a marked coincidence of earthquakes with plate boundaries.

The 1906 San Francisco earthquake lasted for only 40 to 60 seconds; it caused 700 deaths and in its aftermath left 225,000 people homeless.

THE SAN ANDREAS FAULT

Different types of plate motion produce earthquakes with distinct characteristics. The San Andreas Fault, which slices up the western coast of North America is an example of a transform fault—a fault where two plates slide horizontally past each other. Transform faults produce shallow earthquakes. They emanate from a point, or focus, which is generally less than 18½ miles (30 kilometers) below the Earth's surface. The two plates involved in the San Andreas Fault system are moving past each other at a rate of 0.4 inches (1 centimeter) per year. The strains caused by the plates grinding together are absorbed until they reach a critical point. Then, suddenly, fracturing occurs, the rocks slip and an earthquake is released.

CALIFORNIA EARTHQUAKES

There have been several large earthquakes exceeding Richter magnitude 3 along the San Andreas Fault during this century. Only the first, which occurred in San Francisco in 1906, caused major devastation. This earthquake involved movement up to 23 feet (7 meters) along an 186-mile (300-kilometer) stretch of fault. The earthquake fractured the gas mains, leading to a firestorm that was almost impossible to quench, as the water mains had also been destroyed. Large parts of the city were completely wiped out, and 700 lives were lost.

JAPAN'S QUAKE-ZONES

Japan is located close to a point where three subduction zones meet, and is, therefore, very prone to earthquakes. Early documents record the Great Earthquakes of Ansei (1854–1855), and the 1891 earthquake that virtually split the country in two, destroying 200,000 homes. In 1923, over 143,000 people were killed, directly or indirectly, by an earthquake in Tokyo.

EARTHQUAKE MORTALITY

Most earthquake-related deaths are not caused by the earthquake itself, but by its side-effects. Fire, flooding, mud and rock avalanches, and the collapse of buildings can all cause fatalities at the moment of impact. Awareness and preparedness for these risks, as in Japan's 1995 Kobe earthquake, is reflected in relatively low mortality figures. In regions that are unprepared for the eventuality, many more people are killed by exposure, famine, and disease, the result of homelessness, poor water supply, and inadequate or absent sewage treatment before aid and supplies are available.

An earthquake struck the city of Kobe, Japan, in the early hours of January 17,1995. A total of 5,000 people were killed and over 67,000 buildings collapsed causing tens of billions of dollars of damage.

SLEEPING GIANT

The first sign of the reawakening of the Mount Saint Helens volcano in Washington State was an earthquake of magnitude 4.2 that occurred on March 21, 1980. Constant low magnitude quakes during the following April are thought to have been triggered by the ascent of magma beneath the volcano. Then, on May 18 1980, a magnitude 5.1 earthquake triggered a rock avalanche that unbalanced the mountain and precipitated the explosion that blasted almost the entire northern flank of the volcano away.

TSUNAMIS

A side-effect of both volcanic eruptions and earthquakes are giant waves, or tsunamis, which may cause more destruction than the volcano or earthquake itself. Tsunamis can travel at speeds of up to 435 miles per hour (700 km per hour). They are caused by shock waves, mainly generated by submarine earthquakes or volcanic eruptions spreading through water.

PACIFIC WAVES

Most of the world's tsunamis are associated with ocean floor spreading in the Pacific. Since much of the Pacific region is underpopulated, or has been largely isolated from the rest of the world until this century, little is known about the historic frequency of tsunamis. The Japanese islands and Hawaii are both particularly prone to tsunamis. Out in the ocean, submarine shock waves produce small fast-moving waves that are barely noticeable. The waves gain height and destructive power when they move into shallower water near land. Sophisticated warning systems can now detect submarine earthquakes and predict where and when tsunamis might hit populated coasts.

THE KRAKATOA TSUNAMI

Perhaps the most famous tsunami in recent history was generated by the massive volcanic eruption of Mount Krakatau (Krakatoa) in 1883 on an uninhabited Indonesian island, which was almost obliterated by the eruption. The tsunami was set up by the collapse of the island into the sea, creating a trench 5 miles (8 kilometers) wide, and over 600 feet (200 meters) below sea level. The wave spread out towards the neighboring islands of Java and Sumatra, and reached a height of over 130 feet (40 meters) when it approached land, swamping coastal settlements and killing some 36,000 people. Fishermen out at sea did not even notice the wave as it passed but returned to find their coastal villages, families, and livestock swept away. The tsunami caused more deaths than the eruption itself.

The Krakatoan eruption in 1883 was heard 3,000 miles (4,800 kilometers) away. The tsunami it precipitated was 131 feet (40 meters) high.

ALASKA PHENOMENON

Most tsunamis are initiated by earthquakes. These frequently occur under the sea, and the tsunami may harmlessly dissipate without damage. However, if the earthquake is large or unfortunately located, then the results can be catastrophic. An example is provided by the 1964 Alaska earthquake. This large earthquake, of magnitude 8.4, caused little damage in the sparsely populated surrounding area. Several vicious aftershocks, however, set off a series of 33-foot- (10-meter-) high tsunami waves. They spread out into the Gulf of Alaska and caused extensive damage to property.

TRAVELING TSUNAMIS

The waves generated by the Alaska earthquake were later observed off the coast of California, still 23 feet (7 meters) tall and still dangerous, as the deaths of 12 people in the region prove. Their journey continued to Hawaii, where they were still 6½ feet (2 meters). By the time they reached Antarctica, on the other side of the globe, they measured 3¼ feet (1 meter).

A GIANT TSUNAMI

One effect of the 6¼-mile- (10-kilometer-) wide meteorite which hit the Yucatan peninsula, Mexico, at the end of the Cretaceous (65 MA), was the generation of a giant tsunami. The shockwaves from the impact were so great that the estimated height of the tsunami, which spread throughout the Caribbean and Gulf of Mexico, is about 3,000 feet (1 kilometer). There is geological evidence that ocean-floor sediments were ripped up and dumped onshore around the Gulf of Mexico. Such a wave would have destroyed all life around the coastal areas where it struck. It was probably one of the biggest tsunamis ever experienced on Earth.

Volcanoes

A volcano is a vent or fissure in the surface of the Earth through which molten, solid, or gaseous material erupts. The main products of eruption are molten or solidified mineral silicates and related gases. The type of erupted material varies greatly depending on prevailing physical conditions and the chemistry of the molten material generated deep within the Earth's crust (magma). Volcanoes are not found on Earth alone; on Triton, the larger of Neptune's two satellites, volcanoes spout fountains of nitrogen. On Io, the first satellite of Jupiter, plumes of sulfur dioxide and sulfur lavas are produced.

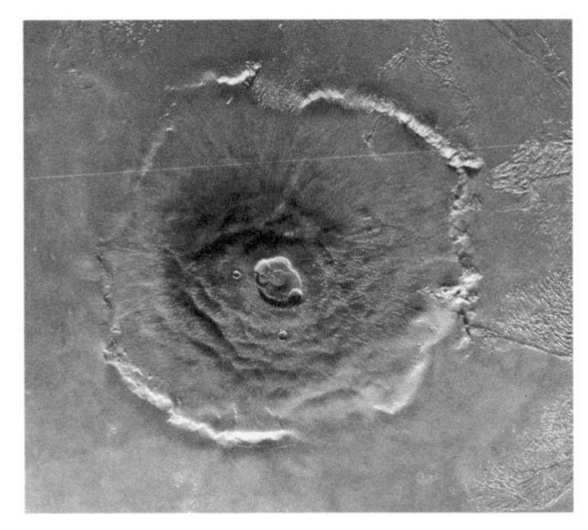

Volcanic activity is not restricted to the Earth. Olympus Mons on Mars, the largest known volcano, is over 15 miles (25 kilometers) high.

THE FORGE OF VULCAN

Not surprisingly, volcanoes, with their often catastrophically unpredictable behavior, have been invested with supernatural powers since prehistoric times. The term volcano is derived from the island of Vulcano, one of the Aeolian Islands off the north coast of Sicily. Because of its frequent eruptions, the Romans regarded the island as the forge of Vulcan, the god of fire and maker of weapons.

VOLCANO DISTRIBUTION

At present the Earth has more than 1,500 active volcanoes. They tend to be distributed around the edges of oceans, for example, on the edge of the continental landmasses around the Pacific rim (the Ring of Fire). There are some obvious exceptions to this, such as the volcanoes of the Hawaiian islands. The global distribution of volcanoes is largely controlled by plate tectonics—the movement of the upper 6 to 50 miles (10 to 80 kilometers) of the Earth's surface in a jigsaw of near-rigid plates.

PLATE BOUNDARIES

Some of these crustal plates are diverging, some are converging, and others sliding past one another. Volcanoes are generally found at the boundaries of the crustal plates, particularly at divergent and convergent margins. At divergent margins, the tectonic plates are stretched and thinned, allowing the hot, semi-molten mantle underneath to well up and melt further, forming magma. The magma may break through in a few places to form volcanoes such as Kilimanjaro, Mt. Kenya, and Oldoinyo Lengai, all found along the East African Rift Valley.

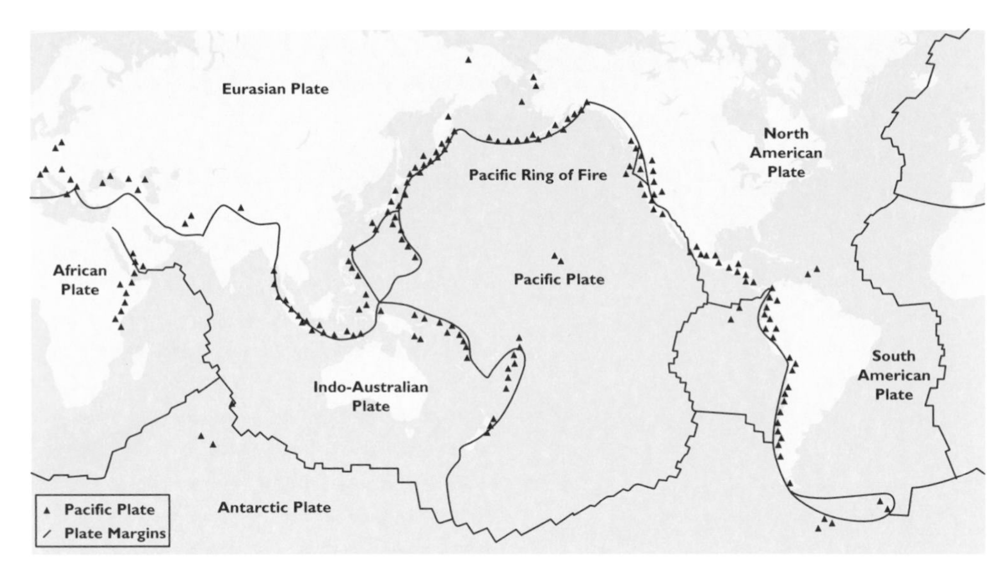

The Ring of Fire, an extensive belt of volcanic activity stretching right around the Pacific Ocean, is the most seismically active area in the world. The volcanoes are located at plate margins, on the edge of continental landmasses. Most major cities have been affected by earthquakes or volcanic activity.

MID-OCEAN RIDGE VOLCANOES

Where plate divergence is extreme, the tectonic plate thins so much that it splits, allowing a more or less continuous chain of volcanic activity along the entire length of the fracture. This process forms the mid-ocean spreading ridges, such as the Mid-Atlantic Ridge, which runs down the middle of the Atlantic Ocean, from Jan Mayen, an island to the east of Greenland, to Bouvet Island in the South Atlantic. Small eruptions occur episodically all the way along the ridges, either from fissures up to about 9 miles (15 kilometers) in length or from more isolated volcanoes within a rift valley in the center of the ridge.

ICELANDIC ERUPTIONS

On the mid-Atlantic island of Iceland, where the mid-ocean ridge rises above sea level, most of the erupted magma, or lava, is fluid. But the volumes of lava expelled tend to be very large because the ridge coincides with an area of active upwelling from the mantle (a so-called mantle hot spot). In 1783–84, the Laki fissure erupted, emitting the longest flow of lava ever recorded—it traveled up to 43 miles (70 kilometers) from the source. Associated emissions of sulfurous gases caused climate change, leading to severe winters in northwest Europe. Crops and livestock were devastated in Iceland, leading to a disastrous famine. Disease and starvation killed 25 percent of the Icelandic population.

HOT SPOTS

Volcanic centers are also found above hot spots in the middle of tectonic plates, such as Hawaii, which lies in the middle of the Pacific plate. Most of the hot spot eruptions are moderately sized, but very long lived. The Pu'u'O'o eruption of Kilauea on Hawaii has been continuous for the last 16 years. The lava covers enormous distances because it is so fluid.

SUBDUCTION VOLCANOES

The volcanic eruptions that occur at convergent margins tend to be much more remarkable and devastating. The most volcanically active convergent margins are those where an oceanic plate is moving under a continental plate (a subduction zone). This is happening around much of the Pacific Ring of Fire. In these areas, the chemical composition of the magma makes it more sticky (viscous) than the magma produced at divergent margins. Consequently, the viscous lava tends to solidify below ground, forming solidified lava plugs in cracks and fissures. The trapped magma under the lava plugs continues to release gas bubbles, building up pressure. Eventually, either the pressure builds up too high or an event such as an earthquake dislodges the plug, forcing it out like a champagne cork.

In AD 79, the eruption of Vesuvius produced a pyroclastic flow which smothered the Roman town of Pompeii in hot ash and gas. The burned bodies left hollows which have been cast in cement.

MOUNT SAINT HELENS

After 123 years of inactivity, on March 21, 1980, earthquakes started to be felt around Mt. Saint Helens, Washington State. On the north slope, a large dome of trapped magma grew at a rate of 5 feet (1.5 meters) a day. When, on May 18, 1980, a magnitude 5.1 earthquake caused the dome to slide away, the pressure that was holding back the underlying magma was released. A gigantic rockslide and avalanche ensued, as well as a major pumice and ash eruption. At least 17 different pyroclastic flows (flowing clouds of ash, rock, and gas), with temperatures of over 2,731°F (1,500°C) surged at over 60 miles per hour (100 km per hour) down the flanks of the volcano. Over 1,300 feet (400 meters) of the mountain peak was blown away.

Seismic activity gave ample warning of the eruption of Mt. St. Helens in 1980. Most of the area was evacuated and the mortality rate was comparatively low—even so, 57 people died.

VOLCANIC HAZARDS

The hazards arising from volcanoes are wide-ranging. Volcanic eruptions destroy housing, crops, livestock, and human lives. But the fertile soils produced by the weathering of lavas attract people to live and work on volcano slopes. The densely populated Soufrihre Hills on the Caribbean island of Montserrat, for example, were totally devastated by eruptions in 1997.

PYROCLASTIC DANGERS

A volcano's eruptive products, such as lava, ash, and pumice, may cause direct damage. Pyroclastic flows, which consist of superheated, suffocating ash, poisonous gases, and large blocks of rock, are particularly deadly. They can travel at 180 miles per hour (300 km per hour) or more over many square miles. Historically, the most famous pyroclastic flows erupted from Vesuvius in southern Italy in AD 79. Many citizens were overcome by flows of burning toxic gases and ash in the towns of Pompeii and Herculaneum.

VOLCANIC POLLUTION

An additional problem associated with large eruptions is the climatic effects of so much material entering the atmosphere. Some 74,000 years ago, the massive eruption of Toba in Sumatra ejected so much volcanic pollution into the atmosphere that its chemical composition was altered and the Earth was cooled.

ASH CLOUDS, MUDSLIDES, AND FLOODS

The side-effects of eruptions can also be dangerous. In 1985, hot ash from the small eruption of Nevado del Ruiz in Colombia melted ice and snow around the summit. Floods of meltwater, mixed with ash, formed rapidly moving mudflows, which poured down the mountainside destroying a small town and killing more than 20,000 people. The eruption of Grimsvvtn in Iceland in 1996 led to a colossal flood (called a *jokulhlaup*), releasing water at the rate of 65,393 cubic yards (50,000 cubic meters) a second.

BENEFITS FROM VOLCANOS

Volcanic activity is not all harmful. In Iceland, the geothermal heat created by the underground activity of the magma is used to generate electricity and to heat glasshouses in which to grow food that would otherwise be imported. Soils produced by the weathering of lavas are often very rich in mineral nutrients and can be highly productive when cultivated.

PREDICTING ERUPTIONS

It is essential to develop some means of predicting the timing and projected magnitude of volcanic activity to avoid catastrophes. Although it is possible to detect the early warning signs of an imminent eruption, it is very difficult to predict precisely when an eruption will begin, or in which direction lava and ash will flow. Eruption is controlled by many geological factors, not all of which are understood or can be monitored easily. Continual monitoring of seismic activity and volcanic gases may lead to a better understanding of some early warning signs, but it is unlikely that precise predictions of volcanic eruptions will be possible for a very long time.

Sedimentation

Submarine slides of rocks the size of city blocks, desert dust storms, avalanches of snow, ice, mud, or rock, incandescent flows of volcanic ash, and meteorite impacts are all occasional and catastrophic sedimentary processes. Although rare, they may have just as much, if not more, long-term impact as the steady settling of sedimentary particles on the floors of the world's oceans and seas. All of these sedimentary processes ultimately produce similar results—the deposition of sediments, in the form of layers of mineral and organic material, which may eventually become solid rock.

In this glacial avalanche in Alaska, suspended ice and snow particles thunder down the mountain. Its destructive power is greatly increased by dislodged rock material that is finally dumped downslope.

THE PROCESS OF SEDIMENTATION

The transport of sediment particles of any size from one place to another is known as sedimentation. Sedimentation may be fast or slow, taking seconds or decades. It may fill a small pond or a region of the ocean floor the size of a large country. Sedimentation can occur in response to catastrophic events, or be a steady, constantly occurring process. Sediment may be deposited on land or underwater, although sediment that forms underwater is by far the most likely to be eventually preserved as strata in the rock record.

GLOWING CLOUDS

One of the most impressive, violent, and destructive forms of sedimentation is the flow of volcanic ash and glass shards, carried in a stream of hot gas, down the side of a volcano. These flows, known as *nuée ardentes* (French for "glowing clouds") can move extremely fast, at up to 180 miles per hour (300 km per hour), causing enormous amounts of damage and loss of life. In 1902, a *nuée ardente* erupting from Mount Pelee, a volcano on the Caribbean island of Martinique, completely destroyed the town of Saint Pierre, killing all but two of its 28,000 residents. The sediment produced by a flow of this nature is known as block and ash deposits. These flows are rare, producing only a very tiny fraction of the Earth's sediment.

ASH FALLOUT

The widespread fallout of ash from explosive volcanic eruptions is a much more common sedimentation process. Ash can be blasted through the atmosphere to heights of 25 miles (40 kilometers). Fine dust-sized particles are carried around the world by high-level winds, eventually raining down over vast areas. Very large individual volcanic eruptions, such as that of Krakatau in 1883, spread dust globally. Periods of intense vulcanicity, such as the outpouring of the Indian Deccan lavas 65 million years ago, propelled enough ash into the atmosphere to actually change global climates and contribute to a major extinction event.

ASHFALL DEPOSITS

Larger ash particles are distributed more locally to form ashfall deposits, called tuffs, ranging from a fraction of an inch to hundreds of feet thick. Tuffs frequently contain minerals such as zircon, which can be dated radiometrically. When they are interbedded with normal terrestrial sediment, as in the Rift Valley of East Africa, they are, therefore, very useful for dating the deposits.

UNDERWATER AVALANCHES

Very similar flows of material are known to occur underwater. These flows, called turbidity currents, consist of sandy, muddy, and silty particles suspended in water. The suspension is triggered by earthquakes, or simply by the overbalancing of some of the vast piles of river-derived sediments that build up in lakes or on the edge of the continental shelves. Once the mass of particles is shaken up into a watery suspension, its density is greater than that of the surrounding water and gravity accelerates its flow below the main body of water, like an avalanche.

DEEP-OCEAN DEPOSITION

Turbidity currents can travel for hundreds of miles down the continental shelf before settling out in the depths of the ocean. On the deep-sea floor they spread out to form sediments known as turbidites. During the height of deposition several feet of sand and silt may be laid down in a very short length of time, ranging from several hours to days. A significant proportion of the sediment that reaches the oceans is eventually transported down the continental shelf by turbidity currents. Turbidite deposits form some of the most common deposits of ocean basins and are often preserved as sedimentary rock.

SPEEDING CURRENTS

An idea of the immense speed at which turbidity currents can move was provided by the earthquake that occurred close to Nova Scotia in 1929. The earthquake initiated a turbidity current, which proceeded, channeled by a submarine canyon. down the Grand Banks continental slope. The flow broke 13 submarine telegraph cables on its way. As the exact time of successive cable rupture was known, the speed of the flow was calculated at up to 60 miles per hour (100 km per hour). The area finally covered by the sediment carried within that single current was more than 108,000 square miles (280,000 square kilometers).

EXTRATERRESTRIAL IMPACT

When meteorites hit the Earth's surface, they melt the surrounding rock, which splashes up and out of the impact crater. The melted droplets, (tektites) may then be distributed over a wide area. Vaporization of the meteorite's outer layers leaves a trail of dust in the atmosphere, which can be distributed over a wide area, forming an almost instantaneous and identifiable deposit.

IRIDIUM DEPOSITS

Dust produced by the fragmentation of a meteorite has a unique chemical signature. It settles out to form a sediment containing traces of the rare element iridium. For example, the worldwide boundary deposits between the Cretaceous and Tertiary periods are enriched in iridium. They are related to the impact and fragmentation of a 6-mile- (10-kilometer-) wide meteorite in the Yucatan Peninsula of Mexico 65 million years ago. The dust cloud it created blocked out the Sun, killing vegetation and contributing to the extinction of the dinosaurs.

MOVING GLACIERS

The movement of glaciers can drastically modify landscapes and build up large deposits very quickly. A moving glacier grinds the underlying rock as it travels, and much of the pulverized material is incorporated into the frozen base of the ice flow. These fragments act like the abrasive grains on sandpaper, scratching and smoothing down rock surfaces.

The crater at Canyon Diablo, Arizona was formed about 50,000 years ago, by a nickel-iron meteorite 197 feet (60 meters) in diameter.

GLACIAL DEPOSITION

When the ice melts, the mixture of boulders and rock fragments is dumped, forming moraines and boulder clay or tillite deposits, which contain a vast range of different materials of varying sizes, all surrounded by a muddy matrix. These sediments, which can be miles long, may be deposited in distinct ridges, parallel to the front of the glacier (terminal moraines), or parallel to the direction of flow of valley glaciers (lateral moraines). They are also deposited in sheets and molded into egg-shaped mounds (drumlins). Crag-and-tail deposits occur when a rock outcrop is too hard to be ground down, forcing the glacier to "climb" over it, dropping a "tail" of debris on its descent down the other side.

GLACIAL ERRATICS

Till deposits may contain a mixture of pebbles, which began their journey hundreds of miles apart, and house-sized boulders, known as glacial erratics, which are often left behind after the finer-grained material of the moraine has been eroded. Norwegian rocks have been transported by ice as far south as Norfolk on the east coast of England. Late Precambrian tillites, over 550 million years old, have been found in Canada, Ireland, and Scotland, indicating that ice ages have occurred throughout Earth history.

The Perito Moreno glacier, Patagonia, Argentina. During the last ice age glaciers were well beyond their present limits; today are retreating.

STEADY SEDIMENTATION

Many sediments are deposited continuously over the surface of the Earth: river-transported sediment builds up on beaches or deltas; coral and other fragments accumulate at the base of reefs; a steady "rain" of dust and organic particles falls in the abyssal plains of the deep sea.

DATING DEEP-OCEAN SEDIMENT

Sedimentary material that reaches the deep-ocean floor is varied. Volcanic ash, cosmic dust, and very fine sand blown by desert sandstorms make up the inorganic component, while the skeletons of swimming or free-floating organisms, which may be made of calcium carbonate or silica, make up the rest. Their skeletons are important for interpreting the deep-sea sediment record, but at great depths the skeletal calcium carbonate dissolves and is not deposited.

ENVIRONMENTAL CHANGE

Sedimentation in lakes with distinct seasonal climatic variations can provide very useful sedimentary records of changing environments in the past. For example, the 200,000 to 400,000-year-old sedimentary rocks now found in the Parana Basin of Brazil record the passage of each year in the form of a pale layer, formed during summers, and a dark layer, rich in the remains of living creatures, that formed during winters.

AFTER DEPOSITION

Once sediment is deposited, it is eroded or transformed by a range of processes. In water, waves may reduce the size of existing particles or winnow through a mixed sand and silt deposit, removing finer material, to leave a sandstone. Once covered by other sediments, grains may react with the water trapped beneath. On land, wind, frost, and rain erode or remove any sedimentary deposits.

HUMAN DEPOSITION

Today, the human race is leaving behind a wide range of indestructible deposits—especially the huge waste deposits rich in bottle glass and plastics and contaminated by a potentially toxic chemical cocktail. They will be examined by future geologists who will be able to decipher them in the same way that they interpret ancient environments from sedimentary rock.

The Present as a Key to the Past

How are mountains formed? Why are shells of sea-dwelling animals enclosed in hard rock, uplifted thousands of feet above sea level, and seemingly carried hundreds of miles inland to form mountains? How are rocks bent and folded as if they were made of soft clay? What turns soft sand and mud into hard rock? Even these basic geological questions have only been satisfactorily answered in the last 200 years. The most important key to the geological past was an understanding of present processes.

Richard Owen (1804–92), anatomist, paleontologist, and pioneer of dinosaur reconstruction. He made extensive studies of extinct vertebrates, and campaigned for a Natural History Museum in London.

CATASTROPHISM

While many geological processes are infinitely slow, some are fast-acting and often dangerously dramatic or even catastrophic. In the past, powerful events such as earthquakes and volcanic eruptions were thought to be responsible for the opening up of valleys and elevation of mountains. For a long time, European natural philosophers believed that the creation of life and history of the Earth followed the Old Testament version of events. The Great Flood was seen as particularly important in shaping Earth's geology. Gradually, as geological understanding developed, this ancient view had to be modified to include successive large-scale catastrophic events.

GRADUALISM

A quite different view came to dominate geological thinking throughout much of the 19th century. Geological processes were seen as both incredibly slow and inexorable and, given enough time, capable of producing the structures observed in rocks and mountains. The models for many of these processes were in fact the common, everyday processes that can be observed all over the Earth's surface.

OBSERVATION AND CALIBRATION

For the first time, geologists observed and measured the processes of weathering and erosion on mountainsides, the sediment-carrying capacity of streams and rivers, the features of deposition by wind, water, ice, and river, and the character of their deposits. Given enough time, these familiar processes were evidently capable of destroying mountains and recycling their rocks into layers of sediments. Just how the mountains were built was still not clear, but many of the intermediary processes were.

A STABLE UNIVERSE

The methodology of this approach was to use the present as a key to the past. Behind these ideas were two famous Scottish geologists, James Hutton (1726–97) and Charles Lyell (1797–1875). Hutton observed the ceaseless and repetitive nature of Earth processes, which fitted an even older Newtonian view of a stable and cyclic universe. Lyell took up this Newtonian approach; natural phenomena could only be reasonably explained by agencies that are seen to be effective. Explanations should always be in terms of actual causes, since only the present can be directly observed and witnessed.

VICTORIAN PRAGMATISM

Victorian geologists were intent on describing and obtaining the facts of the natural world as much as theorizing about them. They initiated the first mapping of the distribution of strata at the Earth's surface, and there was a realization that the layering of strata reflected a historical sequence of events. By drawing vertical sections through the layers, it was possible to work back through time from the youngest, uppermost deposits, into successively older strata. By the 1860s it had become evident that even older strata and, therefore, a deeper past remained to be plumbed.

THE DIRECTION OF LIFE

Adhering to his cyclic view, Lyell expected to find fossil representatives of all kinds of organisms, even in some of the oldest rock. But by the middle of the 19th century it was becoming apparent that there was some overall development of plants and animals from the primitive to the more advanced throughout geological history. Lyell, initially unsympathetic, was converted to Charles Darwin's theory of evolution by the persuasive advocacy of the English biologist, Thomas Henry Huxley.

OLD-WORLD GEOLOGY

Many of the early developments in geology were made in Europe during the 18th century, and in Britain, France, and Germany in particular. For such a small geographical area, the geology of Britain contains a remarkable sample of Earth history, from the Precambrian era through to the present. Several major subdivisions of geological time, such as the Cambrian, Ordovician, Silurian, and Devonian, were named by British geologists, The often abundant fossils of these strata allowed British and European paleontology to advance very quickly in the early part of the 19th century.

NEW-WORLD VISTAS

When it came to larger-scale geological phenomena, however, Europe could not provide a full sense of the geological possibilities. The global scale could only be determined by the vastness of the New World, as revealed by the North American geological pioneers in the latter part of the 19th century. Charles Lyell visited North America four times between 1841 and 1853 and used his new experiences to illustrate subsequent editions of his famous book *Principles of Geology* (which was first published in 1830).

MOVING MOUNTAINS

One of the most important contributions by the North American geologists was to the understanding of the geological complexities of mountain belts. Not only were they sites of enormous thicknesses of sedimentary strata, but structurally they could be complicated by large-scale folds and faults, with an order of magnitude greater than anything seen in Britain. Some of these structural mountain belts, such as the northeastern Appalachians, terminated abruptly with ocean margins. The puzzle was finally resolved by the discovery of plate tectonics, which explained their continuation in the Caledonian Mountains of Ireland and Scotland on the other side of the Atlantic.

This model of an *Iguanodon* was created for the 1854 Great Exhibition at London's Crystal Palace by the artist Benjamin Waterhouse Hawkins under the supervision of paleontologist Richard Owen.

THE BRITISH DINOSAUR

The first dinosaur remains were discovered and described as such from very fragmentary and incomplete fossil remains. The bones were found in Mesozoic strata from the south of England in the first few decades of the 19th century. The first full-scale dinosaur reconstructions were undertaken by anatomist and paleontologist, Richard Owen.

REPTILE RECONSTRUCTION

When Owen attempted to reconstruct this new group of reptiles, the only models available to him were the living reptiles, especially the lizards, crocodiles, and newly discovered iguanas. This was an instance where the simple application of present models for the past did not work at first. Owen realized that it was not possible to simply scale them up to elephant size, so he partly employed mammal-like models. The result was a curious hybrid; massive and lumbering rhinoceroslike reptiles.

THE HEROIC AGE

The discovery in America of more complete dinosaur skeletons suggested that all were not the lumbering quadrupedal beasts that Owen had envisaged. The center of dinosaur investigations shifted away from Europe. In 1858, Joseph Leidy found a skeleton in New Jersey, which he reconstructed in a two-legged, kangaroolike posture. By the 1870s, two schoolmasters, Arthur Lakes and O.W. Lucas, found even better dinosaur remains in Colorado and started what has been called the "heroic age" of dinosaur discovery. As paleontologists have realized the limitations of the comparative anatomy approach, the image of the dinosaurs has continued to evolve slowly.

A painting of marine reptiles by Benjamin Waterhouse Hawkins (1809–89), assistant to Richard Owen. Pictures such as these helped popularize the "denizens of the abysmal slime."

THE NEW CATASTROPHISM

In the last decade or so, geologists have come to understand the potential power of catastrophic events such as storms, floods, gravity flows, tsunamis, and meteorite impacts. The impact of rare natural events, both on land and at sea, can be greater than the cumulative effects of the intervening slow and gradual processes.

COSMIC IMPACT

The most dramatic catastrophic events are the large meteorite impacts that occur at intervals of hundreds of millions of years. Some, such as the Chicxulub impact, which took place 65 million years ago in Mexico's Yucatan Peninsula, are claimed to have been responsible for mass extinctions. The realization that such events are more common than had previously been thought and that they will recur in the future has added a new interest to the study of catastrophic events of geological significance.

What Next? Future Plate Movements and Their Consequences

The study of the Earth's geological history shows an extraordinary record of dynamic change. Oceans have repeatedly opened and closed. Continents have moved about the Earth's surface like pieces of an enormous jigsaw puzzle, colliding with one another, joining up, and then breaking apart again. Understanding of these movements is based on the geological interpretation of the Earth's 4-billion-year-old rock record. There is no indication that these processes have slowed down in recent geological history and it is likely that they will continue into the distant future. Eventually, the gradual cooling and thickening of the lithosphere, the rigid outer layer of the Earth, will slow down the plate tectonics processes. The Earth will lose its dynamic drive and begin to die.

THE PAST AS A KEY TO THE FUTURE

It is possible to use some of the methods employed by geologists to determine the past configurations of the continents to calculate the direction of future continental movements. The basic assumption is that the rate of present movement will continue. The fundamental driving force behind Earth's dynamic processes is the formation of new ocean floor at mid-ocean ridges. Measurement of plate movement is not simple and depends on calculating the rate at which new ocean floor is generated. Two basic methods are used, mapping and measurement of paleomagnetic reversals and radiometric dating of the ocean floor rocks.

PALEOMAGNETIC REVERSALS

The Earth's magnetic field is generated by convection currents in the molten iron of the Earth's core. Every so often, the direction of the Earth's magnetic field reverses and magnetic North becomes magnetic South and vice versa. As new ocean floor lavas are forced out and solidify at the mid-ocean ridges each newly formed strip of lavas records the magnetic field at that time. Continued generation of lavas records any changes in the magnetic field in the form of a linear pattern like a barcode. Two symmetrical linear patterns mirror each other on either side of the spreading ridge. These patterns have been mapped by ship-towed instruments and can be fitted to particular segments of the global history of reversals.

PROVIDING A TIMESCALE

Samples of ocean-floor lava retrieved by submersible can be dated radiometrically. Their ages of formation provide a contextual timescale for the history of magnetic reversals. With an accurate knowledge of when the reversals took place, the precise rate at which the ocean floor is spreading can be calculated. Using this method, it is also possible to see where changes in plate motions have occurred.

MEASURING FAULT MOTION

The measurement of fault movement during an earthquake is another way of calculating present-day plate motion. By recording earthquakes over a period of time in a particular area and using a global network of seismometers, it is possible to determine rates of strain within the Earth's crust, providing a clue to present plate movements.

SPACE OBSERVATIONS

Satellites now provide another method of measuring plate movement. By recording the change of position of particular points in the crustal plates over a period of time, the rate of movement of these points relative to one another can be calculated.

The East African Rift, an incipient mid-ocean ridge. Within 10 million years, the northern rift may have opened out, looking like the Red Sea.

TIME TREK

A computer program called Time Trek has been developed at the University of Cambridge in England to show past plate motions and to predict plate movement, although some unpredictable events, such as rises in sea level caused by global warming and glaciation, cannot be taken into account. The sequence of future scenarios, which reveal that within 20 million years from now (a geologically short period) the surface of the Earth may look very different, can be summarized as follows:

+20 MILLION YEARS: AFRICA DIVIDED

Eastern Africa and Madagascar have split off from the rest of Africa and in the process are opening a new ocean. Spain has cut its connection with France and rotated clockwise slightly. Australia, New Zealand, and Papua New Guinea have moved so rapidly northward, that northern Australia now lies on the equator. The Black Sea is now completely cut off from the Mediterranean Sea and the Gulf of Aqaba has opened up all the way north to Turkey.

+40 MILLION YEARS: WIDENING ATLANTIC

The Persian Gulf is now cut off from the Indian Ocean and the Black Sea has halved in size, on the way to being completely closed. Africa continues its inexorable move northward and is gradually closing the Mediterranean Sea. Sicily has pushed north and is lying offshore within sight of Rome. Spain continues its move clockwise, away from France. East Africa is still pushing eastward away from the rest of Africa, while Australia continues its northward journey towards Southeast Asia. The Americas move farther away from Europe, and the Atlantic Ocean widens.

+50 MILLION YEARS: CALIFORNIA SPLIT

North America (with Greenland) moves further away to the west and starts to rotate clockwise and move southward. From now on, Greenland will begin to be truly green as it creeps south below 60°N. Part of California has finally split away from mainland America, along the line of the San Andreas Fault and is heading northeastward.

+80 MILLION YEARS: DISAPPEARING MEDITERRANEAN

New Zealand has lost any vestiges of Alpine snow

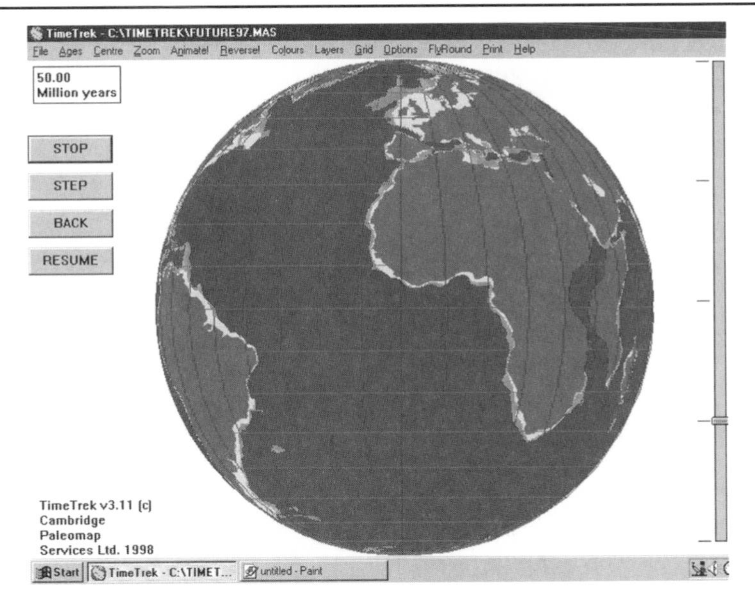

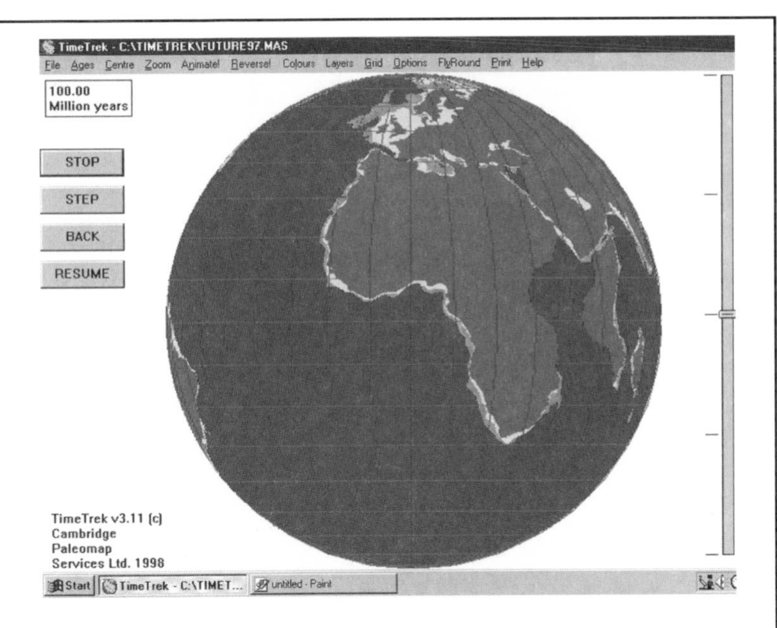

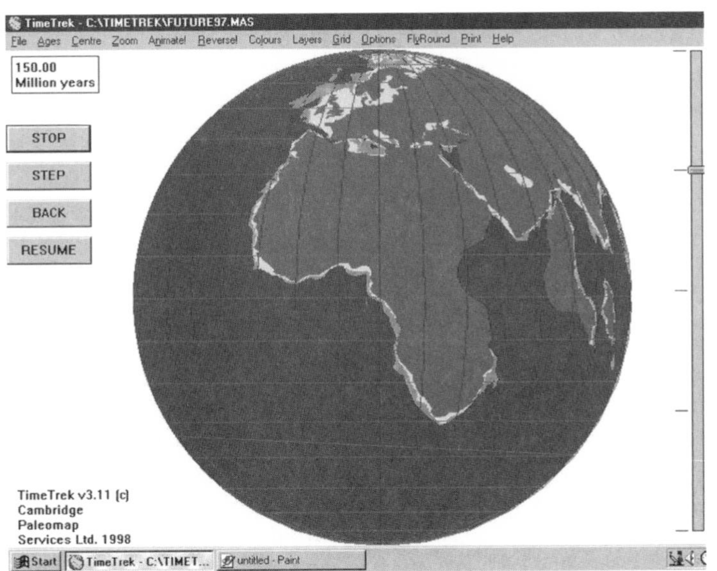

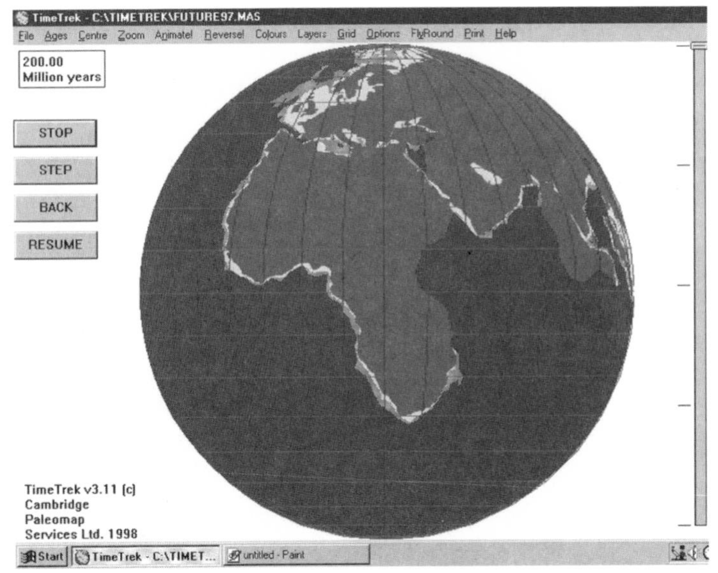

Future scenarios from the Cambridge University Time Trek program monitor the gradual widening of the Atlantic Ocean. Top left +50 million years, top right +100 million years, bottom left +150 million years, bottom right +200 million years.

as it moves into the tropics. Meanwhile, Australia has collided with Japan. Antarctica has started to move toward Australia. Africa has finally collided with southern Italy and Spain, closing the Mediterranean, and destroying the remains of the classical world. The impact is starting a new phase in the long history of mountain building in the Alps.

+90 MILLION YEARS: AMERICAS DIVIDED

North and South America have finally split apart. The southward movement of North America is bringing it alongside South America.

+150 MILLION YEARS: TROPICAL NEWFOUNDLAND

The large continent of Greenland is now entirely south of 60°N and enjoying a climate it last experienced in early Tertiary times (200 million years before the present). Newfoundland is entering the tropics, Mexico now lies on the equator, with Florida a few degrees north. South America is moving southward, leaving Peru at about 30°S.

+200 MILLION YEARS: EQUATORIAL ANTARCTICA

Antarctica now lies very close to Mexico and together they straddle the Equator. Once again Antarctica is luxuriously vegetated as it was in early Mesozoic times (400 million years before the present). East Africa has finally collided with India while Madagascar has moved eastward to join Indonesia in Southeast Asia. Newfoundland, at about 10°N, is moving toward the Equator, which Florida has crossed as it moves south. South America has rotated clockwise through 90°, so that Argentina lies along the latitude of 60°S. During these last 200 million years, the British Isles and Scandinavia have moved slowly southward and eastward.

THE END OF EARTH'S STORY

Tectonic plates are comprised of the brittle and rigid outer layer of the Earth, the crust and upper mantle, known as the lithosphere. Since the Earth is slowly cooling, the lithosphere will become thicker and more resistant to movement. Ocean-floor spreading will slow and subduction of the oceanic crust beneath the continents will cease. The Earth will lose its dynamic drive and start to die. It will take many millions of years for this to happen, but when it does, Earth will eventually become as barren as Venus or Mars.

Fossils: Classification

Scientific attempts to classify the tens of millions of organisms that have lived on Earth both now and in the distant geological past have developed out of very ancient traditions. Scholars of the Classical Greek and early Christian worlds handed down various schemes in which life was organized into hierarchies that progressed from the most primitive to the most advanced (humans). Within these hierarchies, natural divisions of organisms, such as worms, insects, plants, fish, birds, mammals, and humans, were recognized, and have been crystallized in our language for many centuries.

In 1836, English naturalist Charles Darwin (1809–82) embarked on a surveying voyage to South America and the Pacific islands on board the *Beagle* (above). His observations of the geology, fossils, and living organisms that he encountered on his journey led him to develop his theories of evolution, which were later formulated in his controversial work *On the Origin of Species* (1859).

INHERITED CHARACTERISTICS

Human reproduction, family history, and the ancient skills of breeding domesticated plants and animals provided a basic understanding of life processes and their genealogical implications. Cereals, vegetables, and ornamental plants have been bred and cultivated over thousands of years to improve yields and appearance. Similarly cattle, horses, dogs, and cats have been "improved" by human intervention. Although the mechanisms were not understood, it was clear that generally "like begets like." Inheritance of characteristics was understood, at least at a pragmatic level.

CLASSIFYING LIFE

Since 1735, the standard biological method of organizing and grouping plants and animals has been based on the scheme outlined by the Swedish naturalist Carl Linnaeus (1707–78) in his *System of Nature*. Linnaeus believed that species are real and discrete biological units that are unchanged from one generation to another.

NAMING LIFE

Linnaeus adopted a hierarchical system of classification with four ascending levels: species genus, order, and class. Linnaeus introduced the still-used method of giving each species two Latinized names, the first referring to the genus and the second to the species. The human genus, for example, is characterized as *Homo,* and the species as *sapiens*. Linnaeus placed the genus *Homo* in the Order Primates, along with the apes, monkeys, and lemurs. These, in turn, were placed within the Class Mammalia, as part of the Kingdom Animalia.

THE DARWINIAN REVOLUTION

Despite initial criticism, the Linnaean method of classification was generally adopted by scientists. It was, and still is, constantly expanded and modified to accommodate the discoveries of biology. For early 19th-century naturalists, it was a representation of the natural order. However, the publication of the theory of evolution, developed jointly by Charles Darwin and Alfred Wallace in 1858, changed all that. The impact of *On the Tendency of Species to form Varieties; and on the Perpetuation of Varieties and Species by Natural Selection* is still being felt today.

EVOLUTIONARY LINKS

According to the theory, there should be evolutionary links, or transitional forms, between groups of organisms as one evolved into another through time. But Darwin realized that it would be difficult to find support for his proposals from the fossil record. His knowledge and experience of geology indicated that the fossil evidence was too fragmentary to back up his theory. The fossil record seemed to preserve such a small sample of past diversity that it was unlikely that the intermediary links would be found. In the light of subsequent methods of dating and analyzing fossils, Darwin would doubtless have been amazed by the extent to which the fossil record has supported his revolutionary theory of the mid-19th century.

THE PREHISTORIC "FAMILY TREE"

The 19th-century German biologist Ernst Haeckel (1834–1919) was one of the first scientists to portray the complete succession of prehistoric changes in life on Earth through time. He described the history of life as a connected genealogy, or extended family tree, with humans forming the highest branch.

COMMON ANCESTORS

Haeckel also developed the concept of the phylum (from the Greek for "stem"), a new and high rank of classification. All classes of organisms within a phylum are descended from a common ancestor. This concept gave the Linnaean classification a new dimension. All species, living or extinct, could be portrayed somewhere on the phylogenetic tree, with their lines of descent ideally being traced back to a common ancestor.

THE TIME DIMENSION

Darwin and Haeckel developed the classification of organisms into a genealogy in which species evolved through time. The growing understanding of the nature of the fossil record generally supported this view. The different nature of fossils and living organisms, however, often creates problems of affinity. The test of a living species, whether it can breed viable young, cannot be applied to fossil species.

CLADISTICS

Cladistic analysis is a recent development in the understanding of evolutionary and biological interrelationships between organisms. Pioneered by the entomologist (expert on insects) Willi Hennig, it is a formal method of assessing the extent to which organisms, both living and fossil, share characteristics. With this method, the importance of the dimension of time is reduced. The closeness of relationships between species and their most recent common ancestor is represented by a branching diagram, a cladogram.

Analysis of genetic similarity has suggested to some researchers that whales should be grouped with even-toed hoofed mammals (artiodactyls) such as hippopotamuses, although other scientists feel there may be insufficient data to support this conclusion.

SHARED CHARACTERS

A cladogram is constructed by assessing characteristics that are shared between two species exclusively (called shared derived characters, or synapomorphies). The succession of branching points (nodes) on a cladogram shows the relative order in which synapomorphies arise.

MEANINGFUL COMPARISONS

By showing the order in which shared derived features evolved, cladograms can be useful for several purposes. Groups that share more or fewer synapomorphies are considered more or less closely related to each other. Also, the sequence of acquisition of novel abilities or behaviors (for example how birds evolved wings) can be elucidated. It is also important to compare a large number of features and organisms.

THE DNA TREE

The ability to analyze and describe the genetic code (DNA) of organisms has created a new measure of the interrelationships, at the molecular level, between major groups of living organisms. Molecular phylogeny, the assessment of fundamental relationships between organisms, is based on the information held in the genetic code. Measures of the similarity between organisms at this level can be used to check the morphological classification (based on the form and structure of organisms). Assessments of genetic similarity have helped to resolve outstanding questions, such as showing that chimps and humans are probably closer to each other than either is to gorillas.

TESTING THE FOSSIL RECORD

Although this method cannot be used for extinct groups, it provides useful information that can be used to test the fossil record. An accurate assessment of the genetic distance between major invertebrate groups (phyla) such as annelids, mollusks, arthropods, and echinoderms, can be used to estimate how far back in time they diverged. Since representatives of these phyla of multicellular organisms (metazoans) are known from Cambrian strata, it has been estimated that the metazoans must have originated some 800 million years ago in the late Precambrian. This is significantly further back than the fossil record indicates, and paleontologists are now actively trying to test this claim.

Fossil Formation

Fossils are the most direct evidence of past life and its 3.8-billion-year history on Earth. But fossils record the existence, actions, and behavior of a very small sample of that past life—mainly those organisms with preservable hard parts like shells and bones. How representative of past life is the fossil record? Can it be relied upon to give a true picture of past life, the "family" histories of the plants and animals alive today, and all those that are extinct? To assess the shortcomings of the fossil record, it is necessary to understand the process of fossilization.

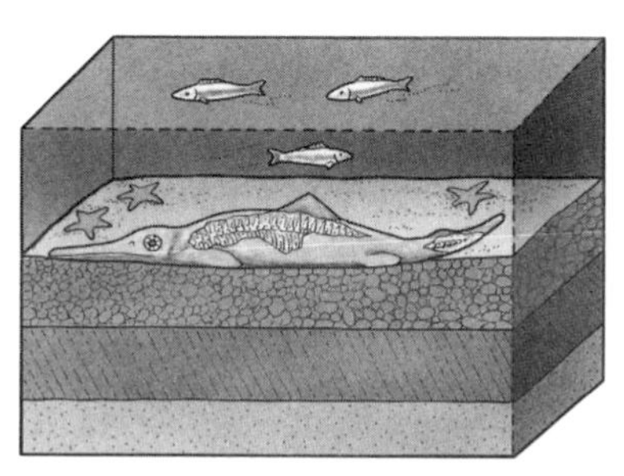

An ichthyosaur dies and is buried in soft sediments on the sea floor.

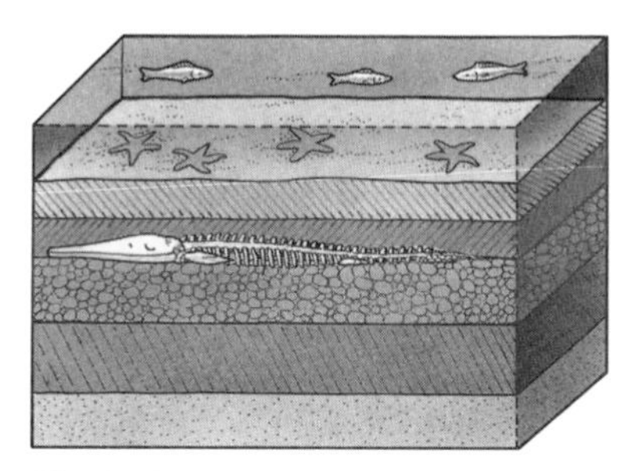

The flesh decays, and the bones, covered by layers of sediment, are mineralized.

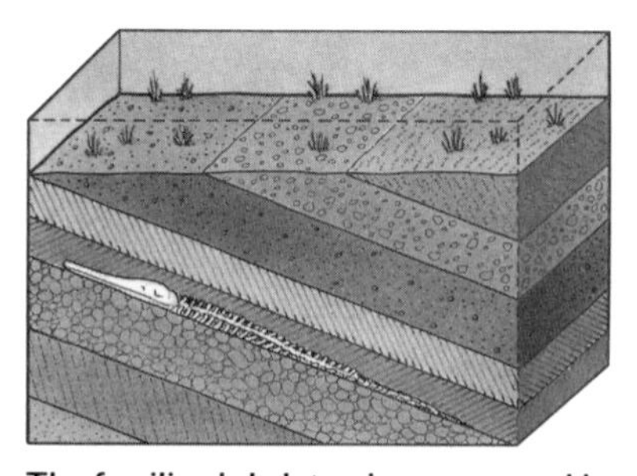

The fossilized skeleton is compressed by the weight and movement of the land.

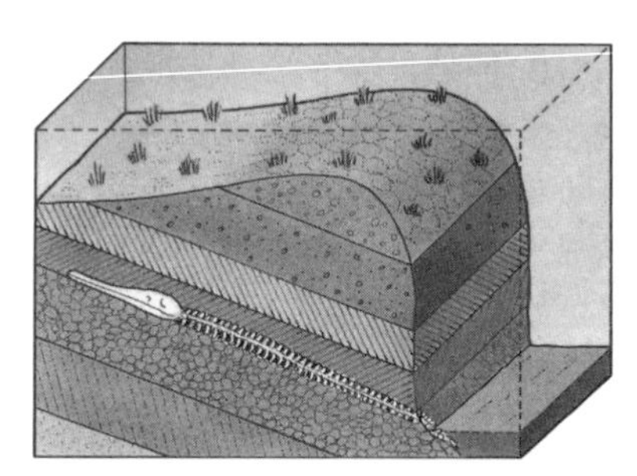

A stream's eroding action exposes the tail, some bones drop into the stream bed.

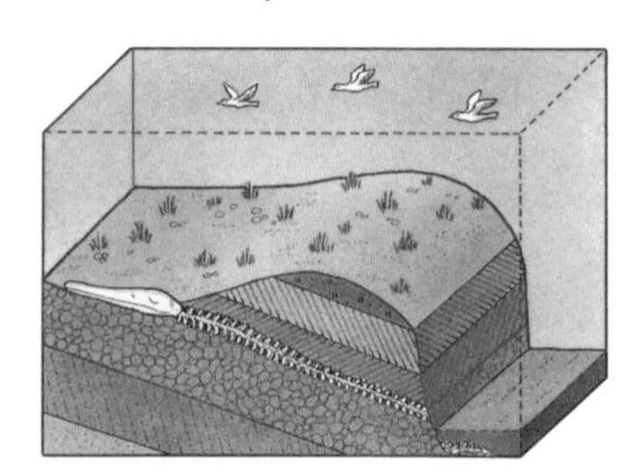

The forces of erosion wear away the land's surface and the skeleton is exposed.

THE DIVERSITY OF LIFE TODAY

There are some 10 million species of organisms alive on Earth today, with an enormous diversity and size range, from viruses and bacteria to giant redwood trees and mammalian blue whales. The majority (some 63%), however, are relatively small arthropods and most of these are insect arthropods (over 85%). Given the plenitude of life today, the fossil record potentially should contain even greater numbers of species. Since species do not exist forever, perhaps between 1 and 15 million years, there has been considerable turnover of life during the Earth's history.

FOSSIL SAMPLE SIZE

Taking the average species duration as 10 million years, there have been over 50 complete turnovers during the 500 million years from the Cambrian to the present. Assuming the same level of diversity of ten million species over that time, there should be in the order of 500 million fossil species buried in the stratigraphic record. So far, paleontologists have described only a few hundred thousand fossil species. At less than 0.01 percent, this represents a very small sample of the estimated total.

FOSSIL RECORD BIAS

In general, organisms without mineralized hard parts are not readily fossilized, discounting from the fossil record most of the single-celled creatures and other microorganisms (bacteria, protists, fungi), algae, vascular plants without woody tissues, worms, jellyfish, and so on. The insects in particular are poorly represented in the fossil record, considering their present phenomenal diversity and numbers.

PRESERVING BODIES

The vast majority of fossils are shells, bones, teeth, pollen, and carbonized plant material, which are the toughest, most easily preserved parts of animal and plant bodies. The organisms most commonly fossilized are marine creatures (such as clams, snails, corals, brachiopods, echinoderms, trilobites, crabs) and most of these live, or have lived, in shallow seas. The original organisms were very abundant, and their remains are resilient and frequently buried by sediment.

VERTEBRATE PRESERVATION

Bony parts of the backboned animals (vertebrates), especially teeth, vertebrae, and skeleton fragments, are all fairly tough and preserve quite well, provided they are buried quickly in sediment. Bone is a mixture of a limy mineral (calcium phosphate) held together by an organic "cement," which can be degraded by bacteria, fungi, and oxidation. The organic component of bones left on the surface of the ground or seabed can, therefore, rot away in a few months or years. Tissue in vertebrate bodies attracts scavengers, and in any case, most soft tissue, such as flesh and organs, starts to decay within hours of death. Consequently, the fossil remains of land-living vertebrates, such as dinosaurs and humans, are relatively rare.

DRYING

Drying, especially in desert environments, can preserve tissues such as skin, hair, and even muscle. Some land-living vertebrate fossils have been preserved by this type of desiccation and there are rare examples of fossilized dinosaur skin impressions. Some entire dinosaur skeletons, buried by desert dust-storms, have been found in Mongolia in late Cretaceous sandstone.

AMBER

Amber is one of the best-known natural preserving mediums. It is a complex aromatic resin produced in the Baltic by araucarian pine trees, and has fungicidal properties that help to prevent the biological degradation of organisms that become trapped in it. As a fossil resin, it is most common in Cenozoic deposits, such as those of the Baltic (30–40 MA) but older Cretaceous amber (up to 120 MA) is known from the northeastern U.S., Siberia, Lebanon, and the Isle of Wight in England.

PRESERVED IN AMBER

A great range of organisms from toadstools to feathers and insect parasites has been found in amber, and since amber persists in the rock record as an organic mineral, entrapment in amber is true fossilization. Although most amber fossils are invertebrate and predominantly insects, a number of small vertebrates (tree-living frogs and lizards) have also been found.

FREEZING

Freezing in permafrost conditions can preserve blood and body organs for tens of thousands of years. Complete bodies of ice age mammoths and other animals such as the woolly rhinos, horses, wolverines, and bisons of Siberia and Alaska (and the occasional human such as the Ice Man of the Tyrol) have been preserved in this way. Although not permanently fossilized, because permafrost will not last indefinitely, they provide an invaluable source of information about ice age conditions. The most remarkable find was the 1977 discovery of the complete baby male mammoth (between 6 and 12 months old), Dima, who lived about 40,000 years ago.

BUGS AND MUD

Bacteria are fundamental to the natural recycling of organic material. They are present in huge numbers in almost all environments on Earth, from the depths of the oceans to hot-water springs on land and even in polar ice. Most bacteria degrade and break down the complex chemicals of organic matter into simpler liquids and gases. In certain circumstances, however, especially where there is a lack of oxygen, bacterial action can enhance fossilization of soft tissues by setting off chemical reactions.

ANAEROBIC PRESERVATION

Conditions where bacterial action enhances fossilization often arise in fine-grained muds at the bottom of lakes or the sea. Minerals are produced, such as calcium phosphate and iron pyrites, that cover and replicate in very fine detail tissues such as muscle fibers, skin, feathers, intestines, and even delicate gill tissues. The early Cambrian Burgess Shale of Canada is a famous fossil locality with this kind of preservation—arthropods with legs and gills, soft-bodied worms, and chordates were all found there.

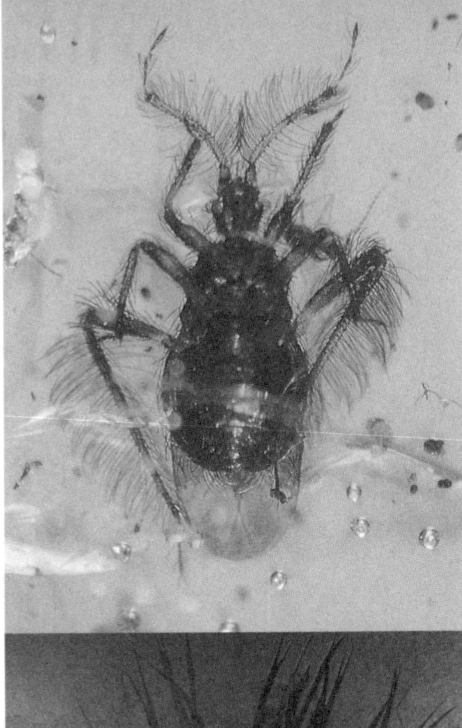

Fossils are a direct record of the evolution of life on Earth. From top to bottom: a late Eocene turtle, *Praecoris*, an ant bug trapped in amber, and *Sabalites*, a fossilized palm frond of early Tertiary age.

A MARINE ENVIRONMENT

Seashore environments, abundant in all kinds of life, are rich in the fossils of common marine invertebrates. Paleozoic marine sandstone is typically full of brachiopods, fragments of trilobites, sea lilies and moss-animals (bryozoans), with occasional snails, clams, and cephalopods (nautiloids). Mesozoic sandstone contains clams, snails, cephalopods, sea lilies, and brachiopods. Cenozoic sandstone contains many different kinds of snails and clams, fragments of echinoderms (sea urchins, starfish), and crabs.

FOSSIL FUELS

Plant remains are generally carbonized during fossilization. They are gradually transformed by increasing pressure and temperature within the Earth's crust from an initial peatlike condition, through lignite to coal and anthracite. This process also releases gases that, under certain geological conditions, may be trapped. Despite intense exploitation throughout the 19th and 20th centuries, coal and gas still form major global reserves of fossil fuels.

PLANT MINERALIZATION

Some woody plant tissues may be altered in different ways by lithification (transformation into solid rock) and replacement by various minerals, from calcium carbonate and iron pyrites to opal or chert. Surprisingly, these modes of mineralization can provide remarkably detailed information on the cell anatomy of extinct plants, many millions of years old.

BURIAL

Fragments of organisms that can be preserved must be buried in sediment in order to become fossils. Most marine preservation takes place in the accumulated sediment on the shallow marine shelves around the continental margins. The land is subject to weathering and erosion, so the preservation of sediment and fossils is dependent on trapped sedimentary deposits, found in inland seas or lake basins, the flanks of rising mountain chains, or fault-bounded troughs such as rift valleys. These environments, known as depositional traps, accumulate so much sediment that, despite later uplift and erosion, some strata, with their buried fossils, remain.

Fossil Discoveries: Reconstructing the Past

Today, fossils are readily accepted as the remains of once-living organisms, brought to life in films, books, and animated museum displays as dramatic reconstructions. Even a hundred years ago, such vivid representations of the life of the past would not have been possible because much of the scientific evidence on which they are based was not available. Fossil discoveries over the last few decades continue to reveal new and often unsuspected aspects of the distant past. We are still just scratching the surface of Earth's 3.8-billion-year-old fossil record.

Steven Spielberg's *Jurassic Park* is famous for its lifelike and animated dinosaur reconstructions.

THE FIRST FOSSIL DISCOVERIES

Fossils have been objects of fascination since they were first discovered by early humans, several thousand years ago. Fossil shells, clearly valued by our prehistoric ancestors, were used as objects of personal adornment and were buried along with their owners. The first discoveries of large fossil bones were generally construed as belonging to some mythical beast or giant.

SEEKING AN EXPLANATION

Within the Biblical tradition of the Western world, the story of the Great Flood provided a persuasive explanation for these enigmatic fossil remains. The apparent explanatory power of this story was so strong that it was not dislodged until the early part of the 19th century. Many eminent early geologists were convinced that there was good geological evidence for the Flood and, therefore, support for the historical truthfulness of the Bible account.

REMNANTS OF THE FLOOD

When the bones of a variety of large animals, such as those of elephants, were found in northern Europe and North America, far beyond the animals' known geographical range, it was assumed that the beasts had been drowned and swept there by the Flood. In addition, the event seemed to provide a reasonable explanation for the discovery of fossils closely resembling the shells and bones of sea creatures buried in rocks found far inland and sometimes even high on mountains. It was not until the mid-19th century that there was a general acceptance that this interpretation was mistaken.

EARLY INTERPRETATIONS OF FOSSILS

Our present well-developed understanding of the nature and history of the fossil record is little more than 300 years old although ancient Greeks such as Aristotle (384–322 BC) and Romans, such as Pliny the Elder (c. AD 23–79) did make enormous progress with accurate observations and deductions of the natural world. Much of this classical learning was not rediscovered until medieval times and it was not until the Renaissance in Europe that much more progress was made.

MEDALS OF CREATION

The location, collection, and illustration of fossils became an accepted pastime and matter of study. From the middle of the 17th century, fossils were increasingly accepted as the genuine remains of once-living creatures rather than objects formed by some force or fluid within the ground in which they were found. The collection and study of fossils was acceptable as long as they could be seen as "medals of creation," which confirmed the prevailing doctrine and world view based on the version of the Creation as presented in the Old Testament of the Bible.

REASSESSING THE PAST

By the early 1800s great thicknesses of fossiliferous strata had been discovered and it became clear that they could not all have been produced by a single flood, however catastrophic. Furthermore, the duration of the Earth's early prehistoric development could no longer be confined within a restricted period of some 6,000 years. In 1650, the Protestant Archbishop of Armagh in Ireland, James Ussher, had used the genealogical accounts in the Old Testament to calculate the date of the Creation as 4004 BC. As the slow rates of many geological processes of erosion and sedimentation became understood, the age of the Earth had to be extended into millions of years. The geological investigation of the Earth's long history now revealed that the burial of organic remains in accumulating layers of sediment was continual, and that types of fossil organisms changed throughout the known succession of strata.

REASSESSING BIBLE NARRATIVES

At this time, scholarship was showing up the many contradictions within the Bible. It was becoming clear that the Bible was not a simple historical document of fact but a complex cumulation of historical narratives of different age that required interpretation. For many Christian divines who were actively involved in the investigation of the natural world and particularly the search for the fossil remains of past life, these revelations were not particularly problematic. New discoveries could still be viewed as the "wondrous works of a benevolent and munificent God." However, cracks were soon beginning to appear, even in this liberal view.

THE PROBLEM OF EXTINCTION

From the latter part of the 18th century, fossil finds of the remains of large and often unrecognizable vertebrate animals were being made in different parts of the world. In 1739 elephantlike bones (named *Mastodon* in 1806) were found on the banks of the Ohio River in North America. In 1796, fossil remains from Paraguay were described as those of a giant ground sloth and named as *Megatherium*. The "Beast of Maastricht," a giant marine reptile, was found in 1786 (finally named as *Mosasaurus* in 1823). The sea dragons of Lyme Regis (*Ichthyosaurus* and *Plesiosaurus*) were first recovered in the early decades of the 1800s. Even by then, the world was sufficiently well explored for naturalists to have to face up to the possibility of extinction. But questions remained; if they were not victims of the Great Flood, how could a benevolent creator allow any of his creations to be somehow deficient enough to die out? The problems of extinction were to pale into insignificance compared with the growing problem of evolution.

CREATING THE IMAGE OF THE DINOSAURS

The first discovery, early in the 19th century, of very fragmentary fossil remains of some large animals that did not compare with any living reptiles, was initially little more than a biological puzzle, of interest to only a small number of the academics and natural historians. But when Richard Owen, an English professor of anatomy, interpreted the fossils as the remains of dinosaurs, a group of extinct reptiles new to science, everything changed. Richard Owen could not have realized what he was creating in 1842. He was to generate a whole new realm of fact and fiction and a renaissance in animal fantasy.

REVIVING THE DEEP PAST

Both the study of fossils (paleontology) and the rocks in which they are found (geology) are academic disciplines which largely belong to the 19th-century development of the sciences. The raw data and information on which this revivification of the "deep" past is based is generally incomplete, often no more than a collection of petrified, broken, and distorted fossil bones. From these unpromising beginnings fossils are brought to life by paleontologists, modelers, and scientific illustrators as convincing animals, often dramatized as ferocious and predatory. The resulting image is generally accepted without much question. But the images, no matter how realistic they might look, are still interpretations with varying degrees of possible resemblance to the original organisms. Their realism depends entirely on the quality of the fossil data and the availability of an appropriate living model.

THE SIGNIFICANCE OF DINOSAURS

The meaning and image of the Dinosauria have changed, almost beyond recognition, since they were first invented by Richard Owen. From being the dragonlike "lowly creeping serpents" of the Bible, dinosaurs have become an extraordinary array of beasts ranging from bird-sized and birdlike to vast lumbering monsters, whose size and strength seem to defy the laws of biology and physics. Some dinosaurs are now thought to have been highly active, warm-blooded killers. Long dead, the dinosaurs have never been observed in action by human beings, so they offer enormous potential for speculative reconstruction. Even so, no matter how fanciful the interpretation, there is still the unalterable proof, provided by the fossil record, of their existence and size. There is no doubt that some dinosaurs really were the largest terrestrial plant-eaters and meat-eaters to have ever existed on the planet.

PREHISTORIC MONSTERS

Furthermore, the dinosaurs were influential and instrumental in helping to destroy a number of the preconceptions of Victorian society. With beasts of such size, it was no longer possible to argue convincingly for the continuing hidden existence of a colony of mysterious monsters in an unexplored region of the Earth—although this notion still persists today in stories of the Loch Ness monster and other refugees from the geological past.

Three extinct reptiles from the deep past of the late Cretaceous times between 65 and 80 million years ago. Counterclockwise from left, *Triceratops*, a horned ceratopsian dinosaur from North America, 30 feet (9 meters) long, weighing up to 5.4 tonnes; *Velociraptor*, a small two-legged theropod dinosaur from Mongolia, 6 feet (1.8 meters) long; *Queztalcoatlus*, a flying pterosaur reptile from Texas, North America, with a wingspan up to 39 feet (12 meters).

Evolution and the Fossil Record

In the early decades of the 19th century, geologists such as Roderick Murchison and Adam Sedgwick discovered that the fossil remains of past life could be found not just in young rock strata near the surface, but also in older strata beneath, stretching far back into the depths of time. The fossils demonstrated that extinction had not just happened once but many times. The idea of a single Flood as the cause for extinction was abandoned, in the same way the idea that the Earth was only a few thousand years old had to be revised. Life had acquired a long history.

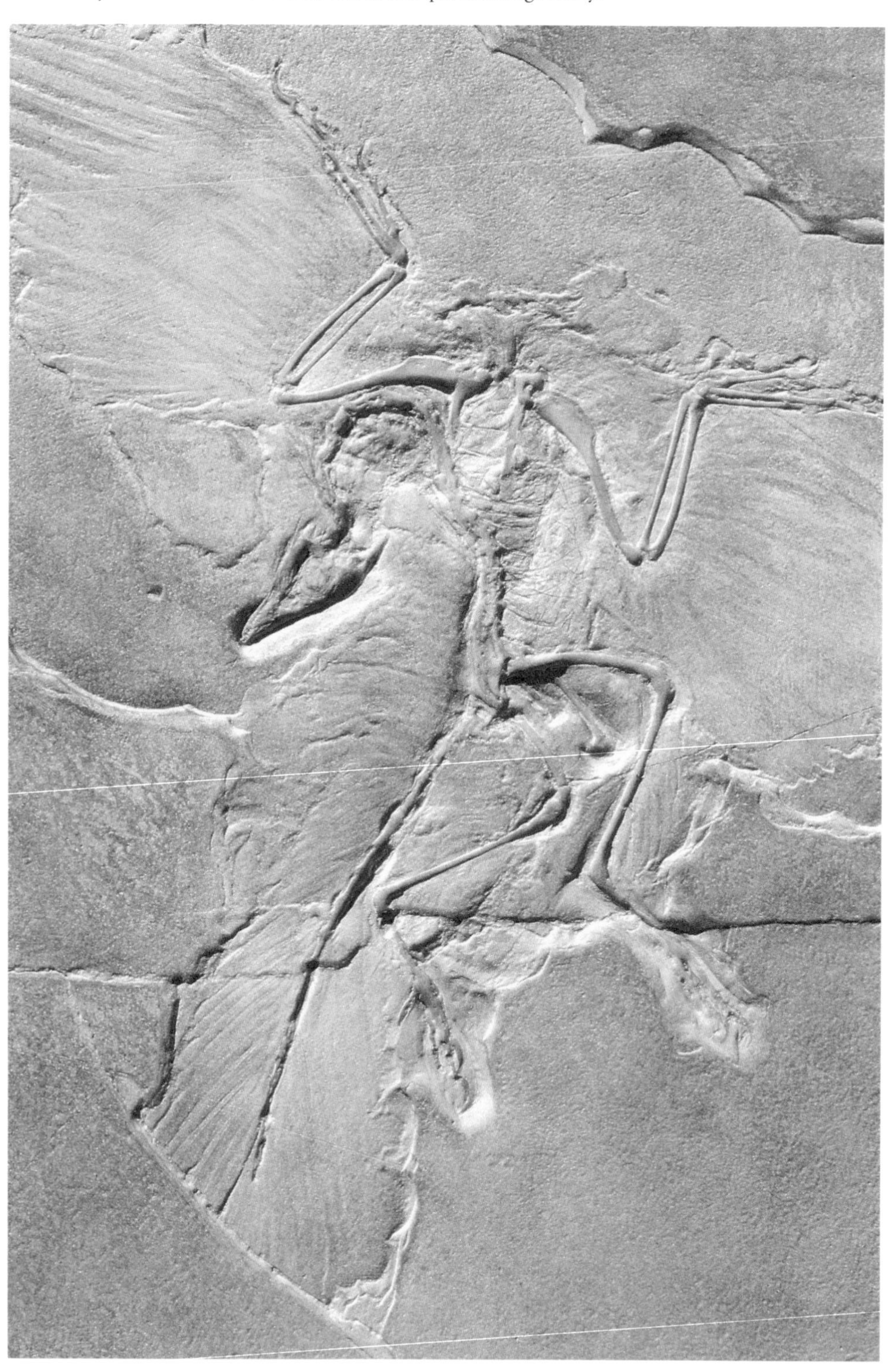

TRANSMUTATION

Growing evidence that individual species and groups of animals and plants appeared in, and disappeared from, the geological record at different times raised questions about just how fixed in form the species were. After all, if new varieties of life could be produced by human intervention in the interbreeding of species, could one species transmute or change into another over the course of time? Ideas about transmutation had been circulating since the end of the 18th century among natural philosophers, such as Georges-Louis Leclerc de Buffon (1707–88) and Jean-Baptiste de Monet de Lamarck (1744–1829) in France and Charles Darwin's grandfather, Erasmus Darwin (1731–1802), in England.

SELECTIVE BREEDING

A species is distinguished by its ability to produce viable young that are fertile. Humans have bred improvements into crops and animals over thousands of years, and it has long been known that by selective breeding of offspring, the chances of increasing particular characteristics can be improved significantly. Most of the different breeds of cattle, dogs, cats, pigeons, and flowers, for example, have been artificially bred in this way. Although the detailed mechanism was not understood, it was clear that over successive generations living organisms could change.

COMMON PATTERNS EMERGE

The idea of a hierarchical succession of life, arranged from the most primitive to the most advanced, has ancient classical roots. But since the time of Linnaeus and his system of classification of organisms, marked similarities between the great apes and humans became evident. Questions arose as to whether apes could be "civilized" and attempts were made to do so. Furthermore, structural comparisons have been made between all the vertebrate skeletons, revealing a common underlying pattern.

COMPARATIVE ANATOMY

The science of comparative anatomy, founded by the Scottish surgeon John Hunter (1728–93) and the French naturalist Georges Cuvier (1769–1832), enabled scientists to reassemble the fragmentary and mixed fossil bones of extinct

Found in Upper Jurassic limestone deposits in Solenhofen, Germany, *Archaeopteryx* shows a mixture of bird and reptile features (bony tail and feathers).

creatures into anatomically viable animals. The acceptance of a common skeletal plan among all vertebrates was the basis for reconstruction. The basic form of a lizard's thigh bone or upper arm bone, for instance, is fundamentally similar to that of a frog or a human.

CUVIER'S MODELS

Cuvier made some of the most innovative and startling reconstructions of extinct mammals, ranging from the giant ground sloth (*Megatherium*, 1796) that lived within the last 2 million years in South America to some of the then earliest known primitive mammals of the Tertiary era from the strata of the Paris basin, including an extinct marsupial mammal (1804) and the tapirlike *Palaeotherium* (1804). However, the widely accepted connection between the skeletal structure of all vertebrates did not immediately lead to an acceptance of the emerging theories of species evolution.

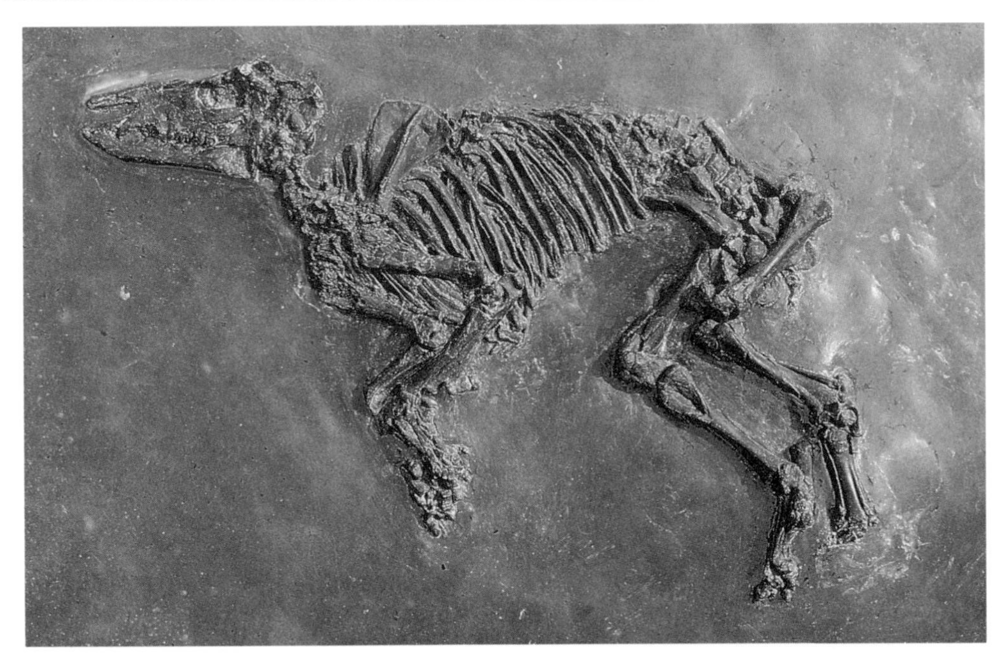

A fossilized horse (*Propaleotherium*) from Eocene deposits in Germany. Paleontologist Othniel Marsh showed that horses' foot bones follow an evolutionary pattern through time for faster running.

THE DARWINIAN REVOLUTION

Charles Darwin was tutored in geology and paleontology by Adam Sedgwick in Cambridge and Wales and by his reading of Charles Lyell's newly published *Principles of Geology*. Darwin also gained firsthand experience of geology during his voyage on board the *Beagle*. He soon realized that the sample of past life provided by fossil evidence was, and still is, fragmentary. In *On the Origin of Species* (published in 1859), he speculated that evolutionary links, or transitional forms, should be found between different groups of organisms as one evolved from another. But the fossil record was such a small sample of the diversity of past life that the likelihood that such intermediaries would be preserved was small, and Darwin largely avoided the fossil evidence.

THE MISSING LINK

In 1860, the discovery of one particular fossil, a single feather in some Jurassic lithographic limestone in Bavaria, Germany, was a breakthrough. Six months later a virtually complete bird skeleton was found. The English biologist and exponent of Darwin's theories, Thomas Henry Huxley (1825–95) realized that this new find, named as *Archaeopteryx* (Greek for "ancient wing"), showed a mixture of reptilian and bird characteristics. It therefore provided the first, surprisingly good, fossil example of a transitional form that clearly linked one major group of animals (the birds) to the ancestral group (the dinosaur reptiles) from which it had evolved in the past.

CHANGING HORSES

Another, and in some ways even better, example of evolution was provided by the fossil record of horses. A French expedition in the 1850s recovered large numbers of horse leg bones from terrestrial deposits at Pikermi in Greece. In the 1860s, a provisional family tree for the evolution of the horses was drawn up by linking the Greek find with previous finds from France. The oldest known form, *Palaeotherium,* was a small ungulate mammal with three toes of nearly equal length. The younger *Hipparion* from Greece still had side toes but they were nonfunctional as they were too small to reach the ground. It was therefore identified as an intermediate between *Palaeotherium* and the modern horse *Equus*, which has an enlarged single-hoofed toe and side toes reduced to insignificant splints. The story of horse evolution was further elaborated in the 1870s by American paleontologist, Othniel Marsh, who discovered a number of other horse species in the Tertiary deposits of North America.

MICRO-EVOLUTION

In the last decade or so, paleontologists have discovered sequences of strata that are exceptionally rich in particular fossil groups. These deposits record detailed changes in the evolutionary lineages within these organisms. Outstanding samples of evolutionary change are provided by Ordovician trilobites from Wales, Silurian graptolites from Poland, Tertiary snails and cichlid fish from East Africa, and recent deep-sea sequences of microfossils.

KEEPING TRACK

Large samples made up of hundreds or even thousands of specimens belonging to successive generations of fossil species can be tracked over millions of years. They appear to acquire and lose characteristics at varying rates, and independently of other closely related lineages. The cichlid fish, which took advantage of the formation of a number of large lakes, show how evolutionary developments can happen very quickly. Even Charles Darwin would have been impressed by the quality of the fossil data. By comparison the fossil records of dinosaurs or hominids are sadly deficient.

LIFE'S PARISH REGISTER

Not long ago, an eminent biologist claimed that so much was known about evolutionary relationships from living organisms that all the fossil record had to contribute was to "fill in the parish register of life." But in the last decade, fossil discoveries have actually provided vital information. In vast areas of the world that have not been geologically explored in any great detail, the fossil sample of the past is very small. Paleontologists now have a much better understanding of the circumstances under which soft tissues can be preserved. Consequently, it is possible to review the past record for new examples of such conditions. The greatest stretch of *terra incognita* in the past is still the Precambrian period, over three billion years of the history and evolution of life about which we know very little.

Fossils and the Molecular Clock

The real missing link for Darwin and Wallace's theory of evolution was the understanding of the underlying mechanisms of inheritance. Even the fundamental patterns by which characteristics are passed from one generation to the next was not generally realized until the turn of the century, after the death of Darwin and Wallace, although these hereditary patterns had, in fact, been discovered in the 1860s by an Austrian monk, Gregor Mendel (1822–84). He had published the results of his botanical breeding experiments with garden peas, but they went unnoticed by the rest of the scientific community and were not rediscovered until some years after his death. Armed with Mendel's discoveries, Darwin would have been able to promote his revolutionary theory with greater confidence.

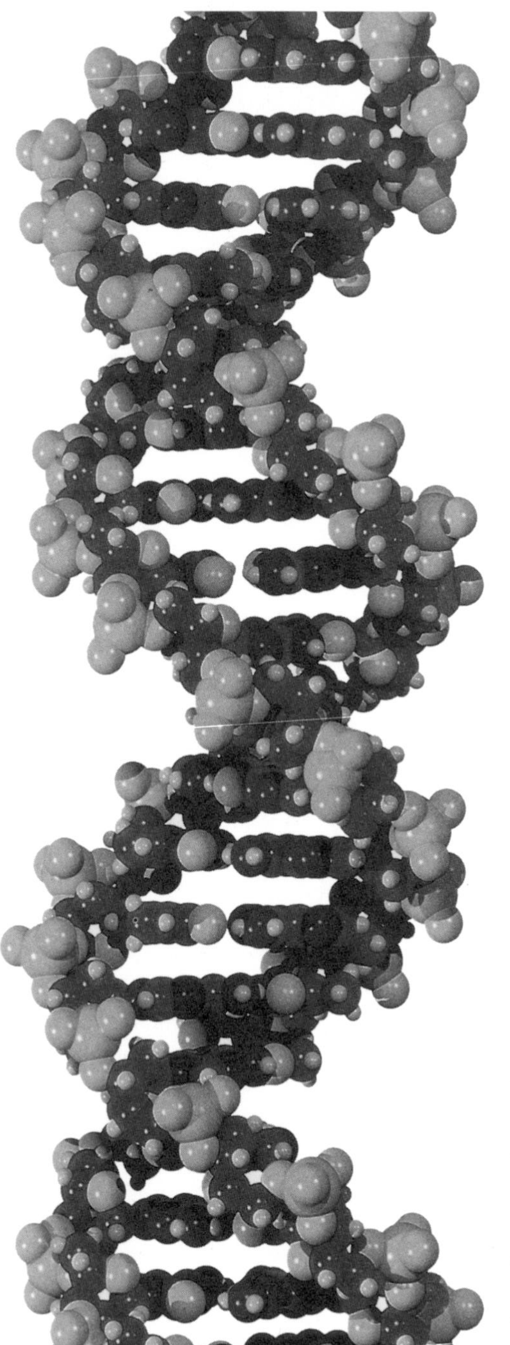

UNDERSTANDING INHERITANCE

At the turn of the century, independent breeding experiments by the British zoologist William Bateson (1861–1926) and Dutch botanist Hugo de Vries (1848–1935) revealed that repeated ratios of inherited characteristics, called "dominant" and "recessive," are distributed among offspring. But scientists had still not discovered the deeper mechanism that actually controls the way in which reproductive cells combine and exchange the information that determines the mixed inheritance of parental characters in the offspring.

CRACKING THE CODE

The underlying mechanism of inheritance, encoded within the chromosomes of each body cell, is replicated during cell division by duplication of the double helix structure of deoxyribonucleic acid (DNA), the main constituent of the chromosomes of all organisms. The genetic code is the order in which the nitrogenous bases of DNA are arranged within the molecule, which then determines the type, and amount, of protein to be synthesized in the cell. This mechanism was finally discovered in 1953 by the American James Watson (1928–), and the Englishman Francis Crick (1916–). They built on the pioneering work of many other scientists working toward the same goal.

EVOLUTIONARY RELATIONSHIPS

The detailed genetic code of each body cell determines the uniqueness of every individual organism. Similarity of cellular codes between organisms determines their ability to interbreed.

A section of the DNA molecule, which is twisted in a double-stranded helix. DNA is responsible for the transmission of hereditary characteristics from parents to offspring.

The analysis of detailed sequences of genetic information encoded within each cell of an organism allows the closeness of evolutionary relationships among living organisms to be assessed. This analysis has confirmed the genetic proximity of humans and chimpanzees.

OUR NEAREST RELATIVES

In the 1960s and 1970s molecular biologists found that chimpanzee genes are closer to those of humans than expected. The fossil record had seemed to indicate that the evolutionary split between the higher apes and humans occurred approximately 15 million years ago. If that had been the case, then there should have been a greater genetic distance between humans and the higher apes than is actually found.

THE MOLECULAR CLOCK

The idea of the molecular clock was based on experimentally determined rates of genetic mutations in living organisms. These rates differ among different biological molecules. At first the hypothesis was tested that mutations occurred at a constant rate through time, but extensive tests in living organisms have shown that different molecules change at different rates. Studies now suggest that some molecules are not very reliable as "clocks," whereas others may keep fairly regular time. In each case, inferences about molecular rates of evolution between groups must be tested against information from the fossil record and elsewhere.

MAMMALIAN RELATIONSHIPS

Despite knowing a great deal about the biology of the different mammalian groups, biologists still puzzle over their interrelationships. For instance, how closely related are the living primitive mammals, the egg-laying monotremes (for example, the duck-billed platypus) and marsupials (for example, the kangaroos) to the more advanced placental mammals (eutherians)? Traditional thinking, based on assessing their form and structure, has suggested that monotremes are far more primitive. New molecular data suggests that monotremes and marsupials may be closer to each other than to the placentals.

USING FOSSILS PLUS MOLECULES

Molecular differences by themselves cannot tell us when groups of organisms diverged from each other. They have to be calibrated against fossil records. For example, based on the first known extinct members of the lineages leading to crocodiles and to birds, the date of crocodile and bird divergence has been estimated at 225 million years ago. Assuming molecular changes have accumulated gradually and regularly over time, molecular studies can then provide an estimate of the divergence times in various bird and crocodile subgroups. New molecular studies have sometimes proposed relatively earlier or later divergence dates than have been known from the existing fossil record, and subsequent fossil discoveries have often supported these molecular estimates. Working in concert, a clearer picture of the relationships of groups and their times of divergence has begun to emerge.

ANCIENT DNA

The problem with genetic analysis is that, despite the recent claims highlighted by Michael Crichton's story *Jurassic Park*, DNA cannot be extracted from fossils of any great age. Most large biological molecules, such as DNA and proteins, break down very rapidly after the death of an organism, unless the tissue is preserved in some unusual way, such as by rapid freezing.

EXPERIMENTING WITH AMBER

The apparently perfect preservation of organisms that are trapped in amber had led to hopes that their DNA would also be preserved. Numerous attempts have been made to extract DNA from insects embedded in amber and there have been claims of success. But all attempts at replication of the analysis have failed, indicating that the samples were contaminated by modern DNA.

FROZEN IN TIME

Rapid freezing of the tissue of extinct organisms happened during the last ice age, when animals such as the woolly mammoth became preserved in permanently frozen ground. Their DNA has been preserved and analyzed; however the cadavers are only some tens of thousands of years old. It may be possible to combine the preserved DNA of these ice age remains with that of modern species, to recreate an "Ice Age Park," populated by animals such as hybrid elephants and mammoths.

The edentate (toothless) armadillos (top) have long been regarded as the most primitive placentals, but analysis of new molecular data suggests that the insectivores, such as the hedgehog, may be the most primitive. Another remarkable molecular discovery suggests that the lagomorphs (such as rabbits) may be closely related to the primates, whereas they were previously classified with rodents, such as rats.

"Progress" and Catastrophe

The fossil remains of the past tell us that the history of life on Earth has been full of dramatic changes of fortune. Entire groups of organisms have come and gone through a wide range of natural causes. The fossil record is punctuated by 54 extinction events over the last 500 million years, which have wiped out 10 percent or more of fossil genera. Climate has always changed, ice ages have come and gone, and we humans will have to continue to adjust to such change in order to survive. Knowledge about the processes that have disrupted life in the past equip us to assess our impact on the planet more accurately; we tamper with climate change at our peril unless we want to follow the dinosaurs into oblivion.

The surface of the Moon is pitted by meteorite impact and volcanic activity—there is no erosion or sedimentation. The large Copernicus and Tycho craters were formed 800 to 400 million years ago.

EVOLUTIONARY DEVELOPMENT

Traditionally, the history of life has been portrayed as one of progress and advance, from the lowest, most primitive organisms to the highest, most advanced organisms. The mammals and, in particular, the hominid primates, have been seen as the high point of this progression. Since the early 20th century and the development of the Darwinian theory of evolution, genetic mutation has been regarded as the driving force behind the potential fitness and adaptation of organisms. The environment and other organisms provide the selective forces that allow the best adapted organisms to survive and reproduce.

NUCLEAR WINTER SCENARIOS

Recently, catastrophic events have been reassessed as factors that may have contributed significantly to the history and development of life and may do so again in the not-too-distant future. One of the effects of the cold war was the development and modeling of nuclear winter scenarios, which predict the aftermath of a nuclear holocaust. These models suggested that during such a catastrophe, so much rock dust from the explosions would be thrown into the atmosphere that winter conditions could prevail for long enough to have a drastic effect on life. Plant growth at the base of the food chain would be damaged, affecting life at all levels.

FLOOD BASALTS

Cold War scenarios made scientists think about other catastrophic events, such as large-scale volcanic eruptions and extraterrestrial impacts on Earth. The geological evidence of lava and ash layers in the stratigraphic rock record shows that both are natural types of events that recur throughout Earth history. There have been 11 vast eruptions of flood basalts over the last 250 million years, taking place at average intervals of 22 million years. Most of the eruptions have coincided with extinction of lifeforms, which is recorded by loss of fossil organisms.

VOLCANIC IMPACT

Volcanic eruptions on a large scale throw out great volumes of ash and gases, especially carbon dioxide, which is a natural greenhouse gas. It allows shortwave solar radiation to enter the Earth's atmosphere, but stops longwave radiation from escaping, a process that traps heat and raises the Earth's temperature. A major eruption can cause initial cooling because of low light levels and acid rain, followed by global warming. All these effects can have a disastrous impact on life on Earth, especially on plants.

LUNAR IMPACT

The pockmarked surface of the Moon is an object lesson in the history of Earth. Both have suffered continuous bombardment from space by a range of extraterrestrial bodies of varying size and composition. However, the surface of the Moon preserves the impact craters, while the geologically dynamic Earth tends to conceal the evidence as its surface is constantly recycled.

EXTRATERRESTRIAL EVENTS

Nevertheless, several hundred measurable impact events have now been identified, spread out over

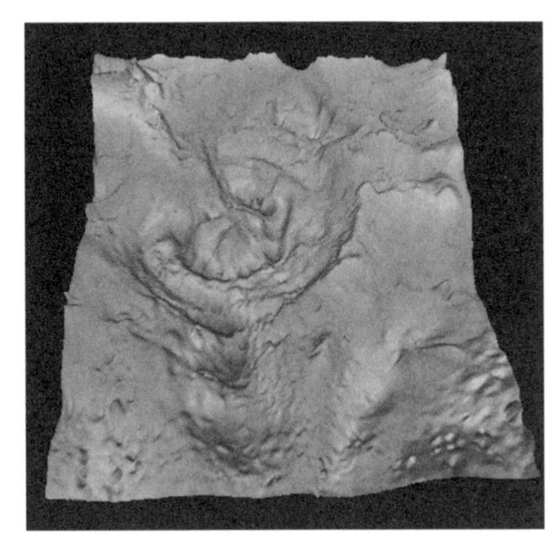

The Chicxulub impact occurred 65 million years ago in the Yucatan Peninsula, Mexico. It is the only impact that has made a crater bigger than 60 miles (100 kilometers) in diameter.

the last 500 million years. Thirty of these have involved objects that have made craters larger than 6 miles (10 kilometers) wide, and events of this magnitude occur with a frequency of less than 10 million years.

EXTINCTION EVENTS

Of the 54 extinction events that have occurred over the last 500 million years, 15 have involved the extinction of 30 percent, or more, of the Earth's genera. Scientists have realized only in the last decade or so that extinction events have been so frequent in the history of life.

THE END OF THE PALEOZOIC

The Permo-Triassic extinction event, which marks the end of the Paleozoic, is the most drastic event in the history of the Earth. It is now known that at least 57 percent of all families of marine organisms died out and possibly as many as 95 percent of all species disappeared. The hardest hit were the common shelly fossils, which lived attached to the seabed in shallow water such as the brachiopods (lamp shells), bryozoans (moss animals), and crinoids (sea lilies). But terrestrial animals also suffered. While it is surprising that life continued at all, it is a reflection of the resilience of living organisms, both plants and animals, that they not only recovered but continued to diversify.

ENVIRONMENTAL FACTORS

The cause of the Permo-Triassic extinction is generally thought to have been environmental. It may well be linked to climate change and the outpouring of the Siberian plateau basalts around 250 million years ago. The involvement of the impact of an extraterrestrial body has also been suggested, but this catastrophic cause has not been verified, and no large impact crater or impact-related debris has been identified of this exact age. The disappearance of species seems to have been drawn out over a period of some 10 million years. A major factor is likely to have been the global assembly of the continental plates to form the supercontinent of Pangea.

FALLING SEA LEVELS

Plate assembly was accompanied by a major fall in sea level. Consequently, the extensive shallow seas that surrounded the continents withdrew oceanward. Living conditions for a great diversity of marine creatures were altered so quickly that many were unable to adapt, especially those that lived attached to the seabed and within reefs built upon it.

ICE AGE EXTINCTION

The most recent extinction event is associated with the last ice age. As the zone of permanently frozen ground spread south across northern Asia, Europe, and North America, glaciers developed in the mountains and sea-ice spread into the Atlantic. The large mammals were forced to retreat southward. Many of them were able to adapt to the cold and therefore survived on the windswept tundra and grassland steppe of Asia and North America.

EVIDENCE OF CLIMATE CHANGE

It is known that woolly mammoth and rhinoceros, bear, wolves, wolverines, giant deer, horses, big cats, and many other mammals occupied the cold regions of Asia, Europe, and North America during the last ice age because their fossils, including butchered bones, remain. There is also the evidence of the vivid Paleolithic cave paintings of western Europe. They shared these habitats with one of the most effective predators of all time, humans.

THE HUMAN IMPACT

Undoubtedly, the rapid climate change and consequent disruption to vegetation that characterized the end of the last ice age was largely responsible for the demise of animals such as the woolly mammoth. In the northern hemisphere the pressure of human hunting on the dwindling population stocks probably soon reduced them to an unsustainable level. Recent genetic analysis suggests that modern Cro-Magnon humans may also have been responsible, albeit indirectly, for the extinction of the Neanderthals. Certainly there is no evidence of Neanderthal genes within our genetic makeup, as would have been the case if there had been any interbreeding.

BAD LUCK AND SURVIVAL

Some paleontologists argue that extinction may well have played a significant and highly unpredictable role in the process of evolution. Evolution has been portrayed as a board game in which chance, or bad luck, is a controlling factor. At irregular intervals extinctions, with their random levels of destruction, impact on the progress of life. Recovery and further progress may depend on which organisms have survived. Their ability to make the best of the opportunity and exploit the vacated ecological space may then determine the direction of evolution until the next random extinction.

PERSISTENCE AND SURVIVAL

Other paleontologists, however, disagree and point to the persistence of certain lineages of more advanced and complex organisms through time. The vertebrates, for instance, that developed from the chordates in the early Cambrian, have survived through the known 54 extinction events and still prospered. Whatever the cause of extinction events, our own survival depend on our learning from the distant past.

Mountains of ivory tusks are burnt in Nairobi National Park, Kenya. Humans, the Earth's most effective predators, are endangering the remaining megaherbivores of Africa and Asia.

Biographies

Douglas Louis Agassiz (1807–1873) Swiss-American naturalist and glaciologist. He trained as a doctor in Germany, attended **Georges Cuvier**'s lectures in Paris, and made important studies on fossil fish, describing more than 1,700 new species. He was one of the first scientists to argue that there had been a recent ice age. He went on to teach at Harvard in 1846 and was an opponent of **Charles Darwin**'s theory of evolution.

Roy Chapman Andrews (1884–1960) American explorer and museum scientist who led the first expedition, from the American Museum of Natural History in New York to the Gobi Desert of Mongolia in the 1920s. The expedition discovered many new dinosaurs, including *Protoceratops*, *Oviraptor*, *Velociraptor*, and the first nests of dinosaur eggs with hatchlings.

Mary Anning (1799–1847) The most famous member of an English family of professional fossil collectors. The Annings recovered fossils of ichthyosaurs, plesiosaurs, fish, and many invertebrate fossils from the early Jurassic strata in the seacliffs around the coastal town of Lyme Regis in southern England.

Luis (1911–1988) and Walter (1940–) Alvarez American father and son team who in 1980 claimed that the thin layer of clay (enriched with the rare element iridium) found at the boundary of Cretaceous and Tertiary rocks (K-T Boundary) marks the impact of a large extraterrestrial meteorite. They also claimed that this event, 65 million years ago, was responsible for the extinction of the dinosaurs. Luis Alvarez was an astrophysicist and Nobel prize-winner for physics in 1968.

Elso Barghoorn (1915–) American paleontologist who in 1956 discovered the 2-billion-year-old Precambrian gunflint microfossils. In 1968, he showed that chemical fossils such as amino acids can be preserved in rocks as old as 3 billion years.

Joachim Barrande (1799–1883) French engineer and naturalist who studied with **Georges Cuvier** and then worked as a tutor to the exiled French royal family. He devoted his life to describing early Paleozoic fossils in Bohemia.

Hugo Benioff (1899–1968) American seismologist (earthquake expert) who gave his name to the Benioff zone. He found that the subduction (see glossary) of oceanic plates causes earthquakes, and that the farther inland this happens, the deeper the center of the earthquake.

Bertram Boltwood (1870–1927) American chemist who showed that measurement of the ratio of the isotopes (see glossary) of lead and uranium in rocks can be used to date them.

Alexandre Brongniart (1770–1847) French naturalist and pioneer of stratigraphy (see glossary). He worked with the naturalist **Georges Cuvier**, mapping the strata around Paris and collecting local fossils.

Adolphe Brongniart (1801–1876) Son of **Alexandre Brongniart**, he was mainly a botanist who pioneered botanical techniques for the investigation of fossil plants. They provided a model for future studies.

Jennifer Clack (1947–) English paleontologist who revised the way we view the first vertebrate animals with legs (tetrapods). Her detailed studies of Devonian fossils showed that legs initially evolved for swimming in fast-moving water. Only later were they adapted for walking on land.

Edwin Colbert (1905–) American expert on Triassic dinosaurs who found and excavated the Ghost Ranch site in New Mexico with its remarkable abundance of *Coelophysis* skeletons.

Edward Drinker Cope (1840–1897) American naturalist who collected mammal and dinosaur fossils and was a great rival of **Othniel Marsh**. Cope's large collection is now in the American Museum of Natural History in New York.

Georges Cuvier (1769–1832) French founder of comparative anatomy, Cuvier was one of the greatest naturalists of his day. He showed how a fossil vertebrate animal can be reconstructed from a few bones and deductions made about its way of life. With **Alexandre Brongniart**, he discovered the principles of stratigraphy (see glossary). He believed that catastrophes occurred at various points in the history of the Earth and that these greatly affected the progress of life.

James Dwight Dana (1813–1895) American geologist who was a collector for the Wilkes Pacific expedition. His reports on the geological and zoological specimens he gathered are famous for their excellent insight and accuracy. He also reported on volcanoes, coral reefs, and the formation of mountain ranges. Dana supported **Charles Darwin**'s theory of evolution.

Raymond Dart (1893–1988) Australian-born zoologist who discovered the first fossil *Australopithecus* (meaning "southern ape") ancestor of humans. The small but well-preserved skull, nicknamed the "Taung child," was found in 1924 in cave deposits in Botswana, southern Africa. Dart's claim that it represented a link between fossil apes and humans was not generally acknowledged until the late 1930s.

Charles Darwin (1809–1882) English naturalist who studied geology and both living and fossil organisms, especially during his five-year round-the-world expedition on *HMS Beagle*. He developed a now widely accepted theory of the evolution of life through natural selection. The outline theory was first published in 1858 with Alfred George Wallace, who had reached the same conclusions independently. Darwin then developed the theory into his famous book *On the Origin of Species by Natural Selection*, published in 1859. The theory met with considerable opposition, especially when he applied his ideas to *The Descent of Man* in 1871. Many of the scientists of the time, such as **Adam Sedgwick**, were bitterly opposed to the theory.

Louis Dollo (1857–1931) French-born paleontologist who studied the famous *Iguanodon* skeletons in Belgium with Louis de Pauw. Dollo made the first reconstruction of *Iguanodon*, modeled on bird and kangaroo skeletons. He also published a theory of irreversibility in evolution in which specialized creatures cannot evolve into unspecialized ones.

Dianne Edwards (1942–) Welsh paleobotanist who found the earliest fossils of vascular plants (see glossary) in Silurian rocks in Britain. She showed how these first land plants evolved and colonized the land.

Maurice Ewing (1906–1974) American marine geologist who showed that ocean crust is thinner than continental crust. In 1953 he discovered the worldwide extent of mid-ocean ridges (see glossary) with **Bruce Heezen**. Then he found the central rift in the mid-Atlantic Ridge and showed that the ridge is being pulled apart.

Martin Glaessner (1906–1989) Australian geologist who produced the first detailed descriptions (from 1958) of the late-Precambrian soft-bodied, Ediacaran fossils from the Flinders Range mountains in South Australia. The fossils had originally been discovered by R.C. Sprigg in the late 1940s.

Stephen Jay Gould (1941–) American paleontologist and evolutionist who developed the idea of "punctuated equilibria" in evolution. This proposes that new species have evolved in rapid bursts followed by periods of little change.

James Hall (1811–1898) American pioneer of the study of Paleozoic fossils, especially in New York State, and mountain building in the Appalachians. He later became director of the Museum of Natural History in Albany.

Bruce Heezen (1924–1977) American oceanographer who showed that powerful, submarine turbidity currents with speeds of up to 55 mph (85 kph) could carry vast amounts of land-derived sediment hundreds of miles out into deep ocean basins.

Harry Hammond Hess (1906–1969) American geologist who advanced the understanding of the geology of the oceans. In 1962, he suggested that molten rock material constantly rises from the mantle to the surface along mid-ocean ridges (see glossary). From there it spreads out horizontally and forms new ocean floor. The farther away from the ridge the ocean floor is, the older it is.

James Hutton (1726–1797) Scottish naturalist whose *Theory of the Earth* (1788) claimed that the Earth was of great age with "no vestige of a beginning, no prospect of an end" and that geological phenomena can and should be explained by the study of present-day processes. This approach was taken up and developed by another Scottish geologist, **Charles Lyell**.

Donald Johanson (1943–) American paleoanthropologist who, in 1973, discovered the knee joint of an australopithecine in Ethiopia. From the bones, he was able to show that these hominid ancestors walked upright in a similar way to modern humans. The following year he found "Lucy" (*Australopithecus afarensis*). This partly complete fossil skeleton was the earliest known human ancestor, some 3.1 million years old.

Mary Leakey (1913–1998) English paleoanthropologist who lived and worked in Kenya. She led the expedition to Laetoli, Tanzania, which found the oldest known australopithecine footprints, dated as 3.6 million years old.

Inge Lehmann (1888–1993) Danish geophysicist who discovered that the Earth's inner core is solid.

Carolus Linnaeus (1707–1778) Swedish physician and naturalist, whose *Systema naturae* of 1735 formed the basis for the classification of organisms. Linnaeus' system grouped organisms with shared characteristics in which the basic unit is the species. He used Latin names for the different groupings from species to genus and order to kingdom.

Katherine Lonsdale (1903–1971) Irish crystallographer who pioneered the study of crystal atomic structure, especially that of organic, carbon-based crystals, using X-rays. Her work helped progress toward unraveling the structure of proteins such as DNA.

Charles Lyell (1797–1875) Scottish barrister and geologist whose *Principles of Geology* (1830–1833) laid down the beginning of the modern approach to the study of Earth science and was particularly influential on the development of **Charles Darwin**'s evolutionary theory. Lyell was opposed to **George Cuvier**'s catastrophist views and supported **James Hutton**'s approach. He showed how the study of present-day processes can be applied to geological phenomena and divided Tertiary time into epochs—Paleocene, Eocene, Oligocene, Miocene, and Pliocene.

Othniel Marsh (1831–1899) American professor of natural history at Yale, Marsh was one of the great pioneers of dinosaur studies. He described 19 new genera of dinosaurs and competed with his rival **Edward Cope** to collect new dinosaurs from the American Midwest. He also worked on vertebrate evolution, especially that of horses.

Drummond Matthews (1931–1999) English co-discoverer, with **Frederick Vine,** of symmetrical patterns of magnetized ocean floor lava on either side of mid-ocean ridges (see glossary). The patterns showed alternating normal and reversed magnetization, reflecting a history of reversals in the Earth's magnetic field, and showed that the ocean floor is formed at mid-ocean ridges.

Motonori Matuyama (1884–1958) Japanese geologist who in1929 discovered that some sedimentary rocks are magnetized with a reversed polarity, concluding that the Earth's magnetic field must have changed in the past. This helped develop the idea that plates have moved over the surface of the Earth throughout geological time.

Stanley Miller (1930–) American chemist who in the early 1950s created complex organic substances such as amino acids by passing an electrical charge through simple gas mixtures that replicated the early atmosphere of the Earth. His results showed how the first lifeforms on the planet could have been created.

Andrija Mohorovicic (1857–1936) Croatian geophysicist who in 1909 discovered differences in the speed with which earthquake waves travel through the Earth. He realized that the Earth's crust overlies a denser mantle that lies about 19 miles (30 kilometers) beneath the surface.

Sir Roderick Murchison (1792–1871) Retired Scottish military officer who pioneered the mapping and study of Paleozoic rocks, defining and naming the Silurian System in 1835, the Devonian System (with **Adam Sedgwick)** in 1839, and the Permian System in 1841.

Alexander Ivanovich Oparin (1894–1980) Russian chemist who pioneered a chemical approach to the origin of life. He argued that simple organic substances were present on the Earth's surface before life itself evolved. His approach influenced **Stanley Miller**.

Richard Owen (1804–1892) English anatomist who first coined the name "dinosaur," in 1842. Owen supervised the first life-size reconstructions made for the world's first theme park—the Crystal Palace Gardens in London. Owen also described *Archaeopteryx*, the oldest fossil bird, but was opposed to **Charles Darwin**'s theory of evolution.

Henry Fairfield Osborn (1857–1935) Paleontologist with the U.S. Geological Survey and former president of the American Museum of Natural History in New York. He promoted **Charles Darwin**'s theory of evolution, and in 1905 described and named *Tyrannosaurus rex* (although the specimen was actually found by the "bone hunter" Barnum Brown in the late Cretaceous sediments of Hell Creek, Montana).

Catherine Raisin (1855–1945) English geologist and one of the first women to become head of a university department in Great Britain (1890). She made advances in the study of minerals and rocks, especially serpentinites, using a microscope. These rocks are important as fragments of ancient ocean floor that have been caught up in mountain building.

Charles Richter (1900–1985) American geophysicist who in 1935 developed a scale (which bears his name) for measuring the absolute strength of earthquakes. The largest earthquakes this century have registered 8.9 on the Richter scale; the earthquake that destroyed San Francisco in 1906 would have registered 8.25.

Adam Sedgwick (1785–1873) English cleric and Woodwardian professor at the University of Cambridge (from 1818). He mapped the Lower Paleozoic strata of Wales and defined the Cambrian System in 1835 and the Devonian System (with **Roderick Murchison**) in 1839. Subsequently Murchison lowered the base of his Silurian System into Sedgwick's Cambrian, and a bitter dispute broke out which was not fully resolved until after both men had died.

William Smith (1769–1839) English canal engineer and self-taught pioneer of geological mapping and stratigraphic geology (see glossary). He discovered and used the principle that the layers (succession) of strata can be characterized by the fossils they contain. Different fossils are buried at different times. The same principle was independently worked out by **Georges Cuvier** and **Alexandre Brongniart** in France. Smith produced the first geological map of England and Wales in 1819.

Marie Stopes (1880–1958) English paleobotanist who showed how plant remains alter to become coal. She subsequently became better known for promoting women's health issues.

Frederick Vine (1939–) English co-discoverer in 1963, with **Drummond Matthews**, of magnetic anomalies across mid-ocean ridges (see glossary). They measured and mapped the repeated symmetrical patterns of polarity reversals in magnetized lavas on either side of the mid-ocean ridges. This provided support for the suggestion by **Harry Hammond Hess** that new ocean floor rocks are formed at spreading ridges (see glossary).

Charles Doolittle Walcott (1850–1927) American paleontologist who specialized in the study of fossil arthropods, especially those of Cambrian times. He discovered the rich Cambrian deposits of the Burgess Shale in British Columbia, Canada, in 1909. Over several years Walcott excavated some 70,000 specimens and had them shipped back to the Smithsonian Institute, of which he became head in 1907. Administrative work left him little time to devote to the study of this remarkable find.

Alfred Wegener (1880–1930) German meteorologist and geophysicist who developed the theory of continental drift. He collected all the available evidence from rocks and fossils to show that South America, Africa, India, Antarctica, and Australia had once been joined together as a supercontinent, which he named Pangea in 1912. However, he could not suggest an acceptable mechanism by which the continents could have moved such great distances over the surface of the Earth. The theory was not widely accepted until the 1960s, when plate tectonic theory (see glossary) provided hard evidence that the continents had indeed moved.

Abraham Gottlob Werner (1749–1817) German mineralogist and teacher who proposed the Neptunist theory of geology, in which minerals that had dissolved in an ancient ocean that covered the whole Earth were gradually deposited as solid rock (precipitated). The lowest and oldest were "Primitive" granites and slates, followed by "Transition," "Flötz" or stratified rocks, then "Alluvial" sediments. His teaching was highly influential at the time.

John Tuzo Wilson (1908–1993) Canadian geophysicist whose work helped develop plate tectonic theory (see glossary). He showed that oceanic islands become progressively older the farther away they are from mid-ocean spreading ridges (see glossary), and in 1965 proposed the concept of "transform" faults that break up mid-ocean spreading ridges into sections. Wilson also suggested the existence of "hot spots" (see glossary) with heat plumes rising within the mantle.

John Woodward (1665–1728) English professor of medicine who collected "natural objects" including fossils and minerals. He left his collection to the University of Cambridge, where it can still be seen in the Sedgwick Museum.

Places and Websites to Visit

The museums and sites below are among those with outstanding collections of fossils of the prehistoric creatures described in this book.

ARGENTINA
Buenos Aires: Argentinian Museum of Natural Sciences
La Plata: Museum of La Plata University

AUSTRALIA
Adelaide, South Australia: South Australian Museum
Brisbane, Queensland: Queensland Museum
Melbourne, Victoria: Museum of Victoria
Perth, Western Australia: Western Australian Museum
Sydney, New South Wales: Australian Museum
Young, New South Wales: National Dinosaur Museum

AUSTRIA
Vienna: Natural History Museum

BELGIUM
Brussels: Royal Institute of Natural Sciences
Bernissart, Hainault: Bernissart Museum

BRAZIL
Rio de Janeiro: National Museum

CANADA
Calgary, Alberta: Zoological Gardens
Drumheller, Alberta: Royal Tyrrell Museum of Paleontology
Edmonton, Alberta: Provincial Museum of Alberta
Ottawa, Ontario: Canadian Museum of Nature
Patricia, Alberta: Dinosaur Provincial Park
Quebec, Quebec: Redpath Museum
Toronto, Ontario: Royal Ontario Museum

CHINA
Beijing: Beijing Natural History Museum; Institute of Vertebrate Paleontology, and Paleoanthropology Museum
Beipei, Sichuan: Beipei Museum

FRANCE
Paris: National Museum of Natural History

GERMANY
Berlin: Humboldt University Museum
Darmstadt: Hessé State Museum
Frankfurt-am-Main: Senckenberg Natural History Museum
Munich: Bavarian State Institute for Paleontology and Historical Geography
Stuttgart: State Museum for Natural History
Tubingen: Institute and Museum of Geology and Paleontology

INDIA
Calcutta: Geology Museum, Indian Statistical Institute

ITALY
Bologna: G. Capellini Museum
Milan: Civic Museum of Natural History
Padua: Museum of the Institute of Geology
Rome: Museum of Paleontology, Institute of Geology
Venice: Civic Museum of Natural History

JAPAN
Osaka: Museum of Natural History
Tokyo: National Science Museum

KENYA
Nairobi: Kenya National Museum

MEXICO
Mexico City: Natural History Museum

MONGOLIA
Ulan-Bataar: Museum of Natural History

MOROCCO
Rabat: Museum of Earth Sciences

NIGER
Niamey: National Museum

POLAND
Chorzow, Silesia: Dinosaur Park
Warsaw: Institute of Paleobiology, Academy of Sciences

RUSSIA
St Petersburg: Central Geological and Prospecting Museum
Moscow: Orlov Museum of Paleontology, Academy of Sciences

SOUTH AFRICA
Capetown: South Africa Museum
Johannesburg: Bernard Price Institute of Paleontology

SWEDEN
Uppsala: Paleontology Museum, Uppsala University

UNITED KINGDOM
Birmingham: Birmingham Museum
Cambridge: Sedgwick Museum, Cambridge University
Cardiff: National Museum of Wales
Edinburgh: Royal Scottish Museum
Elgin: Elgin Museum
Glasgow: Hunterian Museum
Leicester: The Leicestershire Museums
London: British Museum (Natural History); Crystal Palace Park
Maidstone: Maidstone Museum
Manchester: Manchester Museum
Oxford: University Museum
Sandown, Isle of Wight: Museum of Isle of Wight Geology

UNITED STATES
Boulder, Colorado: University Natural History Museum
Buffalo, New York: Buffalo Museum of Science
Cambridge, Massachusetts: Museum of Comparative Zoology, Harvard University
Chicago, Illinois: Field Museum of Natural History
Cleveland, Ohio: Natural History Museum
Denver, Colorado: Denver Museum of Natural History
Jensen, Utah: Dinosaur National Monument
Los Angeles, California: Los Angeles County Museum of Natural History
New Haven, Connecticut: Peabody Museum of Natural History, Yale University
New York, New York: American Museum of Natural History
Pittsburgh, Pennsylvania: Carnegie Museum of Natural History
Princeton, New Jersey: Museum of Natural History, Princeton University
Salt Lake City, Utah: Utah Museum of Natural History
Washington, D.C.: National Museum of Natural History, Smithsonian Institution

ZIMBABWE
Harare: National Museum of Harare

WEBSITES

The World Wide Web is an excellent source for up-to-date information about the latest fossil discoveries, as well as more general information about many different apsects of geology and paleontology. The following websites offer good coverage of one or more of these different fields, but represent only a small proportion of the information that can be found on the Internet.

Sites with general coverage
University of California Museum of Paleontology, Berkeley
www.ucmp.berkeley.edu

Natural History Museum, London
www.nhm.ac.uk

The Geological Society, London
www.geolsoc.org

The Paleontological Association, UK
www.palass.org

American Museum of Natural History
www.amnh.org

The Dinosaur Society, New York
www.dinosociety.org

New Mexico Museum of Natural History
www.aps.edu/htmlpages/nmmnh.html

The Paleontological Institute of the Russian Academy of Science in Moscow, Russia
http://ucmp1.berkeley.edu/pin.html

Natural History Museum, Berne, Switzerland
www-nmbe.unibe.ch/index.html

Sites focusing on particular species or fossil finds
The Dinosauricon
http://dinosaur.umbc.edu

General information sites
Discovery Channel
www.discovery.com

National Geographic
www.nationalgeographic.com

Glossary

A

ADAPTATION
A biological modification that makes an organism better suited for a particular way of life—for example, to feed on a specific diet.

AGNATHANS
A group of jawless and toothless fishlike vertebrates that includes many extinct sea and freshwater forms. Only the hagfish and lampreys survive. (Ordovician to recent.)

ALGAE
The general name given to several unrelated groups of simple organisms that live in moist or wet environments and include some of the most primitive organisms known. There are both single and multicelled forms and, like plants, they need sunlight to build their cells. Fossilized algae first appeared some 3.5 billion years ago.

AMBER
A sticky, scented resin produced by certain trees since Jurassic times as protection against disease. Insects and other organisms can become trapped in the resin and fossilized when it hardens into amber.

AMMONITES
An extinct group of cephalopod mollusks that lived in coiled shells and are often found as fossils in Mesozoic strata. (Jurassic to end Cretaceous.)

AMNIOTES
Living and fossil vertebrates whose embryos develop within a special protective membrane—the amnion. The group includes some early tetrapods, reptiles, birds, and mammals, but not amphibians.

AMPHIBIANS
A major group of vertebrates that includes all the tetrapods with gills for breathing in water when young, but lungs for breathing air as adults. Amphibians develop into tadpoles from an unprotected egg laid in water and then change into the adult form. (Mid-Carboniferous to recent.)

ANAPSIDS
A member of a group of reptiles characterized by having no openings in the skull behind the eye, including turtles, tortoises, and some other primitive groups.

ANGIOSPERMS
Commonly referred to as the flowering plants, this major division of the plant kingdom includes deciduous trees, shrubs, grasses, and weeds as well as flowers. The seeds are enclosed in an ovary. (Late Jurassic to recent.)

ANKYLOSAURIDS
A family of armored dinosaurs with horny beaks for plant-eating. Bony plates and spikes covered the neck, shoulders, and back, and the tail was armed with a bony club. (Mid- to end Cretaceous.)

ANNELIDS
Soft-bodied worms with bodies divided into segments. They have left a fossil record of trace fossils, some calcareous tubes, and organic toothlike structures. (Late Vendian to recent.)

ANTHRACOSAURS
A group of fish-eating, lizard-shaped tetrapods that includes some land-living and some water-dwelling creatures; they may include the ancestors of the reptiles. (Early Carboniferous to Permian.)

APPALACHIANS
An ancient mountain range on the eastern seaboard of North America with a complex geological history extending back to late Precambrian times.

ARACHNIDS
A large group of mostly land-living carnivorous arthropods including the scorpions, mites, and spiders. The earliest fossil forms are Silurian scorpions, with spiders first appearing in the Devonian period.

ARCHAEBACTERIANS
Primitive, single-celled microscopic bacteria, many of which can live in extreme conditions such as acid or very hot water. They are thought to be among the earliest lifeforms to have evolved, around 3.5 billion years ago.

ARCHAEOCYATHANS
An extinct group of early Cambrian spongelike organisms that grew attached to the seabed to form the first reefs. The animals lived in cup-shaped calcium carbonate structures with porous walls and are thought to be related to the sponges.

ARCHEAN
The earliest part of the Earth's Precambrian rock record, dating from about 3.8 to 2.5 billion years ago.

ARCHOSAURS
A group of reptiles that includes the dinosaurs, pterosaurs, and living crocodiles. They originated in the early Triassic; many became extinct in late Cretaceous times.

ARMORICA
An ancient chunk of continental crust made up of the lands that now form France, Switzerland, southern Germany, and parts of Eastern Europe. Originally Armorica was part of the southern supercontinent of Gondwana, but it broke away and drifted northward from Ordovician times.

ARTHROPODS
The biggest group of animals (over a million living species) that includes many extinct groups such as the trilobites and eurypterids, and living groups such as the crabs, insects, and spiders. They have jointed limbs and a hard skin that has to be periodically shed to allow growth. (Lower Cambrian to recent.)

AUSTRALOPITHECINES
An extinct group of small but upright-walking, apelike human ancestors that lived from 4.5 to 1.4 million years ago.

AVALONIA
An early Paleozoic crustal plate consisting of Newfoundland, England, Wales, southeast Ireland, and part of western Europe that broke away from Gondwana in Ordovician times and joined Laurentia at the end of Silurian times.

B

BACTERIA
A large, diverse group of microorganisms consisting of single cells whose nuclei do not have well-defined membranes around them. Together with the blue-green algae, they make up the prokaryotes, organisms that were among the first and most primitive to evolve, 3.5 billion years ago.

BALTICA
An early Paleozoic crustal plate made up of northwestern and central Europe and part of Russia. The plate collided with Laurentia to form the Caledonian mountain belt in Ordovician times.

BASALT
A volcanic rock formed either in sheets on the surface, when lava flows from a vent or fissure in the ground, or underground when lava is injected into cracks in the surrounding rocks. Cracks filled with basalt are called dykes when they are vertical and sills when they are horizontal.

BED
A layer of sediment (a stratum) deposited by wind, water, or gravity-controlled flow to form a more or less flat-lying sheet.

BELEMNITES
An extinct group of squidlike sea creatures with a solid, bullet-shaped structure embedded in the end of the body. (Jurassic to Cretaceous.)

BIOZONE
A subdivision in geological time, characterized by the presence in a series of rock strata of fossils of the same species, or group of species.

BIPEDAL
Standing, walking, or running on two legs. See also **QUADRUPEDAL.**

BRACHIOPODS
Shellfish, common in the Paleozoic, that were similar to the bivalved mollusks but distinguished by different body organs. (Early Cambrian to recent.)

BROWSER
A plant-eating animal that selects leaves and twigs from shrubs and trees. Compare: **GRAZER.**

BRYOPHYTES
Plants, including the mosses and liverworts, that lack true roots and cannot grow much above ground level. They are thought to have been the first plants to have colonized the land, in Ordovician times.

BRYOZOAN see **MOSS ANIMAL**

BURGESS SHALE
A mid-Cambrian marine deposit in British Columbia famous for the diversity and preservation of its fauna.

C

CALCIUM CARBONATE
A naturally occurring mineral that can form at the Earth's surface; used by many animals (corals, trilobites, clams) to build or reinforce their skeletons.

CALEDONIDES
The Paleozoic mountain chain that extends from Scandinavia through the northwest British Isles into Newfoundland, the result of the collision between Avalonia and Laurentia at the end of the Silurian period.

CAMBRIAN
The first geological period of the Phanerozoic Era, from the end of the Precambrian (545 million years ago) to the beginning of the Ordovician (495 million years ago). A time when most of the main invertebrate groups (phyla) appear in the fossil record, along with the first chordates.

CARAPACE
The hard, protective shell or shield enclosing the body of animals such as the invertebrate arthropods and some reptiles such as the turtles.

CARBONIFEROUS
The period of geological time from the end of the Devonian (354 million years ago) to the beginning of the Permian (290 million years ago.) In this time the first extensive forests developed, leaving coal deposits and the remains of the first land-living vertebrate communities of reptiles and amphibians. Divided into Mississippian and Pennsylvanian.

CARNIVORES
A group of mammals that have well-developed, dagger-shaped canine teeth for eating meat. (Early Tertiary to recent.)

CARNIVOROUS
Describing an animal that eats the flesh of vertebrate animals but is not necessarily a true carnivore. See also **HERBIVORES, INSECTIVORES.**

CARNOSAURS
A group of large carnivorous dinosaurs with large skulls and teeth, many of the biggest being bipedal. (Early Jurassic to end Cretaceous.)

CATASTROPHISM
A theory that claims that the history of the Earth and its life is influenced by sudden catastrophic events. Originally associated with the Biblical Flood, the theory has now been modified to include extraterrestrial impacts and environmental events.

CEPHALOPODS
A large group of sea-dwelling animals, including octopus, squid, and cuttlefish, with a well-developed head surrounded by tentacles. (Cambrian to recent.)

CERATOPSIANS
A group of about 20 species of rhinoceroslike, plant-eating dinosaurs protected by bony head shields and horns. (Late Cretaceous.)

CHALK
A soft limestone formed from a "mud" of calcium carbonate, often made up of the shells of tiny marine organisms, as in the Cretaceous chalk deposits of Western Europe.

CHELONIANS
A large group of reptiles, including the turtles and tortoises, that have short, broad bodies protected above and below by shields composed of bony plates overlain by plates of tortoiseshell. (Late Triassic to recent.)

CHERT
A silica-rich mineral deposit that can form in seabed sediments and enclose and then fossilize the remains of organisms, especially microbes. Precambrian chert provides much of the fossil evidence for primitive life.

CHORDATES
Animals with a notochord or backbone. (Mid-Cambrian to recent.)

CLASS
A high-level grouping of similar organisms. A class contains one or more orders; similar classes form a phylum.

CLUBMOSSES
A group of plants that included large, coal-forming trees in Carboniferous times and still survive as much smaller forms. Their stems are covered in small, leaflike structures; they reproduce by means of spores, grouped in conelike structures. (Devonian to recent.)

COAL
A carbon-rich deposit formed from the remains of plants. At first the material becomes peat; as this becomes more and more compressed, it turns into lignite (brown coal), then harder forms such as anthracite. Each successive form contains more carbon and less water.

COELACANTHS
Primitive bony fish with large single and paired fins, thought to have died out in Cretaceous times until the living coelacanth, *Latimeria*, was found in 1938. (Late Devonian to recent.)

COLLISION ZONE
A region where two crustal plates collide, leading to folding and faulting (mountain building) of the rocks and often subduction of one plate, depending on the type of crustal plates.

COLONIAL
A group of animals or single cells of the same species living together to form an organism. Some colonies, like corals, sponges, and graptolites, have a shared skeleton, but others, like the insects, may have a close social organization in which some individuals are specialized for certain specific duties.

CONIFERS
A large group of woody plants with needle or scalelike leaves and single-sex cones for reproduction. (Carboniferous to recent.)

CONODONTS
An extinct group of small, jawless sea creatures with mouths filled with several pairs of tooth-bars made of bonelike material; recently considered to be chordates or possibly primitive jawless vertebrates. The fossil teeth have considerable use in dating strata. (Late Cambrian to end Triassic.)

CONTINENTAL BREAK-UP
Splitting apart of continental crustal plates, caused by large-scale heat flow within the Earth's mantle, to form a rift valley. Volcanoes and fissures erupt dense basalt lavas in the valley bottom and build a ridge that continuously subsides as the rift valley splits apart. Eventually, the low-lying valley floods with seawater, forming a new ocean. See also **MID-OCEAN RIDGE.**

CONTINENTAL CRUST
The uppermost, brittle rock layer of the Earth that forms the continents and varies in thickness from 16 to 56 miles (25 to 90 kilometers); it has an overall composition of granite, but includes a wide variety of metamorphic, igneous, and sedimentary rocks.

CONTINENTAL SHELF
The margin of the continents that is covered by shallow seas and shelves steeply down to the ocean floor at its outer edge; floored by thick piles of seabed and delta sediments, it is home to many important groups of marine life.

CONVECTION (MANTLE)
Heat-carrying currents in the Earth's semimolten mantle. Material becomes hot near the Earth's core and slowly rises through the mantle. At the same time, cooler material descends toward the core. The heat transferred in this way can melt rocks in the crust to produce magma.

CONVERGENT EVOLUTION
The phenomenon whereby animals evolve similar structures in response to the same environmental pressures—the wings of bats, birds, and pterosaurs, for example.

CORALS
A group of soft-bodied and primitive sea creatures that build a supporting calcareous skeleton. They vary in size and shape from small cups (less than an inch in size) to branched and dome-shaped structures up to 3 feet (1 meter) in diameter. Modern corals, called scleractinians, need light and mostly live in shallow, tropical waters; they evolved

in Triassic times from Palaeozoic species that are now extinct. (Ordovician to Permian.)

CORE
The dense, hot center of the Earth, 4309 miles (6940 kilometers) in diameter, composed of the metallic elements iron and nickel in two layers forming an outer liquid and solid inner core.

CRETACEOUS
A period at the end of the Mesozoic, after the Jurassic and before the Tertiary, that lasted from 142 to 65 million years ago.

CRINOIDS see **SEA-LILIES**

CROCODILIANS
An ancient but surviving group of reptiles that are often armored with bony scales. They have front legs shorter than hind and an elongated body with a laterally flattened tail for swimming. (Late Triassic to recent.)

CRUST
The hard and brittle surface rock layer of the Earth that overlies the mantle and varies in thickness and composition depending on whether it is continental or oceanic crust.

CRUSTACEANS
A large class of marine, freshwater, and occasionally terrestrial arthropods (over 35,000 living species), including the crabs and shrimps. They are protected by a tough outer layer, called a carapace. (Late Cambrian to recent.)

CYCADS
Palmlike seed plants with massive stems and a crown of fernlike leaves. They may be short or treelike, growing to 65 feet (20 meters) high. (Permian to recent.)

CYNODONTS
An extinct group of advanced reptilelike tetrapods, abundant in Triassic times, that includes the ancestors of the mammals. (Late Permian to late Jurassic.)

D

DELTA
The mouth of a river where it meets the sea and deposits its sediment, often in huge delta shapes many miles across, depending on the strength of the current flow and its ability to carry sediment. The fossil remains of abundant plant and animal life buried in ancient tropical deltas have formed deposits of coal, oil, and gas.

DEVONIAN
An Upper Paleozoic period of geological time, 417 to 354 million years ago, between the Silurian and Carboniferous periods. Named for the county of Devon, in southwest England, where rocks of this age are well exposed.

DIAPSIDS
A member of a major group of animals that includes the dinosaurs, extinct marine reptiles, crocodiles, lizards, snakes, and birds, characterized by a pair of openings in the skull immediately behind the eye socket. (Upper Carboniferous to recent.)

DICYNODONTS
An extinct group of advanced reptilelike tetrapods with two prominent, downward-pointing tusks. (Permian to Triassic.)

DINOSAURS
The so-called "terrible lizards," members of an extinct and diverse group of land-living reptiles that flourished from the late Triassic to the end of the Cretaceous and may have given rise to the birds.

DIPROTODONTIDS
An extinct family of Australian marsupial mammals. Most were plant-eaters and some grew to the size of hippos. (Late Tertiary to Quaternary.)

DNA
Deoxyribonucleic acid, genetic material that determines the inherited characteristics in most living organisms. When a cell divides, its DNA is duplicated so that each new daughter cell receives the same genetic DNA code. See also **NATURAL SELECTION.**

DRIP TIP
An elongation of the tip of a leaf to form a lip that helps shed heavy rain and avoid damage to the leaf; characteristic of rain-forest plants.

DROMAEOSAURIDS
An extinct group of birdlike theropod dinosaurs 4 to 10 feet (1.2 to 3 meters) in length; active predators, they had light, agile bodies, long fingers, and a long claw on one toe. (Mid- to late Cretaceous.)

DUNE
A large body of sand piled up by the flow of water or wind. Dunes vary enormously in shape, but their form often indicates the direction of flow. Some extend for tens of miles and on land may reach heights of 100 feet (30 meters.)

DYKE
A vertical, wall-like body of igneous rock that has been squeezed (intruded) into older rocks from a magma chamber deep within the Earth. Some dykes of volcanic origin reach the surface and pour out molten lava.

E

ECHINODERMS
Sea-dwelling invertebrates, including the starfish (asteroids), sea urchins (echinoids), sea lilies (crinoids), sea cucumbers (holothurians), and some extinct forms dating back to Cambrian times. They have an unusual, five-rayed symmetry. Many grow a hard, chalky skeleton and form common fossils.

ECOLOGY
The study of the relationships between organisms and the environment in which they live.

ECOSYSTEM
A unit in nature made up of a community or communities of organisms and the environment within which they live and interact.

EDIACARANS
A group of soft-bodied organisms found fossilized within Vendian seabed sediments. Many of them are extinct. It is not yet clear what kind of organisms they were, but some seem to belong to living groups such as the seapens. Named after the Ediacaran Hills in the Flinders Range of South Australia where the fossils are well preserved.

EMBRYO
An animal in its earliest stage of development, between fertilization and hatching or birth.

EOCENE see **TERTIARY**

EROSION
The removal of rock material that has already been broken down by weathering through the transport processes of wind, water, gravity, or ice.

An extinct group of scorpionlike arthropods that lived in both salty and freshwaters from early Ordovician to end Permian times; some grew to 10 feet (3 meters) in length.

EVAPORITE
A sedimentary deposit of minerals, such as salt and gypsum, formed when salty water has evaporated under a hot, dry climate.

EVERGREEN
A plant that retains its leaves throughout the year. The leaves are generally small to reduce water loss and are shed after a year or two.

EVOLUTION
The process of development and change in life that has been going on since life began on Earth. The fossil record shows that from primitive and tiny single-celled creatures life has gradually become larger and more complex. Evolution results from a combination of genetic change or mutation, reproduction, and the interaction of organisms with their environment, and is a process in which some species change and survive while others die out. The first scientific statement of the theory of evolution was made by Charles Darwin and Alfred Wallace in 1858.

EXOSKELETON
The tough and protective "skin" on the outside of arthropods such as insects, crustaceans, and spiders. It is made of soft material that hardens into a shell. Some arthropods, such as the living crabs, have to molt their exoskeleton periodically and produce a new, bigger one.

EXTINCTION EVENT
A geologically brief time when an abnormal number of organisms die off. Causes may be changes in sea level, climate change driven by movement of the Earth's crustal plates, extraterrestrial meteorite impact, or changes in the amount of heat coming from the Sun.

F

FAULT
A fracture in rocks caused by the build up of pressure within the Earth, so that rock on one side of a fault moves relative to rock on the other side. Individual movements, often associated with earthquakes, may be only of a few feet, but over time they may add up to many miles. The San Andreas Fault in California, for example, has moved over 186 miles (300 kilometers) over the last 30 million years.

FERNS
A large group of terrestrial plants that includes many living and extinct species, Ferns originated in Carboniferous times (although fernlike plants are found from early Devonian times) and are still abundant. They have large, divided, frondlike leaves that usually carry the reproductive spore-producing organs.

FERN SPIKE
An abundance of fern pollen found in a single layer within rock strata, indicating that ferns had formed the main plants in the landscapes of the time.

FLASH FLOODS
Unpredictable, powerful, and often catastrophic deluges of water that occasionally flow down dry stream valleys after torrential storms, carrying sediment and drowning anything in the path of the flood.

FLOOD BASALT
Volcanic lava that pours out over the surface of the land in huge quantities from deep cracks (dyke fissures) in the crust; often produced by mantle "hot spot" plumes rising from deep within the Earth.

FLOOD PLAIN
Flat landscape around a river, formed when the river bursts its banks and dumps its load of sediment on the surrounding countryside. Repeated flood layers of sediment can build up very thick deposits

FOOD CHAIN
A way of linking different organisms together according to what each eats, and what each is eaten by. For example, microscopic plants living near the ocean surface are eaten by small swimming animals such as shrimps that, in turn, are preyed on by small fish who are then eaten by bigger fish.

FOSSIL
The remains or trace of a once-living organism, preserved in rock strata. A fossil may be a chemical trace of an organism, a trace of activity, a bit of the original body, or a mineral replica of it.

G

GENUS
A group of closely related organisms (species). For example, *Homo* is the genus to which both the living species *Homo sapiens* and the extinct species *Homo neanderthalensis* belong.

GINKGOS
Living fossils of a group of primitive plants, with fan-shaped leaves and woody stems, that were much more common in the geological past. Represented today by one surviving species—*Ginkgo biloba*, the maidenhair tree. (Permian to recent.)

GLACIAL
A cold phase within an ice age when glaciers advance. See also **INTERGLACIAL.**

GLACIATION
The covering of part of the Earth's surface by ice sheets or valley glaciers and the accompanying processes of landscape erosion and deposition of glacial debris.

GLACIER
A mass of ice and snow, usually infilling a valley, that can flow slowly downhill, erode the landscape, and carry vast amounts of rock debris.

GLOSSOPTERIDS
An extinct group of plants whose fossil leaves are common in Permian and Triassic strata in the lands that once made up the supercontinent of Gondwana. The distribution of the distinctive strap-shaped fossil leaves in India, Australia, South Africa, South America, and Antarctica was part of the original evidence for the existence of the supercontinent. (Permian to Jurassic.)

GONDWANA
A supercontinent formed in the southern hemisphere by the joining together of several large crustal plates (Australia, South America, Africa, Antarctica, India) and numerous smaller crustal fragments such as Florida; the pieces were assembled in Cambrian times and joined by Laurasia in the Permian to form the even bigger supercontinent of Pangea, which began to break up in Jurassic times, having lasted for some 300 million years.

GRANITE
A hard, crystalline igneous rock formed from a molten rock (magma) deep in the continental crust and made up of particular minerals such as quartz, feldspar, and mica.

GRAPTOLITES
An extinct group of tiny animals that lived in the seas of Paleozoic times (Cambrian to Permian) and built tubular skeletons of organic material. Their fossils look like pencil markings on rock surfaces and are useful for telling the age of marine sedimentary rocks.

GRASSES
Flowering plants (family Gramineae) whose evolution in Tertiary times was closely linked to the increase in grass-eating (grazing) mammals, especially ruminants (cud-chewers) such as the deer, cattle, and horses.

GRAZER
A grass-eating animal—mostly mammals but also some birds—that can crop, chew, and digest grass. The vegetation wears down teeth and requires slow fermentation in the stomach.

GREENHOUSE STATE
A time of warm global climates; increased quantities of carbon dioxide and other gases in the atmosphere trap a greater proportion of the energy in sunlight than usual, causing global warming. The gases can be released by human activities, such as burning fossil fuels, or by natural processes, such as volcanism. Compare: **ICEHOUSE STATE.**

GYMNOSPERMS
A group of seed plants such as ferns and conifers whose seeds are not enclosed in ovaries. (Late Devonian to recent.)

H

HADROSAURIDS
A group of large two- and four-legged ornithopod dinosaurs. They had horny beaks for browsing vegetation and batteries of cheek teeth for chewing. (Mid- to end Cretaceous.)

HATCHLING
A baby animal that has just emerged from an egg. Some are well developed and can soon leave the nest (precocial); others first need parental feeding and care (altricial).

HERBIVORES
Animals that feed on grass and other plants, usually with a specially adapted stomach and teeth for eating and digesting tough plant material.

HOMINIDS
A family of primates that includes humans and their fossil ancestors, the australopithecines. Experts argue as to whether the group should include the higher apes such as chimpanzees. (Pliocene to recent.)

HORSETAILS
Members of the family Calamitaceae that were among the most common of the Carboniferous coal-swamp plants. Some were tree-sized, growing to over 60 feet (18 meters) with hollow stems, tiny scalelike leaves, and branches arranged in circlets. (Mostly late Devonian to early Triassic, but with a few surviving species.)

HOT SPOT
An area in the upper part of the Earth's mantle between 70 and 140 miles (100 and 200 kilometers) wide, from which molten rock (magma) rises in a plume to form volcanoes. The volcanic islands of Hawaii were formed by a hot spot.

HYDROTHERMAL VENT
A small, volcanolike opening from which hot water flows and may deposit minerals. Most vents are located along mid-ocean ridges and recirculate seawater

enriched with minerals to form unique seabed communities independent of sunlight.

HYPSILOPHODONTIDS
Ornithopod dinosaurs 6 feet (1.8 meters) high. Fast-moving and ostrichlike but for their long stiff tails, they browsed plants with horny beaks and cheek teeth. (Late Jurassic to end Cretaceous.)

I

IAPETUS
An ocean that grew between Laurentia and Gondwana in early Cambrian times; it was closed and the ocean floor subducted during Ordovician times as continental fragments such as Avalonia broke away from Gondwana and moved north, opening a new ocean, the Rheic.

ICE AGE
A period of several million years with alternating warm and cool global climates leading to the development of polar icecaps, glaciers, changing sea levels, and climatic zones.

ICECAP
A flat, dome-shaped mass of ice that develops over the poles during ice ages and spreads outward, flowing under its own weight.

ICEHOUSE STATE
A period of Earth history with cool climates and ice ages, connected to low intensities of volcanic eruption and low levels of "greenhouse" gases, such as carbon dioxide, in the atmosphere. Compare: **GREENHOUSE STATE**.

ICHTHYOSAURS
An order of fast-swimming and predatory marine reptiles with dolphin-shaped bodies. (Early Triassic to late Cretaceous.)

IGNEOUS
Rocks formed from a molten material (magma).

IGUANODONTIDS
A group of plant-eating ornithopod dinosaurs that walked on two legs. One of the first groups of dinosaurs to be recognized as fossils in the early 19th century by Gideon Mantell in England. (Late Jurassic to late Cretaceous.)

IMPACT EVENT
The result of the collision of a body from outer space with a planet, forming a crater and, depending on the size of the impact, causing extinction among plants and animals.

INSECTIVORES
A group of small and mainly nocturnal mammals, including the living hedgehogs, moles, and shrews, that feed on insects. This group evolved at the end of the Cretaceous and developed enormously during the Tertiary period.

INSECTIVOROUS
All those organisms, including some plants, that feed mainly on insects.

INTERGLACIAL
A warm phase between cold glacials within an ice age.

INTRUSION
An igneous rock that has been injected below ground into the surrounding rocks, often forming wall-shaped dykes, horizontal sills, or rounded plutons.

INVERTEBRATES
Animals without backbones, from single-celled organisms to the arthropods. The invertebrate echinoderms show some relationship to the vertebrates in the development of their larvae.

IRIDIUM
A rare metal element in the Earth's crust. It is present in meteorites and other debris from outer space.

ISLAND ARC
A chain of volcanic islands formed over a subduction zone where ocean crust has been partially melted with the molten rock magma forcing its way to the surface to erupt explosively through volcanoes.

ISOTOPES
Differing forms of the same chemical element, having the same number of protons but different numbers of neutrons in their nuclei. Some of the isotopes of various chemical elements are radioactive (unstable). The individual atoms of these unstable isotopes "decay" (spontaneously convert) into more stable daughter forms at a steady rate. Measuring how much daughter isotope is present in a rock indicates when it was formed.

JK

JURASSIC
The middle period of the Mesozoic era from 206 to 142 million years ago between the Triassic and the Cretaceous period. Named after the Jura Mountains in Europe.

K-T BOUNDARY
The boundary between the Cretaceous and Tertiary periods. The abbreviation is derived from "K" for *kreide*, German for chalk, a widespread late Cretaceous deposit, and "T" for Tertiary. The boundary is dated at 65 million years ago and is marked by a mass extinction.

L

LANCELETS
Small sea creatures that can swim by flexing their bodies sideways, using paired muscles on either side of a stiff internal rod called the notochord. The presence of the notochord identifies them as chordates and ancestors of the vertebrates.

LAND BRIDGE
A narrow stretch of low-lying land that appears when sea levels are low and

connects land masses, allowing land animals to cross but preventing the migration of sea creatures.

LAURASIA
The supercontinent formed in the northern hemisphere by the closure of the Iapetus Ocean in Ordovician times and the joining of Laurentia and Asia (excluding India).

LAURENTIA
The name for the ancient continent of North America that formed around the Precambrian Canadian Shield.

LIMESTONE
A sedimentary rock made from calcium carbonate minerals, often as the shelly remains of sea creatures.

LUNGFISH
A group of primitive bony fish (dipnoans) with both gills and lungs for breathing in water and air. (Devonian to recent.)

M

MAGMA
Naturally occurring molten rock formed deep within the Earth's crust that can flow upward toward the surface and sometimes erupt as lava.

MAMMALS
Warm-blooded and hairy vertebrates that feed their young. The group includes animals living in a variety of habitats from water to land and air. They arose from reptilelike cynodonts in Triassic times.

MANTLE
The layer of hot, solid rock that lies below the Earth's crust and above the core and is some 1800 miles (2900 kilometers) thick. Heat circulates from the core to the crust through the mantle in rising zones known as convection cells and mantle plumes.

MANTLE PLUME
A rising column-shaped zone of heat through the mantle that spreads out sideways when it reaches the base of the crust. A plume heats the crust, causing it to expand, dome upward, and crack, allowing magma to erupt at the surface through volcanoes and fissures.

MARSUPIALS
Mammals that give birth to small, undeveloped young that are nurtured in a skin pouch on the mother's stomach until they can better fend for themselves. They originated in Cretaceous times and survived in Australia and the Americas.

MESOZOIC
The middle era of life, from 248 to 65 million years ago, between the Paleozoic and Cenozoic (comprising the Tertiary and Quaternary). Subdivided into the Triassic, Jurassic, and Cretaceous periods.

METAMORPHISM
A process whereby rocks are altered by heat and pressure within the crust, especially during mountain building.

MICRODIAMOND
Microscopic diamonds formed by the explosive melting of carbon-rich minerals such as limestone as a result of large meteorite impacts.

MID-OCEAN RIDGE
A submarine mountain range of volcanic rocks that rises from the ocean floor, and is often the site of new seafloor creation.

MIOCENE see **TERTIARY**

MISSISSIPPIAN see **CARBONIFEROUS**

MOLECULAR CLOCK
An estimate of the timing of evolution based on known rates of genetic change in particular groups of organisms.

MOLLUSKS
A large group of soft-bodied animals that includes the living snails, clams, squid, octopus, and the extinct ammonites and belemnites. They appear in the fossil record in early Cambrian times and must have evolved before that. Many of them build calcium carbonate shells that are commonly preserved as fossils.

MONOTREMES
A group of primitive mammals with reptilelike features such as egg-laying. Only the platypus and spiny anteater (echidna) survive. (Mid-Cretaceous to recent.)

MOSASAURS
A group of very large and powerful sea-living reptiles. They grew to 33 feet (10 meters) long and were ferocious predators. (Mid- to late Cretaceous.)

MOSS ANIMALS
Tiny animals that live in colonies resembling rafts of moss or seaweed. The colonies form geometric patterns and can contain thousands of individuals, or zooids. The colonies cling to the surfaces of plants such as kelp. (Ordovician to recent.)

MOUNTAIN BUILDING
The process of forming mountains on land by the thickening of crustal rocks during the collision of crustal plates. As plates collide, continental crust is both pushed down into the mantle and up into the air.

MULTITUBERCULATES
The earliest plant-eating mammals, having chisel-shaped front teeth and ranging from mouse to beaver size. (Late Jurassic to mid Tertiary.)

N

NATURAL SELECTION
The key evolutionary process whereby organisms with the most appropriate adaptations to their environment are more reproductively successful. In this way the environment is seen to "select"

the characteristics of species or individuals that succeed best within that environment.

NEANDERTHALS
An extinct group of humans (*Homo neanderthalensis*) who evolved about 150,000 years ago in the eastern Mediterranean region, spread into Europe and western Asia, and died out around 35,000 years ago. Genetic analysis suggests they did not interbreed with modern humans.

NICHE
The space in the environment occupied by a particular organism and defined by its characteristics such as temperature tolerance, feeding habits, and predators.

NOTOCHORD
A flexible rod within the body of chordate animals. Running from head to tail, it forms the basis of the backbone in vertebrate animals.

OCEAN CRUST
A thin but dense layer of volcanic rocks, 4 to 7 miles (6 to 11 kilometers) deep, that forms the floor of the oceans. None of the ocean crust of today is more than 180 million years old. New ocean crust forms at a mid-ocean ridge and then moves slowly away from the ridge.

OCEAN FLOOR SPREADING
The process by which a new ocean forms. A rising plume of hot material from the Earth's mantle stretches the continental crust above, in time opening volcanic rifts on the surface. The rifts widen into a valley that eventually floods and becomes a new ocean as it continues to spread.

OCEANS
Large bodies of salty water that now cover about 60 percent of the surface of the Earth. They first formed around 2 billion years ago and have opened and closed, and risen and fallen, as the continents have moved and the climate has changed.

OLIGOCENE see **TERTIARY**

ORDOVICIAN
A period of early Paleozoic time, 495 to 443 million years ago, between the Cambrian and the Silurian periods. The name comes from an ancient British tribe, the Ordovices.

ORNITHISCHIANS
One of the two main orders of dinosaurs. They have a birdlike pelvis and are entirely plant-eating. They include groups such as the ornithopods, stegosaurs, and ceratopsians. (Early Jurassic to late Cretaceous.) See also **SAURISCHIANS.**

ORNITHOPODS
A group of ornithischian dinosaurs that walked predominantly on their hind limbs and had three-toed, birdlike feet. Examples include iguanodonts and hadrosaurids.

OROGENY
A period of mountain building, caused by the collision of continents. The great mountain chains of the world have all been created this way. Some orogenies, including the Alpine-Himalayan, are still active today.

P

PALEONTOLOGY
The scientific study of fossils, their formation and preservation; the formulation of theories and the history and evolution of ancient life that the fossils represent.

PALEOCENE see **TERTIARY**

PALEOZOIC
The era of ancient life extending from 545 to 248 million years ago, from the beginning of the Cambrian period, through the Ordovician, Silurian, Devonian, and Carboniferous periods, to the end of the Permian period.

PANDERICHTHYIDS
A small group of fish with two pairs of lobed fins and a particular pattern of skull bones. They are considered ancestral to all tetrapod vertebrates. (Late Devonian.)

PANGEA
A global supercontinent formed by the joining of Gondwana, Laurentia, Baltica, and Siberia at the end of Triassic times. Pangea stretched almost from pole to pole, but soon began to break up as the Atlantic Ocean opened.

PANTHALLASSIC OCEAN
Large ocean that surrounded the supercontinent of Pangea, occupying more than half of the Earth's surface.

PELYCOSAURS
A group of reptilelike tetrapods that show some mammalian features such as different tooth shapes. Some pelycosaurs had webbed sail structures on their backs supported by bone that may have helped the animals to warm up or cool off. (Late Carboniferous to late Permian.)

PENNATULACEANS see **SEAPENS**

PENNSYLVANIAN see **CARBONIFEROUS**

PERMAFROST
An area of permanently frozen ground on the fringe of the polar icecaps. The surface may thaw briefly during summer to allow the growth of some hardy plants.

PERMIAN
The last period of the Paleozoic era, 290 to 248 million years ago, from the end of the Carboniferous to the beginning of the Triassic.

PHANEROZOIC
The current eon of historical time, covering the last 545 million years, during which there has been abundant

life. Follows the Proterozoic eon (2,500 to 545 million years ago).

PHOTOSYNTHESIS
The formation of organic compounds by plants to build their body tissue, using light energy from the Sun, carbon dioxide from the atmosphere, and water. Photosynthesis also releases oxygen into the atmosphere.

PLACENTALS
Mammals that develop a special tissue (placenta) by which embryos can exchange nutrients and waste products with their mothers. The placenta supplies nutrients for growth until the offspring are born. (Mid-Cretaceous to recent.)

PLANKTON
Microorganisms that inhabit the surface waters of lakes and oceans and form the basis of the food chain of these environments.

PLATES
The huge slabs into which the rocks of the Earth's crust are divided up, ranging from continent-sized fragments to many smaller pieces. A typical plate includes continent, shelf sea, and ocean areas.

PLATE TECTONICS
The geological process in which the Earth's crustal plates move over its surface, driven by currents within the semimolten mantle. The plates may diverge to form oceans, slide past one another along major faults, or crash into one another forming island arcs and mountain ranges.

PLATEAU LAVA
A great area of basalt lava that has poured out over the continents above rising mantle plumes through rifts in the continental crust.

PLESIOSAURS
A group of marine reptiles, 10 to 40 feet (3 to 12 meters) in length, that lived in Jurassic and Cretaceous times. Many were long-necked, but there were also short-necked varieties called pliosaurs. (Jurassic to Cretaceous.)

PLIOCENE see **TERTIARY**

PLUTON
A mass of igneous rock that has solidified below the surface of the Earth.

POLLEN
Microscopic spores and grains produced in huge numbers by the male reproductive organs of flowering plants (angiosperms) and seed-bearing plants (gymnosperms) for reproduction.

PRECAMBRIAN
An era of the Earth's history from its formation, 4.6 billion years ago, until the beginning of the Paleozoic era, 545 million years ago.

PRIMATES
A group of mammals that includes living monkeys, apes, and humans, and their fossil ancestors. They evolved from small, four-legged, tree-living insect-eaters in early Tertiary times.

PTEROSAURS
An extinct group of flying reptiles. Their wings were formed out of skin that stretched from the body over the forelimbs and along elongated fourth fingers that acted as supporting ribs. (Late Triassic to late Cretaceous.)

QR

QUADRUPEDAL
Walking on all fours.

QUATERNARY
The most recent period of Earth history, 1.8 million years ago after the Tertiary, marked by a major ice age.

RHEIC OCEAN
An ocean that opened up as the crustal plates of Avalonia, Armorica, and Iberia rifted away from the northern edge of Gondwana and swept northward toward Laurentia during Ordovician and Silurian times.

RIFT VALLEY
A valley formed by the sideways stretching, sagging, and then fracture of brittle crustal rocks along two parallel fault lines so that the central area between the fault lines drops down to form a valley floor; often accompanied by volcanic eruptions, and sometimes the precursor to continental break-up.

RODENTS
A group of small mammals including squirrels, beavers, rats, porcupines, and their extinct ancestors. Rodents have sharp, chisel-shaped front teeth that grow continuously for gnawing tough grains and seeds. (Early Tertiary to recent.)

S

SANDSTONE
Rock made up of mineral fragments deposited and layered as sediment by the action of gravity, wind, or water, and then compressed.

SAURISCHIANS
One of two major orders of dinosaurs. They had a reptilelike pelvis and include the large, plant-eating sauropods that walked on four legs, and the generally smaller carnivorous theropods that walked on their two hind limbs. (Early Jurassic to late Cretaceous.) See also **ORNITHISCHIANS**.

SAUROPODS
Saurischian, plant-eating dinosaurs with small heads, long necks and tails, massive bodies, and four trunklike legs. (Early Jurassic to late Cretaceous.)

SAVANNA
Open tropical landscapes in which grasses are the main plants due to a yearly dry season and wildfire. Savannas first

developed in early Tertiary times and have provided plant food for large herds of grazing mammals.

SCABLANDS (CHANNELED)
Landscapes molded by large-scale torrential floodwaters that carve channels in the bedrock several miles wide and up to a hundred feet deep. The floodwaters also form huge sediment ripples on the channel bed.

SEA-LILIES
Plant-shaped echinoderms that live attached to the seabed by roots. They have a long stem ending in a cup with arms, and are made of jointed plates of calcium carbonate. (Early Ordovician to recent.)

SEAPENS (PENNATULACEANS)
Soft-bodied, feather-shaped creatures that live rooted in the seabed by a stalk. They are related to the sea-anemones and corals. (Vendian to recent.)

SEA SQUIRTS (TUNICATES)
Soft-bodied animals that live attached to the seabed as adults but have free-swimming, tadpolelike larvae. The presence of a notochord in the larva shows that they are chordate animals. (Early Cambrian to recent.)

SEED FERNS
An extinct group of gymnosperms called pteridosperms with fernlike leaves on which seeds are developed. (Late Devonian to late Cretaceous.)

SEED PLANTS
Plants with naked seeds (gymnosperms). These contrast with the flowering plants (angiosperms), which have enclosed seeds. The gymnosperms were the dominant land plants until the angiosperms took over in Cretaceous times. (Late Devonian to recent.)

SHOCKED QUARTZ
Grains of the silicate mineral that have had their atomic structure distorted by very high pressure such as that produced by an enormous explosion from a meteorite impact or volcanic eruption.

SILL
A horizontal sheet of igneous rock found between older rocks deep underground. The igneous rock is formed from magma.

SILURIAN
The period of Paleozoic time, 443 to 417 million years ago, that followed the Ordovician period and preceded the Devonian. Named by Roderick Murchison in 1835 after an ancient British tribe, the Silures, for a series of strata in the Welsh Borderlands.

SPECIES
A group of closely related organisms that can interbreed and produce fertile young.

SPREADING RIDGE see **MID-OCEAN RIDGE**

STRATA
A sheet of rock formed from sediment deposited through the action of wind, water, or simply gravity. Successive layers of sediment are layed over each other, becoming buried and compressed to form level strata of sedimentary rock. Subsequently strata can be folded and faulted by geological processes such as mountain building.

STRATIGRAPHY
The study of rock strata, especially their relative ages, character, and correlation across different locations.

STEGOSAURS
A group of plant-eating ornithischian dinosaurs that walked on four legs. Stegosaurs had rows of bony plates or spikes along the back, which were probably for sexual display and perhaps heat regulation. (Mid-Jurassic to late Cretaceous.)

STROMATOLITES
Layered mound structures, several feet high, built up over many years in shallow and warm tropical waters by sheets of bacteria growing over the seabed and trapping sediment. Stromatolites first formed in Precambrian times 3.5 billion years ago.

SUBDUCTION
A plate tectonic process in which dense rocks on the ocean floor are pushed down beneath lighter continental rocks when crustal plates collide. The process releases huge amounts of energy, in the form of earthquakes. In addition, some of the subducted rock melts to become magma that rises to the surface of the continental plate and erupts from volcanoes.

SUPERCONTINENT
The joining together of continental crust plates to form a bigger continental mass, such as Gondwana or Pangea.

SYNAPSIDS
A group of extinct tetrapods with mammalian characteristics, including the pelycosaurs and therapsids, which have a single pair of openings low down in the skull behind the eyes. (Mid-Carboniferous to mid-Jurassic.)

T

TECTONIC THEORY see **PLATE TECTONICS**

TELEOSTS
A very large group of some 22,000 species of bony fish such as cod, salmon, and eels. They are dominant in both the marine and fresh waters of the Earth today. (Late Triassic to recent.)

TETHYS OCEAN
A largely tropical ocean that separated Laurasia and Gondwana between Permian and mid-Tertiary times and was closed by the northward movement of Africa and India.

TERRANE
A fragment of continental crust that has a different origin to the rest of the

surrounding rocks. Terranes have always originated some distance away from their final destination. They were moved into position by plate tectonic movements.

TERTIARY
The period at the beginning of the third era of life after the Cretaceous period and before the Quaternary, between 65 and 1.8 million years ago. It was subdivided by Sir Charles Lyell in 1833 into five epochs—Paleocene, Eocene, Oligocene, Miocene, and Pliocene.

TETRAPODS
A major group of vertebrates including all four-limbed vertebrates. Tetrapods evolved in late Devonian times, and their descendants include the amphibians, reptiles, mammals, and birds. Some early tetrapods cannot be assigned to any of these groups, notably reptilelike tetrapods with some mammalian characters such as the therapsids.

THERAPSIDS
A group of late Permian to early Triassic reptilelike synapsid tetrapods that include the ancestors of the mammals.

THEROPODS
A diverse subgroup of saurischian dinosaurs. They were large and walked on their hind limbs. They were also mostly carnivorous, and included the tyrannosaurs. The theropods make up 40 percent of all known kinds of dinosaurs. (Late Triassic to late Cretaceous.)

TILLITE
A rock that is a glacial deposit left when ice melts. Tillite is composed of mud, sand, and rock debris mixed together without any size sorting. The larger rocks are often scratched by ice. Tillite strata are characteristic of past periods of glaciation.

TRACE FOSSIL
A mark left on or in sediment by the movement of an animal or plant and preserved in the rock.

TREE-FERNS
An ancient group of ferns that grew to the size of trees. There are a few surviving representatives such as *Dicksonia.* (Late Carboniferous to recent.)

TRENCH (SUBMARINE)
A deep submarine valley in the ocean floor that in places may descend to depths of more than 36,000 feet (11,000 meters). Trenches are formed where the ocean floor is pushed down (subducted) below a plate of continental crust in a plate collision zone.

TRIASSIC
The earliest period of the Mesozoic era, lasting from 248 to 206 million years ago, before the Jurassic period and after the Permian period. The Triassic was named in 1834 by Friedrich von Alberti to describe a threefold division of strata in Germany.

TRILOBITES
An extinct and abundant group of Paleozoic sealiving arthropods with a distinct threefold division of the body and hard, shell-like exoskeletons. The skeletons had to be molted for the animals to grow and their remains were readily fossilized. (Early Cambrian to late Permian.)

TSUNAMI
A surface wave caused by earthquakes, submarine faulting, or a large meteorite impact; can travel at speeds of up to 550mph (900kph) across oceans, gaining height and destructive power as it approaches land.

TUNICATES see **SEA SQUIRTS**

TYRANNOSAURS
An extinct group of large-headed theropod dinosaurs. Tyrannosaurs walked on their hind limbs and had unusually short arms and two-fingered hands. They lived in late Cretaceous times and were distributed through North America and eastern Asia.

VW

VARISCAN
A phase of mountain building stretching eastward from the Atlantic seaboard of North America through the southern British Isles and into Germany in late Carboniferous and early Permian times. It resulted from the closure of the Rheic Ocean as Avalonia and northern Gondwana collided.

VASCULAR PLANTS
Plants with special cells for carrying water and nutrients from the soil through a root system, up the stem, and usually to the leaves. The cells are generally strengthened to allow upright growth away from the ground toward the light.

VENDIAN
A late Precambrian period of Earth history, 600 to 545 million years ago, before the beginning of Cambrian times.

VERTEBRAL COLUMN
A long jointed skeletal structure that allows the body to be flexed and supports the head, internal organs, and paired limbs. Commonly known as the backbone in vertebrates,

VERTEBRATES
A major group of animals that have an internal bony skeleton made up of a backbone and paired limbs. (Mid-Ordovician to recent.)

VOLCANIC ASH
Small particles of solidified magma, rock fragments, and mineral crystals that are blasted into the atmosphere during volcanic eruptions and fall back to Earth to form a sediment. Some dust-sized particles may be carried by winds around the globe before falling.

WILDFIRE
Naturally occurring forest and prairie fires caused mostly by lightning, particularly during dry seasons. Wildfires are important for renewing plant growth.

Further Reading and Bibliography

Further Reading:

The following books discuss many of the topics covered in this Atlas, at a level suitable for the casual reader:

Benton, M. J.. *Penguin Historical Atlas of Dinosaurs.* New York and London: Viking Penguin, 1996.

Benton, M. J.. *The Reign of the Reptiles.* London; Kingfisher, 1990.

Elsom, D.. *Earth.* New York: Macmillan, 1992.

Gould, S. J. (ed.). *The Book of Life.* London: Ebury Hutchinson, 1993.

Gould, S. J.. *Wonderful Life: The Burgess Shale and the Nature of History.* London: Hutchinson Radius, 1990.

Lambert D.. *The Ultimate Dinosaur Book.* London: Dorling Kindersley, 1993.

Lister, A. & Bahn, P.. *Mammoths.* New York: Macmillan, London 1994.

Norman, D.. *Prehistoric Life: the Rise of the Vertebrates.* London: Boxtree, 1994.

Norman, D.. *The Illustrated Encyclopaedia of Dinosaurs* London: Salamander, 1985.

Norman, D.. *Dinosaur!.* London: Boxtree, 1991.

Osborne, R. & Benton, M. J.. *The Viking Atlas of Evolution.* New York: Viking, 1996.

Palmer, D.. *Life Before Man.* London: Reader's Digest, 1997.

Taylor, P.. *Eyewitness Guides: Fossil.* London: Dorling Kindersley, 1990.

Walker, C. & Ward, D.. *The Eyewitness Handbook of Fossils.* London: Dorling Kindersley, 1998

Whitfield, P.. *From So Simple a Beginning: The Book of Evolution.* New York: Macmillan, 1993.

Bibliography:

The following books describe some of the issues covered by this book at greater depth, sometimes using academic terms:

Archibald, J. D.. *Dinosaur Extinction and the End of an Era.* New York: Columbia, 1996.

Bakker, R. T.. *The Dinosaur Heresies.* New York: Morrow, 1986.

Benton, M. J. (ed.). *The Fossil Record 2.* London: Chapman & Hall, 1993.

Benton, M. J.. *Vertebrate Palaeontology.* London: Chapman & Hall, 1997.

Benton, M. J.. *Penguin Historical Atlas of Dinosaurs.* New York: Viking Penguin, 1996.

Benton, M. J. & Harper, D.. *Basic Palaeontology.* London: Longman, 1997.

Briggs, D. E. G. & Crowther, P. R.. *Palaeobiology: a Synthesis.* Oxford: Blackwell Scientific Publications, 1990.

Carroll, R. L.. *Vertebrate Paleontology and Evolution.* Oxford: W. H. Freeman, 1988.

Carroll, R. L.. *Patterns and Processes of Vertebrate Evolution.* Cambridge: Cambridge University Press, 1997.

Chernicoff, S. & Fox, H.. *Essentials of Geology.* New York: Worth Publishers, 1997.

Condie, K. & Sloan, R.. *Origin and Evolution of Earth: Principles of Historical Geology.* New York: Prentice Hall, 1998.

Conway Morris, S.. *The Crucible of Creation: The Burgess Shale and the Rise of Animals.* Oxford: Oxford University Press, 1998.

Currie, P. J. & Padian, K. (eds.). *Encyclopedia of Dinosaurs.* San Diego: Academic Press, 1997.

Dingus, L. & Rowe, T.. *The Mistaken Extinction: Dinosaur Evolution and the Origin of Birds.* New York: W. H. Freeman & Co., 1998.

Dingus, L.. *Next of Kin: Great Fossils at the American Museum of Natural History.* New York: Rizzoli, 1998.

Farlow, J. & Brett-Surman, M. (eds.). *The Complete Dinosaur.* Indianapolis: Indianapolis University Press, 1997.

Feduccia, A.. *The Age of Birds.* Cambridge: Harvard University Press, 1980.

Glut, D.. *The New Dinosaur Dictionary.* New York: Citadel, 1982.

Hallam, A. & Wignall, P. B.. *Mass Extinctions and their Aftermath.* Oxford: Oxford University Press, 1997.

Imbrie, J. & K. P.. *Ice Ages.* Cambridge: Harvard University Press, 1986.

Jones, S. & Martin, R. (eds.). *The Cambridge Encyclopedia of Human Evolution.* Cambridge: Cambridge University Press, 1992.

Kemp, T. S.. *Mammal-like Reptiles and the Origin of Mammals.* San Diego: Academic Press, 1982.

Lambert, D.. *The Cambridge Field Guide to Prehistoric Life.* Cambridge: Cambridge University Press, 1985.

Lambert, D.. *The Cambridge Guide to Prehistoric Man.* Cambridge: Cambridge University Press, 1987.

Lewin, R.. *Human Evolution: An Illustrated Introduction.* Oxford: Blackwell Scientific Publications, 1984.

Long, J. A.. *The Rise of Fishes.* Baltimore: John Hopkins University Press, 1995.

MacDougall, J. D.. *A Short History of Planet Earth.* New York: John Wiley and Sons, 1996.

McFarland, W. N., Pough, F. F. H., Cade, T. J. & Heiser, J. B.. *Vertebrate Life.* New York: Collier Macmillan, 1979.

Press, F. & Siever, R.. *Earth (4th edition).* New York: W. H. Freeman, 1986.

Savage, R. J. G & Long, M. R.. *Mammal Evolution: An Illustrated Guide.* London: British Museum (Natural History), 1986.

Scarth, A.. *Volcanoes.* London: UCL Press, 1994.

Schaal, S. & Ziegler, W.. *Messel.* Oxford: Oxford University Press, 1992.

Simpson, G. C.. *Splendid Isolation: The Curious History of South American Mammals.* New Haven: Yale University Press, 1980.

Skelton, P. (ed.). *Evolution: a Biological and Palaentological Approach.* Wokingham: Addison-Wesley, 1993.

Skinner, B. & Porter, S. C.. *Physical Geology.* New York: John Wiley and Sons, 1987.

Tattersall, I., Delson, E. & Van Couvering, J. (eds.). *Encyclopedia of Human Evolution and Prehistory.* New York: Garland Publishing, Inc., 1988.

Van Andel, T. H.. *New Views on an Old Planet: A History of Global Change.* Cambridge: Cambridge University Press, 1994.

Wade, M.. *The Greening of Gondwana.*

Wellnhofer, P.. *The Illustrated Encyclopedia of Pterosaurs.* New York: Crescent Books, 1991.

White, M.. *The Flowering of Gondwana.* Princeton: Princeton University Press, 1990.

Young, D.. *The Discovery of Evolution.* Cambridge: Cambridge University Press, 1992.

INDEX

Page numbers in **bold** indicate a major reference in the Ancient Worlds section (pp. 48–159).

A

B

C

D

E

F

G

H

I

J

K

L

M

N

O

P

Q, R

S

T

U, V

W

X, Y, Z

ACKNOWLEDGMENTS

Picture credits

t=top, b=bottom, c=centre, l=left, r=right
1 François Gohier/Ardea; 2 Vaughan Fleming/Science Photo Library; 4 P. Morris/Ardea; 6l Simon Conway Morris, 6c Sinclair Stammers/Oxford Scientific Films, 6r François Gohier/Ardea; 7l Vaughan Fleming/Science Photo Library, 7c The British Museum, 7r P. Morris/Ardea; 8t The Natural History Museum, London, 8b François Gohier/Ardea; 9t John Reader/Science Photo Library, 9b François Gohier/Ardea; 10-11 Tony Stone Images; 48-49 P. Morris/Ardea; 50t B. Murton/Southampton Oceanography Centre/Science Photo Library, 50b Sinclair Stammers/Science Photo Library; 51 Jean-Paul Ferrero/Ardea; 52 François Gohier/Ardea; 53 Breck P. Kent/Oxford Scientific Films; 54t Simon Conway Morris, University of Cambridge, 54b Dr Peter Crimes; 55t Dr Peter Crimes, 55b Simon Conway Morris, University of Cambridge; 56 Jean-Paul Ferrero/Ardea; 57 Shuhai Xiao and Andrew Knoll, Harvard University; 58l Simon Conway Morris, University of Cambridge, 58r Simon Conway Morris, University of Cambridge; 59t Simon Conway Morris, University of Cambridge, 59b Simon Conway Morris, University of Cambridge; 60 Dr Peter Crimes; 61 Dr Peter Crimes; 62t Simon Conway Morris, University of Cambridge, 62b Royal Ontario Museum; 63t Simon Conway Morris, University of Cambridge, 63b Dr Derek E.G. Briggs, University of Bristol; 64 Simon Conway Morris, University of Cambridge; 65l Simon Conway Morris, University of Cambridge, 65tr Dr Derek E.G. Briggs, University of Bristol, 65br Dr Derek E.G. Briggs, University of Bristol; 66t Gary Bell/Planet Earth Pictures, 66b Simon Conway Morris, University of Cambridge; 67 NHPA; 68t William Campbell/DRK Photo, 68b Jens Rydell/Bruce Coleman; 69t Martin Land/Science Photo Library, 69b Volker Steger/Science Photo Library; 70 Richard Aldridge, University of Leicester; 71t BD/IPR/19-7 British Geological Survey © NERC. All rights reserved, 71b The Natural History Museum, London; 72t Manfred Schauer, 72b Martin Land/Science Photo Library; 73t The Natural History Museum, London, 73b The Natural History Museum, London; 74l Sinclair Stammers/Science Photo Library, 74r Department of Earth Sciences, Cardiff University, Wales; 75l Kaj R. Svensson/Science Photo Library, 75r Sinclair Stammers/Science Photo Library; 76t Breck P. Kent/Oxford Scientific Films, 76b The Natural History Museum, London; 77t Eric and David Hosking/Corbis, 77b The Natural History Museum, London; 78 Zig Leszczynski/Oxford Scientific Films; 79 University Museum of Zoology, Cambridge; 80t G.I. Bernard/NHPA, 80b Sinclair Stammers/Oxford Scientific Films; 81t Sarah Finney, 81b The Manchester Museum, The University of Manchester; 82l Andrew Mounter/Planet Earth Pictures, 82r University Museum of Zoology, Cambridge; 83 National Museums of Scotland; 84 P. Morris/Ardea; 85 Prof. Dr Carsten Brauckmann/Institut für Geologie & Palaeontologie, Clausthal; 86t David Muench/Corbis, 86b The Field Museum, Chicago Neg. No. GEO 81284; 87t David M. Dennis/Oxford Scientific Films, 87b Chip Clark; 88l Dr David Norman, 88r Luiz Claudio Marigo/Bruce Coleman; 89 The Field Museum, Chicago Neg. No. GEO 81027; 90 The Natural History Museum, London; 91 François Gohier/Ardea; 92t P. Morris/Ardea, 92b Sinclair Stammers/Science Photo Library; 93t Specimen: Staatliches Museum für Naturkunde Stuttgart/Dr R. Wild, 93b Specimen: Museo Civico di Scienze Naturali "E. Caffi" Bergamo, Italy/Dr R. Wild; 94 François Gohier/Ardea; 95 Neg. No. 329319 Photo by Bolton Courtesy Dept. of Library Services American Museum of Natural History; 96 The Natural History Museum, London; 97t Geoscience Features Picture Library, 97b James D. Watt/Planet Earth Pictures; 98t David M. Dennis/Oxford Scientific Films, 98b P. Morris/Ardea; 99t François Gohier/Ardea, 99b Vaughan Fleming/Science Photo Library; 100 Robert Harding Picture Library; 101 P.Morris/Ardea; 102b Mary Evans Picture Library; 103t Ken Lucas/Planet Earth Pictures, 103b Peter Scoones/Planet Earth Pictures; 104 The Natural History Museum, London; 105l Ken Lucas/Planet Earth Pictures; 105 François Gohier/Ardea; 106 John Fields/Nature Focus; 107 Anthony Bannister/NHPA; 108t Tony Stone Images, 108b The Natural History Museum, London; 109t François Gohier/Ardea, 109b François Gohier/Ardea; 110 Steve Hutt; 111 Vivek Sinha/Oxford Scientific Films; 112l François Gohier/Ardea, 112r The Natural History Museum, London; 113l The Kobal Collection, 113r Bringham Young University; 114t David Sanders, 114b François Gohier/Ardea; 115t E.R. Degginger/Oxford Scientific Films, 115b Ken Lucas/Planet Earth Pictures; 116 François Gohier/Ardea; 117 François Gohier/Ardea; 118 Jonathan Blair/Corbis; 119 François Gohier/Ardea; 120 Jean-Loup Charmet; 121 Natuurhistorisch Museum Maastricht; 122t François Gohier/Ardea, 122b Paul A. Souders/Corbis; 123t Dr David Kring/Science Photo Library, 123b E. Hanumantha Rao/NHPA; 124 The Natural History Museum, London/Dorling Kindersley; 125 J. David Archibald; 128t P. Morris/Ardea, 128b François Gohier/Ardea; 129t David C. Fritts/Oxford Scientific Films, 129b Wolfgang Kaehler/Corbis; 130t The Stock Market, 130b Ken Lucas/Planet Earth Pictures; 131t Photo: Senckenberg, Messel Research Department, 131b Photo: Senckenberg, Messel Research Department; 132 Photo: Senckenberg, Messel Research Department; 133 Photo: Senckenberg, Messel Research Department; 134 Kevin Schafer/NHPA; 135 Krafft/Planet Earth Pictures; 136t Kathie Atkinson/Oxford Scientific Films, 136b Dr Paul Selden, University of Manchester; 137t David Dilcher and Ge Sun, 137b Steve Hopkin/Planet Earth Pictures; 138t Alex Kerstitch/Planet Earth Pictures, 138b George Poinar; 139t Vaughan Fleming/Science Photo Library, 139b David Maitland/Planet Earth Pictures; 140 NHPA; 141 David Maitland/Planet Earth Pictures; 142 David Paterson; 143 NASA/Science Photo Library; 144t Adrian Warren/Ardea, 144b John Reader/Science Photo Library, 145t John Reader/Science Photo Library, 145b James Balog/Tony Stone Images; 146 Christopher Ratier/NHPA; 147 Anthony Bannister/NHPA; 148 Copyright 1995, Worldsat International and J. Knighton/Science Photo Library; 149 Tony Stone Images; 150t Anup Shah/Planet Earth Pictures, 150b Kenneth W. Fink/Ardea; 151l John Reader/Science Photo Library, 151r Gerald Cubitt/Bruce Coleman; 152t Harald Sund/The Image Bank, 152b Dr D.P. Lane, University of Keele; 153t Mike Newton, 153b Peter Parks/Oxford Scientific Films; 154 Novosti Photo Library; 155t B & C Alexander/NHPA, 155b Jean Vertut; 156 Grotte Préhistorique de Rouffignac; 157t The Natural History Museum, London, 157b The British Museum; 158/159 Images Colour Library; 158t Richard Coomber/Planet Earth Pictures, 158b J.G. Paren/Science Photo Library; 159t Frank Spooner Pictures, 159b Dick Mol; 160-161 David Paterson; 162 Stuart Westmorland/Tony Stone Images, 162 inset Bettmann/Corbis; 163l Bettmann/Corbis, 163c Hulton-Deutsch Collection/Corbis, 163r Hulton-Deutsch Collection/Corbis; 165 David Bayliss/Geoscience Features Picture Library; 166l Bettmann/Corbis, 166r Bettmann/Corbis; 167 G. Brad Lewis/Tony Stone Images; 168t Archiv für Kunst & Geschichte, Berlin/AKG London, 168b Herve Gloaguen/Network; 169t Corbis, 169b The Stock Market; 170 M. Angelo/Corbis, 170 inset Oliver Benn/Tony Stone Images; 171Corbis; 172 Yann Arthus-Bertrand/Corbis; 173t David Muench/Corbis, 173b Yann Arthus-Bertrand/Corbis; 174 Craig Lovell/Corbis, 174 inset Kevin Schafer/Corbis; 176 Bettmann/Corbis; 177t John Dakers; Eye Ubiquitous/Corbis, 177b Mansell/Time Inc.; 178 World Perspectives/Tony Stone Images; 179t Bettmann/Corbis, 179b Prof. Stewart Lowther/Science Photo Library; 180 Tom Bean/Tony Stone Images; 181l François Gohier/Ardea, 181r Robert van der Hilst/Tony Stone Images; 182 Mary Evans Picture Library; 183t The Natural History Museum, London, 183b The Natural History Museum, London; 184 C. Weaver/Ardea; 186 Sinclair Stammers/Science Photo Library, 186 inset Mary Evans Picture Library; 189t Tom Bean/Corbis, 189c George Poinar, 189b Buddy Mays/Corbis; 190 The Kobal Collection; 192 Geoscience Features Picture Library; 193 T.A. Wiewandt/DRK Photo; 194 Richardson/Custom Medical Stock Photo/Science Photo Library; 196 Lick Observatory; 197b Robert Hadley/Impact Photos; 198-224 Ken Lucas/Planet Earth Pictures

If the publishers have unwittingly infringed copyright in any illustration reproduced, they would pay an appropriate fee on being satisfied to the owner's title.

Illustrators

Graham Allen 106/107, 149t, 195; David Bergen 84/85, 100/101, 124/125, 126/127; Richard Bonson 134/135, 142/143, 158/159; Robin Bouttell 78/79, 110/111, 146/147; Jim Channell 60/61, 74/75, 154/155; Bill Donohoe 52/53, 56/57, 70/71, 104/105; Eugene Fleury 90/91; Gary Hincks 157; Steve Holden 148; Rob Jakeway 50/51; Steve Kirk 96/97, 190/191; Kuo Kang Chen 188; Colin Newman 64/65, 82/83, 137; Luis Rey 94/95, 118/119, 140/141; Andrew Robinson 149c & b; Peter David Scott 88/89, 116/117, 120/121, 132/133; Dick Twinney 195; Andrew Wheatcroft 156/157

Maps

Three-dimensional maps produced by Lovell Johns Limited, Witney, using illustration by Hardlines Limited, Charlbury, and based on data supplied by Paleomap Services Limited, Cambridge.

Two-dimensional maps by Eugene Fleury.

The publishers would like to thank the following people for their kind help during the production of this book:
Dr. Alan Smith, Department of Earth Sciences, University of Cambridge
Dr. Norman Macleod, Natural History Museum, London.